Whose Trade Organization?

Corporate Globalization and the Erosion of Democracy

An Assessment of the World Trade Organization

By
Lori Wallach and Michelle Sforza
Public Citizen's Global Trade Watch

Published
by

Joan Claybrook, President
Washington, D.C. 1999
www.citizen.org

Published by Public Citizen, 1999
1600 20th Street, N.W.
Washington, D.C. 20009
www.citizen.org

ISBN 1-58231-001-7

Acknowledgments:

Special thanks go to Patrick Woodall for his research and writing contributions and for his extraordinary effort as ringmaster of the overwhelming process of writing, editing, fact-checking, design, layout and more editing that brought this book to life. Special thanks also go to Mary Bottari for her irreplaceable leadership and fortitude in the preparation of the final manuscript and contributions to research, writing and coordination of this project. Booth Gunter and Angela Bradbery have our eternal gratitude for their excellent editing, which helped make this book accessible and clear. Extra thanks and kudos go to Marianne Mollmann and Katie "Footnote Queen" Burnham and for research assistance and dogged fact-checking. The authors also would like to thank the following Public Citizen staff for their tireless dedication and invaluable contributions to this book, without which it would not have been brought to completion: Dion Casey and also Darci Andresen, Matthew Currie, Alesha Daughtrey, Matilda Lee, Joel Ngugi, Margrete Strand-Ragnes and Jessica Roach. Special thanks also go to Neal Brown for his creative layout work and for designing the cover, and to Paul Levy for his legal review. Several individuals outside of Public Citizen also provided invaluable input: Kiera Costic, Kristen Dawkins, Anton Dembowski, Chris McGinn, Scott Nova, Martin Wagner, Mark Weisbrot, Rob Weissman and Patricia Wu. Additional thanks are extended to Peter Lurie, T. J. Sutcliffe and our other family and friends, whose assistance, patience and support were essential to seeing this project through to completion. Finally, thanks to Ralph Nader and Joan Claybrook for their vision and support.

This book was made possible in part by funding from the Ford Foundation.

Contents

Preface

By Ralph Nader

In this book, Public Citizen's Global Trade Watch team comprehensively documents the five-year record of the World Trade Organization (WTO). Unfortunately, the WTO's performance is considerably more damaging than predicted by WTO critics prior to its approval.

In approving the far-reaching, powerful World Trade Organization and other international trade agreements, such as the North American Free Trade Agreement, the U.S. Congress, like those of other nations, has ceded much of its capacity to independently advance health and safety standards that protect citizens and has accepted harsh legal limitations on what domestic policies it may pursue. Approval of these agreements has institutionalized a global economic and political structure that makes every government increasingly hostage to a global financial and commerce system engineered through an autocratic system of international governance that favors corporate interests.

This new governing system provides enormous generic control over the minute details of the lives of the majority of the world's people. This new system is not based on the health and economic well-being of people, but rather on the enhancement of the power and wealth of the world's largest corporations and financial institutions.

Under this new system, many decisions affecting people's daily lives are being shifted away from our local and national governments and instead are being made by a group of unelected trade bureaucrats sitting behind closed doors in Geneva, Switzerland. These bureaucrats, for example, are now empowered to dictate whether people in California can prevent the destruction of their last virgin forests or determine if carcinogenic pesticides can be banned from their food, or whether the European countries have the right to ban the use of dangerous biotech materials in their food. Moreover, once the WTO's secret tribunals issue their edicts, no independent appeals are possible. Worldwide conformity is required.

At stake is the very basis of democracy and accountable decision-making that is the necessary undergirding of any citizen struggle for just distribution of wealth and adequate health, safety and environmental protections. The erosion of such democratic accountability, and the local, state and national sovereignty that is its embodiment, has taken place over the past several decades. The globalization of commerce and finance has been shaped by multinational companies that, in the absence of global rules, simply conducted their business to suit their needs. Establishment of the WTO marks a landmark formalization and strengthening of this heretofore *ad hoc* system.

Best described as corporate economic globalization, this new economic model is characterized by the establishment of supranational limitations on the legal and practical ability of any nation to subjugate commercial activity to other policy goals. Globalization's tactic is to eliminate democratic decision-making and accountability over matters as intimate as the safety of food, pharmaceuticals and motor vehicles, or the way in which a country may use or conserve its land, water, minerals and other resources.

One cannot open a newspaper today without facing myriad examples of the problems that concentrated power spawns: reduced standards of living for most people in the developed *and* developing world; growing unemployment worldwide; massive environmental degradation and natural resource shortages; growing political chaos; and a global sense of despair replacing hope and optimism for the future.

Conspiratorial meetings have not been necessary to fuel the push for globalization. Corporate interests share a common, perverse outlook. To them, the globe is viewed first as a common market and capital source. Governments, laws and democracy are factors that restrict their exploitation. From their perspective, the goal is to eliminate market barriers on a global scale. From any *other* perspective, such barriers are seen as valued safeguards on unfettered economic activity — that is, every nation's laws that foster their economies, their citizens' health and safety, the sustainable use of their land and resources, and so on. But for multinational corporations, the diversity that is a blessing of democracy and that results from diffuse decision-making is itself the major barrier.

On rare occasions, promoters of the economic globalization agenda have been frank about their intentions. "Governments should interfere in the conduct of trade as little.as possible," said GATT (General Agreement on Tariffs and Trade) Director General Peter Sutherland, in a March 3, 1994, speech in New York City promoting U.S. approval of the WTO.

What makes such statements even more alarming is that what is being characterized as "trade" these days covers a huge portion of each nation's economic *and* political structures. The WTO and other trade agreements have moved beyond their traditional roles of setting quotas and tariffs to institute new and unprecedented controls over democratic governance. Erasing national laws and economic boundaries to foster capital mobility and "free trade," a term that ought properly to be called *corporate-managed* trade (since it produces constraints, not freedom, for the rest of us) has led to rejoicing by the likes of American Express, Cargill, Union Carbide, Shell, Citicorp, Pfizer and other mega-corporations. But the prospect of global commerce without democratic controls is a brewing disaster for the rest of the world left uniquely vulnerable to unrestrained corporate activity amid declining living, health and environmental standards.

As economist Herman Daly warned in his January 1994 "Farewell Lecture to the World Bank," the push to eliminate the nation-state's capacity to regulate commerce "is to wound fatally the major unit of community capable of carrying out any policies for the common good. ... Cosmopolitan globalism weakens national boundaries and the power of national and subnational communities, while strengthening the relative power of transnational corporations."

The philosophy allegedly behind the globalization agenda is that maximizing global economic liberalization will in itself result in broad economic and social benefits. However, anyone who believes this philosophy or that corporate economic globalization has any underpinnings except maximizing short-term profit, need only consider the case of U.S.-China economic relations. When only human rights were at issue in 1994, the Clinton administration ended the historical linkage between favorable trade status and a country's human rights record and supported renewal of China's Most Favored Nation (MFN) status. However, in early 1995, when property rights were in question, McDonald's lease and Mickey Mouse's royalties were cause for $1 billion dollars in threatened U.S. trade restrictions against China. This threat resulted in Chinese government policy changes to enforce intellectual property restrictions.

Similarly, economic globalization's primary mechanisms — the WTO and NAFTA — do not target all "fetters" on commerce for elimination. Rather, the agreements promote elimination of restrictions that protect people, while increasing protection for corporate interests. Regulation of commerce for environmental, health or other social goals is strictly limited. For example, selling products internationally made with child labor is WTO-legal. Proposals to strengthen obsolete or antiquated standards are chilled in their incipiency by the potential of a WTO challenge, thus leading to a *de facto* moratorium on efforts to upgrade and create new standards. Labor rights, which were to be included in the Uruguay Round under congressional orders, were entirely left out as inappropriate limitations on global commerce. But regulation of commerce to protect monopolistic corporate property rights — such as intellectual property — was expanded. The right for capital to be invested in any country in any economic sector without conditions was also strengthened.

By giving up the right to condition investment in a country on certain societal standards or the entry of products into domestic markets on compliance with national rules, countries have eliminated whatever leverage they had on corporate behavior. U.S. corporations long ago learned how to pit states against each other in "a race to the bottom" to profit from whatever state would offer the lower wages, pollution standards and taxes. Often a federal standard would stop such manipulation. Now, through NAFTA and the WTO, multinational corporations can play this game at the global level, pitting country against country. After all, externalizing environmental and social costs is one way to boost corporate profits. It is a tragic lure that has its winners and losers determined before it even gets under way: Workers, consumers and communities in all countries lose; short-term profits soar and big business "wins."

Under the WTO, the race to the bottom is not only in standard of living and environmental and health safeguards but in democracy itself. Enactment of these so-called free trade deals virtually guarantees that democratic efforts to ensure corporations pay their fair share of taxes, provide their employees a decent standard of living or limit their pollution of the air, water and land will be met with the refrain: "You can't burden us like that. If you do, we won't be able to compete. We'll have to close down and move to a country that offers us a more hospitable climate." This sort of intimidation is extremely powerful. Communities already devastated by plant closures and a declining manufacturing base are desperate not to lose more jobs. They know all too well that exit threats of this kind are often carried out.

One of the clearest lessons that emerges from a study of industrialized societies is that the centralization of commerce is environmentally and democratically unsound. No one denies the usefulness of some international trade. But societies need to focus their attention on fostering community-oriented production. Very often such smaller-scale operations are more flexible and adaptable to local needs and environmentally sustainable production methods. They are also more susceptible to democratic control, are far less likely to threaten to migrate and perceive their interests as more overlapping with community interests.

Similarly, allocating power to lower-level governmental bodies tends to increase citizen power. Concentrating power in distant international organizations, as the trade pacts do, tends to remove critical decisions from citizen control. You can talk to your city council representative but not some faceless international trade bureaucrat at the WTO in Geneva.

If local or state decisions can be jeopardized by a foreign country's mere charge that their standards are a non-tariff trade barrier, if a country must pay a tribute in trade sanctions to maintain laws ruled to be trade barriers by closed and autocratic foreign tribunals, if a company's claim that the burden that important citizen safeguards would impose causes them to pick up their stakes and move abroad, then standards of living and the all-important underlying standards of justice worldwide will continue to spiral downward. This is what happens when democratic values are subjugated to the imperatives of international trade.

Following the establishment of the WTO, the corporatists' globalization process and its effects are increasing with a commensurate perpetuation of declining or stagnant economic conditions for most of the world's people. In the U.S., if we do not make the connection between our local problems and the multinational corporate drive for economic and political globalization, then others will blame these unavoidable and increasing problems on other causes. "It's the immigrants!" "It's the welfare system!" "It's greedy farmers or workers!" "It's the regulatory system!" "It's the tort system!" Allowing such camouflage for the real causes of these multifaceted problems means a massive diversion of proper focus, dividing citizens against each other to the benefit of the agenda of mega-corporations.

Thus, what we face now is a race against time: How will citizens reverse the expanding globalization agenda while democratic instincts and institutions remain, albeit under attack? The degree of suppression and subterfuge necessary to continue the globalization agenda will be hard to maintain in the presence of any vigorous democratic oversight. However, actually reversing NAFTA, the WTO and the push toward globalization will require a revitalized citizen democracy here and abroad.

What follows in this ground-breaking volume is the experience under the WTO since 1995, which demonstrates the ever-mounting verification in one area after another that the caveats by the critics of GATT and NAFTA were indeed prophetic.

Introduction

After decades of promotion by corporations that make infant formula, the world was faced with a plague of needless infant deaths that occurred when mothers in developing countries mixed the formula with unsanitary water. Reacting to this public health crisis and a global campaign by religious and human rights activists, UNICEF created a global code on infant formula marketing. More than a hundred countries implemented the code, which banned infant formula packaging that depicted healthy, fat babies. The idea was to ensure that women, particularly illiterate ones, wouldn't associate baby formula with healthy infants and be discouraged from breast-feeding.

Not everyone liked the law. Gerber Foods, the company whose trademarked logo includes a pudgy, happy infant, took particular exception to it. When Guatemala insisted that Gerber remove the baby from the packaging of products distributed in Guatemala, the company refused and threatened action under an international trade agreement known as the General Agreement on Tariffs and Trade (GATT).

Unbeknownst to most people in Guatemala and other countries, negotiations were nearly complete to establish a phenomenally powerful new global commerce agency, the World Trade Organization (WTO). This organization would be empowered to enforce 700-plus pages of rules covering numerous issues previously under the purview of domestic governments. Among these rules was a new agreement on intellectual property rights that required countries to give precedence to corporate trademarks over other national priorities.

The new organization would have extraordinarily potent enforcement capacity not included in global arms control, environmental, human rights or other major treaties. It created a new system of global governance under which countries can challenge another country's laws before secretive WTO tribunals of trade bureaucrats in Switzerland. Policies found to violate WTO rules would have to be eliminated or changed, or the country enforcing the policies would have to pay higher tariffs or other financial compensation to the winning country.

As a signatory to GATT, the Guatemalan government knew about the nearly complete expansion of GATT and proposed establishment of the WTO. Faced with the prospect of a long and costly fight before a WTO tribunal, Guatemala backed down and exempted imported baby food products from its labeling restrictions. Today, Gerber's pudgy baby face remains in stores throughout the country.

This is but one story of how the WTO can affect the lives of people around the globe, most of whom have likely never heard of it, much less realized that its establishment amounted to a slow-motion *coup d'etat* over democratic governance worldwide.

Unlike past trade pacts, the WTO and its underlying agreements move far beyond traditional commercial matters such as tariffs, import quotas or requirements that foreign and domestic goods be treated equally. Rather, the WTO's provisions, for example, can limit the strength of a country's food safety laws and the comprehensiveness of product labeling policies. They can prevent a country from banning products made with child labor. They can even regulate expenditure of local tax dollars (for instance, prohibiting environmental or human rights considerations in government purchasing decisions). The WTO's constraints apply to state and local laws as well as national ones.

Promises vs. Reality:
Documenting the WTO's Effects

The WTO was established on January 1, 1995, as part of the Uruguay Round Agreements of the General Agreement on Tariffs and Trade and now has 134 Member countries. When the Uruguay Round was being negotiated, environmental, labor and consumer groups warned that the GATT system, which had existed for decades, was being dramatically recast and expanded in a way that would subjugate broad public interest goals – such as accountable governance, environmental protection, health and safety, and human and labor rights – to corporate interests.

Proponents of the Uruguay Round and the WTO dismissed these concerns as ill-informed doomsday prophesies. They promised that the Uruguay Round and the WTO would pose no threat to domestic sovereignty or democratic, accountable policymaking. They also promised enormous economic gains worldwide if the Uruguay Round were implemented: The U.S. trade deficit would decrease by $60 billion in ten years. Latin American countries would boom and Asian growth would keep pace. Then-U.S. Treasury Secretary Lloyd Bentsen even predicted that passage of the Uruguay Round would result in an additional $1,700 in annual income per U.S. family.

Now, nearly five years later, it is clear that public interest policies have been undermined, and health and environmental safeguards are being threatened in the United States and around the world. The promised economic gains have not materialized. Not only has the WTO failed to live up to its proponents' promises, but it is wreaking continuing damage.

This book, the result of a yearlong investigation by Public Citizen's Global Trade Watch, examines the results of nearly five years of WTO operations. It examines the WTO's impacts on environmental protection and conservation; food and product safety; public health, worker safety and access to medicines; jobs, livelihoods, economic development and standards of living; and human and labor rights.

This book documents an insidious shift in decision-making away from democratic, accountable forums — where citizens have a chance to fight for the public interest — to distant, secretive and unaccountable international bodies, whose rules and operations are dominated by corporate interests. Ironically, the U.S. — which has one of the world's most open and accountable government systems — is a leader in using the WTO to undercut in other nations the democratic institutions and mechanisms that have served it so well.

Much of the information presented here about the disputes adjudicated by the WTO and a series of corporate and government threats of WTO action has not been publicized previously and was obtained only after extensive investigation. The trend that emerges is of the WTO silently eroding the hard-won balance between public interests in economic equity, environmental protection, health and safety on the one hand and short-term corporate interests in market control and profitability on the other.

Proponents of this system have called it "free trade," yet the WTO's rules (some of which set broad monopoly-style limits on trade in such areas as medicines and technology) have little to do with the 19th century free trade philosophies of Adam Smith or David Ricardo. Rather, the rules create a model of corporate economic globalization that would be most accurately dubbed "corporate managed trade."

The full magnitude of this new global governance system is yet to be seen because some WTO rules have not taken full effect. But it is now time to ask: *Whose trade organization is it?* It does not appear to belong to or benefit the majority of the world's citizens. Rather, as this book begins to document, the emerging system favors huge multinational companies and the wealthiest few in developed and developing countries.

This still-emerging system is not a foregone conclusion. Despite the public relations efforts of those who benefit from this arrangement to convince us otherwise, the WTO setup is merely one design; it is not inevitable like the moon's pull on the tides or some other force of nature. Putting into place the WTO and the globalization it implements required its proponents to undertake an enormous amount of planning, public relations and political work. If we do not like the outcomes of this design, we can choose alternatives to it.

The goal of this book is to shed light on the impacts of the current system for those who will be most affected by whether we keep this model or replace it. We have written this book for people who know very little about the WTO's rules or its five-year track record and who have no idea what a threat the current agreement poses to their health, safety, livelihood, food, environment and future.

If after reading this book you agree with us that the WTO's outcomes are undesirable and unacceptable, please act. Working together, citizens around the world can create the demand to replace the WTO model with a more equitable, environmentally sustainable and democratically accountable system.

Promised Economic Gains Fail to Materialize

We must await full implementation of the Uruguay Round Agreements before we can assess their long-term economic impacts. But the economic trends that have emerged so far indicate serious problems. These trends would have to abruptly reverse course to merely return the developing world to better, pre-Uruguay Round conditions, much less to fulfill many of the outlandish predictions of broad benefits served up by Uruguay Round boosters.

What we do know today is that since the WTO was created, the world has been buffeted by unprecedented financial instability. Economic growth in the developing world has slowed. Income inequality is rising rapidly between and within countries. Despite productivity gains, wages in many countries have failed to rise. Commodity prices are at all-time lows, causing the standard of living for many people to slide, particularly in Asia, Latin America and Africa. Indeed, in most countries the period under the Uruguay Round has brought dramatic reversals in fortune.

Latin America is foundering, mired in its deepest economic slump since the debt crisis of the 1980s. A report by the United Nations Conference on Trade and Development (UNCTAD) found that, "In almost all developing countries that have undertaken rapid trade liberalization, wage inequality has increased, most often in the context of declining industrial employment of unskilled workers and large absolute falls in their real wages, on the order of 20-30% in Latin American countries."

East Asia is paralyzed by an economic crisis caused in part by the very investment and financial service sector deregulation that WTO rules intensify and spread to other nations. While the U.S. media have announced that the crisis is over, people living in South Korea know better. There, the crisis has quadrupled unemployment and precipitated a 200% increase in absolute poverty, effectively rolling back decades of economic progress.

Global economic indicators generally paint a tragic picture: The income gap between the fifth of the world's people living in the richest countries and the fifth in the poorest was 74-to-1 in 1997, up from 60-to-1 in 1990 and 30-to-1 in 1960. By 1997, the richest 20% captured 86% of world income, with the poorest 20% capturing a mere 1%.

In the U.S., the trade deficit is at an all-time high, $218 billion and climbing, having ballooned — not declined as promised — from $98 billion in 1994. The median family income has not risen by $1,700 per year during *any* of the past four years as the Clinton administration promised, despite the fact that the U.S. economy is growing at a record pace.

While the economic numbers paint a telling picture, they are but one part of the story. Of equal importance, but less well known, is the WTO's consistent record of eroding public interest policies designed to safeguard the environment, our families' health and safety, human rights and democracy.

WTO Challenges and Threats Undermine the Public Interest

The expansive Uruguay Round Agreements' constraints on the ability of governments to maintain public interest regulations are enforced through a freestanding WTO tribunal system empowered to judge countries' laws for WTO-compliance.

Since it was created in 1995, the WTO has ruled that every environmental, health or safety policy it has reviewed is an illegal trade barrier that must be eliminated or changed. Nations whose laws were declared trade barriers by the WTO — or that were merely threatened with prospective WTO action — have eliminated or watered down policies to meet WTO requirements. In addition to undermining important policies, this trend has a chilling effect on countries' inclinations to pass new environmental, human rights or safety laws because they want to avoid new challenges.

The very mechanics of the WTO, which are skewed in favor of corporations and trade, pre-ordain this outcome. WTO business is conducted by committees and panels that meet behind closed doors in Geneva, Switzerland. In sharp contrast to domestic courts and even other international arbitration systems, there is a startling lack or "transparency" – public disclosure and accountability. This leads to overwhelming industry influence. *As one WTO staffer admitted to the Financial Times, the WTO "is the place where governments collude in private against their domestic pressure groups."[1]*

Even the dispute resolution tribunals meet in secret. The panels rely on documents never made public and on anonymous "experts" to make decisions and issue reports that cannot be accessed by the public until the hearings are over and a binding judgment is handed down. WTO panelists are selected for their trade credentials, not their knowledge of such areas as public health, environmental protection or development policy. Most disturbing is the fact that these decision-makers are trade advocates, not unbiased judges.

The WTO's tribunals systematically rule against domestic laws challenged as violating WTO rules. Defending countries have won just three of the 22 WTO challenges completed to date. (The U.S. lost two of those three anomalous cases.) The string of public interest laws ruled against and developing countries are among the biggest losers in this system. Developing countries generally do not have the money and expertise either to bring cases to the WTO or defend themselves before the WTO. Many simply amend their laws before the matter even reaches the WTO, thus enabling powerful companies and countries to flex their muscles, make threats and force smaller nations to change laws and regulations that comply with WTO rules.

Because the WTO is still so young, the cases described in this book are merely the beginning, offering a frightening glimpse of what is still to come unless significant changes are made.

The primary problem stems from the fact that countries' goals and policies must pass muster with the WTO, which, among other tests, requires laws and regulations to be the least restrictive to trade as possible.

Consider what happened to the U.S.'s attempt to reduce emissions from automobiles. The U.S. has relaxed standards designed to limit gasoline contaminants after Venezuela won a WTO challenge against Clean Air Act regulations it claimed unfairly affected its gasoline industry. In a classic example of WTO double-talk, the panel in this case ruled that a country was free to *choose* any environmental policy it desired, but only could *implement* policies that were consistent with WTO rules.

Further, WTO rules prohibit countries from treating physically similar products differently based on how they are made or harvested. For instance, in the eyes of the WTO, tuna caught in dolphin-safe nets should be treated no differently than tuna caught in nets that ensnare dolphins. This is why the Clinton administration worked with some of the Congress' leading anti-environmental members to water down a popular U.S. law designed to prevent dolphins from being killed in tuna nets. The change came after Mexico threatened to go to the WTO to enforce an earlier GATT ruling against the U.S. dolphin-safe tuna policy. This backwards logic put in limbo laws banning drift net fishing or requiring manufacturing processes that cause less pollution. It also jeopardizes laws banning trade in goods made with child labor or trade with countries where human rights abuses take place.

WTO philosophies also undermine global cooperation on the environment, health and human rights. If a country is a WTO member, its domestic implementation of other international commitments must comply with WTO rules. For instance, the WTO ruled against provisions of the U.S. Endangered Species Act that required shrimpers to protect endangered sea turtles — a law that implemented U.S. commitments under the global environmental treaty called Convention on Trade in Endangered Species (CITES). Now, the U.S. and EU are threatening Japan's attempt to enact laws to implement the Kyoto Treaty on global climate change as WTO-illegal.

WTO rules set a ceiling on safety by making certain international standards the only presumptively WTO-legal standards. Domestic standards on health, the environment and public safety that are higher than international ones must pass a set of stringent tests in order *not* to be considered trade barriers. Meanwhile, there is no *floor* on health or safety that all countries must meet; there is no requirement that international standards be met, only that they cannot be exceeded.

France, for example, has joined nine other European countries in banning asbestos, a known human carcinogen. Canada has insisted that the WTO gives it a new right to market its asbestos and has filed a WTO challenge against France's ban. WTO rules require that domestic standards be based on international standards. The international standards, which are heavily influenced by industry, permit "controlled use" of asbestos. Canada thus argues that a ban, by providing more health protection than international standards, violates the WTO. The case now lies before a WTO panel.

The cases also clearly show that the WTO system effectively turns the very premise by which most some progressive governments have handled food safety and other human health-related policies on its head. Generally, manufacturers are required to prove that a product is safe before it can be sold, and countries ban the product until the company has submitted the proof. Under WTO rules, however, the burden is completely reversed. Governments must prove that a product is unsafe before they ban it and must clear near-impossible procedural and evidentiary hurdles to prove that products pose a risk to people. The WTO rules also make trade a priority over health by explicitly requiring that domestic regulations be the least restrictive to trade as possible.

With the establishment of the WTO, control over such key areas as food safety has been snatched from the hands of domestic legislatures and effectively ceded to international corporate interests. A WTO ruling against Europe's ban on beef containing residues of artificial growth hormones is a vivid and alarming illustration of the WTO's unacceptable approach to human health and safety. The WTO declared that Europe's ban on meat tainted with artificial growth hormones had to go because the Europeans had not first scientifically proved that the artificial hormone residues in meat pose an explicit threat to human health, although it is known that the hormones themselves do. The EU has refused to cave in to U.S. pressure to accept the beef its consumers do not want. Now it has been hit with $115 million in WTO-authorized trade sanctions.

Another alarming aspect of this new WTO system is the fact that nations are effectively used by corporations to challenge regulations in other countries. The U.S. went to bat for Chiquita, the banana giant, when it successfully attacked Europe's preferential treatment of bananas from former EU colonies. The U.S. does not produce bananas for export and most of Chiquita's employees are underpaid farm workers laboring on its vast central American plantations. The EU has announced that it has no choice but to rescind its preferential treatment, an action that could have a devastating impact on the small, independent banana farmers in the Caribbean. The result could be a destabilization of the very economic foundation of the Caribbean's numerous small democratic nations. The U.S. national interest in the region — in drug interdiction, political stability, trade and tourism — will be undermined by this outcome.

But a country need not always actually challenge another country's laws to change them. Often, the mere threat of a challenge suffices. For instance, after the U.S. threatened WTO action, South Korea weakened two food safety laws — one pertaining to the shelf life for meat, the other dealing with fruit and vegetable inspections. And while many Americans saw news coverage of Vice President Al Gore's campaign events being protested by AIDS activists, few people realized that a WTO threat was at the base of this brouhaha. South Africa's efforts to make medicines, especially AIDS treatments, more accessible to its population came under fire from international pharmaceutical companies and the Clinton administration, which claimed that the policy violated intellectual property rights granted to the companies under the WTO. South Africa's proposal encourages compulsory licensing — so that less expensive generic versions of drugs can be produced — and parallel importing of cheaper drugs from other countries.

Because developing countries generally lack the resources and expertise to defend challenges, these threats can be particularly devastating. However, developing countries haven't been the only losers. Rich countries have seen some of their valuable policies gutted too. The threats of WTO action described in this book are merely the tip of the iceberg, given that so much of the activity is shrouded in secrecy.

WTO Trend: Commerce Always Takes Precedence

Beyond these cases, which are sufficiently disturbing in and of themselves, lies an overall theme that is even more unnerving: In the WTO forum, global commerce takes precedence over everything — democracy, public health, equity, the environment, food safety and more.

Indeed, under WTO rules, global commerce takes precedence over even small *business*. As described in the chapter on the WTO's impacts on developed country economies, the Uruguay Round Agreements provide corporations new rights to establish themselves in every WTO Member country. Obviously, small enterprises cannot take advantage of new rights to acquire the telecommunication system of a country, set up a branch abroad or relocate production to another country to avoid the U.S. minimum wage or the costs of environmental or workplace safety requirements. What is worse, however, is that WTO rules forbid small business promotion policies that could have the effect of discriminating against large *foreign* businesses — the only businesses likely to enter another country's market.

In recent years, foreign direct investment has shifted dramatically away from the establishment of new enterprises and toward global consolidation through mergers and acquisitions between existing entities. As documented in the following pages, this trend has been most intense in the economic sectors in which WTO agreements have been completed — financial services and telecommunications. This global merger mania is leading to problems with market concentration and, absent some countering force, will increasingly affect consumer prices and access to services. Not only has this trend led to the absorption of small enterprises into global giants, but under WTO rules developing countries have lost many of the safeguards for their infant industries that, for instance, the U.S. enjoyed in its economic development.

Indeed, the explicit plan of the WTO is to bring every country in the world — ready or not — into an existing global market that has been designed by the *ad hoc* activities of corporations established in rich countries and now formalized in the WTO rules. In five years of the WTO's existence, the least developed countries' share of world trade flows has dropped.

In addition, WTO rules seek to commodify everything — to turn everything into a form of property — so that it can be traded. For instance, the new system gives patents — and thus exclusive marketing rights — for life forms and indigenous knowledge. Consider what has happened in India, where the indigenous population has used the neem tree for medicinal purposes for generations. After a U.S. importer discovered the tree's pharmaceutical properties, multinational companies from the U.S. and Japan sought and received numerous patents on products made from the tree, leaving the indigenous populations unable to profit from knowledge they have developed over centuries.

Consider, too, the plight of subsistence farmers. Despite enormous growth in food trade, only 15% of the world food supply is traded. A large share of the world's population relies on subsistence farming for its food supply. Subsistence farmers are able to grow crops each year by saving seeds from the previous year. However, under the WTO's new intellectual property guarantees, a company can obtain ownership rights — literally a patent — over the knowledge and effort of the local farmers who bred the perfectly adapted seed over generations. Once a company holds the patent for a particular seed variety, it can force cashless farmers either to pay an annual royalty, buy new seeds each year or no longer use the variety, which may be the only one available or effective in that region. In addition, through an innovation called "terminator technology," companies can alter plants to make their seeds sterile so that a farmer literally cannot save the seed of one year's crop to plant the next year. This effectively gives companies license to rob subsistence farmers of their ability to feed themselves and their families.

Another overarching WTO characteristic is the push for "harmonization." Harmonization is the word industry has given to the replacement of the varied domestic standards of many nations with uniform global standards to allow companies to produce goods and services for a single global market. Harmonization gained a significant boost with the establishment of the WTO, which requires or encourages national governments to harmonize standards on issues such as food and worker safety, pharmaceutical patents, environmental rules and informational labeling of products.

The premise underlying harmonization is that the world is one huge market. Differences in standards, even if they express differences in cultures and values, are deemed inherently undesirable because they fragment the global market. But this core premise is false. When a single standard is forced on the world, it is impossible to respect the various choices that people in societies throughout the world make about the standards by which they want to live. Consumer groups are skeptical about harmonization because it creates an inherent conflict between industry's goal of unified global markets, and consumer power and democratic government.

A disturbing mechanism of harmonization is illustrated by the U.S. decision to accept imports of company-inspected Australian meat as "equivalent" to U.S. government-inspected meat. U.S. consumers will have no way of knowing which meat is which because both will bear the U.S. Department of Agriculture's seal of approval. Yet, salmonella poisonings in Australia have skyrocketed since industry inspection was first permitted there. This extraordinary increase deserves extra close scrutiny by the U.S. before allowing shipments of the company-inspected meat — not a blanket announcement that Australia's new system is equivalent to U.S. practice and thus an open door for imports.

Under "equivalence," significantly different – and often lower – standards from other countries can be declared equivalent to a country's domestic standards. The WTO provides for equivalence determinations based on subjective comparisons without clear procedural guidelines or an enumeration of the factors considered. Once countries declare each other's standards to be "equivalent," they must be treated as if they were domestic standards.

The WTO established more than 50 committees and working groups to work on harmonization. These working groups do not provide an opportunity for interested individuals or potentially affected communities to submit information or analysis or to participate, and they generally conduct their operations behind closed doors. Yet, under current trade rules, these standard-setting processes can directly affect national, state and local policies. In the U.S., the government must have an open, on-the-record rulemaking proceeding with public participation. International harmonization under the WTO, though, undercuts this process.

The Choice Is Ours:
The Seattle WTO Ministerial Meeting

In late November 1999, the 134 countries that are WTO Members were to meet in Seattle, Washington, for a Ministerial Summit to determine the future work plan of the WTO. At this writing, numerous countries were determining their positions for the meeting. Most corporate interests sought a major expansion of WTO rules to cover education and health services and to establish new rights for currency speculators and foreign investors (bringing into the WTO the Multilateral Agreement on Investment, a controversial proposed treaty killed by broad public and legislative opposition in 1998).

The U.S. scaled back its already modest agenda for labor or environmental safeguards at the WTO and instead is focused on obtaining an agreement at the Ministerial to:

• launch new negotiations to expand the scope of the WTO to include new service sectors, such as health and education;

• expand the rules concerning government procurement to all WTO countries, first by requiring all WTO Member countries to publicly list all of their procurement activity and to agree to future negotiations limiting the ability of governments to take non-commercial considerations (such as environmental protection or economic development) into account when making purchasing decisions;

• sign a global "Free Logging" pact that could increase deforestation by 4% per year;

• launch new negotiations on WTO protections for biotechnology products (such as genetically modified organisms); and

• further deregulate agricultural trade.

Much of the U.S. government's plan to expand the current WTO model runs contrary to U.S. public opinion and would undermine citizen participation under existing law. A recent survey showed that 81 percent of Americans believe Congress should oppose trade pacts that give one nation the power to overturn consumer safety, labor or environmental laws in another.

A global coalition of citizens groups — labor, religious, consumer, environmental, family farm and others — is calling for a "turnaround" to replace the WTO's damaging provisions. "No New Round, Turnaround" is the rallying cry issued by this large coalition of nongovernmental organizations worldwide.

These concerned groups seek an objective review of the performance under the current WTO rules, with an eye toward scaling back areas that inappropriately invade domestic policymaking, removing some issues from WTO jurisdiction altogether and replacing other WTO rules with versions aimed at serving the broad public interest.

We hope that after reading this book, you will be motivated to join others in a movement to halt the spread of the corporate economic globalization trade agenda in favor of democratic and accountable government.

Notes:

[1] Guy de Jonquieres, "Network Guerillas," *Financial Times*, Apr. 30, 1998, at 12.

In this chapter ...

CASES:

- **U.S. Clean Air Act:** The U.S. weakened regulations limiting gasoline contaminants that cause pollution after Venezuela won a WTO challenge against its Clean Air Act regulations.

- **U.S. Dolphin Protections:** The Clinton administration pushed amendments through Congress gutting the Marine Mammal Protection Act's dolphin-safe tuna provisions after Mexico threatened a WTO enforcement action on a 1991 GATT case it had won on the issue.

- **U.S. Endangered Species Act (Sea Turtles):** The WTO ruled against Endangered Species Act provisions that require U.S. and foreign shrimpers to equip their nets with inexpensive turtle excluder devices if they seek to sell shrimp in the U.S. market. Not yet implemented.

- **Japan Kyoto Treaty Implementation:** U.S. and EU governments and automakers have threatened WTO action against new fuel efficiency rules implementing Japan's Kyoto Treaty (on climate change) commitments. Also in this chapter is the **U.S. CAFE fuel efficiency rule GATT case.**

- **EU Toxics and Waste Reduction Policy:** The electronics industry got the U.S. to issue a WTO threat against a new EU environmental proposal that bans use of some toxic substances and makes companies responsible for disposal of used electronics products.

- **EU Ban on Cruel Steel Jaw Leg-Hold Traps:** U.S. and Canadian WTO threats resulted in a Europe-wide ban on steel jaw leg-hold traps and sale of furs caught using them being stalled for years and then being dramatically weakened.

- **U.S. Pushes Industry Case Against Eco-labels:** The Clinton administration pushed an industry-drafted proposal at the WTO that would have recast most eco-labeling programs as illegal trade barriers. EU opposition to the U.S. proposal has resulted in a deadlock to date.

- **U.S. Invasive Species Containment (Asian Longhorned Beetles):** The U.S. is fighting an infestation of the voracious, tree-eating beetle, which has arrived in raw wood packing crates from China and Hong Kong. Hong Kong has complained to the WTO about U.S. rules requiring treatment of wood packaging to kill the moths.

CONCEPTS:

WTO's Anti-Environment Bias: The WTO ruled against every environmental or conservation law it has reviewed, judging them to be illegal trade barriers that must be eliminated or changed.

Multilateral Environmental Agreements: Their implementation by signatory countries is susceptible to challenge as violating WTO requirements.

GATT Article XX: Provisions can be invoked to defend a law that otherwise violates GATT/WTO rules, but the WTO has rejected these defenses each and every time they have been invoked in an attempt to save a WTO-challenged environmental, conservation or health law.

Committee on Trade and Environment: This was established in an attempt to calm unanimous environmental opposition to the WTO. It has made no proposals to limit WTO damage to the environment or green policy and now is refocusing its attention to seek trade liberalization that also would be environmentally beneficial.

The WTO's Environmental Impact

When the legislation implementing the GATT Uruguay Round and establishing the World Trade Organization was approved in the U.S. Congress in 1994, it was done without the support of a single environmental, conservation or animal welfare group.

While the year before, several environmental groups had split away from the majority of U.S. nongovernmental organizations to support NAFTA, environmentalists were unified in opposition to the Uruguay Round Agreements. Then-U.S. Trade Representative Mickey Kantor claimed that no U.S. environmental or health laws would be undermined by the WTO, testifying, "The ... [WTO] clearly recognizes and acknowledges the sovereign right of each government to establish the level of protection of human, animal and plant life and health deemed appropriate by that government."[1] But these assurances failed to persuade the environmental community.

The environmentalists' skepticism was not surprising. Some of the groups that had supported NAFTA the year before – in exchange for an environmental "side agreement" – felt betrayed. First, early indications were that the side agreement would be ineffective.[2] Second, the groups had been promised by the Clinton administration that the NAFTA model would establish a "floor" for environmental protection in trade agreements that would be strengthened in subsequent trade pacts.[3] Instead, NAFTA's environmental side pact turned out to be the high water mark. The next year it became clear that the Uruguay Round Agreements contained numerous provisions limiting the actions governments could take to protect the public and the environment – but included no environmental safeguards at all.

In addition, environmentalists had witnessed the negative impacts of GATT provisions in effect *before* the Uruguay Round. In several instances, countries had challenged environmental laws as violating GATT rules. GATT dispute resolution tribunals had agreed that the environmental laws violated GATT rules and

Environmental standards in the WTO are "doomed to fail and could only damage the global trading system."[4]

— WTO Secretary General
Renato Ruggiero

also made extremely narrow interpretations of several GATT "exception" provisions that theoretically could be relied upon to protect environmental safeguards from such challenges.

Environmentalists feared that the expansive new powers of enforcement that were to be granted to the WTO, combined with the anti-environmental bias already inherent in the GATT, would produce dire consequences for global environmental protection. Environmentalists implored the Uruguay Round negotiators to refashion their approach to environmental issues.[5]

These entreaties were ignored by the negotiators, who produced an agreement that built upon the GATT's foundation of rules prioritizing commercial prerogatives over conservation and environmental protection. In an effort to counter the potential political problems that environmental concerns could cause with parliaments faced with approval of the Uruguay Round, the future WTO Member countries made a last-minute decision at the Marakesh, Morocco, WTO signing ceremonies to establish a Committee on Trade and Environment (CTE). The committee was given the mandate to study ways to make trade and environmental goals mutually compatible. The CTE was designated a WTO study group (not a negotiating group, meaning it was not empowered to develop new WTO rules for environmental protection). It has proven entirely ineffective as a mechanism for promoting environmental interests within the WTO.

Five years of experience under the WTO have confirmed environmentalists' fears. In case after case, the WTO is being used to threaten or has upheld formal challenges to environmental safeguards, doing far more damage than occurred under the pre-Uruguay Round regime.

Threats – often by industry but with government support – of WTO-illegality are being used to chill environmental innovation. Increased trade flows also are leading to greater biodiversity problems caused by invasive species infestations, and the status of multilateral environmental agreements is being undermined by the WTO. These cases include Japan's Kyoto Treaty implementation, a European toxics and recycling law, the Hong Kong WTO threat against U.S. longhorned beetle infestation policy, the U.S. threat against EU eco-labels, enforcement action on the GATT dolphin ruling and a quashed EU humane trapping law. Also described in this chapter are prominent WTO panel decisions on the U.S. Endangered Species Act (turtles) and the U.S. Clean Air Act. We now turn to a review of the GATT/WTO's environmental track record.

Through the threat of sanctions, the WTO has compelled countries to repeal or

> **"N**on-tariff barrier" is trade jargon for any law or policy that is not a tariff but affects trade. For instance, from the GATT/WTO perspective, a law that prohibits import of food containing carcinogenic pesticide residues would be considered a non-tariff barrier to trade. Depending on the specific GATT rules, it might be deemed an acceptable non-tariff barrier. Unfortunately, the Uruguay Round GATT rules provide for few such allowances, even when a law treats domestic and foreign goods the same.

rewrite key environmental laws or has chilled innovations. Particularly disturbing, most challenges to date have merely involved the application of the WTO's new enforcement powers to long-standing, anti-environmental GATT rules. The new, stronger anti-environmental provisions developed through the Uruguay Round have, with limited exceptions, only been brought to bear in the context of threats. These new agreements, as they are fully implemented, will provide new, far broader opportunities for anti-environmental interests to use the WTO to attack environmental safeguards – a process already under way.

GATT and the Environment: Pre-Uruguay Round

The GATT's anti-environmental bent was apparent prior to negotiation or approval of the Uruguay Round, as exemplified by high-profile challenges to two key U.S. environmental laws – the Marine Mammal Protection Act (MMPA) and the Corporate Average Fuel Efficiency (CAFE) standards for automobiles.

In 1991, GATT Article III on National Treatment (nondiscrimination) was interpreted to prohibit governments from treating goods differently based on the way they are produced or harvested. This interpretation arose from a successful GATT challenge by Mexico to the MMPA – an effective, long-standing U.S. statute banning the U.S. sale of tuna caught by domestic or foreign fishers using purse seines. Purse seines are massive nets that are laid over schools of dolphins to catch tuna swimming below. The technique had resulted in millions of dolphin deaths.[6] A GATT tribunal ruled that the U.S. law violated GATT rules by distinguishing tuna caught in a dolphin-safe manner from tuna caught using deadly encirclement seines.

Then, in 1994, a GATT panel ruled against U.S. CAFE regulations on a challenge brought by the European Economic Community (EEC). The GATT panel concluded that although the CAFE rules were facially neutral – i.e., they treated domestic and foreign cars alike – they had a discriminatory *effect* on European cars. Under the regulation, a manufacturer's entire fleet of cars sold in the U.S. was required to meet a combined average fuel efficiency. European auto manufacturers had made the marketing decision to sell only the larger, high-end (and thus more profitable) models of their cars in the U.S. An unintended consequence of that marketing decision was the requirement under the CAFE standards that such models be more fuel efficient than comparable American or Japanese luxury cars, whose efficiency could be averaged against smaller, cleaner models that the American and Japanese makers also sold on the U.S. market.

In both the dolphin and automobile fuel efficiency cases, the U.S. tried to invoke exceptions to the GATT that are contained in Article XX of the agreement. Article XX "exceptions" are supposed to allow countries to adopt and/or maintain laws that contradict GATT rules in certain narrowly defined circumstances.[7] In theory, the exceptions protect countries from inappropriate infringements on the capacity of policymakers to protect the public interest in vital areas such as national security and, theoretically, health or environmental protection. However, in both of these cases, the exceptions were so narrowly interpreted as to render them moot.

Thus, before Uruguay Round talks were complete, environmentalists had witnessed successful attacks on environmental laws using GATT rules and had seen that the existing GATT exceptions provided no protection for such laws.

The WTO and the Environment: Strong Enforcement of Anti-Environmental Rules

Mindful of this disturbing pre-Uruguay track record, environmentalists urged Uruguay Round negotiators to strengthen the weak Article XX exceptions so that they might be used effectively to safeguard WTO-challenged environmental laws. They also sought to amend GATT provisions that had been – or could be – the basis for attacks on environmental policies. Since a central objective of the Uruguay Round

GATT Article XX:
Useful as an Environmental Exception?

GATT Article XX contains "exceptions" that countries can invoke to defend a challenge to a law or policy that otherwise violates GATT rules. Several provisions of Article XX have been employed by the U.S. and other countries in an attempt to defend challenged environmental rules. For instance, Article XX(b) refers to laws that are "necessary to protect human, animal or plant life and health," and Article XX(g) refers to laws "related to the conservation of exhaustible natural resources." Yet because of their ambiguous textual construction and the way past GATT panels have interpreted them, these provisions have proved to be of no use in defending environmental laws.

For instance, the requirement that a law be "necessary" in Article XX(b) has been interpreted to require that the environmental laws in question be the *least trade restrictive* way to achieve the environmental goal. Also, the general *chapeau* (opening clause) of Article XX has been interpreted to undercut the application of all of the underlying provisions. Indeed, Article XX has never been successfully used by any country trying to defend an environmental law from GATT or WTO challenge.

Industry groups are well aware of this fact. In threatening the EU with a WTO challenge for proposing strict new environmental guidelines relating to electronics products, the American Electronics Association noted: "So far, no panel called to apply Article XX(b) has accepted the necessity of a measure otherwise inconsistent with other GATT provisions."[8]

was to make the GATT and other related agreements strongly enforceable through the WTO by use or threat of trade sanction, environmentalists considered it to be critical that the new regime not include provisions that could undermine domestic and international environmental laws and policy.

Uruguay Round negotiators refused to remedy the existing problems. Rather, in the Uruguay Round Agreements, they added a vast array of new anti-environment, anti-conservation provisions to the existing GATT rules. These new rules subject a wider array of hard-won environmental laws to scrutiny as so-called "non-tariff barriers" to trade. ("Non-tariff barrier" is trade jargon for any law or policy that is not a tariff but affects trade. For instance, from the GATT/WTO perspective, a law that prohibits import of food containing carcinogenic pesticide residues is considered a non-tariff barrier to trade.)

The WTO Agreement on Sanitary and Phytosanitary Measures (SPS) explicitly restricts the actions that governments can take relating to food and agriculture in an ef-

---

Potential GATT "Exceptions" Rejected in Each Environmental Challenge

- *MMPA/Tuna-Dolphin I (Mexico v. U.S.):* A 1991 GATT panel ruled that the U.S. embargo on tuna caught in a manner harmful to dolphins was illegal because, among other grounds, GATT Article XX did not apply to U.S. actions to protect dolphins taken outside of its territorial waters and because the U.S. had failed to show the policy was "necessary" to conserve dolphin populations.

- *MMPA/Tuna-Dolphin II (EEC v. U.S.):* A 1994 GATT panel ruled that the U.S. secondary tuna embargo was not "necessary" to protect dolphins and thus failed the "least trade restrictive test." The panel also ruled that under GATT Article XX(g), countries can implement only those environmental laws meant to influence the producers' practices. Countries cannot implement laws meant to influence the policies of foreign governments, because the panel decided that the term "relate" in Artice XX(g) required a law to *directly* relate to the goal of resource conservation.

- *Clean Air Act/Venezuela Gasoline:* In 1996 the WTO Appellate Body ruled that air qualified under GATT Article XX as an "exhaustible natural resource" worthy of protection but that the U.S. government-set gasoline cleanliness requirements discriminated against foreign gasoline and thus failed to satisfy Article XX's *chapeau.*

- *Endangered Species Act/Shrimp-Turtle:* In 1998 the WTO Appellate Body ruled that while the U.S. law protecting sea turtles caught in shrimp nets was theoretically protected by GATT Article XX, in the specific case in question, the U.S. law's certification requirements were not covered because they forced sovereign governments to adopt specific regulatory regimes regarding shrimp fishing and were applied differently among trading partners.

fort to protect the environment, human, plant and animal health, and the food supply. As a result, many policies that governments use to avoid or contain invasive species infestations from undermining biodiversity can run afoul of SPS rules. The WTO Agreement on Technical Barriers to Trade (TBT) requires that product standards — a nation's rules governing the contents and characteristics of products — be the least trade restrictive version and, with extraordinarily limited exceptions, be based on international standards. The WTO Agreement on Government Procurement (AGP) requires that governments take into account only "commercial considerations" when making purchasing decisions. The Agreement on Trade Related Aspects of Intellectual Property (TRIPs) requires that WTO Members provide property rights protection to genetically modified plant varieties even though their long-term environmental impacts have not been established. All of these agreements are enforceable, by threat of sanction, through the WTO's dispute resolution system.

A crucial difference between the GATT and the WTO trade regimes is the legal status of their respective dispute settlement panel rulings. Both systems include the possibility of challenging other countries' laws before trade tribunals, when one country thinks another's law violates GATT rules. Under GATT, however, the emphasis was on cooperation and negotiated settlements to trade disagreements. The WTO, in contrast, is "self-executing," which means its panels are empowered to make binding decisions, enforceable through trade sanctions.

Under pre-Uruguay Round rules, a dispute panel report was adopted only if there was a consensus by all GATT Contracting Parties. Requiring consensus for action is a typical sovereignty protection found in many international agreements. Under the previous GATT rules, a country whose domestic regulations were under fire could essentially block the enforcement of a ruling (although, in order to avoid undermining GATT's legitimacy, countries rarely exercised this option).

The Uruguay Round Agreements turned the sovereignty safeguard of consensus on its head by requiring unanimous consensus to *stop* adoption of any WTO panel's ruling. This would require 134 WTO Members, including the victorious country, to all agree to stop adoption of a panel ruling. The intention of this change was to create a rule-based system in which all WTO Members were equal, since the former cooperative system was seen to give too much negotiating power to the financially stronger countries who had more political ability to decide to follow or ignore rulings. Unfortunately, the effect of the new binding system has been to consolidate the dominant position of countries that can afford permanent representation at the WTO and expert help at the panel hearings.[9] Worse still, the outcomes of trade battles are now being sold to the public as technical, legal interpretations of commercial law and not recognized as what they are: political and policy decisions.

While the WTO publicly states its support for the principles of sustainable development in the WTO ("the [environment] has been given and will continue to be given a high profile on the WTO agenda"),[10] the track record suggests an altogether different set of priorities. Indeed, in a revealing attack of candor, then-WTO Secretary General Renato Ruggiero stated that environmental standards in the WTO are "doomed to fail and could only damage the global trading system."[11]

WTO's New Binding Rules Have Weakened Environmental Safeguards

Case 1: U.S. Weakens Clean Air Rule to Implement WTO Order

The WTO had been in operation only for several months when the first attack on an important environmental law was launched. In response to a challenge initiated by Venezuela and Brazil, a WTO dispute panel in January 1996 found that U.S. Clean Air Act regulations adopted under 1990 amendments to the Act violated trade rules.[12] The U.S. was instructed by the WTO to amend its gasoline cleanliness regulations,[13] which it did by adopting a policy toward limiting contaminants in gasoline that the U.S. Environmental Protection Agency (EPA) earlier had rejected as effectively unenforceable.[14]

This case generated significant press coverage as an example of how the WTO could be used to skirt a country's democratic policymaking and judicial systems. It was the first concrete evidence of the WTO's threat to environmental policy and to national sovereignty in setting and effectively enforcing important policies.

The EPA gasoline regulation struck down by the WTO had withstood all the challenges available through the U.S. legislative, regulatory and judicial systems. First, opponents of the rule, including the Venezuelan government represented by the prominent U.S. lobbying firm Arnold & Porter, lobbied Congress.[16] Failing there, they intervened in the rule-making process.[17] When the EPA ultimately passed a regulation the Venezuelan industry did not like, its lobbyists went back to Congress to try to get the rule changed.[18]

After failing to change the regulation, domestic oil refiners began to comply. They claimed to have invested $37 billion to implement the law.[19] Venezuela and Brazil, on the other hand, renewed their attack at the WTO. Only there, in a closed WTO tribunal, out of the public eye and before unaccountable, unelected trade bureaucrats, did opponents of the Clean Air Act amendments find success.

> **"WTO Members were free to set their own environmental objectives, but they were bound to implement those objectives only through measures consistent with [WTO's] provisions."[15]**
>
> — WTO Clean Air Ruling

The clean air ruling actualized environmentalists' gravest fears about the WTO. In typical WTO double-speak, the panel rhetorically affirmed the right of nations to sovereignty over environmental matters while acknowledging that, in practice, countries' environmental laws must conform to WTO rules: "WTO members were free to set their own environmental objectives, but they were bound to implement those objectives only through measures consistent with [WTO's] provisions."[20]

The Clean Air Rules in Question: The amendments to the 1990 Clean Air Act were designed to empower the EPA to regulate pollution attributed to motor vehicle fuels, which, with the exception of the phase-out of leaded gasoline, had been neglected in previous U.S. pollution eradication programs.[21] Gasoline contaminants (known as "aromatics") produce emissions that result in ozone, smog and toxic air pollutants and are a principal cause of ground-level ozone.[22]

The reasons for the amendments were well documented. The adverse human health effects of ground-level ozone include respiratory irritation, breathing problems, aggravation of asthma, inflammation and damage to the lining of the lungs, as well as a reduction in the immune system's ability to fight off bacterial respiratory infections.[23] A severe increase in the incidence of asthma in the U.S. corresponded to the increase in smog due to toxic emissions from gasoline in the 1980s.[24]

In 1994, the EPA issued the rule implementing Congress' 1990 Clean Air Act amendments requiring reduction of gasoline contaminants.[25] The rule required the cleanliness of gasoline sold in the most polluted cities in the U.S. to improve by 15% over 1990 levels, and all gasoline sold elsewhere in the U.S. to maintain levels of cleanliness at least equal to 1990 levels.[26]

The difficulty in designing the regulation was finding an enforceable, trustworthy and economically feasible way to ensure that all gasoline sold in the U.S. met the standards. Had the EPA simply set a single, absolute cleanliness target and required all refiners to comply immediately, the gasoline market would have suffered from shortages and price hikes. In addition, the EPA needed to gather more data to quantify the extent to which some of the contaminants in reformulated gasoline led to increased emissions before setting a single, absolute cleanliness standard.

> **T**he EPA will implement clean air rules as long as they are "consistent with the obligations of the United States under the World Trade Organization."[27]
>
> — EPA Guidelines on new Clean Air Rules

On the other hand, a flexible approach — setting cleanliness standards based on each refinery's past performance — was problematic because some gas refiners (including U.S. refiners that had been in business less than six months and most foreign refiners over whom the EPA had no enforcement authority) lacked sufficiently reliable data upon which EPA could determine an individual baseline standard from which to calculate the required improvement.

In an attempt to minimize market disruptions and maximize health protection, the EPA settled on an interim solution: Those gasoline producers with EPA documentation of their 1990 gasoline cleanliness levels set their improvement target from that data. Gasoline from foreign refiners that sold less than 80% of their gasoline in the U.S. (those selling 80% or more were required to file with the EPA) and from domestic refiners without documentation (new ones or those with filing violations) had to match the average actual 1990 contaminant level of all gas refiners able to provide full documentation. This rule was set to expire in 1998, giving EPA five years to determine a single cleanliness target.

The WTO Challenge: Venezuela and Brazil claimed that the EPA rule put their gasoline industries at an unfair disadvantage because the structure of the rule created a possibility that imported gasoline that failed to meet the average could be rejected while equally dirty gasoline from a U.S. refiner whose individual baseline was at the bottom end could be allowed.

The WTO panel sided with Venezuela and Brazil's oil industries, holding that the EPA's mechanism to enforce the congressionally mandated air standards could result in discriminatory *effects* favoring U.S. refiners over foreign refiners.[30] The U.S. appealed, but the WTO Appellate Body upheld the lower panel's decision.[31] In its submission defending the Clean Air Act regulation, the U.S. claimed that if the regulation were changed it would be possible for annual nitrous oxide (NOx) emissions from imported gasoline to increase 5 to 7%.[32] The final 1996 WTO Appellate Body ruling, however, held that although air qualified under Article XX as an "exhaustible natural resource" worthy of protection, the U.S. government-set gasoline cleanliness requirements discriminated against foreign gasoline and therefore failed to trigger the GATT Article XX exception clause.[33] The WTO instructed the U.S. to change the policy.

U.S. Implements WTO Ruling:

The WTO's rulings forced the U.S. to choose between repealing the EPA regulation and permitting imports of dirtier Venezuelan gasoline (and possibly placing U.S. refiners at a competitive disadvantage for having made the investments to implement the EPA regulations), or keeping the EPA regulation and facing the $150 million in trade sanctions each year in the form of higher Venezuelan tariffs on U.S. products that WTO would authorize for failure to comply.

> *I n August 1997, the EPA replaced the regulation with a new one that was "consistent with the obligations of the United States under the World Trade Organization"[28] to implement the WTO ruling. The new WTO-consistent rules are identical to an oil industry proposal that the EPA had previously contended was unenforceable and too costly.[29]*

The decision had major implications; Venezuela is the single largest exporter of oil products to the U.S., supplying 16% of the total U.S. crude oil product imports and 19% of all gasoline imports.[34] In August 1997, the EPA replaced the regulation with a new one that was "consistent with the obligations of the United States under the World Trade Organization"[35] to implement the WTO ruling. The new WTO-consistent rules are identical to an industry proposal that the EPA had previously contended was unenforceable and too costly.[36]

The gasoline case inspired a run of successful challenges against hard-won environmental and public health laws. To date, all GATT/WTO rulings on environmental laws have led (or will lead, if implemented) to the weakening of the measures in question.

Green Groups Sue U.S. EPA for Capitulating to WTO on Clean Air Act Regulations

In early May 1998, Earthjustice Legal Defense Fund filed a federal lawsuit on behalf of Friends of the Earth, Defenders of Wildlife and the Center for International Environmental Law charging that EPA had exceeded its congressional mandate by weakening the U.S. standard for gasoline cleanliness based on a WTO panel ruling.[37] "While the EPA has explicit authority to consider cost and other factors in determining the 'greatest reduction in emissions achievable' ... the agency has no authority" to relax the standard for economic reasons, the lawsuit said.[38] The Earthjustice brief further noted: "there must be an air-quality purpose for regulatory action ... in order for the EPA to consider economic feasibility. ... [I]n relying on international trade rules and economic factors to justify the new rule, EPA violated the law and relied on factors that Congress did not intend the agency to consider."[39] The groups also argued that WTO panel reports create no international obligation for the U.S. to change its laws.

In early 1999, the court ruled that the EPA was within its mandate to change the standard. The court said that the WTO decision was a good reason to interpret the Clean Air Act to allow the EPA to take factors other than that of air degradation into account when formulating the new gasoline cleanliness rule.[40] The court also implied that the WTO panel ruling creates a treaty obligation for the U.S. that should not be contravened.[41] Environmentalists are concerned that the court's decision could be used to justify other changes to U.S. laws as these become subject to successful WTO challenges in the future.

Case 2: Clinton Administration Guts Dolphin Protection

Under amendments to the U.S. Marine Mammal Protection Act (MMPA), the sale by domestic or foreign fishers of tuna caught with encirclement nets, known as purse seines, was banned in the U.S. in 1988 because the nets killed millions of dolphins in the Eastern Tropical Pacific.[42] For reasons marine biologists have never determined, schools of tuna in that region congregate under schools of dolphins. Thus, the fishing industry began using mile-long nets deployed by speedboats to encircle the dolphins on the surface. In this method, the weighted bottoms of the massive nets are drawn shut, creating huge sacks in which both the dolphins and the tuna are trapped. Over 30 years, seven million dolphins were drowned, crushed or otherwise killed as a result of purse seine tuna fishing.[43]

The slaughter was captured on videotape by an environmentalist who slipped aboard a fishing boat as a cook.[44] The resulting furor – including millions of children writing to Congress to "Save the Dolphins" – led to the dolphin-safe tuna provisions of MMPA.[45] Two of four affected species of dolphin, the eastern spinner and northeastern offshore spotted dolphins, have been designated "depleted" under the MMPA due to purse seine fishing methods.[46]

The Gatt Dolphin Cases: In 1991, a GATT panel ruled against Section 101(a)(2) of the U.S. MMPA[47] – which excluded from the U.S. market tuna caught by domestic or foreign fishers using purse seines. The panel interpreted language in GATT's Article III, which prohibits discrimination between products on the basis of *where* they are produced to also forbid distinguishing between products based on *how* they are produced (called production processes and methods or PPMs). Specifically, the GATT panel interpreted language in GATT Article III requiring "like products" produced domestically or abroad to be given equal treatment. By deciding that the notion of "like product" only pertained to a product's physical characteristics, the panel ruling placed a long list of U.S. and other countries' laws that focus on *how* tuna is caught or *how* paper is manufactured in violation of GATT's rules. Thus, unless there is literally dolphin meat *in* a can of tuna, making it physically different, a can of tuna caught with dolphin-deadly nets must be treated exactly the same as one caught by dolphin-safe methods.

The next year the European Community, which sought to export prepared tuna processed from fish obtained from Pacific Ocean stocks, launched its own challenge to the law.[48] In its 1994 ruling, the GATT panel on the European challenge again ruled against dolphin protection.[49]

In both cases, the U.S. argued that because dolphin protection is a legitimate environmental objective and the embargo was applied to both the domestic and foreign tuna industries, the law would fall well within the protections of GATT Article XX. Both GATT panels rejected this argument. The first panel found that the law was not "nec-

Production and Processing Methods

GATT dispute resolution panels have ruled that products cannot be treated differently on the basis of how they are produced or harvested. The ability to distinguish among production methods is essential to environmental protection and environmentally sensitive economic policies. A key component to setting sustainable policies is the ability to change the conditions and processes under which goods are produced and commodities grown, harvested and extracted to more environmentally friendly ones. Trade rules that forbid the differentiation between production methods make it impossible for governments to design effective environmental policies.

GATT: Nations Cannot Restrict Goods Made with Child or Forced Labor

Under GATT rulings banning distinctions among products based on the way they are produced, the U.S. can't maintain an embargo on tuna harvested in a way fatal to dolphins but allow dolphin-safe harvested tuna into U.S. markets. This same rule, if applied to bans on products made with child labor, would hamstring citizens' attempts to make corporations and governments accountable to fundamental, universally recognized human and labor rights. For instance, the U.S. could not ban soccer balls from Pakistan that the International Labor Organization has documented as being produced by young children under abusive conditions. Under GATT, a soccer ball is a soccer ball no matter how different the conditions of its manufacture. In addition, the WTO Agreement on Government Procurement (AGP) explicitly prevents the U.S. or any other WTO Member that has signed on to the agreement from using its purchasing power to withhold lucrative government contracts from companies engaging in labor, human rights or environmental violations. The WTO therefore erects a huge obstacle to enforcing ILO Conventions and basic human rights through government and consumer activism.

essary" to protect dolphin health because, in the panel's opinion, the U.S. could have attempted to protect dolphins through other measures that would not have violated GATT.[50] It also found that the U.S. law targeted tuna fishing largely outside U.S. borders and ruled that Article XX applied only to actions taken inside a nation's borders.[51] This ruling is astounding, given that fish are migratory and are not confined to the territory of one country.

The panel in the European challenge disagreed with the first panel's conclusion that a country can never, under GATT rules, protect resources outside of its territory if such protections limit trade. However, it agreed with the first panel that the dolphin-safe law was not "necessary" to protect dolphin health and thus that the U.S. law was GATT-illegal.

In addition, the panel in the European challenge concluded that a nation cannot require another country to change domestic laws — in this case adopt regulations on tuna fishing to protect dolphins — in exchange for market access.[52] The U.S. could pressure individual tuna producers to change their behavior but could not condition access to the U.S. market for these producers on their home country *governments'* taking concrete action to enforce U.S. dolphin protection standards. This line of reasoning would be recycled in a similar WTO case involving a U.S. embargo on shrimp from countries that do not require fishers to protect sea turtles (see below).

Given that the rulings against the U.S. dolphin-safe law were issued by GATT – and not WTO – panels, they were not automatically enforceable. Indeed, worried that implementation of the controversial 1991 GATT case that had been dubbed *GATTzilla vs. Flipper* could threaten NAFTA's 1993 congressional approval, the U.S. and Mexico originally agreed to block further GATT action.

However, in 1995, with NAFTA already implemented and the WTO enforcement mechanism now in effect, Mexico threatened a WTO enforcement case against the U.S. for continuing failure to implement the 1991 GATT dolphin ruling. In order to avoid the political embarrassment of having the WTO order the U.S. to rescind the highly popular dolphin protection (or face millions of dollars in trade sanctions) the Clinton administration launched a two-year campaign that ultimately resulted in the gutting of the MMPA.

Clinton Administration Guts Dolphin Law to Comply with GATT: President Clinton was so anxious to avoid the public spectacle of a dolphin protection law being eviscerated again by the WTO, he sent a letter to Mexican President Ernesto Zedillo declaring that the weakening of the standard "is a top priority for my Administration and for me personally."[53] Clinton promised to take action within the first thirty days of his second term.[54] It would not prove easy to comply with the ruling or this promise, as this required the U.S. to amend the Marine Mammal Protection Act through an act of Congress.

The administration recruited several members of Congress with notoriously bad environmental voting records, such as Rep. Randy "Duke" Cunningham, a California Republican, and Sen. John Breaux, a Louisiana Democrat, to introduce a bill weakening the MMPA to make it conform to the GATT ruling. That legislation was quickly nicknamed the "Dolphin Death Act" by many environmental groups.[55]

Under the leadership of the Marine Mammal Protection Act's original champions, such as Sen. Barbara Boxer and Rep. George Miller, both California Democrats, a coalition of environmental, consumer and other public interest groups – the Dolphin Safe Fair Trade Campaign – was able to stall the Dolphin Death Act in 1996. However, a slightly different version of the legislation was passed in August 1997[56] after a huge push by the Clinton administration, led by then-Undersecretary of State Timothy Wirth and Vice President Al Gore. The amendment would allow tuna caught with the deadly nets to be sold in the U.S. Moreover, it would even allow tuna caught with such nets to carry the "dolphin safe" label that consumers have come to know and trust – provided the tuna is certified as coming from a catch where a single monitor on a football field-length fishing boat did not observe any dolphin deaths.

On April 29, 1999, the Commerce Department announced that based on the results of a study by the National Marine Fisheries Service (NMFS)[57] in consultation with the Marine Mammal Commission and the Inter-American Tropical Tuna Commission (IATTC), it would implement the 1997 law and weaken the labeling standard

> **T**hanks to a GATT ruling, tuna caught with dolphin-deadly purse seines will be back on the U.S. market by the fall of 1999 – for the first time in over a decade.

for "dolphin safe" tuna.[58] The study, mandated by the 1997 legislation, concluded that dolphin mortality has declined in areas where purse seines are used but monitors are aboard fishing fleets.[59] The study also found, however, that the dolphin population in the Eastern Tropical Pacific was not recovering, despite the use of monitors. The study showed that although mortality rates declined *relative* to unmonitored purse seine fishing, the decline was not sufficient to replace the damage that purse seines had already wrought on the dolphin population. Nonetheless, the Commerce Department decided to move ahead, and tuna caught with purse seines was slated to be back on the U.S. market by the fall of 1999 – for the first time in over a decade. (Meanwhile, the IATTC will continue to study dolphin mortality until 2002, at which time, if the results are the same, the U.S. will make the new U.S. standard permanent.)[60]

The U.S. Commerce Department claims that the new regulation will allow only tuna from catches during which no dolphin deaths were observed to bear the "dolphin safe" label.[61] However, tuna boats are a football field in length, the nets are miles in circumference and only one observer is required per ship – making it physically impossible to monitor thoroughly. Moreover, to enforce this policy, the U.S. would have to track all tuna imports from the moment they are caught in the Eastern Tropical Pacific to the time they enter the U.S. consumer market. This presents an enormous task for regulators, which is why the old law operated on a country-by-country basis, not on a catch-by-catch basis. It remains unclear how the U.S. can, with any confidence, distinguish among tuna shipments that have involved the death of dolphins and those that have not. Instead, regulators will have to rely on the "dolphin safe" reports of the producers themselves – those with the greatest incentive to downplay dolphin deaths. Consumer and environmental groups say that this new policy degrades the "dolphin safe" label from an effective way in which to hold the tuna industry accountable to consumers to a cynical marketing ploy rewarding unsafe fishing practices.[62]

The precedent set in the GATT panel's ruling has widespread implications.[63] It declares import bans designed to further a legitimate social or environment aim by eliminating objectionable production methods to be outside GATT/WTO permissible policy. Under such reasoning, prohibiting the use of fur harvested by clubbing of harp seals could be GATT-illegal. Similarly, bans on products involving child labor or even slave labor could be prohibited by the WTO.

Case 3: The WTO Rules Against Endangered Species Act

Provisions of the Endangered Species Act allow sale of shrimp in the U.S. only if the shrimp is caught in nets equipped with turtle excluder devices, or TEDs.[65] These devices are designed to allow sea turtles to escape from shrimp nets. In late 1998, a WTO panel ruled that the U.S. law violated trade rules and ordered the U.S. to rewrite its sea turtle protection policy.

On the WTO Shrimp-turtle ruling: *"Good dicta for environmentalists, but I wouldn't want to be a sea turtle."*[64]

— Jack Nash,
Trade Analyst

Worldwide, the turtle population has plummeted, and all sea turtles that inhabit U.S. waters are listed as endangered or threatened.[66] Shrimp nets entangle, drown, dismember and kill as many as 55,000 endangered or threatened sea turtles each year.[67] Indeed, shrimping kills more sea turtles than all other human threats to turtles combined.[68]

In an effort to minimize the decline in the sea turtle populations, the National Marine Fisheries Service promoted the use of TEDs to U.S. shrimpers. After few shrimpers installed TEDs in their nets, U.S. law was changed in 1989 to require shrimpers to operate in a manner that did not harm turtles.[69] Under section 609 of the Endangered Species Act,[70] all shrimp sold in the U.S. must be caught using TEDs, any of several trapdoor-like devices that shunt turtles out of shrimp nets before they drown. Costing from $50 to $400, TEDs are a relatively inexpensive way to reduce sea turtle deaths by as much as 97% – without appreciably decreasing shrimp catches.[71]

The governments of India, Malaysia, Pakistan and Thailand joined forces to challenge the U.S. law, arguing that WTO rules prohibit limitations on imports based on the way products are produced.[72] Australia, El Salvador, the EU, Guatemala, Hong Kong, Japan, Nigeria, the Philippines, Singapore and Venezuela made third-party submissions to the WTO panel arguing that the U.S. law violated WTO rules.

Under the argument used by these nations – the same one used in the tuna-dolphin case – all shrimp are "like products" and therefore must be allowed into the U.S. market, regardless of whether the shrimp are caught using methods that kill sea turtles.

The U.S. argued that it was allowed under WTO rules to protect animal life, as long as the law applied equally to U.S. and foreign shrimp producers. Indeed, unlike the MMPA challenged in the tuna-dolphin case, which had a potential for technical discrimination in how one aspect was implemented, the turtle policy was *exactly* the same for foreign and domestic fishers. Thus, the U.S. argued that the shrimp law qualified for an exception under Article XX.

The WTO panel disagreed. "We note that the issue in dispute was not the urgency of protection of sea turtles. ... It was not our task to review generally the desirability or necessity of the environmental objectives of the U.S. policy on sea turtle conservation. In our opinion, Members are free to set their own environmental objectives. However, they are bound to implement these objectives in such a way that is consistent with their WTO obligations, not depriving the WTO Agreement of its object and purpose."[73]

The panel ruled that the U.S. law was *designed* to interfere with trade and thus the Article XX exceptions were inapplicable. Of course, this interpretation eviscerates the entire exceptions clause of GATT. The panel also declared that because the regulations were uni-

> " **W**TO Members are bound to implement [environmental] objectives in such a way that is consistent with their WTO obligations, not depriving the WTO Agreement of its object and purpose. " [73]
>
> — WTO Shrimp Turtle Ruling

laterally imposed on U.S. trading partners, the law deprived the WTO of its object and purpose of establishing a multilateral trade regime, regardless of the non-trade related objective that was being pursued and the lack of discrimination between domestic and foreign fisheries.

Major U.S. environmental organizations quickly denounced the decision and urged the Clinton administration to continue to implement the sea turtle protections and attempt to reform the WTO substantially – or withdraw from it.[74] Even the pro-WTO *New York Times* editorialized about the "Sea Turtles Warning," contradicting its past admonitions about WTO critics' unfounded concerns by urging the WTO to reconsider and the U.S. not to change the law.[75] The U.S government appealed the WTO decision.[76]

In October 1998, the WTO Appellate Body reaffirmed the decision that the U.S. law is WTO-illegal.[77] However, the Appellate Body reversed the lower panel as to whether the Endangered Species Act theoretically could be covered by Article XX exceptions.[78] Reaching impressive heights of legal sophistry, the panel held that the law could indeed have qualified for an environmental exception under Article XX but did not do so in this case because the law was implemented in a way that was unjustifiably and arbitrarily discriminatory.[79]

The Appellate Body's ruling has been viewed as an attempt to defuse the criticism of environmentalists while still advancing the GATT agenda of primacy of trade over all other policy goals. The panel acknowledged that sea turtles are endangered and that there is a legitimate interest in protecting and preserving them. It also acknowledged the appropriateness of the U.S. turtle excluder device policy. The ruling included language aimed at pacifying environmentalists, stating, "We have not decided that the protection and preservation of the environment is of no significance to the Members of the WTO. Clearly, it is. We have not decided that the sovereign nations that are Members of the WTO cannot adopt effective measures to protect endangered species, such as sea turtles. Clearly, they can and should."[80] Despite the positive sounding political rhetoric, the WTO Appellate Body ultimately ruled that the U.S. measure violated WTO rules.

The Appellate Body then recommended that the U.S. change its turtle protection measures to comply with the ruling, leading one trade policy expert to quip, "Good dicta for environmentalists, but I wouldn't want to be a sea turtle."[81]

If implemented, the WTO ruling against the Endangered Species Act could severely hamper efforts to protect sea turtles. Perversely, it could also put U.S. producers who have already invested in TEDs technology at a competitive disadvantage for having complied with the law of the land. According to one shrimper, "We are the ones who have to pay the price to save the turtle. I thought we were going to have a level playing field to compete, but apparently not." [82]

As domestic industry learns the lesson that the WTO is hostile to strong environmental safeguards affected domestic industries will question environmental legislation on the basis that it disadvantages them *vis-à-vis* their foreign competitors, whose noncompliance is effectively sanctioned by the WTO. The combination of WTO environmental hostility and related industry pressure will make it increasingly difficult for countries to assert environmental leadership in the absence of often slow or impossible international consensus.

Initially, the U.S. agreed to comply with the WTO ruling against the Endangered Species Act by revising regulations to allow shipment-by-shipment certification of

TEDs use. Under the original regulation, a country seeking to send shrimp to the U.S. was responsible for requiring its shrimp fleet to have sea turtle protections comparable to the Endangered Species Act standard. Environmental groups charged that the new regulation would violate the Endangered Species Act. In April 1999, the U.S. Court of International Trade (CIT) sided with environmental groups, interpreting Section 609 of the ESA as requiring countries to have fleet-wide TEDs regulations in place *before* any boat could export shrimp to the U.S.[83] That would stop shrimpers who don't use TEDs from evading U.S. law by purchasing export permits that say they do or by shipping their product on boats that do use TEDs.[84]

The Clinton administration faces a stark choice. The administration agreed to comply with the WTO ruling by taking regulatory action, thus limiting the role of Congress and the public. The Court of International Trade ruling removes this option. Now, the administration must bow to the WTO and prepare for a bruising congressional battle to change the Endangered Species Act or face WTO sanctions.

What's Next? Special Interests Threaten WTO Action to Thwart Environmental Initiatives

To the consternation of citizens advocating on behalf of the environment, health and safety, new Uruguay Round texts, such as the Agreement on Technical Barriers to Trade (TBT), contained provisions rendering nondiscriminatory policies based on production and processing techniques that advance important social and environmental objectives inconsistent with trade obligations.

The TBT Agreement outlines the procedures WTO Members must follow when promulgating product standards or other technical regulations. Its provisions apply to all products, including industrial and agricultural products,[85] but not to health-related food rules or agricultural product regulations dealing with plant pests or animal health.[86] The TBT Agreement limits how governments can regulate trade in the interest of environmental protection by requiring that regulations not be more trade restrictive than is necessary[87] and not differ from international standards.[88]

Although the TBT Agreement has not yet been the subject of a WTO panel ruling, its provisions have already been used by the U.S. to pressure Japan to weaken clean air laws designed to comply with internationally agreed upon targets for CO_2 reduction[89] and to attack an EU prohibition on leg traps deemed cruel to animals.[90] The U.S. government also has argued that labeling products as environmentally friendly to raise environmental awareness among consumers – called eco-labeling – is a technical regulation that should be subject to TBT scrutiny.[91] Canada also has used the TBT Agreement to file a WTO challenge to France's ban on asbestos (*See* Chapter 7 for more information on the Canadian asbestos case). These and other threats of WTO action are examined in detail below, as they provide an indication of how the TBT Agreement can be used over time on behalf of narrow economic interests hostile to environmental regulations.

Threat 1: U.S. Pressures EU to Abandon High Standards for Curtailing Electronics Industry Pollution

In what will be an important test case, the American Electronics Association (AEA) has attacked an EU proposal to control electronics pollution. The AEA claims the EU proposal is WTO-illegal because it restricts trade in certain heavy metals used to make electronics products, is not based on an international standard, and is more trade restrictive than necessary to satisfy its objective.[92] The U.S. State Department quickly sent a *demarche* to the EU, suggesting that the high-standard proposal runs afoul of WTO rules and urging the EU to adopt the less-stringent U.S. standard for electronics pollution.[93]

The EU proposal is designed to minimize pollution caused by electronic products and to shift the cost of subsequent environmental cleanup from the public to the electronics industry.[94] This high-standard environmental package would require electronic companies to take responsibility for their products from cradle to grave.[95] First, the EU proposes to ban electronic products containing lead, mercury, cadmium, hexavalent chromium and halogenated flame retardants by the year 2004.[96] The EU also proposes a 5% recycled content rule for plastic electronic components. Electronics manufacturers would also be made responsible for the recovery and disposal of electronic equipment.[97]

The electronics industry and the U.S. government have gone on a major offensive against the EU proposal. The AEA — with 3,000 member companies, including Motorola and Intel — wrote to the EU charging that the proposal would violate a number of WTO rules.[98] In assailing the proposal, the AEA makes the astounding claim that there is no evidence that heavy metals, like lead, pose a threat to human health or the environment.[99] U.S. law and regulation recognizes, however, that lead solder and the solvents used in electric manufacturing have a number of significant health risks, including cancer.[100]

The AEA also argues that the EU recycled content requirement violates the WTO Agreement on Technical Barriers to Trade (TBT).[101] According to the AEA, the EU cannot impose recycling requirements on foreign producers because the EU has no interest, or right, to advance environmental protection in the foreign country in which the components are made.[102] However, given that these products will eventually be disposed in the EU, the EU claims to have a significant interest in regulating their content.

The AEA also charges that the proposed ban on heavy metals would violate GATT's Article XI, which prohibits import quotas, and that Article XX exceptions would not apply. "So far, no panel called to apply Article XX(b) [allowing exceptions from the GATT/WTO for measures designed to protect human, animal and plant life and health] has accepted the necessity of a measure otherwise inconsistent with other GATT provisions," the AEA pointed out.[103]

The U.S. Department of State *demarche* to the EU was only slightly more moderate in tone than the industry letter.[104] While opening with the familiar theme that the U.S. "supports the overall objectives" of hazardous waste reduction, the *demarche* goes on to state that the proposed regulations are too trade restrictive and that they violate WTO trade rules. Specifically, the U.S. criticized the recycled content and recovery/disposal requirements for electronics products as being "trade distorting," implying that these would violate the WTO Agreement on Trade Related Investment Measures (TRIMs) by forcing U.S. companies to purchase recycled materials and build collection facilities in Europe.[105]

Even while acknowledging that heavy metals in electronic equipment are hazardous, the U.S. is primarily concerned that the EU proposal requirements that the electronics industry collect, treat and dispose of end-of-life equipment are not "market-driven."[106] The U.S. argues that since not all of the costs can be passed on to consumers, the EU proposal would impose onerous obligations on the electronics industry.[107] It advises the EU to adopt the "U.S. approach" of regulating, rather than banning hazardous wastes.[108]

In the *demarche*, the U.S. also cynically and erroneously suggests that the EU proposal may conflict with a multilateral environmental agreement called the Basel Convention on the Transboundary Movement of Hazardous Wastes.[109] Specifically, the U.S. implies that the requirement that the electronics industry be responsible for waste recovery and disposal could lead to the increased transport of toxic materials across national boundaries because foreign-based companies will repatriate the waste instead of dealing with it on location.[110]

Perhaps because the U.S. has not signed the Basel Convention, State Department officials are confused about its requirements. The Basel Convention specifically relates to the practice of rich, industrialized countries disposing of industrial waste in developing countries, which often lack the technological and regulatory infrastructure to handle it properly.[111] While the Basel Convention does encourage countries to dispose of waste in its country of origin, there is nothing in the proposed EU regulation requiring waste to be shipped across borders. The EU's proposal would simply require electronics manufacturers — domestic and foreign — to shoulder more of the responsibility and expense of disposing of waste. It does not tell them where they may dispose of it. Indeed, this requirement would provide an incentive for the industry to develop cleaner technologies to manage waste.

In contrast with the U.S. government, environmental groups in the U.S. applauded the EU proposal for setting a high standard of environmental protection for the electronics industry that should be replicated in other countries.[112] However, the threats of a WTO challenge could lead to the downward "harmonization" of the EU standard – to the U.S. standard — in order to avoid a WTO challenge.

This case is a perfect illustration of how WTO rules empower industry and the trade ministries that represent them to chill progress on improved environmental standards. As governments struggle to address environmental hazards, industries in producing nations will issue WTO threats designed to deter action. The regulating countries face a choice between protecting their population or facing WTO dispute panels and the possibility of sanctions.

Threat 2: U.S., EU Auto Industries Attack Japanese Clean Air Rules Implementing Kyoto Treaty

The growing international concern over climate change led to voluntary agreements to limit the production of greenhouse gases, such as the CO_2 produced by automobiles and other fossil fuels, which trap heat in the atmosphere, warming the climate.[113] When voluntary measures failed to constrain the growing use and production of greenhouse gases, a treaty was signed in Kyoto, Japan, formally committing countries to reduce emissions to 1990 levels.[114] The Kyoto Protocol requires countries to implement measures to limit and reduce emissions of greenhouse gases.

The Japanese government committed itself in the Kyoto Protocol to cut greenhouse gases by 6% from 1990 levels.[115] Japanese emissions of greenhouse gases have been on the rise, with CO_2 emissions increased by 8.1% from 1990 to 1995.[116] A major cause of the rise in emissions has been the increased use of cars, which were responsible for 88% of CO_2 emissions in the transportation sector.[117] Japan launched a comprehensive plan to cut CO_2 emissions that included revising its "Law Concerning Rational Use of Energy," which among other things, sets standards for fuel efficiency for automobiles. Japan set new fuel efficiency standards for all cars, particularly cars in the medium weight category, where the standards were less rigorous when compared to those applied to smaller and larger autos.[118] Japan set its new fuel efficiency standard using the best available technology. The law requires emissions levels equal to those achieved by the most non-polluting

U.S. Fuel Efficiency Hypocrisy: Japan Feels WTO Heat

The WTO arguments being made by the U.S. and the EU against Japan's Kyoto Protocol implementation echo those made against the U.S. Corporate Average Fuel Economy (CAFE) standards by the European Community (EC) during its successful 1994 GATT challenge. Now the U.S. argues that fuel efficiency standards implementing a treaty concerning ozone depletion have a discriminatory *impact* on foreign-made cars because these vehicles happen not to comply with the high standard. In both the U.S. CAFE and Japanese Kyoto Protocol standards cases, the standards apply equally to all vehicles – domestic and foreign.

In 1994, a GATT panel ruled against the U.S. CAFE standards requiring that the fleets of both U.S. manufacturers and importers of foreign vehicles meet an average fuel efficiency standard.[125] The standards emerged from the 1973-74 OPEC oil embargo and aimed at doubling the average fuel economy of passenger cars from less than 14 miles per gallon to 27.5 miles per gallon by 1985.[126] By 1993, when the law was GATT challenged, the average fuel economy of passenger vehicles in the U.S. had reached 28.3 mpg[127] and the U.S. Department of Transportation projected that the law would save 9.4 billion barrels of oil from 1978 through 2000.[128] Further, the CAFE rules had been considered a success in reducing emissions of carbon dioxide and other gases contributing to global warming and ozone depletion,[129] and were consistent with the UNCED Framework Convention on Climate Change.[130]

The explicit goal of the U.S. CAFE standards was to reduce the proportion of fuel-inefficient vehicles in the U.S. market. The law applied equally engine existing in the middle range weight class. That engine is designed by Mitsubishi.[119]

In 1999, the EU cried foul, shooting off a letter to the WTO TBT Secretariat complaining about the new rules.[120] The U.S. followed suit on behalf of Daimler-Chrysler and the Ford Motor Company.[121] In a March 8, 1999, letter to the Japanese Ministry of Foreign Affairs, the U.S. voiced its support for the objective of reducing CO_2 emissions, while claiming that Japan's new rules may be WTO-illegal.[122] Both the U.S. and the EU question Japan's basing of the new standard on the performance of the Mitsubishi engine; they argue this discriminates against foreign manufacturers that do not use that engine. They cite the Technical Barriers to Trade prohibitions on standards that are discriminatory and more trade restrictive than necessary.[123] In its letter, the EU states: "[A]lthough the use of these technical criteria for the definition of the scheme does not appear to be *per se* discriminatory, the regime ... puts a comparatively heavier burden on imported products."[124] The U.S. and EU also complain that the new Japanese fuel efficiency standards shift the greatest burden to European automobiles, since almost 90% of the cars in Japan of that category are of European origin. The U.S. requested a

---

to all manufacturers.[131] If a domestic manufacturer was also an importer of foreign vehicles, each fleet – domestic and foreign – had to meet the requirements.[132] A domestic car is defined as having 75% domestic content.[133] This was done to ensure that domestic and foreign cars weren't averaged together. For example, some foreign cars were more fuel efficient than domestic ones, and if averaged with a domestic fleet, would enable the less fuel efficient domestic cars to meet the standards, reducing the need for domestic automakers to produce more fuel efficient cars.[134] Many U.S. manufacturers began producing smaller, more efficient models to meet the CAFE standards.

Many European manufacturers chose not to comply, adopting a marketing strategy of selling their more profitable and less fuel efficient cars in the U.S. luxury car market.[135] Manufacturers like Mercedes, Volvo and BMW, whose cars once had bettered CAFE standards in the late 1970s and early 1980s, decided to export large, high-end cars that were less fuel efficient.[136]

The EU challenged the CAFE standards on the basis that they discriminated *in effect* against EU auto manufacturers.[137] The average fuel economy requirements and the penalties imposed for non-compliance were identical for domestic and foreign fleets.[138] However, the EC argued that not one U.S. "big three" vehicle had been burdened by what it referred to as the "CAFE tax," and that of the "nearly $263 million in CAFE penalties imposed ... 99.99% was paid on European cars."[139] The GATT panel agreed, stating that the separate fleet requirements violated GATT's nondiscrimination provisions because of the *impact* they had on foreign cars.[140]

meeting with Japan, urging it to postpone enactment of the new standards until amendments taking into account U.S. concerns could be introduced.[141]

Japan argues that cars not equipped with the best emissions-reducing technology should be targeted because they are responsible for CO_2 emissions that make it difficult for Japan to meet its obligations under the Kyoto Protocol. Japanese industry data indicate that most of Japan's domestic automakers also would have to improve fuel efficiency to comply with the new standards.[142] Further, Japanese officials claim that the new regulation has been written flexibly, allowing EU and U.S. automakers to meet the standards however they wish, and that it does not require them to use the Mitsubishi engine, just to meet a similar level of fuel efficiency.

It remains to be seen whether the EU or the U.S. will mount a formal challenge in the WTO. Given its long struggle against successful EU challenges to its Corporate Average Fuel Economy standards, it would be ironic to see the U.S. challenge Japan's similar fuel efficiency standards on behalf of two companies.

If the Kyoto Protocol – which itself doesn't contain any trade restrictions – does conflict with WTO rules, then the WTO threat to human health and environmental protection is much broader than previously expressed. Regardless of the outcome, this case demonstrates how mega-corporations like Daimler-Benz-Chrysler expect the WTO to be used: as a bogey man to scare away environmental regulation. A developing country would not necessarily have the resources to fight to protect its environmental safeguards.

Threat 3: Europeans Weaken Ban on Cruelly Trapped Fur

The European Union has long been concerned with animal welfare issues and has enacted progressive anti-cruelty laws relating to farming, animal transport and slaughter practices. In 1991, the EU tried to extend this tradition to fur trapping but encountered WTO-challenge threats by the U.S. and Canada that ultimately undermined the new proposal.

The EU prohibited the use of steel jaw leg-hold traps for 13 fur bearers as of 1995.[143] Importation of such pelts would be banned starting in 1995 unless the exporting country forbid the use of steel jaw leg-hold traps or met other humane trapping standards.[144]

North American and Russian trappers and furriers contended that these laws and rules constituted unfair trade barriers. Few of the species covered by the EU law were native to Europe.[145]

Steel jaw leg-hold traps are allowed in many U.S. states and in Canada and Russia. More than four million wild animals are trapped for the fashion industry every year in the U.S.; the majority of them are caught with steel jaw leg-hold traps.[146]

Steel jaw leg-hold traps operate with a powerful spring that snaps a metal jaw shut, pinning an animal by its leg. This technique avoids damaging the animal's pelt, but unlike snare leg-hold traps, the steel jaw is painful, restraining the animals to await the trappers, who may not come for days, to bludgeon them to death. Some studies estimate that as many as one in four animals trapped in steel jaw leg-hold traps chew off their own limbs to escape.[147]

Before the EU rule went into effect, the U.S. already was moving to protect U.S. trappers, and Canada was expected to file a GATT challenge. In 1994, as the Clinton administration faced a tough fight in Congress over the proposed Uruguay Round, then-U.S. Trade Representative Mickey Kantor reassured members of Congress from trapping states that the U.S. would ask for a one-year waiver to the EU import ban.[148] The EU granted a one-year delay of the regulations.[149] Negotiations continued between the trapping countries and the EU, but as the January 1996 extended deadline grew closer, the Clinton administration informed Canada that it would join a WTO challenge if negotiations broke down.[150]

Shortly before the ban was to go into effect, EU External Trade Minister Leon Brittan independently extended the waiver for another year, citing the threat of a WTO challenge and ongoing negotiations with the U.S., Canada and Russia.[151] The move triggered outrage in Europe. A week after Brittan's postponement, the European Parliament reaffirmed support for the ban by vote. The EU Commission instructed customs officials to continue ignoring the ban, despite the lack of European Parliamentary approval for such action.[152] Only the Netherlands upheld, implemented and enforced the ban on time.[153]

Negotiations continued throughout 1996 but proceeded slowly, with Canada and Russia leaning toward a watered-down phaseout of leg-hold traps, which U.S. negotiators did not support.[154] By May 1997, Russia and Canada had signed off on a deal.[155] The European Parliament delayed a vote on the deal because it did not go far enough and indeed undermined the policy it had approved twice, and because the U.S. refused to join the pact.[156]

A letter from U.S. Trade Representative Charlene Barshefsky (who inherited the dispute from Kantor) to the EU's Leon Brittan stated that the U.S. would not participate in "an arbitrary ban on certain traps,"[157] although this was not the law's requirement.[158] When the U.S. offered to phase out steel jaw leg-hold traps over eight years, Europe initially rejected it.[159]

After more WTO saber rattling, a final weak deal was struck with the U.S. The proposal allowed a six-year phase-out of steel jaw leg-hold traps while the U.S. continues to export fur to Europe.[160] Animal welfare advocates were critical of the EU's willingness to negotiate with the trapping industry. They argued that the language in the U.S.-EU agreement is sufficiently vague as to make it unenforceable. For instance, the deal covers "conventional" leg-hold traps, but does not define "conventional" so as to allow slippery definitions in the future. Second, the agreement explicitly provides for "Best Management Practices," allowing steel jaw leg-hold trapping to continue if the U.S. government determines that it is the best way to manage some American species.[161]

Carlos Pimenta, a Portuguese member of the Parliament and animal welfare proponent, slammed the U.S. agreement noting, "It is especially bad as regards to observation and enforcement."[162] Said Anita Pollack, another member of European Parliament, "In reality it is a non-agreement. I would liken it to the Cheshire Cat, because all you can see is its smile."[163]

The WTO threat succeeded in halting the EU humane policy. The outcome allows fur caught with steel jaw leg-hold traps to continue to be sold in Europe, providing no incentive for the U.S. fur industry to switch to less cruel techniques. In the future, the threatened WTO action and subsequent weak agreement could have implications for other policies concerning humane treatment of animals, such as slaughter rules, transport and testing of consumer products on laboratory animals, and fur farming techniques.

Threat 4: U.S. Threatens Voluntary Eco-Labeling as WTO-Illegal

Eco-labels communicate product differences based on environmental or social criteria. Eco-labeling programs can be voluntary or mandatory, with certifying bodies either inside government or privately run. Familiar mandatory eco-labels with government certifications include energy ratings on appliances and the recently WTO-gutted "Dolphin Safe" label. Voluntary programs with certifications done by private organizations include the U.S. Greenseal, the Nordic Swan label and Germany's Blue Angel. In 1992, the European Union put in place an EU-wide voluntary eco-labeling program.[164]

Eco-labels promote informed consumer choice by making it possible for consumers to identify ecologically responsible products. Environmental advocates hail eco-labeling as a way to encourage and then reward companies for producing environmentally sound products.[165] Eco-labels represent the most "hands-off" approach to environmental policy in that they merely present consumers with information allowing them to choose an environmentally responsible product as opposed to one that is not.

Critics see the potential for invidious trade restrictions and distortions in such schemes.[166] A common industry charge is that even voluntary eco-labeling is trade distorting and should be considered the equivalent of mandatory labeling, because even though products without eco-labels technically have the same access to the market, consumers are less likely to buy those products.[167]

Given that voluntary, nongovernmental eco-labels comprise a "market approach" to environmental policy, the vociferous attack against eco-labels launched by a U.S. corporate front group in 1996 was revealing. The Coalition for Truth in Environmental Marketing Information included timber, plastics, chemical, electronics and packing industry associations in addition to the Grocery Manufacturers of America and the National Food Processors Association.[168]

The Coalition for Truth in Environmental Marketing Information launched a multifront campaign. A major target of its ire was European eco-labeling, which the companies charged was done in a closed process that excluded their participation and resulted in standards and approval processes that were harmful to their interests. However, the corporate group's main focus was to push for a U.S. position at the WTO that would effectively end voluntary eco-labeling by making it WTO-illegal, as well as many mandatory eco-label systems — undoubtedly "fixing" the European problem as well.

The WTO was a strategic target for the corporate group. Eco-labeling is an inherently controversial topic at the WTO because eco-labels explicitly make distinctions among physically similar products based on the way they are produced (called non-product related production and process methods or PPMs) and many WTO rules forbid such distinctions. In 1996, heated debate ensued on eco-labeling at both the Committee on Technical Barriers to Trade and the Committee on Trade and Environment (CTE).[169]

In February 1996, the two WTO committees[170] meeting jointly considered a submission by the Canadian government setting out principles for eco-labeling that would submit most eco-labeling schemes — whether public or private, mandatory or voluntary — to the WTO Agreement on Technical Barriers to Trade's strict rules governing product standards.[171] Getting eco-labels covered by the TBT Agreement was a goal of the corporate coalition. The WTO system is supposed to be aimed at trade barriers between countries, so obtaining WTO jurisdiction over voluntary programs that pose no constraint on actual market access would be a massive expansion of WTO powers.

The TBT Agreement requires governments to use the least trade restrictive alternative available when setting product standards and to rely on international standards where these exist.[172] Thus, if eco-labeling were judged to fall under TBT Agreement jurisdiction, programs could be challenged in the WTO on a variety of grounds. The technical question at issue is whether the TBT Agreement's definition of "product standards" can be interpreted to cover regulations based on non-product related standards. If the Joint Committee decided that production method regulations fell under TBT rules, all eco-labeling schemes could be brought under WTO jurisdiction.[173] The EU, Norway and Australia were in clear opposition to this proposal, maintaining that only directly product-related characteristics were covered by the WTO rules.[174] From their perspective, to use the tuna example, TBT rules would apply to how one classifies "albacore" versus "chunk light" tuna but not to how governments label the same type of tuna based on how it is caught.

The corporate coalition was lobbying for an anti-eco-label U.S. position. In March 1996, the U.S. submitted a proposal with six criteria for WTO-legal eco-labels and the presumption that eco-labels fall under the TBT Agreement.[175]

Happily, a nearly identical six-point "Suggested Basis of U.S. Proposal Regarding Principles Applicable to Eco-labelling Programs" was accidentally released outside the U.S. government with the fax imprint of the corporate law firm that drafted it still visible. The controversy over the source of the proposal helped fuel a quick campaign by environmental and consumer groups working together as the "Save the Seals" coalition and their allies in Congress.

Five of the six points in the industry proposal being presented as U.S. policy would devastate both voluntary and mandatory consumer information labels. First, the proposal applied assorted subjective and intentionally non-attainable tests to eco-labeling programs, such as ensuring that the programs did not have the effect of "deny[ing] equivalent competitive opportunities to imports."[176] That a U.S. government proposal should demand that other countries ensure equivalent consumer appeal for non-eco-labeled imports *vis-a-vis* all eco-labeled products is both absurd and obviously unattainable.

Second, the proposal tried to impose a "sound science" subjective standard of evidence going beyond the TBT Agreement.[177] Third, the proposal placed an unattainable burden on the certifying bodies, private or government, to "demonstrate" or prove assorted negatives — for instance that the program "is not an unnecessary obstacle to international trade."[178] Finally, inclusion of voluntary and private eco-labeling schemes under WTO jurisdiction would represent an enormous (and perhaps First Amendment-violating) expansion of WTO powers beyond government policy and into activities of the private sector. The result would be WTO jurisdiction over Good Housekeeping Seal of Approval decisions and *Consumer Reports* ratings. Similarly, private programs such as "Local Exchange Trading Systems" would also be dragged under WTO rules.[179]

The eco-labeling question was never resolved. Intractable disagreement among countries led to the adoption of a non-committal report, simply recognizing the importance of transparency on the subject and stressing the importance of adherence to TBT Agreement rules, notwithstanding the considerable differences of opinion as to how these rules should be interpreted.[180]

However, the U.S. and Canada recently raised labeling again in the Committee on Technical Barriers to Trade with respect to proposals in Britain and other European countries to label genetically modified foods.[181] (*See* Chapter 3 for more on GMO labeling). The U.S. battle with the EU over GMO regulation is becoming so heated that the question of the WTO-legality of certain types of labeling schemes may end up in front of a WTO dispute panel before it can be decided in a WTO committee. The U.S. position is that "foods obtained through bio-technology do not warrant mandatory labeling," and that "providing information regarding the method of production on the food label would be highly impractical and inequitable."[182]

The U.S. also has already announced it plans to challenge EU country-of-origin labeling at the WTO.[183]

Threat 5: Hong Kong Complains About U.S. Anti-Invasive Species Rule at WTO

Increased commerce resulting from the lowering of tariffs, as well as WTO rules restricting quarantine and other Sanitary and PhytoSanitary (SPS) measures, pose serious new risks to biodiversity as exotic pests and other species increasingly infest non-native territories. Invasive pests that out-compete native species are the second leading cause of species extinction.[184] However, a recent policy to combat a particular invasive species raises an additional concern about WTO constraints.

On November 11, 1998, Hong Kong registered a complaint at a meeting of the WTO SPS Committee against the U.S. over a 1998 rule requiring solid wood packing materials from China and Hong Kong to be heat treated, fumigated or treated with preservatives before being exported to the U.S.[185] The Animal and Plant Health Inspection Service (APHIS)adopted the rule in response to infestations in the U.S. near ports and airports of the Asian longhorned beetle, which was traced to wooden packing materials from China and Hong Kong.[186] Many goods are shipped on wood crates and wood pallets, and these packing materials and raw imported logs can carry a variety of damaging wood-eating insects that have no natural predators in the U.S. to keep them in check.

The wood-boring Asian longhorned beetles, indigenous to Japan, Korea and China, cannot be eradicated by pesticides once they have infested a tree.[194] The only way to get rid of them is to uproot and burn the affected trees.[195] APHIS officials already have had to uproot and burn thousands of trees in Brooklyn, New York, after discovering an infestation of the beetles.[196] More than 500 maple trees were cut and burned in Chicago's Ravenswood neighborhood to stop an infestation. The beetle has been detected at 30 other sites, including warehouses in Madison, Wisconsin, and Morton Grove, Illinois.[197] U.S. Department of Agriculture officials predict that damage from the beetle infestation could reach $138 billion.[198] This figure focuses on direct losses – to the Wisconsin and Michigan maple syrup producers and in board-feet of timber. It does not include biodiversity and aesthetic considerations.

As international trade has brought an increasing number of exotic species – from sea lampreys in the Great Lakes to gypsy moths and zebra mussels, U.S. government agencies have stepped up efforts to catch infestations early to avoid irreversible environmental damage or monumentally expensive eradication programs.

Being a member of the WTO may make it more difficult for the U.S. to respond to the beetle crisis. China, which is not in the WTO, has criticized the rule but has no recourse to the WTO dispute body, and thus must accept U.S. treatment guidelines or face an embargo of its goods packed in untreated wood.[199] Hong Kong, as a WTO Member, on the other hand, is empowered to challenge the U.S. policy – and can only benefit from the stringent evidentiary requirements imposed on the U.S. by the SPS Agreement (*See* Chapter 2 on food safety). The U.S. included Hong Kong in the ban because "about half of [China's] exports to the United States come through Hong Kong."[200] To date, Hong Kong has not filed a formal WTO challenge. Should Hong Kong initiate and win a case against the U.S., the U.S. would be left with only two choices – face sanctions or lift the treatment requirement, endangering forests across the U.S.

Exotic Pests Threaten Biodiversity

ZEBRA MUSSELS

Zebra mussels – native to eastern Europe – were introduced into the U.S. in the mid-1980s when a vessel traveling from Europe discharged ballast water into Lake St. Clair.[187] The mollusks, which can produce up to 100,000 eggs each year, colonized almost every firm object in Lake Erie within a year.[188] Zebra mussels pose a public health risk because their tissues accumulate pollutants – such as PCBs – and pass the pollutants up the food chain.[189] Zebra mussels pose a threat to native species as well. In western Lake Erie, for example, unionids have become exterminated by these exotic pests.[190]

GYPSY MOTHS

Scientists estimate that infestations of Asian gypsy moths associated with imports of Siberian logs could cost the forest and farm economy of the Pacific Northwest as much as $58 million.[191] Native to Europe and Asia, the gypsy moth is a major pest in America responsible for defoliating millions of acres of trees in the U.S. annually.[192] Gypsy moth caterpillars eat tree leaves, especially oak. After defoliation, the trees produce new leaves. However, refoliation uses enormous amounts of moisture and energy, causing trees to lose twigs and branches. Most trees die if this defoliation/refoliation process occurs for two consecutive years.[193]

Multilateral Environmental Agreements Run Afoul of WTO

The negotiation of multilateral environmental agreements (MEAs) represents a recognition of the fact that natural resources like air, water and wildlife are not constrained by national borders. When these resources are threatened by pollution or with extinction, nations must cooperate to forestall the damage. There are numerous multilateral efforts under way to address global environmental issues such as climate change, air pollution, endangered species and the trade in hazardous waste.

MEAs are the embodiment of global progress toward, and commitment to, the preservation of the environment. Yet many WTO rules explicitly contradict MEAs, including those in effect long before the WTO's formation. As a matter of international law, the WTO automatically supersedes MEAs signed before the WTO. Uruguay Round negotiators refused to include language in the WTO to make MEAs and their domestic enforcement immune to WTO challenge.

There are several ways in which MEAs can run afoul of WTO rules. First, some of the international environmental agreements explicitly restrict trade. For instance, the Convention on International Trade in Endangered Species (CITES) bans trade in endangered species; the Basel Convention on the Transboundary Movement of Hazardous Waste bans the export of toxic waste from rich countries — which produce 98% of the world's hazardous waste — to developing nations; and the Montreal Protocol bans trade in ozone-depleting chemicals and also in products made with those chemicals. Second, these treaties and others sometimes employ the use of trade sanctions to enforce their objectives. Still other multilateral environmental agreements do not involve trade sanctions but may require countries to adopt policies that affect the potential products (asbestos, for example) of one country more than those of another. Thus, MEAs of all stripes have a significant chance of coming into conflict with GATT/WTO rules.

In addition, conflicts now have arisen between WTO rules and MEAs that don't even relate to trade. As discussed earlier in the chapter, the U.S. and the EU have used WTO obligations to attack the Japanese government for strengthening its fuel efficiency laws as required under the Kyoto Protocol to the United Nations Framework Convention on Climate Change.

Finally, unlike the WTO, which is self-executing (i.e., has built-in enforcement mechanisms), the MEAs provide commitments that each country agrees to enforce. For instance, CITES lists species for which its signatory countries have agreed that protection is needed. But, the enforcement of CITES comes not through a central CITES tribunal but rather under the domestic laws of each signatory. Thus, many U.S. CITES obligations are enforced through the Endangered Species Act (ESA). ESA provisions ban import of CITES-listed species and products made from them and endorse embargoes against countries that violate the rules.[201] Other countries have similar domestic laws implementing their CITES obligations. Yet, under WTO rules, such domestic laws can – and have – been challenged as illegal trade barriers.

WTO dispute panels are not required to interpret the existence of MEAs as evidence in favor of environmental laws that are challenged as WTO violations. Indeed, the rules of international law stipulate that the "latest in time" of international obligations trumps previous obligations unless an exception is taken.[202] While a very limited "saving" clause — giving some precedence to three MEAs over conflicting rules — was forced into the North American Free Trade Agreement,[203] it is conspicuously absent in the WTO or other Uruguay Round Agreements. To date there have been several rulings both under GATT and the WTO that have been detrimental to domestic efforts to implement obligations undertaken under MEAs.

Examples of the WTO Ignoring MEAs

Dolphins: Two GATT panels refused to consider the U.S. law designed to halt depletion of dolphins by encirclement tuna fishing in the context of existing multilateral agreements on dolphin protection and on the plurilateral Inter-American Tropical Tuna Commission's work on tuna fishing process and production methods (PPMs). Even though the U.S. and several challenging countries were party to these other agreements, the panels treated the U.S. measure as a unilateral action that did not sufficiently relate to the internationally shared goal of dolphin conservation.

Turtles: Similarly, in a WTO ruling on a U.S. prohibition on sales of shrimp harvested in a manner harmful to endangered sea turtles, WTO panels ignored the fact that the U.S. law conforms with the objectives of the CITES, which lists sea turtles as a protected species[204] and which allows the imposition of trade sanctions to protect them.[205] Sea turtles are also protected under the U.N. FAO Code of Conduct on Responsible Fisheries[206] and under the Bonn Convention on Protecting Migratory Species of Wild Animals.[207] Despite the existence of these international environmental agreements to which the U.S. *and* several of the countries challenging the law were signatories, the WTO Appellate Body faulted the U.S. for not negotiating with each of the then-132 Members of the WTO to come up with a mutually acceptable regime on shrimp fishing methods to safeguard sea turtles.

Yet, under this WTO logic, if countries resist participating in MEA negotiations, they are essentially able to hold conservation efforts hostage. For instance, the U.S. is trying to negotiate an Indian Ocean sea turtle protection treaty that would include all four of the countries that challenged the shrimp embargo.[208] Only Australia and Thailand have expressed any interest in participating. The WTO's ruling implies that each country must wait for the whole world to act before it decides to implement environmental policies. Indeed, by ruling that particular national environmental regulations are WTO-illegal, the WTO removes the incentives for countries to participate in MEAs. WTO rulings against environmental laws thus present sizable obstacles to the formation of international consensus on environmental issues.

Misguided WTO Committee on the Environment

Environmentalists had hoped that the WTO's Committee on Trade and the Environment (CTE) would provide a forum for WTO Members to devise new WTO rules to safeguard MEAs. Indeed, the original CTE work plan prioritized the issue. But when the European Union offered proposals in 1996 for WTO recognition of MEAs that allow the imposition of trade sanctions, the U.S. neither supported the EU nor produced any proposals of its own.[209] Other countries grew bitter at the lack of leadership from the U.S., the country that had called for the creation of the CTE in the first place.[210]

Indeed, in its somewhat beleaguered four years of operation, the CTE has failed to agree to any recommendations for pro-environment changes to the GATT/WTO system. Some environmentalists criticize it as being used primarily to identify environmental measures that distort trade and to propose ways to get rid of them.[211]

Recently, the CTE has shifted the entire approach to its work. Dubbed the "win-win" strategy, the new approach abandons the goal of protecting environmental regulations from WTO challenge and instead focuses on identifying and eliminating trade barriers (like subsidies for fisheries) that are also bad for the environment.

> **W**hen the European Union offered proposals in 1996 for WTO recognition of MEAs that allow the imposition of trade sanctions, the U.S. neither supported the EU nor produced any proposals of its own.

At the March 1999 high-level WTO meeting on the environment in Geneva, WTO officials sought out environmental groups to give this strategy their support.[212] A few groups such as World Wildlife International did issue positive statements on the idea of cutting fisheries subsidies,[213] but the environmental community as a whole criticized the WTO's failure to make progress on the issue of safeguarding existing environmental policies coming under increasing WTO attack worldwide.[214]

Now the Clinton administration is shifting its environmental strategy for WTO in the same direction, specifically as regards to its position in the WTO's Seattle Ministerial, where the WTO's future agenda will be set.[215] Indeed, some environmental groups view the shift to the so-called "win-win" strategy as a way to try to buy off environmental opposition to the European proposal to launch further liberalization talks and to make use of environmentalists to further aspects of the WTO's agenda.[216] Ironically, even as the WTO staff and now the Clinton administration are calling for such a "win-win" strategy, the U.S. is moving forward with its efforts to make liberalization in forest products – which is vigorously opposed by environmentalists and has been estimated by the industry to increase depletion of forests by 3-4%[217] — a high priority for future WTO negotiations.[218]

———————— CHAPTER ⬤ ENDNOTES ————————

[1] U.S. Trade Representative Michael Kantor, Testimony to the House Ways and Means Committee, Jan. 26, 1994.

[2] The North American Agreement on Environmental Cooperation (NAAEC) is ancillary to NAFTA, meaning its terms are not binding over any of NAFTA's core provisions. The NAAEC created the Commission for Environmental Cooperation (CEC), which can investigate citizens' complaints that a NAFTA member-country is not enforcing its environmental laws. The side agreement does not cover environmental problems caused by the *absence* of regulation. The NAFTA environmental side agreement also specifically excludes laws on natural resources, endangered species and other vital environmental issues. The process for seeking review of the limited areas covered is long and tortured. In the five years that NAFTA has been in effect, the CEC has issued a total of two fact-finding reports out of over 20 citizen submissions alleging government non-enforcement of environmental laws. The first report took the CEC over two years to complete, and though it found that Mexico was not enforcing its environmental laws in allowing the construction of a pier requiring the destruction of ecologically critical coral reefs in the port of Cozumel, the pier had been built and the reefs had been destroyed for over a year before the report was even issued. *See* "NAFTA Environmental Agreement: A Paper Tiger?," *News-Journal Wire Services,* Jul. 29, 1998. All petitions to use the limited provision that could result in actual enforcement actions (versus the issuance of reports on the matter) have been refused to date.

[3] The Clinton Administration, *The NAFTA: Expanding U.S. Exports, Jobs and Growth*, U.S. Government Printing Office, Nov. 1993, at 1.

[4] Robert Evans, "Green Push Could Damage Trade Body – WTO Chief," *Reuters*, May 15, 1998.

[5] Letter to President Clinton, Apr. 21, 1998, signed by the Center for International Environmental Law, Center for Marine Conservation, Community Nutrition Institute, Defenders of Wildlife, Earth Island Institute, Earthjustice Legal Defense Fund, Friends of the Earth, Humane Society of the United States, National Audubon Society, National Wildlife Federation, Natural Resources Defense Council, Sierra Club, on file at Public Citizen.

[6] Between 1958 and 1994, at least 6 million dolphins in the Eastern Tropical Pacific have been killed by purse seine nets. *See* Shannon Brownlee, "A Political Casserole of Tuna and Greens," *U.S. News & World Report*, Aug. 11, 1997, at 53.

[7] For instance, Article XX allows countries to restrict trade in "national treasures" and products made with prison labor, as well as to "protect public morals." The Article XX terms considered relevant to the environment allow governments to take measures "necessary to protect human, animal or plant life or health" (Article XX(b)) and those "relating to the conservation of exhaustible natural resources" (Article XX(g)). However, to date such departures from GATT restrictions have never been permitted when an actual case has been decided. This results in part from language in the chapeau (or introductory clause) to the Article XX exceptions, which significantly narrows their scope. The chapeau clause states: "Subject to the requirement that such measures are not applied in a manner which would constitute a means of arbitrary or unjustifiable discrimination between countries where the same conditions prevail, or a disguised restriction on international trade, nothing in this Agreement shall be construed to prevent the adoption or enforcement by any contracting party of measures. . . " (Article XX). Among other things, the chapeau has been interpreted by GATT/WTO panels to mean that environmental laws must use the least trade restrictive means available to meet their goals.

[8] American Electronics Association (AEA), *Legality Under International Trade Law of Draft Directive on Waste from Electrical and Electronic Equipment*, Mar. 1999, prepared by Rod Hunter and Marta Lopez of Hunton & Williams, Brussels, on file with Public Citizen.

[9] *See* Chapter 8 on the WTO's dispute resolution system.

[10] WTO, "Trade and the Environment in the WTO," Press Brief, Apr. 16, 1997.

[11] Robert Evans, "Green Push Could Damage Trade Body – WTO Chief," *Reuters*, May 15, 1998.

[12] WTO, United States - Standards for Reformulated and Conventional Gasoline (WT/DS2/R), Report of the Panel, Jan. 29, 1996.

[13] *See* WTO, United States - Standards for Reformulated and Conventional Gasoline (WT/DS2/AB/R), Report of the Appellate Body, May 20, 1996.

[14] 62 *Fed. Reg.* 24776, May 6, 1997, at Appendix 19.

[15] WTO, United States - Standards for Reformulated and Conventional Gasoline (WT/DS2/R), Report of the Panel, Jan. 29, 1996, at Para 7.1.

[16] Foreign Agent Registration Unit data shows Arnold and Porter representing Venezuela from Jun. 1992. Data on file with Public Citizen.

[17] Petroleos de Venezuela, S.A. (PDVSA), the state-owned oil company of Venezuela, submitted comments on EPA's proposed gasoline rule on April 16, 1992; November 20, 1992; and May 17, 1993. Docket A-91-02.

[18] 103rd Congress, H.R. 4953, Sponsored by Rep. Kim (R-CA), introduced Aug. 12 1994.

[19] The National Defense Council Foundation, *Domestic Refining: Target of a WTO Power Grab*, Feb. 21, 1996.

[20] WTO, United States - Standards for Reformulated and Conventional Gasoline (WT/DS2/R), Report of the Panel, Jan. 29, 1996, at Para 7.1.

[21] 42 U.S.C. Sec. 7401; *see also* WTO, United States – Standards for Reformulated and Conventional Gasoline, First Submission by the United States, Jun. 27, 1995.

[22] *See id.*

[23] *See* U.S. Environmental Protection Agency (EPA), Office of Air and Radiation, *1997 Air Quality Status and Trends,* December 1998.

[24] National Institutes of Health (NIH), National Asthma Education and Prevention Program data cited in "The Attack of Asthma," *Environmental Health Perspectives*, Vol. 104, No. 1, Jan. 1996. According to the National Institutes of Health (NIH), between 1982 and 1993, the prevalence of asthma in the United States increased 46% overall and 80% among those under age 18. NIH estimates that more than 7 percent of American children now have the disease. A New Jersey study found that emergency room visits for asthma increased by 28% when ozone concentrations reached only half the federal limit. Clifford P. Weissel, Ronald P. Cody, Paul J. Lioy, "Relationship between Summertime Ambient Ozone Levels and Emergency Department Visits for Asthma in Central New Jersey," Environmental Health Perspectives, supplement 2, Mar. 1995, on file at Public Citizen.

[25] 59 *Fed. Reg.* 7716, Feb. 16, 1994.

[26] *Id.*

[27] 62 *Fed. Reg.* 24776, May 6, 1997, at Appendix 19.

[28] *Id.*

[29] WTO, United States – Standards for Reformulated and Conventional Gasoline, Second Submission of the United States, Aug. 17, 1995, at 22-24.

[30] WTO, United States – Standards for Reformulated and Conventional Gasoline (WT/DS2/R), Report of the Panel, Jan. 29, 1996, at Para. 6.10.

[31] WTO, United States – Standards for Reformulated and Conventional Gasoline (WT/DS2/AB/R), Report of the Appellate Body, May 20, 1996, at 32.

[32] WTO, United States –Standards for Reformulated and Conventional Gasoline, Second Submission of the United States, Aug. 17, 1995, at 3-5; *see also* Appendix at 387-89.

[33] WTO, United States – Standards for Reformulated and Conventional Gasoline, (W/DS2/9), Consolidated Report of the Panel and the Appellate Body, May 20, 1996, at Part C (Conclusions).

[34] U.S. Department of Energy, *Petroleum Supply Annual 1998*, Vol. 1, Table 21, on file with Public Citizen.

[35] 62 *Fed. Reg.* 24776, May 6, 1997, at Appendix 19.

[36] WTO, United States – Standards for Reformulated and Conventional Gasoline, Second Submission of the United States, Aug. 17, 1995, at 22-24.

[37] *See* George E Warren Corporation and the Independent Refiners Coalition vs. EPA, D.C. Circuit No. 97-1651, as consolidated with 97-1656, Brief of Intervenor-Petitioners, Friends of the Earth, Inc., filed on May 1, 1998, on file with Public Citizen.

[38] *Id.* at 26.

[39] *Id.* at 31.

[40] *See* D.C. Cir. No. 97-1651, Ginsburg, J. ruling , delivered Nov. 3, 1998.

[41] *See id.*

[42] Shannon Brownlee, "A Political Casserole of Tuna and Greens," *U.S. News & World Report*, Aug. 11, 1997, at 53.

[43] John Malek and Dr. Peter Bowler, *Dolphin Protection in the Tuna Fishery*, Interdisciplinary Minor in Global Sustainability, Seminar, Irvine: University of California Press (1997), at 1.

[44] *Id.*

[45] The key provision that was the target of challenges under GATT is 16 U.S.C. Section 1371(a)(2), prohibiting the importation of tuna from countries that harvest tuna using purse seine nets.

[46] *See* Statement for the Inter-American Tropical Tuna Commission Meeting, Oct. 21-23, 1996.

[47] GATT, United States - Restrictions on Imports of Tuna (DS21/R), Report of the Panel, Sep. 3, 1991.

[48] *See* GATT, United States - Restrictions on Imports of Tuna (DS29/R), Report of the Panel, Jun. 1994.

[49] *See id.* at Para. 6.1.

[50] *See* GATT, Findings on U.S. Tuna Ban, Report of Dispute Panel, Aug. 16, 1991, at Paras. 5.24-5.29.

[51] *See id.* at Paras. 5.30-5.34.

[52] GATT, United States - Restrictions on Imports of Tuna (DS29/R), Report of the Panel, Jun. 1994, at Para. 5.24.

[53] "Clinton Pledges Early, Renewed Effort to Pass Tuna-Dolphin Bill," *Inside U.S. Trade*, Oct. 1996.

[54] *Id.*

[55] *See* 104th Congress, HR. 2179, Sponsor: Rep. "Duke" Cunningham (R-CA); *see also* S.1420, Sponsors: Sen. Ted Stevens (R-AK), Co-sponsor: Sen. John Breaux (D-LA).

[56] *See* 105th Congress, H.R. 408, Sponsor: Rep. Gilchrest (R-MO); *see also* S.39, Sponsor: Sen. Ted Stevens (R-AK).

[57] *See* 64 *Fed. Reg.* 24590, May 7, 1999. In its initial finding, NMFS concluded that there was insufficient evidence to show that catching tuna by encircling dolphins has a significant adverse impact on dolphin stocks.

[58] *See* U.S. Department of Commerce, "Commerce Department Issues Initial Finding on Tuna/Dolphin Interactions - Will Adopt New Dolphin-Safe Label Standard," Press Release, Apr. 29, 1999.

[59] 64 *Fed. Reg.* 24590, May 7, 1999.

[60] *Id.*

[61] *See* U.S. Department of Commerce, "Commerce Department Issues Initial Finding on Tuna/Dolphin Interactions - Will Adopt New Dolphin-Safe Label Standard," Press Release, Apr. 29, 1999.

[62] Scott Harper, "Rule Revised for Tuna Fishing, Encirclement Will be Allowed with Oversight to Help Protect Dolphins," *The Virginian Pilot*, May 18, 1999. A campaign by Earth Island Institute has resulted in commitments by some major tuna canners to use only tuna caught without purse seine nets.

[63] A WTO Appellate Body has stated that adopted reports of either GATT or WTO "create legitimate expectations among Members and, therefore, should be taken into account where they are relevant to a dispute." Japan - Taxes on Alcoholic Beverages, (WT/DS10/AB/R), Report of the Appellate Body, Oct. 4, 1996, at 14. In practice, panels have cited previous reports as precedents and have supported subsequent rulings by referring to previous decisions.

[64] Jock Nash, Trade Analyst, written communication with Michelle Sforza, Research Director, Public Citizen's Global Trade Watch, Oct. 13, 1998.

[65] Public Law 93-205, 16 U.S.C. 1531 *et.seq.*; *see also* 52 *Fed. Reg.* 24244, Jun. 29, 1987.

[66] 52 *Fed. Reg.* 24244, Jun. 29, 1987. Five species of sea turtles fell under the Endangered Species Act regulations: loggerhead (*Caretta caretta*), Kemp's ridley (*Lepidochelys kempi*), green (*Chelonia mydas*), leatherback (*Dermochelys coriacea*) and hawksbill (*Eretmochelys imbricata*).

[67] National Research Council, Committee on Sea Turtle Conservation, *Decline of the Sea Turtles: Causes and Prevention* (1990), at 5.

[68] *Id.*

[69] *Id.* at 17-18.

[70] Pub. L. 101-162.

[71] National Research Council, Committee on Sea Turtle Conservation, *Decline of the Sea Turtles: Causes and Prevention* (1990), at 11.

[72] WTO, United States - Import Prohibition of Certain Shrimp and Shrimp Products (WT/DS58), Complaint by India, Malaysia, Pakistan and Thailand.

[73] WTO, United States - Import Prohibition of Certain Shrimp and Shrimp Products (WT/DS58/R), Final Report, May 15, 1998, at Para. 9.1 (Concluding Remarks).

[74] *See* Letter to President Clinton, Apr. 21, 1998, signed by the Center for International Environmental Law, Center for Marine Conservation, Community Nutrition Institute, Defenders of Wildlife, Earth Island Institute, Earthjustice Legal Defense Fund, Friends of the Earth, Humane Society of the United States, National Audobon Society, National Wildlife Federation, Natural Resources Defence Council, and Sierra Club, on file at Public Citizen.

[75] "The Sea Turtles' Warning," *The New York Times*, Apr. 10, 1998.

[76] WTO, United States - Import Prohibition of Certain Shrimp and Shrimp Products (WT/DS58), Appealed on Jul. 13, 1998.

[77] WTO, United States - Import Prohibition of Certain Shrimp and Shrimp Products (WT/DS58/AB/R), Report of the Appellate Body, Oct. 12, 1998, at Para. 187.

[78] *Id.* at Para. 122.

[79] *Id.* at Para. 184.

[80] *Id.* at Para. 185.

[81] Jock Nash, Trade Analyst, written communication with Michelle Sforza, Research Director, Public Citizen's Global Trade Watch, Oct. 13, 1998.

[82] "Louisiana Shrimpers Threatened By Ruling On Turtle Excluder," *States News Service*, Apr. 14, 1998.

[83] *Earth Island Institute v. William M. Daley*, U.S. Court of International Trade, Case No. 98-09-02818, Apr. 2, 1999, at 35.

[84] The U.S. government had initially refused to implement the shrimp-turtle policy's country-based certification requirements in favor of shipment-by-shipment certification. In 1996, three environmental groups sued to force implementation of the law as written. The U.S. Court for International Trade (CIT) ruled in 1997 for the environmentalists, and ordered the State Department to rewrite the rule to require country-based certification. This CIT ruling triggered the WTO challenge. The CIT overturned its earlier ruling on a technicality in 1998, but in April 1999, an appellate judge ruled that the law allowed U.S. sale of shrimp only from countries that have regulations mandating TEDs. If the CIT affirms its interim ruling, the State Department will have no choice but to scrap its proposal to certify shrimp on a shipment-by-shipment basis.

[85] WTO, Agreement on Technical Barriers to Trade at Article 1.3.

[86] *Id.* at Article 1.5.

[87] *Id.* at Article 2.2.

[88] *Id.* at Article 2.4.

[89] *See* description of case on page 31.

[90] *See* description of case on page 34.

[91] "TBT Committee Discusses Labeling, Standards," *BRIDGES Weekly Trade News Digest*, Vol. 3, No. 23, Jun. 14, 1999.

[92] American Electronics Association, *Legality Under International Trade Law of Draft Directive on Waste from Electrical and Electronic Equipment*, Mar. 1999, prepared by Rod Hunter and Marta Lopez of Hunton & Williams, Brussels, on file with Public Citizen.

[93] U.S. Department of State *Demarche* to DG1, DGIII (industry) and DGXI (environment), Jan. 11, 1999, at 4, on file with Public Citizen.

[94] *See* Second Draft Proposal for a Directive on Waste from Electrical and Electronic Equipment, issued Jul. 1998 by DGXI.

[95] *Id.* at Articles 3-7.

[96] *Id.* at Article 4.4.

[97] *Id.* at Article 7.

[98] American Electronics Association, *Legality Under International Trade Law of Draft Directive on Waste from Electrical and Electronic Equipment*, Mar. 1999, prepared by Rod Hunter and Marta Lopez of Hunter and Williams, Brussels, on file at Public Citizen.

[99] *Id* at 10.

[100] *See* 15 U.S.C. Chapter 53, Toxic Substance Control Act, Subchapter IV (Lead Exposure Reduction); *see also* 43 U.S.C. Chapter 85, Subchapter 1, Part D, Subpart 5 (Additional Provisions for Areas Designated nonattainment for sulfur oxides, nitrogen, dioxide, or lead).

[101] American Electronics Association, *Legality Under International Trade Law of Draft Directive on Waste from Electrical and Electronic Equipment*, Mar. 1999, prepared by Rod Hunter and Marta Lopez of Hunton & Williams, Brussels, on file with Public Citizen, at 17.

[102] *Id.* at 13.

[103] *Id.* at 11.

[104] *See* U.S. Department of State *Demarche*, 1999 to DG1, DGIII (industry) and DGXI (environment), Jan. 11, 1999, on file with Public Citizen.

[105] *Id.* at 2.

[106] *Id.* at 8.

[107] *Id.* at 4.

[108] *Id.* at 8.

[109] *Id.* at 5.

[110] *Id.* at 4.

[111] Basel Convention on the Transboundary Movement of Hazardous Wastes at Article 2(e), "Each Party shall take the appropriate measures to ... not allow the export of hazardous wastes or other wastes to a State ... particularly developing countries ... if it has reason to believe that the wastes in question will not be managed in an environmentally sound manner, according to criteria to be decided on by the Parties at their first meeting."

[112] An April 22, 1999, letter to the Vice President Gore, signed by over 75 environmental and other public interest groups applauded the EU electronics pollution abatement proposal, on file with Public Citizen.
[113] The Climate Control Action Plan is a comprehensive inter-agency plan, composed of more than 50 voluntary programs. It was created during the Framework Convention on Climate Change at the Rio Summit on Environment and Development in June, 1992 and went into effect on March 21, 1994.
[114] *See* 1997 Kyoto Protocol to the United Nations' Framework Convention on Climate Change, U.N. Document FCCC/CP/1997/L.7/Add.1.
[115] *See* Embassy of Japan Backgrounder on Amendments to its Law Concerning Rational Use of Energy Law 1999, on file with Public Citizen.
[116] *Id.,* citing OECD data.
[117] *Id.*
[118] The system employs lean-burn technology that reduces fuel used by means of air intake larger than the theoretical air-fuel mixture ratio, in order to achieve fuel economy. *See id.*
[119] Japan, Law Concerning Rational Use of Energy, Jun. 22, 1979, revised Jun. 5, 1998.
[120] *See* "TBT Notification 99.003," Letter from European Commission Industrial Secretariat, 1999, on file with Public Citizen.
[121] According to Japanese Government sources, the U.S. first weighed in against Japan's fuel efficiency law on behalf of Daimler-Chrysler. At the U.S.-Japan summit in May 1999, Japanese officials reported that the President of Ford Motor Company also complained about the law to the Prime Minister of Japan. Official with Japanese Embassy in Washington, D.C., personal communication with Michelle Sforza, Research Director, Public Citizen's Global Trade Watch, May 13, 1999.
[122] *See* Letter from Ferial Ara Saeed, First Secretary of the Economic Section of the U.S. Embassy to Mr. Kazuyoshi Umemoto, Director of the First International Organizations Division of the Economics Affairs Bureau of the Ministry of Foreign Affairs, Mar. 8, 1999.
[123] *See* "TBT Notification 99.003," Letter from European Commission Industrial Secretariat, 1999, on file with Public Citizen; *see also* Letter from Ferial Ara Saeed, First Secretary of the Economic Section of the U.S. Embassy to Mr, Kazuyoshi Umemoto, Director of the First International Organizations Division of the Economics Affairs Bureau of the Ministry of Foreign Affairs, Mar. 8, 1999.
[124] "TBT Notification 99.003," Letter from European Commission Industrial Secretariat, 1999, on file with Public Citizen.
[125] The U.S. Energy Policy and Conservation Act, U.S.C. 2001 et seq. CAFE regulations in 49 C.F.R. Part 500.
[126] U.S. Department of Transportation, *Summary of Fuel Economy Performance,* Sep. 1993; *see also* Public Citizen and Center for Auto Safety, *United States – Taxes on Automobiles: Dispute Pending Before GATT Panel,* Submission on the European Communities' Challenge to CAFE Penalties & Gas Guzzler Tax, Oct. 14, 1993, at 5.
[127] *See* U.S. Department of Transportation, *Summary of Fuel Economy Performance,* Sep. 1993.
[128] *Id.* at 3.
[129] International Energy Agency, *Energy Efficiency and the Environment* (1991), at 80, 151, and 159.
[130] The Climate Control Action Plan is a comprehensive interagency plan, composed of more than 50 voluntary programs. It was created during the Framework Convention on Climate Change at the Rio Summit on Environment and Development in June 1992 and went into effect on March 21, 1994.
[131] GATT, United States – Taxes on Automobiles (DS31/R), Report of the Panel, Oct. 11, 1994, at 60, Para. 3.230.
[132] 15 U.S.C. Sec. 2003(b)(1).
[133] *Id.* at Sec. 2003(b)(2)(E).
[134] GATT, United States – Taxes on Automobiles (DS31/R), Report of the Panel, Oct. 11, 1994, at 111, Para. 5.47.
[135] The effect of the separate fleet rule has actually been to disadvantage U.S. car-makers *vis a vis* foreign competitors. The domestic manufacturers have had much higher average fuel economies for their imported fleets than for their domestic fleets. *See, e.g.,* 53 *Fed. Reg.* At 39288, Oct. 6, 1988; U.S. Department of Transportation, *Summary of Fuel Economy Performance,* Sep. 1993; *see also* Public Citizen and Center for Auto Safety, *United States – Taxes on Automobiles: Dispute Pending Before GATT Panel,* Submission on the European Communities' Challenge to CAFE Penalties & Gas Guzzler Tax, Oct. 14, 1993, at 22-23.
[136] *See* U.S. Department of Transportation, *Summary of Fuel Economy Performance,* Sep. 1993.
[137] GATT, United States – Taxes on Automobiles (DS31/R), Report of the Panel, Oct. 11, 1994, at 63, Para. 3.220.
[138] *Id.* at 9, Para. 2.19.

[139] *Id.* at 63, Para. 3.220.

[140] *Id.* at 111-112, Paras. 5.47-5.49.

[141] Letter from Ferial Ara Saeed, First Secretary of the Economic Section of the U.S. Embassy to Mr. Kazuyoshi Umemoto, Director of the First International Organizations Division of the Economic Affairs Bureau of the Ministry of Foreign Affairs, Mar. 8, 1999.

[142] Embassy of Japan Backgrounder on Amendments to its Law Concerning Rational Use of Energy Law 1999, on file with Public Citizen.

[143] European Economic Council (EEC) Regulation No. 3254/91, Nov. 4, 1991, at Articles 2 and 3, Annex I.

[144] *Id.* at Article 3, Para. 1.

[145] Willem Wijnstekers, "Implementation of Regulation 3254/91, Leg-hold Traps and Fur Imports," Memo for European Parliament, Nov. 24, 1993. Only Sweden and Finland have wolves or ermines native to their countries; both have introduced muskrats and Finland has introduced beavers

[146] Simon Coss, "Critics Deride Leg-hold Trap Deal," *European Voice*, Dec. 4-10, 1997.

[147] *See* "Trapping: the Inside Story," U.S. Humane Society, 1998.

[148] John Maggs, "U.S. to Protest EU Fur Ban involving Use of Leg-Hold Trap," *Journal of Commerce*, Jun. 22, 1994; *see also* Letter from U.S. Trade Representative Michael Kantor to Senators Stevens (AK), Breaux (LA), Murkowski (AK), Danforth (MO), Baucus (MT) Burns (MT), Johnston (LA), Rockefeller (WV) and Wallop (WY) and Representatives Young (AK), Hayes (LA), Dingell (MI), Tauzin (LA) and Brewster (OK), *cited in Inside U.S. Trade*, Aug. 26, 1994, at 21.

[149] EEC Regulation No. 1771/94, Jul. 19, 1994, at Article 1.

[150] Letter from U.S. Trade Representative Michael Kantor to Canadian Minister of International Trade Roy MacLaren, Aug. 10, 1995; *see also* "EU: Canada to Take Action if EU Bans Its Fur Exports," *European Report*, May 10, 1995.

[151] Gillian Handyside, "MPES Want Brittan's Head Over Leghold Trap," *Reuters*, Dec. 11, 1995.

[152] "EU Leghold Trap Ban Delayed Without Council, Parliament Approval," *Inside U.S. Trade*, Dec. 22, 1995.

[153] Ronald van de Krol, "Dutch Ban Leg-Hold Fur Imports," *Financial Times*, Jan. 12, 1996.

[154] "EU States Delay Fur Ban for Fourth Time," *Inside U.S. Trade*, Feb. 28, 1997.

[155] Emma Tucker, "Brussels Reaches Pact on Leg-Hold Traps, *Financial Times*, May 30, 1997. The deal would prohibit leg-hold traps on land for more than half the specified species, phase out leg-hold traps on land for the remaining species over three years, and permit padded leg-hold traps underwater.

[156] "EU Blocking Minority Forces Delay of Vote on Fur Ban," *Inside U.S. Trade*, Jun. 27, 1997.

[157] Letter from U.S. Trade Representative Charlene Barshefsky to Sir Leon Brittan, reprinted in *Inside U.S. Trade*, Jul. 11, 1997.

[158] Willem Wijnstekers, "Implementation of Regulation 3254/91, Leg-hold Traps and Fur Imports," Memo for European Parliament, Nov. 24, 1993, at 2-3. The original law clearly states that the leg-hold trap need not be banned entirely, only regarding specified species.

[159] Neil Buckly, "U.S. Fur-Trapping Offer is Rejected," *Financial Times*, Nov. 28, 1997.

[160] Neil Buckly, "New Offer by U.S. on Leg-Hold Traps," *Financial Times*, Dec. 1, 1997.

[161] Animal Welfare Institute, "True Trapping Reform Won't Come from Vague, Weak Agreements," *American Welfare Institute Quarterly*, Winter 1998, at 12.

[162] *Id.*

[163] *Id.*

[164] *See* U.S. Trade Representative, *1999 National Trade Estimate Report on Foreign Trade Barriers* (1999), at 115.

[165] *See* Community Nutrition Institute, *Environmental Labeling in the Trade and Environment Context*, Discussion Draft Prepared for Joint Dialogue on Environment and Trade, in Oct. 1996, at 13; *see also* National Wildlife Federation, *Guarding the Green Choice: Environmental Labeling and the Rights of Green Consumers* (1996), both on file with Public Citizen.

[166] *See, e.g.,* John Zarocostas, "'Eco-labeling' is a Sticky Issue, Say Developing Nations at WTO Talks," *Journal of Commerce*, Aug. 20, 1996.

[167] *See* Community Nutrition Institute, *Environmental Labeling in the Trade and Environment Context*, Discussion Draft, Prepared for Joint Dialogue on Environment and Trade in Oct., 1996, at 12.

[168] *See* Signatories to Feb. 6, 1996, Open Letter to Policymakers from Coalition for Truth in Environmental Marketing Information, on file with Public Citizen.

[169] *See* 1997 Trade Policy Agenda and 1996 Annual Report of the President of the United States on the Trade Agreements Program (1997).

[170] *See* WTO Committee on Trade and Environment Document WT/CTE/W/23; *see also* WTO Committee on Technical Barriers to Trade Document G/TBT/W/23, "Eco-labeling Programmes," Mar. 19,

1996.

[171] *Id.*

[172] WTO, Agreement on Technical Barriers to Trade at Article 2.4.

[173] WTO, "WTO Trade and Environment Committee Discusses Proposals on Trade Measures in Multilateral Environmental Agreements and on Eco-Labelling," Press Release 96-711 PRESS/TE 008, Apr. 29, 1996.

[174] John Zarocostas, "'Eco-labeling' is a Sticky Issue, Say Developing Nations at WTO Talks," *Journal of Commerce*, Aug. 20, 1996.

[175] WTO Committee on Trade and Environment Document WT/CTE/W/27, "U.S. Proposals Regarding Further Work on Transparency of Eco-Labeling," Mar. 25, 1996.

[176] Suggested Basis of U.S. Proposal Regarding Principles Applicable to Eco-labelling Programs, May 22, 1996, at Item 2, on file with Public Citizen.

[177] *Id.* at Item 5.

[178] *Id.* at Item 2.

[179] LETS (Local Exchange Trading Systems) are a simple system of expanded barter that allow participants to trade with each other without using conventional money. *See* Helen Barnes, Peter North, and Perry Walker, *LETS on Low Income*, New Economics Foundation (1996). If the WTO TBT Agreement covers voluntary eco-labeling schemes as barriers to trade, LETS could by the same logic be subjected to WTO rules.

[180] *See* USTR, *1997 Trade Policy Agency and 1996 Annual Report of the President of the U.S. on the Trade Agreements Program* (1997).

[181] "TBT Committee Discusses Labelling, Standards," *BRIDGES Weekly Trade News Digest*, vol. 3, no. 24, Jun. 14, 1999.

[182] Codex Alimentarius Commission, Proposed Draft Recommendations for the Labeling of Foods Obtained Through Biotechnology (Alinorm 99/22, Appendix VIII), CX/FL 99/6, Government Comments at Step 3 from the U.K. and the U.S., Jun. 1999, on file with Public Citizen.

[183] Keith Koffler, "Adminstration to Bring Seven Trade Complaints to the WTO," *Congress Daily*, May 3, 1999.

[184] Sierra Club, "Protect Our Neighborhood, Don't Trade Away Our Trees," Summer 1999.

[185] Douglas P. Norlen, "Hong Kong Registers WTO Complaint Over U.S. Wood Crate Ban; Canada to Follow," *Bureau of National Affairs*, Nov. 18, 1998.

[186] 63 *Fed. Reg.* 50099.

[187] "Zebra Mussels: the Invasion and Its Implications," Fact Sheet 045, Ohio State University, Ohio Sea Grant College Program, Fact Sheet 045, on file with Public Citizen.

[188] *See* "Zebra Mussels," Gulf of Maine Aquarium, Fact Sheet, Dec. 12, 1998, on file with Public Citizen.

[189] *See id.*

[190] *See* G. Thomas Watters, "North American Freshwater Mussels," Ohio Biological Survey and the Ohio State University Aquatic Ecology Laboratory.

[191] *See* Sierra Club, "Protect Our Neighborhood, Don't Trade Away Our Trees," Summer 1999.

[192] *See* Fact Sheet: Asian Gypsy Moths, (AFI-USDA-APHIS-PPQ), May 25, 1993.

[193] *See* F. William Ravlin and Kenneth J. Stein. "What Will the Gypsy Moth do to My Trees?," Virginia Polytechnic Institute and State University, Department of Entomomolgy, on file with Public Citizen.

[194] Tom Baldwin, "Bug Casts Giant Shadow," *Journal of Commerce*, Sep. 28, 1998.

[195] 63 *Fed. Reg.* at 50101.

[196] *Id.*

[197] *See* Sierra Club, "Protect Our Neighborhood, Don't Trade Away Our Trees," Summer 1999.

[198] Tom Baldwin, "Bug Casts Giant Shadow," *Journal of Commerce*, Sep. 28, 1998, and P. T. Bangsberg, "China Criticizes 'Unfair' Beetle Ban," *Journal of Commerce*, Sep. 22, 1998.

[199] P. T. Bangsberg, "China Criticizes 'Unfair' Beetle Ban," *Journal of Commerce*, Sep. 22, 1998.

[200] 63 *Fed. Reg.* at 50101.

[201] 16 U.S.C. Chapter 35, Section 1538.

[202] 1969 Vienna Convention on the Law of Treaties at Article 30(2).

[203] North American Free Trade Agreement (NAFTA) at §104.

[204] Convention on International Trade in Endangered Species (CITES) at Appendix I.

[205] *Id.* at Article VIII, "1. The Parties shall take appropriate measures to enforce the provisions of the present Convention and to prohibit trade in specimens in violation thereof. These shall include measures: (a) to penalize trade in, or possession of, such specimens, or both; and (b) to provide for

the confiscation or return to the State of export of such specimens . . . ."

[206] U.N. F.A.O. Code of Conduct on Responsible Fisheries at Article 7.2.2: "[M]easures should provide *inter alia* that . . . endangered species are protected."

[207] *See* 1979 Bonn Convention on Protecting Migratory Species of Wild Animals at Article III.4: "Parties that are Range States of a migratory species listed in Appendix I [including sea turtles] shall endeavour . . . to prevent, remove, compensate for or minimize, as appropriate, the adverse effects of activities or obstacles that seriously impede or prevent the migration of the species . . . ."

[208] "CIT Ruling Complicates Shrimp-Turtle Case," *BRIDGES Weekly Trade News Digest*, Double Issue, vol. 2, nos. 15 & 16, Apr. 26, 1999.

[209] Dan Seligman, *Broken Promises: How the Clinton Administration is Trading Away Our Environment*, Sierra Club Responsible Trade Campaign, May 13, 1998.

[210] *Id.*

[211] *See* "U.S. Business, Environmental Groups Divided on Shrimp-Turtle Case," *BRIDGES Weekly Trade News Digest*, vol. 2, no. 15, Apr. 27, 1998.

[212] "WTO Enviro Groups Getting Closer Together," *Washington Trade Daily*, Mar. 17, 1999.

[213] "Green Groups Challenge WTO," *Financial Times*, Mar. 17, 1999.

[214] "Cuts Urged in Fishing and Farm Aid," *Financial Times*, Mar. 16, 1999.

[215] Statement by the U.S. delegation to the WTO General Council Session, Geneva, Switzerland Jul. 29, 1999.

[216] *See, e.g.,* Friends of the Earth International. The U.S. government was speaking about reconciling the WTO and the environment at the WTO high-level environmental meeting while it was negotiating with other countries in an attempt to secure a final forestry deal as an "early harvest" at the Seattle Ministerial.

[217] The American Forest & Paper Association, "Forest Industry Leader Urges Worldwide Tariff Elimination," Press Release, Apr. 28, 1999, citing study by the international consultant firm of Jaakko Poyry.

[218] Statement by the U.S. delegation to the WTO General Council Session, Geneva, Switzerland, Jul. 29, 1999.

In this chapter ...

CASES:

- **EU Artificial Hormone Residues in Beef:** The WTO ruled against a ban on beef containing artificial hormone residues because the EU could not prove scientifically that *residues* in meat harm human health (the actual hormones are known to do so.) The WTO approved $116.8 million in sanctions after the EU refused to cave in and accept the meat.

- **Company-Inspected Australian Meat Declared Equivalent to U.S. Government Inspection:**. Applying WTO rules, the U.S. deemed Australian company-inspected meat to be "equivalent" to U.S. government-inspected meat. Both products will bear the same U.S. Department of Agriculture seal of approval although a dramatic rise in salmonella cases paralleled the implementation of the new system.

- **Australian Quarantine on Raw Salmon:** The WTO ruled against Australia's strict rules governing importation of uncooked salmon, designed to prevent foreign bacteria from infecting domestic salmon stocks. Australia scientifically proved risk, but not the precise probability that it would occur, thus failing the WTO's prohibitive evidentiary rules.

- **Japan Codling Moth Testing:** Japan is free of the agriculturally devastating codling moth. The WTO ruled that Japan could not invoke strict testing requirements on all fruit based on experience with one type of fruit *unless* it could prove scientifically that such tests were necessary for all fruit.

- **South Korean Shelf Life for Meat:** To avoid a U.S. WTO challenge on its 30-day shelf life limit for meat, South Korea weakened its food safety policy by extending shelf life to 90 days.

- **South Korean Produce Inspection:** To avoid a U.S. WTO challenge, South Korea agreed to dramatically shorten the duration of its produce inspection process. Now produce is sold to consumers before test results on its safety are in.

- **EU Toxic Teething Ring Ban:** The U.S. threatened WTO action on behalf of the toy industry against an EU-wide policy regulating certain plastic softeners used in teething rings and other toys. This was a unique instance in which a WTO threat backfired, thanks to joint efforts of the European governments and U.S. consumer groups.

- **Danish Lead Ban:** The U.S. has threatened a WTO challenge if Denmark implements an intended ban on lead compounds in pigments and chemical processes to avoid lead's threat to child development.

CONCEPTS:

Sanitary and Phytosanitary Agreement: Contains WTO rules on food safety, inspection and labeling, and animal and plant health (e.g., quarantines, invasive species countermeasures.)

Precautionary Principle: The WTO undermines this widely used principle, which calls for action to *avoid* uncertain and possibly irreversible harm. Under the precautionary approach, industry is required to prove a product's long-term safety before it is approved for the market. The WTO puts the burden of proof on governments to show scientifically that a risk exists *prior* to taking action and exposes laws based on precaution to successful WTO attack.

Harmonization: Is the replacement of varied national standards with uniform global standards to facilitate trade. The WTO requires or promotes harmonization of food, product safety, environmental and other standards. Harmonization undermines the value choices that people in different societies make about the standards by which they want to live.

Equivalence: Significantly different, often lower, standards from other countries can be declared equivalent to domestic standards based on subjective comparisons without clear procedural guidelines or an enumeration of the factors to consider. Once a standard is declared "equivalent," it must be treated as if it were a domestic standard.

Codex Alimentarius Commission: Is the industry-influenced international body that the WTO recognizes as setting the presumptively WTO-legal food standards.

The WTO, Food Safety Standards and Public Health

U.S. regulatory agencies have intervened in the market to save the lives of millions of Americans who otherwise would have been exposed to dangerous food, products and work environments.[1] In this chapter, we will review how new WTO rules are undermining key food

Cartoon by Gary Hallgren
New York Times, Sept. 14, 1994

safety, public health, and plant and animal health policies. In addition to successful WTO challenges to the EU's ban on artificial beef hormone residues in meat and several other countries' quarantine laws, threats of WTO action have led South Korea to kill two food safety rules. Outstanding WTO threats include U.S. charges against a Danish ban on lead in many products and on a Europe-wide policy on plastic softeners in children's teething rings. Meanwhile, WTO requirements to "harmonize" different national standards towards uniform international standards have led the U.S.

to declare company-inspected beef from Australia equivalent in safety to U.S. government inspected meat. These imports can enter the U.S. labeled as if they met the U.S. law. Finally, the WTO empowers assorted industry-influenced international organizations to set standards presumed to comply with WTO rules.

While U.S. regulatory standards are not perfect, the Food and Drug Administration (FDA), the Department of Agriculture's Food Safety and Inspection Service (FSIS), the National Highway Traffic Safety Administration (NHTSA), the Occupational Safety and Health Administration (OSHA) and the Consumer Product Safety Commission (CPSC) have suc-

The Uruguay Round moved GATT beyond simply requiring equal treatment of foreign and domestic products. It set limits on which issues countries can set policy and how stiff health, safety and environmental regulations can be.

WTO Sanitary and Phytosanitary (SPS) Agreement: Unaccountable Trade Bureaucrats Make Public Health Decisions

The Sanitary and Phytosanitary (SPS) Agreement is one of the Uruguay Round Agreements. It sets strict limits on WTO Members' abilities to enact laws pertaining to food safety and such things as plant pests, animal diseases and quarantines, otherwise referred to as animal and plant health. Article 2.2 of the WTO SPS Agreement declares WTO-illegal measures that are based on "insufficient" scientific evidence — thus effectively eviscerating the Precautionary Principle, which says that potentially dangerous substances must be proven *safe* before they are put on the market. Governments rely on this principle to protect the public and environment from suspected health risks, particularly in the absence of scientific certainty. No country's SPS measure challenged in the WTO has ever been upheld by a WTO panel. In fact, WTO panels have consistently interpreted Members' SPS measures to be barriers to trade that must be weakened or eliminated, rather than public health safeguards.

cessfully regulated the industries under their purview largely to the benefit of consumers. However, more remains to be done.[2]

As many as 9,000 Americans die and 6 million become ill every year from food-borne illnesses.[3] This number is likely to increase as international trade in food increases and consumers are exposed to foods produced under different or weaker safety standards, less stringent inspections and long-distance shipping.

A 1996 report by the World Health Organization (WHO) noted that globalization of the food supply was a growing cause of illness worldwide.[4] The report attributes outbreaks of *shigella sonnei* in Britain, Norway and Sweden in 1994, and a 1991 outbreak of cholera in the southern U.S. to the import of foods from countries with lower safety standards.[5]

Another reason for the increased occurrence of food-borne illness is that food inspection has not kept up with food imports. For instance, under the North American Free Trade Agreement (NAFTA), U.S. agricultural imports from Canada and Mexico have increased by 57%.[6] During this same period, FDA inspections of imported food declined from 8% of total imports to less than 2%, increasing the risk that contaminated produce reaches the public.[7] Thus, consumer and public health groups, as well as the U.S. General Accounting Office, have recommended that the U.S. adopt stricter food safety inspection standards and provide the funding necessary to implement them.[8]

Increased trade has made the strengthening of border food safety inspection particularly important, since poor countries that are under severe pressure from the International Monetary Fund both to export food and to cut public health and sanitation spending[9] often cannot afford to properly enforce their laws or inspect food products themselves. And often funding for such regulatory systems is the first to be cut in times of financial difficulty. For instance, in 1992, Mexico's spend-

Five Years of the WTO: Changing Consumers' Perspectives

An international organization composed of numerous consumer groups from around the world, then known as the International Organization of Consumers Unions (IOCU), came out in favor of the Uruguay Round in 1994. While noting concerns about certain provisions, the federation of groups now known as Consumers International concluded that consumers could expect significant benefits from the Uruguay Round and that the potential threats were not likely to materialize.

"The creation of a World Trade Organization with strengthened powers for settling trade disputes should provide a major boost for open, multilateral world trade rules over unilateral actions by individual countries or trading blocs,"[10] the International Organisation of Consumers Unions said in a statement. However, many other consumer groups, including all but one U.S. consumer organization, joined the unanimity of environmental and other nongovernmental organizations in opposing the Uruguay Round Agreements.[11]

Now, almost five years later, the results of the Uruguay Round have caused some of the consumer groups that supported it to re-evaluate their position. Consumers International has issued a position paper on the pending Seattle WTO Ministerial that is critical of the Uruguay Round's record to date. The paper calls for an objective review, with consumer participation, of the results of the Uruguay Round Agreements, with an eye toward repairing aspects that threaten fundamental consumer rights and are leading to an unbalanced distribution of potential benefits of world trade expansion.[12] The paper also notes that the WTO rules are increasingly affecting domestic regulations and are undermining the ability of governments to ensure effective consumer protection.[13] The federation warns that while the aim of trade should be meeting the needs of consumers and producers, the multilateral trading system established by the Uruguay Round has not resulted in the promised economic gains for poor consumers and has not improved consumer access to information, safe goods or competitive services. In some instances, in fact, it has undermined pre-existing consumer rights.[14]

ing on food safety inspection was $25 million, but three years later, with Mexico reeling from the peso crash and obligated by new loan agreements to implement further "structural adjustment," food inspection funding was slashed to $5 million.[15] Yet U.S. imports of Mexican produce have steadily increased; as of 1998, 52% of all U.S. fruit and vegetable imports came from Mexico.[16]

The increase in food-borne illnesses and the need to improve food safety standards and inspections has not discouraged the efforts by special interests to restrain regulatory agencies and roll back the important public interest safeguards put into place over the past century. In 1996, outraged U.S. consumer groups defeated a bill, dubbed the "Regulatory Rollback Act," that would have required regulatory agencies to conduct costly risk assessments and cost-benefit analyses any time they wished to adopt a consumer safeguard.[17] The bill would have required agencies to prove a risk scientifically *before* regulating products and strengthening inspection procedures. This would place an enormous burden on agencies seeking to establish policy on public health issues such as toxics and worker safety and prevent a quick response to life-threatening outbreaks of food-borne illnesses.

For example, the U.S. adopted new standards for contaminants in meat after a number of children died eating hamburgers infected with *E. coli* bacteria. However, no scientific study exists proving that reducing the level of contaminants in meat is directly linked to reducing the risk of illness and death from food poisoning. Thus, despite proven evidence of deaths due to contaminated hamburger meat, had the proposal been accepted, the Food Safety Inspection Service (FSIS) would not have met the risk assessment prerequisite necessary to issue stronger meat inspection regulations.[18] A somewhat weaker version of the legislation is currently in the U.S. Congress, and consumer groups vow to defeat it.[19]

What many citizens' groups participating in the effort against the "Regulatory Rollback Act" did not know was that the concept they defeated in the U.S. Congress in 1996 had been adopted *globally* in 1994 – embodied in the WTO's SPS Agreement. The SPS Agreement provides parameters within which WTO Members must constrain their domestic policies concerning food safety and animal and plant health (regulations with respect to pests, veterinary drugs, contaminants, additives, food inspection, etc.). A series of WTO rulings on food standards and quarantine rules demonstrates how the SPS Agreement has limited the ability of governments to protect the public from actual and potential health threats and respond to consumer demands for safe food.

Codex Standards Permit Artificial Hormone Residues

A vital element of the WTO ruling against the EU's ban on meat containing artificial beef hormone residues is the requirement that the EU standard be based on international standards set by the Codex Alimentarius, the international food-standard-setting body empowered by the WTO.[20] The Codex standard, which is extremely controversial, allows for residues of artificial hormones in beef.[21]

Codex procedures allow for undue industry influence and politicization of what should be health-based rule-making.[22] Codex issued a standard permitting residues of artificial hormones in beef only after a four-year U.S. campaign to gain approval of these chemicals. The U.S. forced two votes on the issue, which is almost unheard of at Codex (usually, the body sets standards by consensus). The U.S. lost the first vote, and Codex refused to permit the hormones. The U.S. forced a second vote and won. The hormone residue standard was adopted by a slim majority — 33 countries in favor, 29 against, and seven abstaining.[23] The insistence of EU consumers, over opposition by EU farmers, that their meat be free of artificial hormone residues has become a major WTO test: consumer rights versus the WTO and its Codex international food standards.

The WTO SPS Agreement: Trade Trumps Health

The primary goal of the SPS Agreement is to facilitate trade by eliminating differences in food regulations that serve to fragment the global market. [24] It covers WTO Members' food safety rules, as well as livestock, fisheries and plant health, including quarantine, inspection and testing requirements. It sets strict rules governing both permissible policy goals and the means by which nations can pursue these goals. WTO Members can challenge each other's regulations as exceeding these limits.

To facilitate international uniformity in food regulations,[25] the SPS Agreement contains a series of criteria and tests that food, animal and plant health policies must pass to be WTO-legal. First, SPS measures cannot be employed to achieve goals other than human, plant or animal life or health. A country could not, for example, ban a pesticide because it causes wild bird eggs to have thin shells and justify the ban as a legitimate SPS measure. Nor would other animal welfare laws, such as those addressing the humane slaughter of animals, be deemed WTO-legitimate SPS regulations. Such policies would be subject to other, even more restrictive WTO rules governing non-food safety product standards (spelled out in the Agreement on Technical Barriers to Trade, or TBT Agreement).

Second, under the SPS Agreement, the level of protection a country chooses for its citizens is also a matter for WTO review – even when the standard is applied equally to domestic and foreign goods.[26] The SPS Agreement directs countries to use a technique called "risk assessment"[27] in setting their domestic food standards. Yet, some U.S. standards, for example, are based not on assessing a *tolerable* amount of risk, but in forbidding public exposure to a risk altogether. Such "zero tolerance" standards, while safer for consumers, are inherently problematic under WTO rules because they are not developed using the internationally recognized version of risk assessment approved by the WTO. The SPS Agreement also requires that a policy not be any more restrictive to trade than is necessary to obtain its WTO-allowed goal.[28] This provision, taken in combination with the risk assessment requirement, means that in almost every case, nations cannot adopt a "zero risk" standard for pesticide residues, bacterial contaminants and other human pathogens.

Third, the SPS Agreement sharply restricts the right of countries to adopt or maintain standards that exceed those promulgated by international bodies.[29] The WTO empowers specific, named international standard-setting agencies to create standards for food safety and plant and animal health (as well as product safety and technical standards). Countries wishing to maintain higher standards face prohibitive evidentiary hurdles.[32]

Danish Lead Ban Faces U.S. WTO Threat

The U.S. has threatened to challenge Denmark before a WTO panel if it implements an intended domestic ban on lead compounds.[30] The Danes claim that lead compounds can cause brain damage in young children and have notified the European Commission and the WTO of their intention to ban approximately 200 lead compounds used in pigments and chemical processes.[31]

Genetically Modified Organisms in Food

As scientific innovation outpaces the ability of regulators to anticipate the adverse human health effects of new technologies, the potential threat WTO trade rules pose to public health and safety will increase. For instance, barely discussed at the time the SPS Agreement went into effect, but of vital importance, are the potential human health and environmental threats posed by new biological technologies. For instance, more and more commodities for human consumption are being genetically altered to improve appearance or enhance resistance to agricultural chemicals. Biotechnology companies are pushing for the unregulated sale and trade of these "genetically modified organisms" (GMOs) in the absence of a full understanding of their impacts on human and environmental health. Emerging data indicate that some GMOs cause allergic reactions in humans and that some are fatal to benign insects that feed on GMO crops. But the onerous burden of proof placed by the WTO on governments that try to establish or enforce regulations severely undermines their ability to protect the public from the possible dangers of GMOs or respond to public demand to ban, or at least label, such products. (*See* Chapter 3 for more on the WTO and genetically modified organisms).

Unfortunately, these standard-setting bodies – the Codex Alimentarius in the case of food safety and the International Organization on Standardization (ISO) in the case of technical, product and environmental standards – are dominated by industry and operate in a closed manner, insulated from public oversight or accountability. (Indeed, the ISO is a purely private-sector, industry-funded, industry-membership organization.) From a public and environmental health perspective, these bodies tend to set weaker standards than those set by governments with strong regulatory systems and accountability to involved citizens and consumer movements.

Legitimate public interest safeguards thus can be cast as "barriers to trade" by any WTO Member country that can make a *prima facie* case that a food safety law is stronger than international standards or violates other SPS goals or means tests. The burden of proof then switches to governments to prove that the level of protection they set meets WTO requirements and that there is no other way to achieve their WTO-legal goal without affecting trade. Thus, these WTO rules not only eliminate differences in national laws but also cap the strength of food safety protections.

The WTO SPS rules have the cumulative effect of moving key decisions about food and human risk exposure away from democratically elected national governments to international bodies that are heavily influenced by industry and trade bureaucrats who staff WTO dispute panels. The effect is to constrain the power of national legislatures to act in the public interest and to disenfranchise ordinary citizens, who have far more capacity to make their voices heard nationally than in international forums.

WTO Record On Food Safety and Quarantine Laws

After five years, a trend in the food arena has emerged. WTO panels have ruled against all food safety regulations under review on the grounds that they restrict trade more than necessary. These include the EU's consumer protection ban on artificial hormone-treated beef, Japan's testing requirements designed to keep fruit pests out of the country and Australia's quarantine on raw salmon imports, which was designed to protect the health of indigenous fish population. Threats of action under the SPS Agreement have resulted in South Korea lowering food standards.

> **" A**s you recommended, we have initiated action against the EU ban under the dispute settlement procedures of the World Trade Organization. "[33]
>
> — Letter from U.S. Trade Representative Mickey Kantor to the National Cattlemen's Association

Case 1: The WTO Insists Europe Accept Artificial Hormone-Treated Beef

In a major defeat for health and safety policies based on the premise that potentially dangerous substances should be proven safe before they are marketed, a WTO panel ruled in 1997 against an EU ban on artificial hormone-treated beef. The decision was the first involving the WTO SPS Agreement and amply illustrates the adverse effects of shifting the focus of public health policy making away from democratically elected and accountable national officials to the WTO.

Since 1988, the EU has banned the sale of beef from cattle treated with artificial hormones and has applied the ban in a nondiscriminatory fashion to both domestic and imported beef products.[34] Exposure to the artificial hormones themselves have been linked to cancer and premature pubescence in girls,[35] although the risk to humans of artificial hormone residues in the meat they consume is uncertain. On the basis of the known risks and the public's demand for a ban on meat from cattle treated with artificial hormones, the EU adopted a "zero risk" standard: Rather than trying to assess a tolerable amount of an indeterminable risk or waiting for negative human health affects to accrue over time, the EU chose to eliminate public exposure to the risk altogether. The EU made this policy choice after prolonged and effective consumer campaigns in numerous EU member countries.

The U.S. beef and biotechnology industries have long opposed this EU policy.[36] In January 1996, the U.S. challenged the ban at the WTO.[37] In 1998, a WTO panel ruled that the beef hormone ban was an illegal measure under SPS rules in part because it was not based on a WTO-approved risk assessment.[38] The WTO Appellate Body affirmed the original panel's decision, and the EU was ordered to begin imports of U.S. artificial hormone-treated beef by May 13, 1999.[39]

The EU interpreted the WTO ruling as requiring it to produce a risk assessment that backed up the ban. So the EU started a new risk assessment that it claimed would meet the WTO critique and support the ban. The U.S., on the other hand, interpreted the WTO ruling as finding that the EU's beef ban was *prima facie* incompatible with SPS rules because there was no scientific evidence that artificial hormone residues are not fit for human consumption. Thus, the U.S. argued, the EU was required to lift the import prohibition, regardless of any new risk assessment.[40] After the EU refused to comply with the WTO panel ruling by the May 1999 deadline, the WTO on July 12, 1999, approved a U.S. request to impose retaliatory sanctions but lowered the amount from the $200 million requested by the U.S. to $116.8 million worth of European-made products.[41]

Meanwhile, preliminary findings of the EU's new risk assessment were leaked to the press in early May 1999. The assessment established the artificial hormone 17 beta-oestradiol, one of the six artificial growth hormones used in U.S., as a potential carcinogen.[42] The EU's full risk assessment was not complete by the WTO deadline, so the EU offered to compensate the U.S. for maintaining the beef hormone ban until the assessment was done and the issue could be judged on the basis of more complete evidence.[43] U.S. Trade Representative Charlene Barshefsky responded that the U.S. would accept a deal only if the EU pledged to open its beef market in the near future.[44] No deal was struck, and the U.S. levied 100% tariffs on a variety of important EU exports including truffles, mustard, cheeses and foie gras.

The Implications of the Beef Hormone Ruling: In its beef hormone ruling, the WTO effectively declared that health regulations enacted in advance of scientific certainty were not allowed under WTO provisions. The WTO attempted in effect, to eliminate from the standard-setting process such factors as the cultural values, attitudes and priorities of individual societies, as well as the desire to shield people from unnecessary exposure to potentially dangerous substances. The WTO ruling in this case poses a direct challenge to one of the pillars of contemporary public health policy, the Precautionary Principle. Under this principle, potentially dangerous substances must be proven safe before they are put on the market. The principle is based on the fact that science does not always provide the information necessary for authorities to avert environmental or public health threats in a timely manner. Safety regulation based on this approach has saved the lives of thousands of people in the U.S. alone. Many areas of U.S. law, such as our system for approving new pharmaceuticals,[45] are based on the Precautionary Principle; it is also widely recognized in international environmental law.

For instance, by refusing to approve the morning sickness drug thalidomide, the U.S. averted a disastrous epidemic of birth defects. In other countries, thalidomide is estimated to have caused deformities in more than 10,000 babies – even though at the time of its approval for sale in Europe and Canada, tests in laboratory animals showed no negative effects.[46] Thalidomide's damage was revealed only over time — not in the drugs' users but in the children of women taking the drug.

However, because U.S. pharmaceutical law put the burden on the manufacturer to prove that thalidomide was safe, and given that its long-term effects were not known, the U.S. never approved the substance. Yet SPS rules only permit public health measures that are based on "sound science." Thus the absence of a conclusive body of scientific evidence means a nation cannot meet its WTO burden of proof to show that a regulation is necessary.[47]

Thus, the WTO stood the Precautionary Principle on its head, shifting the burden of proof from the manufacturer of the product to the government seeking to regulate the product. By rejecting a popular consumer safeguard solidly grounded in the Precautionary Principle, the WTO sent a powerful message about its priorities.

Even when scientific data is robust, value judgments and social priorities play the central role in policymaking. People make judgments about whether exposure to a risk is avoidable (whether there are acceptable, affordable substitutes) and how much risk is reasonable in exchange for whatever rewards a new product promises. Legislatures may decide to allow zero risk from a particular hazard, rather than establishing an allowable level of risk.

For example, the U.S. has a zero tolerance level for *listeria* in cold smoked fish, canned lobster and ready-to-eat seafood.[48] *Listeria* is a bacterium that can cause blood infections, meningitis, encephalitis, and intrauterine or cervical infections in pregnant women, which may result in miscarriage or stillbirth.[49] Canada considers the U.S. policy to be unnecessarily severe and thus enumerated the *listeria* policy in its 1996 Register of United States Barriers to Trade.[50] Indeed, under the SPS Agreement, the U.S. *listeria* regulations could be challenged as illegitimate trade restrictions.

Determining risk relies on the notion that scientists can accurately and quickly predict the effects on human health of a long and ever-expanding list of new pesticide residues and food additives. In fact, scientists acknowledge that they may never be able to make these determinations. The data on many emerging toxins (e.g., *E-coli H:0157*) and technologies (e.g., genetically modified organisms) is scant at best. For these reasons, many scientists, regulators, and consumer and environmental organizations are calling for public health policies that prevent exposures — particularly to readily avoidable risks — in the face of scientific uncertainty.[51] The WTO's policies ignore current scientific trends and flout public sentiment.

Even far less stringent regulatory approaches to food safety than a ban could run afoul of the WTO. A possible alternative to a ban on artificial hormone-treated beef sales in the EU and elsewhere is labeling. The U.S. argues that this relatively weak strategy may also be WTO-illegal. The Agreement on Technical Barriers to Trade (TBT), which governs all non-food safety, plant or animal health product standards, requires technical regulations to be based on the performance of a product rather than its design or descriptive characteristics. This could be interpreted to prevent labeling based on the manner in which cattle are raised, since the presence of hormone residues does not change the end use of the product.[52] In addition, in the beef hormone case, the WTO already has ruled that artificial hormone residues on food have not been shown to pose a danger to human health. Thus, under the TBT Agreement, mandatory labeling of beef hormones could be determined to serve no legitimate WTO human health objective and thus could be ruled to be an unjustifiable discrimination against U.S. beef.[53]

Case 2: Australian Salmon — WTO Adds Difficulty, Cost to Animal Health Protections

In addition to placing prohibitive obstacles to the adoption of human health safeguards, the WTO also has set strict requirements for standards that protect plant and animal health. In 1998, the WTO Appellate Body ruled that an Australian quarantine on raw salmon imports, designed to protect the nation's indigenous fish population, was an illegal barrier to trade.[54] Australia has restricted the import of uncooked salmon since the 1960s.[55] The rule requires Australia's director of quarantine to ban raw salmon imports unless they have been subjected to treatment that would prevent the introduction into Australia of any infectious or contagious diseases affecting persons, animals or plants.

When Canada and the U.S. requested access to Australia's uncooked salmon market in 1994, Australia conducted a risk assessment as required by Article 5 of the WTO SPS Agreement. In 1996, on the basis of the risk assessment, the director of quarantine concluded that Australia should not permit uncooked salmon imports.[56] Among other findings, the risk assessment revealed that some 20 bacteria not present in Australia were present in Canadian and U.S. salmon. The Australian government concluded that the introduction of these contaminants to its salmon population could cause disease and found that Canada had not developed a treatment to eliminate the bacteria. Moreover, bacteria often can remain in animals after they have been killed, and food prepared for human consumption has in a number of cases ended up in the animal food supply. The final Australian risk assessment report thus confirmed that it was possible that Canadian uncooked salmon could infect live Australian salmon.[57] Indeed, Australia noted that Canada had not disagreed that there was a risk of disease spread through uncooked salmon[58] and had refused to produce relevant scientific data pertaining to the diseases particular to Canadian salmon.[59]

In response to Australia's final report, Canada in June 1998 filed a complaint with the WTO, arguing that the salmon ban violated the SPS Agreement.[60] The WTO Panel ruled that the ban was not based on sound science, exceeded international standards and therefore was arbitrarily and unjustifiably discriminatory.[61]

Australia appealed, arguing that its risk assessment, which was conducted as required by the SPS Agreement and which established that there was a risk of disease from uncooked salmon, allowed it to determine for itself the level of risk to which it would expose its fish stocks[62] in accordance with Article 2 of the SPS. The Appellate Panel concluded that the Australia's risk assessment was unsatisfactory because it failed to calculate the likelihood of salmon disease entry and transmission.[63] "It is not sufficient that a risk assessment conclude there is a possibility of entry, establishment or spread ... A proper risk assessment ... must evaluate the *likelihood*, i.e. the *probability*, of entry, establishment and spread."[64] Thus, the decision required that the risk be quantifiable rather than "merely" present. It also was a prime example of how a democratically elected government's policy judgment was subordinated to the WTO's definition of scientific validity.

The Appellate Panel established strict guidelines for conducting risk assessments relating to non-human disease spread, ruling that they must be conducted each time prior to a WTO Member's introduction or enforcement of a regulation relating to plant and animal pests and diseases.[65] These guidelines impose a significant financial burden on countries wishing to pass such regulations and thus discourage countries from doing so. Scarce fiscal resources will be at stake each time a country contemplates adopting a regulation involving pests and diseases. According to an Australian government official, "There are not a lot of scientists around who are able to do these [types of risk assessments]. A thorough assessment requires a lot of time and resources."[66]

Australia had until July 1999 to lift the ban. In late July, Canada asked the WTO to authorize sanctions on the basis that the new measures put in place by Australia were not compliant with the WTO panel ruling. It requested that the original panel rule on this question of whether new measures were WTO-consistent. Australia made a counter-request that the WTO panel determine how much Canada was actually harmed by the Australian quarantine.[67] Meanwhile, the U.S, which also wants access to the Australian raw salmon market, has initiated a WTO case dealing with the exact same subject matter.[68] A panel to hear this case was established in June 1999.[69]

The WTO's SPS rules do not allow countries to err on the side of caution. The ruling against the Australian law set a precedent requiring WTO Members to adopt SPS standards relating to plant and animal health only when precise risk to animals or plants can be quantified and the likelihood of infection or infestation can be established with scientific certainty. However, as in the Australian case, health agencies often adopt SPS measures precisely because the *exact* likelihood of a danger is unknown at the time.

In its ruling against Australia's salmon measure, as in the beef hormone case, the WTO panel shifted the entire burden – financial and scientific – to the country whose law was being challenged, requiring it to show that prohibited products were unsafe. Exporting countries – or companies located therein – on the other hand, cannot under WTO rules be asked by importing countries to demonstrate that their products are disease-free before they are allowed into the country. In the salmon case, the ruling effectively requires Australia to hire a specialist to conduct research on aquatic disease spread, conduct tests on Canadian salmon and calculate a precise probability of spread to live Australian salmon.

Canada, on the other hand, is not required to do anything to ensure that its salmon exports are free of bacteria that are known to afflict North American salmon. Only *after* Australia completes its lengthy studies and releases an authoritative assessment that successfully quantifies a risk of disease transmission to its salmon stocks can it impose any requirements on Canada under WTO rules. Thus, the WTO ruling requires years of costly tests before countries can adopt measures in response to identified risks to plant and animal health.

A recent development demonstrates the potentially very serious problems with this approach. The U.S. identified a serious infestation of Asian longhorned beetles, voracious tree-eaters with no natural predators in the U.S., which were entering the country in untreated wood pallets and packaging from China. The U.S. immediately banned the untreated wood containers and took severe actions to cut and incinerate hundreds of contaminated trees in Chicago, New York and other locations — the only way to halt the beetles' spread. Had the U.S. been required to conduct a long risk assessment prior to taking action, irreversible harm could have occurred. Yet, Hong Kong, which ships a significant amount of Chinese products to the U.S., has registered a complaint at the WTO's SPS Committee about the U.S. policy. (*See* Chapter 1 on the WTO's impact on the environment). If Hong Kong files a formal WTO challenge, the jusrisprudence of the salmon case will apply.

Case 3: Japan's Moth Quarantine — WTO Limits the Duration of Precautionary Measures

Just as the U.S. is concerned about the invasion of destructive Asian longhorned beetles, Japan has adopted strict quarantine requirements to ensure that imported agricultural products infested with codling moths do not enter the country.[79] Codling moths are known to cause severe agricultural damage.[80] The moths lay their eggs on leaves, nuts and the like. After the eggs hatch, the larvae burrow into the trees' fruit to mature, a process that takes between three and five weeks, depending on the climate.[81] During this process, there is no known practical and effective inspection method to

---

South Korea Lowers Food Safety Standards After U.S. WTO Threats

The U.S. threatened South Korea in 1995 with a WTO complaint for the length of its food safety inspection procedures for fruit.[70] The real target for this warning was Japan and China. South Korea was just the instrument for the U.S. "to set a WTO liberalization precedent on an issue it can win."[71] At the time, then-U.S. Trade Representative Mickey Kantor justified the possible WTO action by testifying to the Senate that "bilateral agreements [between the U.S. and South Korea] were frequently ignored or reinterpreted."[72] The Korean government, however, said that the case had been blown out of proportion and commented that WTO cases should be brought on major — not minor — issues given the expenses involved.[73] The cost of defending against a WTO case makes WTO threats a major concern, especially to developing countries. The U.S. brought the complaint to the WTO, but South Korea settled the case before it reached a panel.[74] South Korea decided that it was cheaper to lower food safety standards than to take on the U.S. In April 1995, inspection time for fruit imported into South Korea was lowered from 25 to five days, and the South Korean government started to allow shipments of fruit to consumers before the test samples were analyzed.[75]

But the U.S. had not finished with South Korea. In May 1995, it filed another complaint over food safety regulations in South Korea, this time related to shelf life of meat products.[76] South Korea, like Egypt and the United Arab Emirates, mandates a short shelf life for meat products for food safety reasons.[77] The U.S. complained that under South Korean law, the mandated shelf life might be shorter than the "sell-by-date" set by the manufacturer. Again, South Korea preferred to back down rather than face a lengthy and expensive battle in the WTO. It offered to substantially lengthen shelf life limits on meat from 30 to 90 days.[78]

detect the presence of the moths inside fruit.[82] Because Japan is currently free of codling moths, the insect is a significant concern to Japan.[83]

In 1950, Japan enacted the Plant Protection Law. Under this law, Japan prohibits the importation of eight agricultural products because they are potential hosts for codling moths: apples, cherries, peaches, nectarines, walnuts, apricots, pears, plums and quince.[84]

Japan provides an exception to its prohibition when the exporting country proposes fumigation treatment that is proven to ensure no codling moths enter Japan.[85] Under its procedures, spelled out in the *Experimental Guide for Cultivar Comparison Test on Insect Mortality – Fumigation*, countries with codling moths must test their fumigation treatment on each variety of every type of fruit they seek to export to Japan (i.e., each variety of apple –red delicious, granny smith, etc.). Japan argued that it required varietal testing because codling moth eggs are less susceptible to fumigation in some fruit varieties than in others.[86] Japan had submitted a risk assessment entitled *1996 Pest Risk Assessment of Codling Moth*, evaluating the likelihood of the entry, establishment and spread of the codling moth through the import of agricultural products.[87] A number of varieties of U.S. apples were allowed into Japan after undergoing treatment to eliminate the codling moth.[88]

However, in 1998, the U.S. filed a complaint with the WTO, arguing that Japan's varietal testing requirement adversely affected the export of agricultural products.[89] It alleged that Japan's policy was inconsistent with its obligations under the SPS Agreement, that it was not based on scientific evidence, and that it was more trade-restrictive than necessary to keep the codling moth out of the country.[90] The U.S. contended that its own evidence concluded that there was no difference in the effectiveness of the fumigation treatment on varieties of the same fruit.[91]

The WTO panel's ruling in this case extended the logic of the ruling in the salmon case.[92] The panel rejected Japan's risk assessment and ruled that available data indicated that there was no scientific basis for the ban.[93] The panel ruled that although there was a risk of introducing the codling moth into Japan through trade in agricultural products, Japan's risk assessment did not establish a rational link between this risk and the rigorous Japanese testing requirements.[94] It thus ruled against Japan's testing requirements on the four commodities — apples, cherries, nectarines and walnuts — for which the U.S. had provided alternative scientific evidence establishing no difference in response to fumigation among varieties.[95]

Japan was aware that its requirements may have exceeded available scientific evidence. But Japan argued that it should be able to adopt safeguards it thought fit, given that it was now free of codling moths and needed to stay that way,[96] considering its limited arable land and national memory of widespread hunger during World War II. Indeed, in its appeal of the ruling, Japan claimed that the WTO should overturn only those measures that were "patently inconsistent" with the SPS Agreement's requirement that measures be based on scientific evidence.[97]

The testimony of one of the technical experts consulted by the WTO panel emphasizes that Japan's law, although extremely cautious, is logical and rational, given the risk posed by the codling moth. The expert, Dr. Patrick Ducom, testified that Japan's absence of scientific evidence to support its varietal testing rules did not mean that Japan's contention about the need to test different varieties was necessarily wrong, but rather that it was unproved.

"The arguments put forth by Japan for requiring varietal trials are not based on scientific data," he said. "They are supported by a few experimental data in which varietal difference exists. ... [Although] each test [for fumigation treatment among varieties] has revealed sufficient efficacy [as an insecticide]... *[e]xtrapolation [of these results] to all available varieties is no more scientific than the Japanese's contrary assertion [that all varieties should be assumed to respond differently to fumigation].* ... It is unfortunate that there has not been a research program on the subject in order to try to present some scientific proof." [98] *(emphasis added)*

The lack of conclusive scientific data in this instance supports the enactment of precautionary regulations. Yet, in this case, the WTO further narrowed the conditions under which such regulations can survive WTO challenge. The WTO panel ruled that the one SPS provision that might have been used to justify measures based on the Precautionary Principle can be invoked only for a limited period of time.[99] The question of how much time is permitted was left unanswered.

Japan appealed its case, but the Appellate Body affirmed all of the lower WTO panel's conclusions and went further, concurring with the U.S. request to extend the ruling to the other quarantined fruits: apricots, pears, plums and quince.[100] The Appellate Body's move was significant, because, unlike the other four varieties of fruit, there is no evidence showing that all varieties of these fruit respond to codling moth fumigation treatment.[101] The Appellate Body argued, however, that precautionary fumigation testing should not be applied to these fruits for the same reason they should not be applied to the other four fruits: The testing requirement itself was not based on a proper risk assessment.[102]

Under the SPS Agreement, countries are forced either to drop a policy in question or pay compensation while collecting scientific data. Japan informed the WTO on April 13, 1999, that it was studying ways to implement the codling moth ruling. In a joint communication, the U.S. and Japan informed the WTO on June 15, 1999 that they had agreed to an implementation period of nine months and twelve days from the date of adoption of the reports.[103] The decision could cause widespread damage to Japanese agriculture if it leads to an infestation of the codling moth, yet the WTO cannot be held accountable for the consequences. Japan agreed to amend its law by December 31, 1999.

Threat 1: U.S. Threat Over EU Toxic Teething Ring Ban Backfires

As global trade rules have encroached on issues traditionally dealt with in the domestic policy realm, the U.S. and the EU are more likely to have a trade fight over public health and environmental policies than tariffs and quotas. One example of this is the U.S. attack on behalf of its toy industry on the EU's proposed ban on baby teething rings containing the controversial plastic softener phthalate, the additive that makes hard plastics pliable instead of brittle. This case is unique because a massive media campaign by public interest groups has so far stopped the EU from lowering public health standards. Indeed, advocacy groups used negative publicity about the U.S. trade threats to pressure U.S. industry to begin voluntarily phasing out phthalates.

In an attempt to limit the exposure of infants to toxic substances in their toys, the EU moved to regulate the prevalence of certain chemicals in children's toys, especially teethers and toys that are put into the mouth, by restricting phthalates and labeling the content of the toys.[104] American toy producers suggested that the proposal may be an illegal barrier to trade.[105]

Several European countries recommended that industry voluntarily stop using plastic softeners in toys marketed to children under three years by 1997.[106] In April 1998, the EU Scientific Committee on Toxicity, Ecotoxicity and the Environment con-

cluded that teething rings made from polyvinylchloride (PVC) leach impermissibly high levels of phthalates into the mouths of infants, potentially causing liver and kidney damage.[107] Beyond concerns with the phthalates already on the market, the committee suggested that before new plastic softeners are introduced into the market, their risks should be assessed.[108] Studies collected by the U.S. Consumer Product Safety Commission found that phthalates caused some cancers in laboratory animals.[110] Despite health concerns that PVCs may be environmentally damaging organic pollutants,[111] the toy manufacturing industry opposed regulatory actions on PVC softeners in teethers and other toys.[112]

While the EU Committee on Science, Toxics, Ecotoxics and the Environment was studying the issue of PVC and plastic softeners in toys, the U.S. Commerce Department was communicating its con-

PVC in Autos: U.S. Threat

The U.S. automotive industry had solicited and received help from the U.S. government to stop any PVC-related EU regulatory action well before the toy issue arose. In November of 1996, the U.S. ambassador to the EU wrote EU regulators criticizing efforts to make certain products and substances, including PVC and lead in automobiles, illegal. These actions "undermine the goals of free trade" and hinder efforts by the TransAtlantic Business Dialogue,[109] the ambassador said.

cerns about possible regulatory action over toys to the U.S. State Department. In an action memo to European station chiefs, the State Department said that "leading toy manufacturers contacted the Commerce Department ... to rectify a problem."[113] The problem was not just the proposed voluntary bans already in place in Denmark, Holland and Belgium, but proposed marketing bans in other European states and the possible "establishment of a ban in Europe."[114]

Beyond articulating the U.S. view on the policy's trade conflicts, the alert suggested that the Europeans were being too stringent and noted that Americans already limit phthalates in toys. The memo noted that the Toy Manufacturers of America voluntarily limits phthlates to 3% in pacifiers and teethers. The memo went on to criticize the marketing ban for exceeding the U.S. standard.[115]

Indeed, concern over one phthalate (diethylhexylphthalate, or DEHP) was significant enough for the Toy Manufacturers of America to "voluntarily ban" it entirely from toys in 1985.[116] However, other phthalates are still prevalent in teethers. One scientific analysis found that some toys contained more than 30% of the phthalate diisononyl phthalate (DINP).[117]

The State Department alert urged the consulates and embassies to press for a withdrawal of the marketing bans "in time for the Christmas purchasing season."[118] *The Los Angeles Times* reported that the Clinton administration was "acting at the behest of Mattel Inc. and other[s]."[119]

Days before the EU Committee on Science, Toxics, Ecotoxics and the Environment came out with its report, a memo sent by A. Vernon Weaver, the U.S. ambassador in Brussels, to Hans Bessler, the director general of the European commission for external affairs, warned that it would be ill-advised for the EU to act on any report "based on incomplete and perhaps erroneous information."[120] The letter warned that even an interim ban "could cause trade misunderstandings between the United States and the European Union."[121]

Even as the U.S. government continued to pressure the EU to drop its public health proposal, efforts by nongovernmental organizations (NGOs) such as Greenpeace and U.S. Public Interest Research Group (PIRG) have created public pressure to eliminate infants' needless exposure to plastic softeners found in toys. In July 1999, the EU decided to let Members regulate phthalates on a nation-by-nation basis.[122] The toy industry finally announced it would begin phasing out pthalates from those products designed to be put in the mouths of children and infants.[123] In September 1998, Mattel, the world's largest toy manufacturer, announced that it would eliminate phthalates in teething toys by 1999.[124] The U.S. government finally backed down after the American television network ABC interviewed Danish Environmental Minister Svend Auken on the damage the U.S. chemical industry could be doing to European children.[125] In December 1999, the U.S. Consumer Product Safety Commission started the rulemaking process to ban PVCs in toys and other children's products.[126]

WTO "Harmonization" Requirements: Environment, Health, Safety and Accountable Governance Threatened

Harmonization is the name given to industry's efforts to replace the variety of product standards and regulations adopted by nations with uniform global standards.[127] The harmonization effort gained a significant boost with the establishment of the WTO, which not only explicitly requires harmonization of food[128] and technical standards[129] but which also lists only certain international standards as presumptively WTO-legal.

The WTO's SPS Agreement requires WTO Member governments to base their domestic standard-making on international standards and on international standard-setting techniques. Countries shall "base their sanitary and phytosanitary measures [food standards] on international standards, guidelines or recommendations."[130] The SPS Agreement permits countries to have food safety measures that achieve a higher level of health protection than relevant international standards only in very limited circumstances.[131]

The WTO's TBT Agreement also requires member countries to base their non-food safety technical standards on international standards, even when those standards are not yet complete but their completion is imminent.[132] As with food standards, the

WTO says that only technical regulations conforming to international standards are presumed not to create unnecessary obstacles to trade. Standards providing more protection to consumers, public health, local communities and the environment are subject to a trade challenge. The WTO's acceptable reasons for exceeding international standards in non-food areas are limited to fundamental climactic, geographical or technical factors.[133]

Harmonization Can Take Many Forms

The WTO has established more than 50 committees and working groups to harmonize standards and regulations. Unfortunately, these working groups do not provide an opportunity for input from most interested individuals or potentially affected communities. In addition, they are staffed by trade experts, not health and safety experts, and generally conduct all operations shielded from accountability and oversight. Yet, under WTO trade rules, these standard-setting processes can directly affect national, state and local policies.

Company Inspection of Beef Declared Equivalent to Government Inspection

On June 1, 1999, the U.S. Department of Agriculture (USDA), following WTO equivalency requirements, declared imports of company-inspected meat from Australia to be equivalent to meat inspected by the U.S. government. Agriculture Secretary Dan Glickman designated a three-year-old Australian meat inspection program, which greatly reduces the role of government inspectors, to be "equivalent" to the U.S. system of mandatory government meat inspection.[134] The decision will permit Australia to export to the U.S. beef that does not meet the inspection requirements of beef produced domestically under the terms of the Wholesome Meat Act of 1968, which requires beef carcass and other meat products to be examined by a federal inspector.[135] This requirement builds on U.S. safety policies instituted in 1906 after exposés of the meat-packing industry, such as that written by Upton Sinclair in his famous book "The Jungle." The U.S. policy of requiring government inspections was designed to take responsibility for public health protection away from company employees, who had the greatest incentive to minimize scrutiny. U.S. consumers will have no way to distinguish between meat that has been inspected by U.S. government employees and meat that has not been, because both products will bear the USDA's seal of approval.

The experimental Australian company-conducted meat inspections were begun in 1997. The first year, salmonella poisonings increased 20% from the previous year, from 5,819 cases to 7,004, according to the Australian Department of Health.[136] In 1998, they jumped to 7,892, an additional 5% increase.[137] The salmonella poisoning rate continued to increase in the first few months of 1999.

While not all the salmonella cases can be traced to meat products, the dramatic increase in cases demands close scrutiny before the U.S. begins to treat Australian company-inspected meat as "equivalent" to meat inspected by U.S. federal employees.

International Standards: The WTO requires that domestic standards be based on international standards. To facilitate this process, the SPS and TBT Agreements name specific international standards that are presumed to be WTO-legal, such as those established by the quasi-governmental Codex Alimentarius Commission (Codex) in Rome[138] or the industry-funded International Organization on Standardization (ISO) in Geneva,[139] Hundreds of committees in each of the WTO-specified institutions and dozens of other international standard-setting organizations are working diligently on the WTO harmonization mandate. Rarely are public interest advocates or the general public invited to participate. The vast majority of international harmonization proposals are being drafted behind closed doors, typically with private industry representatives at the table. Domestic standards that provide greater public health or environmental protection must pass a series of severe WTO tests and criteria not to be considered WTO-illegal.

Equivalence Determinations: In addition to the adoption of uniform international standards, another mechanism of harmonization required by WTO rules is "equivalence determination."[140] Under the notion of "equivalence," significantly different — often lower — standards from other countries can be declared "equivalent" to domestic standards. The WTO provides for equivalence determinations based on subjective comparisons without clear procedural guidelines or enumeration of the factors to consider. Once a foreign standard is declared to be "equivalent," it must be treated as if it were a domestic standard. Under this policy, countries accept other countries' standards and allow "free passage" of goods declared equivalent to domestic standards even if these don't achieve the same level of protection required under domestic law. An example that may soon be affecting all Americans is U.S. Secretary of Agriculture Dan Glickman's June 1999 announcement declaring company-inspected Australian meat to be equivalent to U.S. government-inspected meat.

Mutual Recognition Agreements: Another tool in the international harmonization arsenal is the so-called mutual recognition agreement, or MRA. MRAs are a little-understood but powerful new tool for trade liberalization and deregulation. The U.S. is involved in MRA negotiations with the countries of the Asia-Pacific Economic Cooperation (APEC) forum in the area of telecommunications and has completed MRA negotiations with the EU.

The U.S.-EU MRA was signed on June 20, 1997, and consists of an umbrella agreement incorporating six sectoral annexes, which are more detailed agreements on particular issues. The annexes cover telecommunications, electromagnetic compatibility, electrical safety, recreational craft safety, medical devices and pharmaceutical good manufacturing practices.[141] A new MRA between the U.S. and the EU was signed July 20, 1999.[142] It is a wide-ranging agreement covering veterinary practices and other issues intended to facilitate trade in live animals and animal products.

MRAs are among the newest and least understood components of trade-related global health and safety deregulation. On the surface, the existing MRAs appear to lay out a framework for the harmonization of testing standards and good manufacturing practices. Yet they seem designed in some circumstances (e.g., in the medical device area) to lead to product approval or, at a minimum, mutual recognition of each other's regulatory systems and free passage of goods. The legal status of the MRAs is questionable. In the U.S., it is unclear whether MRAs should be classified as treaties requiring congressional approval, as executive level trade agreements, or as cooperative agreements between regulatory agencies.

One need only take a look at one of the sectoral annexes to see how the MRA will soon begin to affect consumers. The medical device annex covers the exchange of inspection reports for medical devices manufacturers and premarket notification (510 (k)) reports for selected medical devices.[147] Under the MRA, a European conformity assessment body (CAB) can be trained to conduct inspections for all classes of devices and 510 (k) evaluations based on Food and Drug Administration re-

---

International Harmonization Undermines Open, Accountable U.S. Policymaking Process

The international institutions empowered by the WTO to set WTO-legal international standards provide few opportunities for citizen input or oversight. In sharp contrast, U.S. law requires that the public be notified and offered an opportunity to comment on policy proposals. Domestic policymaking also must be conducted "on the record" with a publicly accessible docket required under laws such as the federal Administrative Procedures Act (APA),[143] which includes a process for advance notice about proposed regulations, several opportunities for public comment and open review of draft regulations. The APA also requires the agency making a regulation to describe in writing how and why it came to its conclusion and on what basis it dismissed alternative proposals.

Public access to information and decision-making also is guaranteed by the Freedom of Information Act (FOIA),[144] which permits individual citizens to get copies of most government documents; the Government in the Sunshine Act,[145] which ensures that important agency meetings are publicly noticed; and the Federal Advisory Committee Act (FACA).[146] FACA requires balanced representation on — and open operations of — government advisory committees.

In contrast, even the quasi-governmental organizations identified by the WTO, such as the Codex Alimentarius Commission, have no such due process and openness requirements for their hundreds of committees and working groups. While some Codex subgroups operate on the record and try to make documents available to nongovernmental organizations and concerned members of the public, others are not so helpful, and there is no requirement to compel their cooperation. In the instances of WTO organizations dominated by industry, such as the ISO, there is no avenue for the public to obtain information, much less influence the decision-makers. With the international harmonization of health and safety standards, U.S. federal agency adherence to the domestic procedure for notification, balance, openness and public input has been spotty at best. In a manner both subtle and powerful, the recent trade agreements have redefined the relationships in policy making between governments, industry and the public interest.

quirements for certain devices destined for the U.S market. Similarly a U.S. CAB can conduct quality system evaluations based on EU requirements for devices destined for the EU market.

However, there are many differences between the U.S. and the EU medical device inspection systems. In the U.S., medical devices are regulated by the FDA, and the agency's sole charge is to ensure that devices are safe and effective. In the EU there is a double mandate: to ensure safety and to facilitate trade by creating a single review process that permits devices to be marketed in all member states.[148] Additionally, the U.S. relies primarily on a government inspection system for medical devices. Under the EU system, however, both governmental and private entities – called "notified bodies" – review medical devices.[149] In Europe, manufacturers can select and pay a notified body of its choice to conduct assessments of the devices they would like to market. While reviewers in both the U.S. and the EU are subject to conflict-of-interest rules, the rules that govern FDA reviewers are more comprehensive than those that apply to notified-body employees.[150] The fact that a significant portion of U.S.-bound medical device inspection and product evaluation will soon be turned over to private entities, paid for by the manufacturers, operating under weak conflict-of-interest standards, has raised concerns among U.S. consumer advocates.

While the legal status of this harmonization tool is in question, one thing is clear: The U.S.-EU MRA will have a wide-ranging impact on consumers on both sides of the Atlantic. Yet it was negotiated for years in secret, without input by health advocates or the public. Prior to the signing of the agreement, there was no public notice, and there were no public hearings or other "government in the sunshine" practices usually required by U.S. law.

WTO SPS Agreement Leads to Downward Harmonization

The WTO's SPS Agreement provisions on "harmonization" and "equivalence" threaten to force countries to lower food safety and animal and plant health standards. First, the SPS Agreement requires domestic standards to be based on international ones.[151] It establishes a separate, more rigorous set of tests that domestic laws, which provide greater public health protection than international standards, must pass. This creates strong incentives to avoid exceeding international standards and discourages innovative solutions to public health problems.[152] Second, under the SPS Agreement, the listed international standards serve as a ceiling on food safety, not a floor. It is not possible to challenge a standard for being too weak. In other words, the SPS Agreement contains no incentives, let alone any mandates, that countries provide a minimum level of protection and discourages standards higher than the international status quo. Such downward harmonization has alarming potential public health consequences.

Harmonization's Inherent Limitations

Beyond the specific examples of downward harmonization of food standards, the concept of harmonization has significant inherent limitations. First, harmonization moves decision-making away from accessible, accountable state and national governing bodies to international forums that are largely inaccessible to citizens and generally operate without accountability to those who are affected by their decisions. Shifting decision-making to inaccessible international bodies has a corrosive effect on democratic, accountable governance and almost guarantees that industry will dominate the process. This in turn leads to weaker standards.

Second, a core notion underlying harmonization is that it is possible to establish a uniform global standard appropriate for numerous different cultures. Yet, standard-setting is based on numerous considerations, not the least of which is cultural differences and the extent to which people choose to be exposed to a particular risk. Pasteurized cheese, for example, is standard in the U.S., but regarded with disgust by many French citizens.

Third, setting relevant standards requires consideration of data that differ with geography and culture. Setting acceptable levels of pesticide residues for a commodity such as rice, for example, requires consideration of actual intake levels – which vary enormously between consumers in the U.S., Asia and Latin America.

Health and environmental experts worldwide believe that in the limited instances when harmonization might be acceptable, the process must have as its goal the strengthening of public health, natural resource conservation and worker safety standards, not the weakening of them. Thus, harmonization mandates in the context of trade agreements are especially troubling given that their primary goal is to maximize trade flows by eliminating barriers to trade, including some legitimate public health and environmental laws.

Recent Codex Standards Lower Than Required Under U.S. Law

The overwhelming industry influence over Codex decision-making has led to the adoption by the Codex of standards that provide less health protection than U.S. food safety regulations. For instance, at its July 1999 meeting, the Codex approved pesticide residues that do not take into account their health impacts on children, as is required under U.S. law.[153] It also approved a safety standard for dairy products that does not require pasteurization. The FDA requires pasteurization for all milk and milk products. The Codex also is considering a standard for bottled mineral water that permits higher amounts of lead and other contaminants than are allowed by the FDA.[154]

International Standard-Setting Organizations Empowered by WTO Have Conflicting Mandates

The Codex Alimentarius Commission

Codex Alimentarius is Latin for "food law." The Codex Alimentarius Commission is the Rome-based body established in 1962 jointly by the World Health Organization and the U.N. Food and Agriculture Organization "to facilitate the world trade in foods [through] internationally accepted standards."[155] It establishes food standards that the Uruguay Round recognized as the WTO-legal standard.[156] This means that when WTO Member countries' food safety laws are challenged under the WTO SPS Agreement, a WTO tribunal will evaluate the laws' legitimacy by establishing whether they exceed standards set by the Codex. If they do, the challenged country must bear the burden of proving that their domestic standard meets a series of WTO tests applied only to measures providing stronger health or safety protections than international standards.

The WTO's designation of Codex standards as the world's food trade rules creates a powerful new role for the institution. Until it was empowered by the WTO, the Codex published only voluntary standards for the hygienic and nutritional quality of food and for food additives, pesticide residues, contaminants, labeling and methods of analysis and sampling.[157] The Codex standards initially were designed to help developing countries establish food safety systems so as to facilitate trade.

At its inception, Codex's focus was to assess the trade — not the health — implications of varying pesticide tolerances.[158] Indeed, at one point, the World Health Organization almost terminated its support for Codex on the grounds that Codex's activities were not sufficiently related to the primary mission of the WHO: improved world health.[159] Indeed, Codex is poorly suited to establish global food *safety* standards because its mandate to protect public health often takes a back seat to its competing mandate to promote international trade. The initial motivation behind Codex was to avoid the disruption of international trade through discriminatory application of food standards.[160] Indeed the Codex describes its charge as:

> [T]o guide and promote the elaboration and establishment of definitions and requirements for foods, to assist in their harmonization and, in doing so, to facilitate international trade.[170]

Although Codex now recognizes that its standards must protect public health, those goals are not given preference over Codex's trade-promoting agenda:

> The Codex was set up because of a widely perceived need to facilitate the world trade in foods and internationally accepted standards were seen as the means. At the same time it was realized that if such internationally acceptable standards could be developed then these standards must be based on added protection for consumers' health. Such standards would also promote fair practice in the food trade. It hardly needs saying that the objectives of freer trade and better consumer protection are mutually dependent and mutually supportive.[171]

The Folpet Example: WTO Rules and Codex Standards Complicate the Elimination of Toxics in the Food Supply

Folpet is a broad-spectrum fungicide that EPA had registered for use in paints, stains and plastics.[161] In addition, two Folpet products were registered for food use.[162] Folpet's registration classified it as a B2 (probable) human carcinogen.[163] In 1987, EPA issued a Notice of Intent to Suspend Folpet's registration for all non-industrial uses because no data had been submitted — including residue data for the food uses initially registered — to support Folpet's non-industrial use.[164]

After Folpet's producer indicated that it would only provide data regarding the substance's industrial uses, EPA suspended the food registration of the chemical, except for Florida avocados, for which data was submitted in 1990.[165]

In 1993, Folpet registrant Makhteshim-Agan (America), Inc. wrote the EPA indicating that it desired imported food residue tolerance for some of the uses that were suspended in the U.S. and arguing that Folpet is an important pesticide product in many countries.[166] However, the data to support such tolerances was not supplied, and EPA posted notice in the Federal Register that it was requesting revocation of all Folpet food tolerances (food residue limits) except for avocados in 1994.[167]

Typically such notices do not receive much comment. In this instance, a seemingly coordinated campaign of filings flooded in. A slew of U.S. and European chemical and agribusiness producers submitted comments to the EPA, arguing that the EPA's proposal would violate the WTO's new food rules. The majority contended that it was WTO-illegal for the U.S. to have a higher food safety standard than Codex's international standard (which allows Folpet residues on food) without scientific proof to support the higher U.S. standard. Ironically, one of the reasons that use of Folpet was restricted in the first place was that its producer was unwilling to provide documentation countering the finding of carcinogenicity as relates to human consumption of residues on food.[168] Thus EPA's WTO dilemma: Absent the denied company data, U.S. law requires EPA to eliminate food residue tolerances of the substance, but under WTO rules it cannot ban a Codex-permitted substance without data to meet stringent WTO tests.

In the end, the company provided data on nine additional food items and tolerance levels were set in 1996 for the following: apples, cranberries, cucumbers, grapes, lettuce, melons, onions, strawberries and tomatoes.[169]

This focus on facilitating international trade contrasts sharply with certain domestic mandates in the U.S., such as the federal Food, Drug and Cosmetic Act,[172] in which trade concerns play only a secondary role to public health. Codex's focus is completely at odds with the U.S. standards that are based solely on public health.

Codex has no codified standard that spells out how to assess whether consumer health is adequately protected. Codex also lacks the power to compel industry to produce data necessary for standard-setting.[173] As a result, its standards depend on the particular scientific opinions offered and policy judgments made by the drafters of the Codex standards and member countries that review a particular issue. This reliance on individual judgements gives Codex participants enormous discretion.

Yet, Codex delegations, committees and working groups often are dominated by food industry giants. Codex is composed of government representatives who participate with the active and formal assistance of official industry advisors. Codex meetings are closed to the public. While agribusiness and food industry representatives are encouraged to participate actively, a limited number of nongovernmental organizations (NGOs) have been granted "observer status." At the 26th Codex Alimentarius Commission meeting in Rome in July 1999, representatives from Coca Cola and Proctor & Gamble were part of the official U.S. delegation, as were representatives from trade groups such as the National Food Processors Association, the Corn Refiners Association, the International Dairy Foods Association and the National Milk Producers.[174] No NGO was part of the official U.S. delegation, although a handful of American NGOs were granted "observer status" for the meeting, including representatives from Consumers Union in New York and the Center for Science in the Public Interest in Washington, D.C.

Industry representatives have a central role in developing the U.S. positions presented at international Codex meetings and providing scientists and scientific data to numerous Codex working committees.[175] Draft Codex standards are not made public until well into the process, if at all.[176] To provide input, members of the public must persuade a governmental participant to provide them with a draft proposal and then persuade a governmental participant to present their positions to other delegates. In contrast, industry representatives can present their views directly to delegates.

A systematic comparison of U.S. and Codex pesticide residue rules has not been done in eight years. When a comparative study was completed by the U.S. General Accounting Office in 1991, not surprisingly, many Codex standards were weaker than public health-based food standards in the U.S. For example, some Codex standards allowed residues of pesticides that have been banned completely in the U.S.[177] Others allowed higher residues for pesticides such as heptachlor, aldrin, diazinon, lindane, permethrin and benomyl.[178] In some cases, Codex standards allowed residue levels that were five times as high as U.S. standards.[179] In addition, some Codex standards allowed pesticide residues that have been banned in some U.S. states.[183]Codex has not undertaken major revisions of its pesticide standards, although a consumer campaign to highlight Codex's DDT tolerances resulted in tighter rules for fruits and vegetables. Still, Codex permits DDT residue levels in milk, meat and grain.[184]

International Organization on Standardization

The other major international standards-setting organization recognized by the WTO is the International Organization on Standardization (ISO). ISO is a private-sector body comprised of industry members and funded by industry that has been empowered by the WTO to set standards for all non-food products. When ISO started in the 1950s, its goal was to standardize sizes for light bulbs, screws, batteries and other consumer products to help industry expand markets. In the past six years, ISO's areas of focus have expanded to include environmental products, eco-labels (labels identifying products as being manufactured in an environmentally friendly manner) and humane fur trapping. ISO is now nearing completion of additional

TABD v. TACD: Business As Usual, Or Not?

Years after then-Commerce Secretary Ron Brown had pushed for the formation of the TransAtlantic Business Dialogue (TABD), the EU approached the Clinton administration about forming U.S.-EU consumer, environmental and labor dialogues.[181] Initially the administration viewed establishment of the other dialogues as a cost-free, partial solution to an array of political problems it was having in the trade area.

First, the administration had suffered a set of humiliating political defeats in its attempts to push its backward trade policy, including congressional rejection of Fast Track. The Clinton administration knew it needed to change the political dynamic — by appearing to change its policy — in order to change the outcome in Congress. Second, ever since an exposé in *The New York Times* had revealed the TABD's operations,[180] some political advisors in the administration had called for creating the appearance of a more balanced approach to U.S.-EU trade policymaking. Third, the administration believed that by carefully selecting the U.S. consumer and environmental groups to organize the dialogues, it could control the substance of the dialogues. Thus, the administration selected several groups it believed were more closely aligned with administration policy.

After a tumultuous start and to the dismay of the Clinton administration, the TransAtlantic Consumer Dialogue (TACD)[181] has helped reunite the international consumer movement that had been split over its position on the GATT Uruguay Round. TACD, with its first formal summit in Brussels in early 1999, has prepared numerous detailed consensus U.S.-EU consumer positions on many of the issues on which TABD is demanding action. While the TACD is not behaving like the lap dog as some U.S. government officials had hoped, unfortunately its only role may be as a TABD watchdog. It remains to be seen if TACD or the other dialogues will have anything but a defensive role or an effect on the TransAtlantic Economic Partnership (TEP) negotiations. Both TACD and the environmental dialogue were excluded by the governments from the U.S.-EU Summit in the summer of 1999 even as the TABD industry co-chairs were given private audiences with the heads of state.[182]

standards, called the "ISO 14,000" series, that focus on management practices, including providing a best "environmental practice" seal. To date, this proposal does not include environmental quality measures.[185] ISO's recent expansion into these new issues has begun to concern some environmental and consumer groups that have sought to participate in the ISO process. Unfortunately, the ISO is designed for and operated by industry, making meaningful non-profit group participation nearly impossible.

Other international standard-setting organizations may come into play on an *ad hoc* basis as challenges mount to nations' regulatory laws. For instance, Canada is challenging France's ban on asbestos as a violation of the TBT Agreement. The outcome of the case could turn on the question of internationally formulated standards on asbestos exposure and safety. However, the asbestos industry plays a prominent role in the International Program on Chemical Safety, which sets policy on worker safety for the World Health Organization and the International Labor Organization. This could prove to influence the outcome of Canada's challenge to France's ban on asbestos. Under WTO TBT rules, France must prove it qualifies for one of the limited exceptions permitting variation from these international standards.

Transatlantic Harmonization Under TEP & TABD: The Wrong Model

The TransAtlantic Economic Partnership (TEP) is the name given to U.S.-EU trade negotiations launched in late 1998.[186] One of TEP's primary goals is international harmonization. The launch of such U.S.-EU trade liberalization and standards deregulation was a demand of the TransAtlantic Business Dialogue (often called "TabD"). U.S. Trade Representative Charlene Barshefsky has pointed to the TEP's harmonization activities as a "model" for what can be accomplished in the rest of the world.[187]

The TABD is a forum established in 1995 at the request of the U.S. government for industries on both sides of the Atlantic to develop harmonization proposals of mutual interest that they then present — almost as a *fait accompli* — to the U.S. and EU governments for implementation. It provides an opportunity for industry to make high-level contacts with U.S. and EU government officials and ensures consideration by those officials of each item the industry coalition presents. Indeed, in the U.S., an interagency process chaired by the Commerce Department has been developed simply to respond to TABD demands. The government team issues its own scorecard documenting how many of the industry requests it has satisfied.

The TABD may be considered a new paradigm for trade liberalization because it largely eliminates the middlemen from policymaking. In this case, the middlemen are the U.S. and EU governments, and, by extension, U.S. and EU citizens and consumer, labor and environmental NGOs. Despite its end run around normal policymaking procedures, the TABD has had a great deal of success implementing proposals internationally.

In May 1999, the TABD released its mid-year report.[188] The report contains TABD's scorecard of the progress the U.S. and European governments have made on past

TABD recommendations. The TABD report also proposes further harmonization or deregulation in dozens of areas, including: product liability, economic sanctions, climate change, intellectual property, taxation, services, government procurement, privacy in electronic commerce transactions, dietary supplements, medical devices, pharmaceuticals, chemicals, and automobile and aviation standards. Given that the TABD and the TEP actually take a step *beyond* the WTO harmonization agenda to literally privatize standard-setting, it can be considered among the worst models of harmonization.

——————— CHAPTER 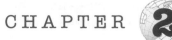 ENDNOTES ———————

[1] *See* John Canham-Clyne, Patrick Woodall, Victoria Nugent and James Wilson, *Saving Money, Saving Lives: The Documented Benefits of Federal Health and Safety Protections*, Public Citizen's Congress Watch, Jun. 1995. The authors conclude that over the past 30 years, standards for motor vehicle safety alone has saved at least 250,000 lives and OSHA regulations have saved over 140,000 lives at *Id.*

[2] *See id.*

[3] U.S. Centers for Disease Control (CDC) "Food and Water Borne Bacterial Diseases," Mar. 9, 1995, on file with Public Citizen.

[4] *See* World Health Organization (WHO), "Emerging Foodborne Diseases," *Factsheet No. 124*, Jul. 1996.

[5] *See id.*

[6] U.S. Department of Commerce, International Trade Administration, "U.S. Total Agricultural Imports to Individual Countries, 1991-97," on file with Public Citizen.

[7] Joan Murphy, "Food Safety Import Bill Introduced by Dingell, Waxman," *World Food Chemical News*, Mar. 3, 1999 at 16.

[8] *See* U.S. General Accounting Office, "Food Safety: Federal Efforts to Ensure the Safety of Imported Foods Are Inconsistent and Unreliable," May 1998.

[9] *See* Robert Naiman and Neil Watkins, "A Survey of the Impacts of Structural Adjustment in Africa: Growth, Social Spending, and Debt Relief," Preamble Center, (unpublished), on file with Public Citizen.

[10] International Organisation of Consumers Unions, Director General's Office, "A Statement on the Outcome of the Uruguay Round by the International Organizations of Consumers Unions (IOCU)," Dec. 20, 1993.

[11] *See* Consumers Union, "Consumers Union Supports GATT Uruguay Round Ratification," Press Release, May 11, 1994.

[12] Consumers International, "Consumers Rights and the Multilateral Trading System: What Needs to be Done Before a Millennium Round," 1999, at 8 on file with Public Citizen.

[13] *Id* at 4.

[14] See *id.*

[15] Organization for Economic Cooperation and Development (OECD), *Examen de las Politicas Agricolas de Mexico* (1997).

[16] *Id.*

[17] 105th Congress, S. 981 (Regulatory Improvement Act of 1998), Lead sponsor: Sen. Carl Levin D-MI).

[18] *See* Public Citizen, "S. 746 Creates a 'Regulatory Obstacle Course' for Public Safeguards," Background Paper, Jun. 1999, on file with Public Citizen.

[19] 106th Congress, S. 746 (Regulatory Improvement Act of 1999), Lead sponsor: Sen. Carl Levin (D-MI).

[20] WTO, European Communities - Measures Concerning Meat Products (Hormones) (WT/DS26/R), Report of the Panel, Aug. 18, 1997, at Para. 9.2.

[21] *Id.* at Paras. 2.17-2.25.

[22] Patti Goldman, J. Martin Wagner, (Sierra Club Legal Defense Fund), World Trade Organization Dispute Settlement Proceeding, European Communities - Measures Concerning Meat and Meat Products (Hormones), Comments on Behalf of Cancer Prevention Coalition, Public Citizen, Institute for Agriculture and Trade Policy, Oct. 4, 1996, at 7-9. The artificial hormone issue was first considered by Codex in 1991, but after considerable debate no consensus was reached. Twenty-eight of the 37 countries represented objected to the adoption of growth hormone standards.

[23] *Id.*

[24] WTO, Agreement on Sanitary and Phytosanitary Measures (SPS Agreement), Preamble at Para. 6: "[T]o further the use of harmonized SPS measures.;" *see also* Article 3 on Harmonization.

[25] *Id.*

[26] *Id.* at Article 5.

[27] *Id.* at Article 5.1.

[28] *Id.* at Article 5.6.

[29] *Id* at Article 3.

[30] *See* Paul Brown, "Danes Fear Bid to Block Ban on Lead," *The Guardian*, May 3, 1999.

[31] *See id.*

[32] WTO, SPS Agreement at Article 3.3

[33] Letter from U.S. Trade Representative Michael Kantor to Bob Drake, president of the National Cattlemen's Association, Feb. 8, 1996, on file at Public Citizen.

[34] *See* European Economic Council Directive 88/146/EEC cited in European Community measures affecting meat and meat products (WT/D526/ABR), Report to the Appellate Body, Apr. 16, 1998 at 2.

[35] "Brie and Hormones," *The Economist*, Jan. 7, 1989, at 22; Samuel S. Epstein, "The Chemical Jungle," *International Journal Health Services* (1990) at 278; A.L. Fisher, *et al.*, "Estrogenic Action of Some DDT Analogues," 81 *Proc. Soc. Expt'l Med.* at 449-441; and W.H. Bulger & D. Kupfer, "Estrogenic Activity of Pesticides and Other Xenobiotics on the Uterus and Male Reproductive Tract," in J.A. Thomas, *et al.*, Eds., *Endocrine Technology* (1985) at 1-33.

[36] Among the most vocal critics of the EU ban has been the National Cattlemen's Beef Association (NCBA). After the ban, NCBA president, George Swan, said, "Ten years of false accusations. Ten years of lost markets for U.S. cattlemen and lost opportunities for European consumers...." National Cattlemen's Beef Association, "Government Must Retaliate if EU Continues to Ban American Beef," Press Release, May 10, 1999.

[37] *See* WTO, European Communities – Measures Affecting Meat and Meat Products (Hormones) (WT/DS26), complaint by the United States.

[38] *See* WTO, European Communities - Measures Affecting Meat and Meat Products (Hormones) (WT/DS26R), Report of the Panel, Aug. 8, 1997, at Para. 8.159.

[39] *See* WTO, European Communities - Measures Affecting Meat and Meat Products (Hormones) (WT/DS26/AB), Report of the Appellate Body, Apr. 16, 1998.

[40] *See* Elizabeth Olson, "$253 Million Sanctions Sought in Beef Fight with Europe," *The New York Times*, Jun. 4, 1999. The U.S. argues that the risk assessment merely recycles the same data rejected by the WTO panel as inconclusive. *Id.*

[41] USTR, "USTR Announces Final Product List in Beef Hormones Dispute," Press Release, Jul. 19, 1999.

[42] *See, inter alia,* "EU Rules Out Lifting Ban on Hormone Treated U.S. Beef on New Evidence," *AFX (UK)*, May 4, 1999, and Adrian Croft, "EU and U.S. Face Another Trade Showdown, First Bananas, Now Beef: EU Won't Lift Ban on Hormone Treated Beef Imports," *Financial Times*, May 14, 1999.

[43] Elizabeth Olson, "$253 Million Sanctions Sought in Beef Fight with Europe," *The New York Times*, Jun. 4, 1999, and "EU Offers Beef Payoff," *The Guardian*, May 11, 1999.

[44] *Id.*

[45] 21 U.S.C. Ch. 9 (Food Drugs and Cosmetics Act) at Section 355.

[46] Morton Mintz, "'Heroine' of FDA Keeps Bad Drug Off Market," *The Washington Post*, Jul. 15, 1962.

[47] WTO, SPS Agreement at Articles 2.2 and 5.1.

[48] U.S. Department of Agriculture, Food Safety and Inspection Service & U.S. Department of Health and Human Services, Food and Drug Administration, "Preventing Foodborne Listeriosis," Mar. 1992, at 5.

[49] Information provided by the U.S. Food and Drug Administration, Center for Food Safety and Applied Nutrition, at vm.cfsan.fda.gov, on file with Public Citizen. The 1987 incidence data shows that there are at least 1,600 cases of listeriosis with 415 deaths per year in the U.S. *Id.*

[50] Government of Canada, Ministry of Trade, *1996 Register of United States Barriers to Trade*, on file with Public Citizen, at 17.

[51] *See* Center for Science in the Public Interest, "Modify Trade Agreement to Improve Food Safety," Press Release, Jul. 26, 1999; *see also* Center for Science in the Public Interest, "Consumer Groups Call for Stronger International Food Safety, Labeling Rules," Press Release, Jun. 28, 1999.

[52] *See* Douglas Jake Caldwell, "Environmental Labeling In The Trade & Environment Context," Community Nutrition Institute, Oct. 1996.

[53] WTO, TBT Agreement at Article 2, Para. 2.2.

[54] *See,* WTO, Australia - Measures Affecting Importation of Salmon (WT/DS18/AB/R), Report of the Appellate Body, Oct. 20, 1998.

[55] WTO, Australia - Measures Affecting Importation of Salmon (WT/DS18/R), Report of the Panel, Jun. 12, 1998 at Paras. 8.10-8.19.

[56] *Id.*

[57] The Australian Final Report had concluded that there were extensive gaps in data relating to disease spread in fish. The Final Report therefore extrapolated data from studies demonstrating that other products for human consumption, such as meat and poultry, have been known to have spread diseases to live animals. Australia thus concluded that given both the difficulty of proving the spread of aquatic animal diseases through salmon meat and the very short history of aquatic animal medicine, it would be prudent to presume that it was only a matter of time and attention until there was definitive proof of the spread of aquatic animal disease via product for human consumption, rather than assume it was unlikely. WTO, Australia - Measures Affecting Importation of Salmon (WT/DS18/R), Report of the Panel, Jun. 12, 1998, at Paras. 2.27-2.30.

[58] *Id.* at Para. 4.42.

[59] *Id.* at Para. 4.43.

[60] *Id.* at Para. 4.52.

[61] *Id.* at Para 9.1.

[62] WTO, Australia - Measures Affecting Importation of Salmon (WT/DS18/AB/R), Report of the Appellate Body, Oct. 20, 1998, at Para. 13.

[63] *Id.* at Para. 137.

[64] *Id.* at Para. 129.

[65] *Id.* at Para. 127. According to a Geneva-based trade official, the Appelate Body move suggests that WTO Members must have conduct a risk assessment before adopting trade-restrictive measures. See, "WTO Salmon Ruling Clarifies Conditions For Banning Food Imports, Experts Say," BNA Daily Report for Executives, Oct. 28, 1998.

[66] "WTO Salmon Ruling Clarifies Conditions For Banning Food Imports, Experts Say," *BNA Daily Report for Executives*, Oct. 28, 1998.

[67] *See* WTO, "State of Play of WTO Disputes," at www.wto.org; on file with Public Citizen.

[68] WTO, Australia - Measures Affecting the Importation of Salmonids, complaint by the United States (WT/DS21).

[69] *See* WTO, "State of Play of WTO Disputes," at www.wto.org; on file with Public Citizen.

[70] *See* Mark Magnier, "WTO Test Case Held Goal in U.S.-S. Korea Flap," *Journal of Commerce*, Apr. 12, 1995.

[71] *Id.*

[72] *Id.*

[73] *Id.*

[74] WTO, Korea - Inspection of Agricultural Products (WT/DS3/1), Complaint of the U.S., Apr. 4, 1995.

[75] Mark Magnier, "WTO Test Case Held Goal in U.S.-S. Korea Flap," *Journal of Commerce*, Apr. 12, 1995.

[76] Korea - Measures Concerning the Shelf-life of Products (WT/DS5), Complaint of the U.S., May 3, 1995.

[77] Mark Magnier, "WTO Test Case Held Goal in U.S.-S. Korea Flap," *Journal of Commerce*, Apr. 12, 1995.

[78] *Id.*

[79] WTO, Japan - Measures Affecting Agricultural Products (WT/DS76/R), Report of the Panel, Oct. 27, 1998, at Para. 4.65.

[80] Celeste Welty, "Codling Moth on Fruit Trees," Ohio State University Extension Factsheet HYG-2203-92.

[81] *See id.*

[82] Michigan State University Extension, "Codling Moth," Fruit IPM Fact Sheet, May 20, 1998.

[83] WTO, Japan - Measures Affecting Agricultural Products (WT/DS76/R), Report of the Panel, Oct. 27, 1998, at Para. 4.65.

[84] *Id.* at Para. 4.13.

[85] WTO, Japan - Measures Affecting Agricultural Products (WT/DS76/AB/R), Report of the Appellate Body, Feb. 22, 1999, at Para. 2.

[86] *Id.* at Para. 4.70.

[87] *Id.* at Para. 52.

[88] WTO, Japan - Measures Affecting Agricultural Products (WT/DS76/R), Report of the Panel, Oct. 27, 1998, at Table 2.

[89] *See* WTO, Japan - Measures Affecting Agricultural Products (WT/DS76/1), Request for Consultations by the U.S.

[90] WTO, Japan - Measures Affecting Agricultural Products (WT/DS76/R), Report of the Panel, Oct. 27, 1998, at Para. 1.2. The United States specifically alleged that, for each agricultural product for which Japan required quarantine treatment, Japan prohibited the importation of each variety of that product until the quarantine treatment had been tested for that variety, even though the treatment had proven effective with respect to other varieties of the same product. The United States claimed that Japan's measure was inconsistent with the obligations of Japan under the SPS Agreement, the GATT 1994 and the Agreement on Agriculture. *See id.*

[91] *Id.* at Para. 4.

[92] *See* the analysis of the Australian Salmon Case above; *see also* WTO, Australia - Measures Affecting Importation of Salmon (WT/DS18/AB/R), Report of the Appellate Body, Oct. 20, 1998, at Para. 123. (The WTO Panel ruled that it is not enough for a risk assessment to establish the possibility of infestation, but it must establish its likelihood.)

[93] WTO, Japan - Measures Affecting Agricultural Products (WT/DS76/R), Report of the Panel, Oct. 27, 1998, at Para. 8.42.

[94] *Id.* at Paras. 8.29 and 8.42.

[95] *Id.* at Para. 9.1.

[96] *See id.*

[97] WTO, Japan - Measures Affecting Agricultural Products (WT/DS76/AB/R), Report of the Appellate Body, Feb. 22, 1999, at Para. 7.

[98] WTO, Japan - Measures Affecting Agricultural Products (WT/DS76/R), Report of the Panel, Oct. 27, 1998, at Para. 8.83, emphasis added.

[99] *Id.*

[100] WTO, Japan - Measures Affecting Agricultural Products (WT/DS76/AB/R), Report of the Appellate Body, Feb. 22, 1999, at Para. 147.

[101] *Id.* at Para. 37.

[102] *Id.*

[103] Pursuant to Article 21.3 of the WTO Understanding on Rules and Procedures Governing the Settlement of Disputes (DSU).

[104] James Gerstenzang, "U.S. Urges European Union to Avert Toy Restrictions," *Los Angeles Times*, May 28, 1998, at A1.

[105] *See* U.S. Department of State, "USG Concerns Over Regulation of Toys Made with Polyvinyl Chloride," Action Cable, Dec. 12, 1997 on file with Public Citizen.

[106] *Id.* at Paras. 3-5. Denmark, the Netherlands, and Belgium had already instituted voluntary bans on phthalates, PVC-softened toys, or PVC toys.

[107] *See* "Phthalate Migration from Soft PVC Toys and Child-Care Articles," Opinion expressed at the EU Committee on Science, Toxicity, Ecotocicity and the Environment (CSTEE), Apr. 24, 1998.

[108] *Id.* at 1.3.

[109] Letter from U.S. Ambassador to the EU Stuart Eizenstadt to Director General for External Affairs Hans Beseler, Nov. 27, 1996, at 1, on file at Public Citizen. The TransAtlantic Business Dialogue (TABD) is a U.S.-EU industry group initiated at the suggestion of then-U.S. Commerce Secretary Ron Brown. TABD industry sector committees develop common positions on regulatory issues which are then presented to U.S. and EU governments. The Clinton administration has set up a special inter-agency process to handle TABD requests and issue a report card annually documenting the progress on the industry demands. Consumer and environmental groups have criticized the TABD harshly for evading accountable, on-the-record U.S. regulatory process.

[110] *See* Michael A. Babich, Ph.D., "The Risk of Chronic Toxicity Associated with Exposure to Diisononyl Phthalate (DINP) in Children's Products," U.S. Consumer Product Safety Commission, Dec. 1998.

[111] "Denmark Plans Radical PVC Phthalate, Curbs," *Environment News Service*, Environmental Data Services (London), Jun. 18, 1999.

[112] James Gerstenzang, "U.S. Urges European Union to Avert Toy Restrictions," *Los Angeles Times*, May 28, 1998, at A1.

[113] U.S. Department of State, "U.S. Concerns over Regulation of Toys Made with Polyvinyl Chloride," Action Cable, Dec. 12, 1997, at Para. 2.

[114] *Id.* at Para. 11.

[115] *Id.* at Para. 8.

[116] James Gerstenzang, "U.S. Urges European Union to Avert Toy Restrictions," *Los Angeles Times*, May 28, 1998, at A9.

[117] Determination by Stat. Analysis of Chicago, IL and First Environmental of Naperville, IL, *cited in* Joseph Di Gangi, *Toxic Chemicals in Vinyl Children's Toys*, Greenpeace, Nov. 1998, at Table 1.

[118] U.S. Department of State, "U.S. Concerns over Regulation of Toys Made with Polyvinyl Chloride," Action Cable, Dec. 12, 1997, at Para. 15.

[119] James Gerstenzang, "U.S. Urges European Union to Avert Toy Restrictions," *Los Angeles Times*, May 28, 1998, at A1.

[120] Letter from A. Vernon Weaver to Director General for External Affairs Hans Beseler, Feb. 27, 1998, on file with Public Citizen.

[121] *Id.*

[122] Stacy Kraver, "Mattel Is Phasing Out Teething-Toy Additive," *The Wall Street Journal*, Sep. 24, 1998.

[123] Susan Warren, "Toy Makers Say Bye-Bye to 'Plasticizers,'" *The Wall Street Journal*, Nov. 12, 1998, at B1.

[124] *See* Mattel Inc., "Mattel Commits to the Elimination of Phthlates in Teething Toys for Children Under 36 Months," Press Release, Sept. 23, 1998, on file at Public Citizen.

[125] *See,* Paul Brown, "Danes Fear Bid to Block Ban on Lead," *The Guardian*, May 3, 1999.

[126] 63 *Fed. Reg.* 70756, Dec. 22, 1998.

[127] For more information, *see* Lori Wallach, *International "Harmonization" of Social, Economic and Environmental Standards*, Public Citizen, July 1998, or visit www.harmonizationalert.com.

[128] WTO, Agreement on the Application of Sanitary and Phytosanitary Measures (SPS Agreement) at Article 3.

[129] WTO, Agreement on Technical Barriers to Trade (TBT Agreement) at Article 2.4.

[130] WTO, SPS Agreement at Article 3.

[131] *Id.* at Article 3.

[132] WTO, TBT Agreement at Article 2.4.

[133] *See id.*

[134] 64 *Fed. Reg.* 30299-30303, Jun. 7, 1999.

[135] Pub.L. 90-201, Dec. 15, 1967, 81 Stat. 584 (Title 21, Sec 601 et. seq.).

[136] Australian Department of Health and Aged Care, National Centre for Disease Control, "Notification of Salmonellosis (NEC) Received by State & Territory Health Authorities in the Period of 1991 to 1999," Jun. 4, 1999, on file with Public Citizen.

[137] *Id.*

[138] WTO, SPS Agreement, Preamble, at Para. 6.

[139] WTO, TBT Agreement, Annex 1 at Para. 1, and Annex 3.

[140] *Id.* at Article 2.7.

[141] Agreement on Mutual Recognition Between the United States of America and the European Community, signed Jun. 20, 1997, on file with Public Citizen.

[142] *See* Animal and Plant Health Inspection Service, "U.S., EU Sign Veterinary Equivalence Agreement to Facilitate Trade," Press Release, Jul. 20, 1999, on file with Public Citizen.

[143] 5 U.S.C. Sec. 551, *et seq.*

[144] 5 U.S.C. Sec. 552.

[145] 5 U.S.C. Sec. 552b.

[146] *See* 5 U.S.C. Sec. 562, *et seq.*

[147] *See* Agreement on Mutual Recognition between the United States of America and the European Community, signed Jun. 20, 1997, on file with Public Citizen.

[148] Government Accounting Office, *Medical Device Regulation: Too Early to Assess European Systems Value as a Model for the FDA,* Mar. 1996, at 2.

[149] *Id.*

[150] *Id.*

[151] WTO, SPS Agreement at Article 3.1: "[M]embers shall base their sanitary or phytosanitary measures on international standards, guidelines or recommendations, where they exist . . . ."

[152] *Id.* at Article 3.3: "Members may introduce or maintain sanitary or phytosanitary measures which result in a higher level of sanitary or phytosanitary protection than would be achieved by measures based on the relevant international standards, guidelines or recommendations, if there is a scientific justification, or as a consequence of the level of sanitary or phytosanitary protection a Member determines to be appropriate in accordance with the relevant provisions of paragraphs 1 through 8 of Article 5." Article 5.4 reads, "Members should, when determining the appropriate level of sanitary or phytosanitary protection, take into account the objective of minimizing negative trade effects."

[153] *See* Center for Science in the Public Interest, "Representatives Tell White House 'Modify Trade Agreement to Improve Food Safety,'" Press Release, Jul. 26, 1999, on file with Public Citizen; *see also* U.S. law at Section 405 of the Food Quality Protection Act of 1996, amending section 408(b) of the Federal Food Drug and Cosmetic Act, 21 U.S.C. Sec. 346a(b).

[154] FDA's limits of contaminants in bottled water are: .005 milligrams per liter (mg/l) for lead, 10 mg/l for nitrate, and .05 mg/l for manganese. 21 C.F.R. Sec. 165.110(b)(4)(iii)(A). In comparison, the World Health Organization (WHO) standards for bottled water, which the Codex is considering, are: .01 mg/l for lead, 50 mg/l for nitrate, and .5 mg/l for manganese. International Association of Consumer Food Organizations, Comments on the Draft Standard for Health Related Limits for Certain Substances in the Codex Standard for Natural Mineral Waters, found at www.cspinet.org/reports/Codex/agenda_item9c.htm on Aug. 23, 1999, on file with Public Citizen.

[155] FAO/WHO Food Standards Programme, *Introducing Codex Alimentarius* (1987); and Goldman and Wiles, *Trading Away U.S. Food Safety*, Public Citizen and the Environmental Working Group, Apr. 1994, at Ch. 6 detailing Codex standard-setting procedures.

[156] WTO, SPS Agreement at Annex A, Para. 3.

[157] *See* Natalie Avery, Martine Drake, and Tim Lang, *Cracking the CODEX: An Analysis of Participation on CODEX Alimentarius Commissions Which Set International Food Standards* (1993).

[158] David Kay, *The International Regulation of Pesticide Residues in Food* (1976) at n. 18, and pgs. 33 and 46.

[159] *Id.* at 44.

[160] *Id.* at 24.

[161] 59 *Fed. Reg.* 61859, Dec. 2, 1994.

[162] *Id.*

[163] *Id.*

[164] *Id.*

[165] *Id.*

[166] *Id.*

[167] *Id.*

[168] *Id.*

[169] 40 C.F.R. Ch. 1 at Sec. 180.91.

[170] FAO/WHO, *This is Codex Almentarius* (1993) at 2.

[171] *Id.* at 3, n. 1.

[172] 21 U.S.C. Sec. 301, *et seq.*

[173] Goldman and Wiles, *Trading Away U.S. Food Safety*, Public Citizen and the Environmental Working Group, Apr. 1994, at 48.

[174] Joint FAO/WHO Food Standards Programme, *Codex Alimentarius Commission, 23rd Session, FAO Headquarters*, Rome, Jun. 28 - Jul. 3, 1999, at 41, Appendix 1, on file with Public Citizen.

[175] FAO/WHO, *This is the Codex Alimentarius*, (1993), at 3, n. 1.

[176] *See*, FAO & WHO, "Procedures for the Elaboration of Codex Standards & Related Texts," *Procedural Manual of the CAC*, 9th Ed. (1995).

[177] *See* General Accounting Office, *International Food Safety: Comparison of U.S. Codex Pesticide Standards* (Aug. 1991).

[178] Mark Ritchie, "GATT, Agriculture and the Environment: The Double Zero Plan," 20 *The Ecologist* 214, at 216-17 (Nov./Dec. 1990).

[179] *Id.*; *see also* General Accounting Office, *International Food Safety: Comparison of U.S. & Codex Pesticide Standards* (Aug. 1991) at 4.

[180] Jeff Gerth, "Where Business Rules, Forging Global Regulations That Put Industry First," *The New York Times*, Jan. 9, 1999.

[181] Transatlantic Consumer Dialogue, Transatlantic Environment Dialogue and Transatlantic Labor Dialogue.

[182] TACD, "EU-US Summit Rejects Environment and Consumer Groups Participation, Invites Business Representatives," Press Release, Jun. 18, 1999.

[183] *See, e.g.*, Minn. Stat. 18B.115 (1990) (heptachlor).

[184] *See* Food & Agriculture Organization of the United Nations (FAO), *Operation of the Prior Informed Consent Procedure for Banned or Severely Restricted Chemicals in International Trade*, Rome (1991); *see also* FAO, *1994 Joint Meeting of the FAO Panel of Experts on Pesticide Residues in Food and the Environment and the WHO Expert Group on Pesticide Residues*, Rome, Sep. 19-28, 1994.

[185] *See* Benchmark Environmental Consulting, *ISO 14001: An Uncommon Perspective - Five Public Policy Questions for Proponents of ISO 14000 Series*, Report for the European Environment Bureau, Nov. 1995.

[186] White House Office of the Press Secretary, Dec. 18, 1998, "US-EU statement on Cooperation in the Global Economy," on file with Public Citizen.

[187] U.S. Trade Representative Charlene Barshefsky, "Service in the Trading System", Speech to the World Services Congress, Washington DC, Jun. 1999, on file with Public Citizen.

[188] Transatlantic Business Dialogue, *TABD Mid-Year Report*, May 10, 1999, on file with Public Citizen, found at www.tabd.com/about/MYMTechnicalAnnex.html, at 36.

In this chapter ...

CASES:

• **Genetically Modified Organisms (GMOs):** Governments in Europe, Japan and Australia, worried about the safety of genetically modified food for humans and the environment, have begun to require labeling or otherwise regulate GMOs until more is known of their long-term effects. The U.S. explicitly has threatened several EU GMO rules with WTO action, but to date has not filed a formal WTO challenge.

CONCEPTS:

Biosafety Protocol: In early 1999, 140 countries met in Cartegena, Columbia, to sign a treaty permitting countries to prohibit GMO imports, require segregation of GMOs and make GMO producers legally liable for any future economic or environmental damage. The U.S. led an effort to stall the treaty's signing, in part by getting a group of countries to demand that no commodities be covered by the agreement — effectively eviscerating it. The U.S. also sought a declaration that WTO rules would be given priority over the Protocol's terms. Negotiations continue.

GMO Labeling: The U.S. had led an effort to stop countries from adopting mandatory GMO labeling. The U.S. argues that there is no safety difference between GMO food and non-GMO food and that only products that are substantially transformed should be labeled. Yet, GMOs are sufficiently transformed to be patented as original creations.

Biotech Negotiations: The U.S. is pushing for negotiations to be launched at the Seattle Ministerial to set new WTO rules to protect trade in GMOs and other biotech products.

The WTO's Impact on Emerging Health and Environmental Issues: Genetically Modified Organisms

The rapid development of ever newer technologies in the area of biology, agriculture, medicine and food production exceeds the speed with which we are able to assess their public health, social, environmental and economic impacts and thus hampers our ability to create adequate public policies to address their impacts. In no case has this become more evident than with the development of genetically modified organisms (GMOs).

The Uruguay Round Agreements and the establishment of the WTO have altered the way decisions are made about public policy, shifting the emphasis from domestic, elected bodies to international rules. Because the WTO focuses on maximizing trade flows, its rules systematically sacrifice other policy goals to commerce. The inevitable collision between the primacy WTO's rules give global commerce and the public's concern over GMOs, guarantees to spotlight how the WTO conflicts with accountable public policymaking.

GMOs are living organisms created through genetic engineering that permits scientists to transplant the genes of one species to another species for the purpose of transferring desirable characteristics.[1] For example, scientists have transplanted fish genes into tomatoes to improve their anti-freezing characteristics.[2] Multinational corporations, such as Monsanto, Novartis, Dupont and Avantis, have applied this process primarily to agricultural crops, including cotton, soya and corn, to improve resistance to disease, pesticides and herbicides, enhance nutritional value and increase yield.[3]

In the U.S., products containing GMOs are completely unregulated. Consumers have no idea which products contain GMOs. Consumers also have no way of knowing what threats GMOs pose to human health, given that neither the U.S. government nor the companies producing GMOs have dedicated resources to examining — much less explaining — their health and environmental impacts.

GMO technology raises serious public interest concerns in many areas where the WTO has proven most hostile: food security and safety, ecological sustainability and environmental protection. Thus, a future conflict over GMO regulations could become emblematic of the WTO's emerging pattern of tying the hands of policymakers who wish to err on the side of caution and regulate the trade of such products until more is learned about their impacts.

Three WTO agreements may make it difficult for countries to maintain or strengthen their domestic safeguards regarding GMOs: the Agreement on Sanitary and Phytosanity Measures (SPS), the Agreement on Technical Barriers to Trade (TBT) and the Agreement on Trade Related Aspects of Intellectual Property Rights (TRIPs). The first two agreements put heavy burdens on governments wishing to restrict the entry of GMOs into their countries. As demonstrated in Chapter 2, the SPS Agreement requires that the GMO-regulating nation provide scientific data proving a threat to justify a regulation,[4] even though the lack of scientific certainty concerning GMO impacts is precisely why governments have begun to regulate them. The TBT Agreement requires governments to minimize trade impacts when setting standards regulating products, including GMO products, under the least trade restrictive rule.[5] In addition, the mere labeling of a product to identify it as containing GMOs may fall under TBT rules, possibly undermining even this relatively modest form of product regulation. The TRIPs Agreement allows GMO agricultural products to be patented, creating new commercial rights for such products that may conflict with government policy goals regarding biodiversity and food security.

The U.S. has threatened a challenge to the EU's GMO regulations.[6] And international efforts to develop responsible regulations of GMOs, for instance under the auspices of the UN Biosafety Protocol, have been waylaid in the name of WTO consistency. Meanwhile, even the threat of WTO trade sanctions could be enough to discourage many of the 134 WTO Member nations from seeking national or multilateral solutions to the GMO question.

Despite Growing Evidence of Health and Environmental Impacts, U.S. Insists That GMO Restrictions and Labeling Are WTO-Illegal

Preliminary evidence about the possible threats posed by GMOs is coming to light. Consumer groups, environmentalists and scientists note that emerging data indicate that GMOs may have adverse consequences for human health, biological diversity and the environment. Ethicists and religious groups also have raised ethical questions about the genetic manipulation of living organisms. Groups urging caution with GMOs raise a number of compelling concerns suggesting that nations have a responsibility to regulate GMOs until they are proven safe.

First, crops engineered to resist pesticides and herbicides perpetuate reliance on those chemicals, threatening the environment.[7] In fact, increasing demand for such products may be a goal of some corporations producing GMOs. For example, Monsanto, manufacturer of the popular Roundup line of herbicides, also genetically engineers Roundup Ready cotton seeds designed to resist its herbicides. The seeds allow increased application of the herbicide without damaging the intended crop. In 1998, Monsanto bought two of the world's top ten seed companies for about $6 billion and is now the second-largest seed company in the world.[8]

Second, scientists believe that crops engineered to resist pesticides and herbicides could pass those traits on to weeds, resulting in herbicide- and pesticide-tolerant "superweeds."[9] Scientists in the U.S. and Denmark have shown that the herbicide-tolerance gene can be readily passed from cultivated canola plants to closely related wild plants, like wild mustard, in nearby fields.[10] If pesticide resistance were transmitted to pest plants, it would force farmers to use more and more herbicides to control plant pests, with unknown effects on the environment and added threat to public health.

Third, GMOs may upset biological diversity. According to a report written for the British government, if GMOs eradicate weeds and insects, species that depend on them for food or habitat, including such birds as the corn bunting, partridge and skylark, will suffer.[11] In fact, researchers funded by the British government found that plants genetically engineered to resist aphids had serious effects on the fertility and life span of ladybirds, which feed on aphids.[12] Furthermore, crops engineered to resist insect pests also may be toxic to harmless or beneficial insects, such as green lacewings and springtails, thereby reducing insect diversity.[13]

In May 1999, Cornell University researchers reported that when pollen from genetically altered corn lands on neighboring milkweed plants, it kills monarch butterfly caterpillars, which live on the milkweed plants.[14] This report prompted environmentalist groups such as Greenpeace and the Union of Concerned Scientists to ask the Environmental Protection Agency (EPA) to pull the genetically altered seeds off the market.[15] The EPA said it would look into the matter.[16]

Fourth, genetically modified foods may run afoul of consumers with allergies and those who have specific dietary requirements because of ethical, religious or cultural beliefs. For example, people allergic to fish could have a reaction to tomatoes with transplanted fish genes. And vegetarians and persons of the Islamic and Jewish faiths may not want to eat food containing transplanted pig genes.

Fifth, GMOs might pose human health risks. British scientist Dr. Arpad Pusztai first suggested this after he conducted a study on the effects of consumption of genetically modified potatoes on rats. He found that rats fed the altered potatoes suffered stunted internal organ growth and weakened immune systems.[17] After publicizing his findings, Dr. Pusztai, despite his stellar reputation, was suspended by the Monsanto-funded[18] Rowett Research Institute. The institute said that it suspended Pusztai because he went public with his findings without sufficient scientific evidence to substantiate them.[19]

A specially convened group of U.K. scientists later concluded that Dr. Pusztai's study, though possibly "flawed," underlined the uncertainty as to the safety of genetically modified foods.[20] Indeed, the British Medical Association, representing Britain's doctors, promptly called for a moratorium on the planting of genetically modified crops in the U.K.[21]

U.S. Trade Demands Jam Biosafety Protocol Talks

Reflecting the growing international concern with the possible risks of GMOs, representatives of more than 140 nations met in Cartagena, Colombia, in February 1999 for ten days to complete a Biosafety Protocol covering GMOs.[22] The conference was to be the culmination of almost seven years of international effort among countries to formulate a policy to safeguard the public against a technology whose long-term effects are essentially unstudied. From the adoption of the U.N. Convention on Biological Diversity in 1992, it had taken concerned countries more than three years to overcome U.S. and industry criticism that a Biosafety Protocol was unnecessary.[23] In December 1996, however, a formal negotiation group assigned to draft a protocol finally was inaugurated under the auspices of the U.N. Convention on Biological Diversity.[24] Thereafter, this working group met frequently, and the final Biosafety Protocol was scheduled to be signed in February 1999.

Throughout the drafting period, both nongovernmental organizations and industry representatives had taken an active stance in trying to persuade governments to adopt their respective positions.[25] The overwhelming majority of countries were seeking a treaty that would permit countries to prohibit imports of GMOs, require segregation of genetically modified grain from conven-

Justifying U.S. opposition to a strong Biosafety Protocol: "This is about a multibillion-dollar industry!"[28]

—Rafe Pomerance,
U.S. Deputy Assistant Secretary of State for Environment and Development

tional grain and make producers of GMOs legally liable for any future environmental or economic damage.[26] The U.S.-led[27] "Miami Group," composed of major exporters of GMOs, including Canada, Argentina, Chile and Australia, how-

U.S. Considers GMO-Labeling a WTO-Illegal "Trade Barrier"

The U.S. has not stopped at merely opposing limitations on GMOs. It also has used the WTO to oppose mandatory labeling of genetically modified foods. The U.S. claims that labels would prejudice consumers and constitute an illegal trade barrier under the Technical Barriers to Trade (TBT) Agreement.[32] The U.S. "does not support a mandatory requirement that in all cases the method by which the food was obtained be disclosed in labeling."[33]

At a recent meeting of the Codex Committee on Food Labeling in Ottawa, support for the U.S. position forbidding mandatory labeling was weak.[34] In fact, only Argentina agreed with the U.S. that food containing GMOs should not be labeled as such. Meanwhile Brazil, Australia and New Zealand, which previously had supported the U.S. stance, reversed their decisions, announcing that they favored mandatory labeling.[35] Furthermore, polls show that 93%

ever, wanted to protect industry interests by writing into the Biosafety Protocol the WTO SPS Agreement provisions requiring nations seeking to prohibit GMOs to justify their decisions on "sound science."[29] Limits on trade based on unproven biosafety concerns, the U.S. argued, should be considered barriers to trade, and the Protocol should explicitly mention that WTO rules prevail over the Protocol.[30]

According to observers attending the negotiations, Rafe Pomerance, deputy assistant secretary of state for environment and development, exclaimed in support of a weak Protocol, "This is about a multibillion-dollar industry!" to which Tewolde Egziabher, Ethiopia's conservation strategy director of the National Herbarium, responded, "This is about the environment!"[31]

The undisguised desire by the U.S. delegation to protect industry at any cost in negotiations that were ostensibly designed to protect the environment angered not only environmentalists but also many other delegates.[41] Indeed, as one commentator said in reference to the trade challenges of U.S. environmental safeguards in the Shrimp-Turtle and the Tuna-Dolphin cases, "it is ironical ... that the U.S. should spout this free trade mantra at an environmental negotiation, [as] it does not fight shy of imposing unilateral trade sanctions on developing countries based on environmental considerations."[42] The comment highlights the hypocrisy of the U.S. Biosafety Protocol position.

In the end, the Miami Group blocked adoption of the Biosafety Protocol by refusing to include commodities (e.g. soya and corn) in the negotiations.[43] According to a statement from the European Commission, "This would in practice mean excluding 99 percent of the genetically modified organisms that the protocol is supposed to cover," reported an environmental journal.[44] The Miami Group then proposed to extend the negotiations by a period of 18 months so that any adoption of the Biosafety Protocol would occur after the WTO Seattle Ministerial in November 1999.[45] As the built-in agenda for the Ministerial included a revision to the WTO

---

of Americans[36] and 74% of Europeans[37] favor labeling to identify GMO products. The U.S. government has admitted that "many consumers in the U.S. have indicated to government agencies such as the USDA and the FDA that labeling [for GMOs] should be mandated."[38]

In its latest proposal to the Codex, the U.S. "moderated" its stance somewhat. It supports mandatory labeling for foods that contain GMOs only "to the extent that the new food compared to an appropriate existing counterpart has undergone significant changes as regards composition, nutritional value, or intended use [and] to disclose the presence of new allergens."[39] This position, however, is logically inconsistent, as GMOs by definition involve genetic alteration and have undergone "significant changes as regards composition." Indeed, GMOs are patentable under WTO TRIPs provisions precisely because they have been altered.[40] The U.S., however, responds that it has no evidence showing that genetically modified foods are any less safe than conventional foods.

Confusing Double-Talk From U.S. Secretary of Agriculture

Recent statements by U.S. Secretary of Agriculture Dan Glickman may suggest that he is modifying his previously unyielding position that other countries must accept products with GMO contents. In a speech delivered on April 29, 1999, at Purdue University, Glickman said that the U.S. cannot "force-feed GMOs down peoples' throats," whether foreign or domestic.[48]

The "new" Glickman position may, however, be only marginally different from the "old" one. GMO patents are worthless unless consumers buy the resulting products. Initially, Glickman's strategy was to attempt to force consumption. Indeed, the U.S. Department of Agriculture proposed rules that would have allowed genetically engineered food to be labeled as organic.[49] However, after the department received 270,000 letters from concerned citizens criticizing this proposal, it abandoned this proposal.[50]

Now Glickman is changing strategies, aiming to encourage consumer acceptance of GMOs through a so-called "arms-length" – i.e., "independent" – regulatory process designed to heighten consumer confidence.[51] Specifically, he is calling for the negotiation of terms under which countries would be permitted to regulate GMOs. However, one of Glickman's key goals is to ensure GMO rules are not based on "unwarranted scientific claims."[52] Thus, it appears the purpose of the new strategy is the same: the unfettered trade of genetically modified products.

Agreement on Agriculture, the Miami Group hoped by this move to be able to deal with most biosafety issues in a forum focusing on trade rather than the environment.[46] The other countries rejected this proposal, and negotiations on the Biosafety Protocol were scheduled to resume in September 1999 in Montreal.[47]

U.S. Moves on GMO Labeling at Codex

The U.S. opposition to the regulation of GMOs has extended even to proposals that products containing GMOs be labeled. The latest U.S. proposal to the Codex Alimentarius Commission listed conditions for a mandatory GMO food labeling program to be WTO-consistent. (Codex is the international standard-setting body empowered by the WTO to set the presumptively WTO-legal standards regarding food.) Under the U.S. proposal, the new food must have "undergone significant changes as regards composition, nutritional value or intended use" compared to its existent counterpart, or the purpose of the labeling must be "to disclose the presence of new allergens."[53] That the seeds, plants and food that result from genetic engineering have undergone "significant change" relative to the seeds, plants and foods obtained through traditional methods is made clear by one simple fact: The corporations that genetically engineer the seeds are able to patent them. To obtain a patent, an inventor must prove that the product is significantly different from all other products.[54] Thus, the continued U.S. opposition to broad mandatory GMO labeling seems logically flawed, or the U.S. proposed Codex conditions are not what they seem on their face.

The U.S. explanation for this strange position: It "has seen no evidence to support that, as a class, foods obtained through bio-technology are inherently less safe or differ in quality or any other manner from foods obtained through conventional methods."[55] In fact, the U.S. Delegation to Codex compares genetic engineering to traditional crossbreeding.[56] Thus, the U.S. position is one reason why commentators predict the GMO issue will become a major WTO battle.

GMO Regulations Proliferate
While U.S. Explicitly Threatens WTO Action

Despite the U.S. sabotage of the Biosafety Protocol signing, in increasing numbers nations are taking steps to regulate GMOs. As early as 1992, the EU had approved a voluntary labeling scheme.[57] Then, in May 1997, the EU adopted the "Novel Foods Regulation" requiring labeling of all new processed foods and food ingredients, including those made with GMOs. In September 1998, an EU policy requiring the labeling of genetically modified corn and soybeans went into effect.[58] The June 1999 amendments to the EU Directive on Deliberate Release of Genetically Modified Organisms included a broad mandatory labeling scheme.[59]

Similarly, in February 1999 the Supreme Court of India prohibited field trials of genetically modified cotton until rules ensuring protection of the environment, human health and biological diversity were implemented.[60] In December 1998, Australian and New Zealand health ministers recommended that genetically modified foods be labeled.[61] In May 1999, Australia introduced a mandatory food standard program prohibiting the sale of food produced using gene technology unless officially tested and included in a "safe-list."[62]

The U.S. considers such regulations to be unnecessary and also illegal barriers to trade.[63] Even Japan, which has previously taken a hands-off approach similar to that of the U.S. to the regulation of GMOs, was criticized by the U.S. trade representative for proposing mandatory labeling requirements on agricultural biotechnology products such as GMO corn, potatoes, cotton, tomatoes and soybeans.[64]

Rather than requiring extensive testing of GMOs at the expense of the U.S. agribusiness industry, the U.S. government instead has tried to downwardly "harmonize" GMO regulations adopted by the rest of the world to the U.S. "non-standard." For example, after the EU rejected Monsanto's application to market two genetically engineered cotton seeds, Frank Loy, U.S. undersecretary of state for global affairs, reserved the right to challenge the decision in the WTO because, he claimed, the EU's decision was not based on "sound science."[65]

Despite the U.S.'s admission that it has not researched the safety of GMO products,[66] the U.S. continues to insist that GMO regulations proposed and enacted around the world may be WTO-illegal because GMOs have not yet been proven dangerous. Unfortunately, nations desiring to prohibit, restrict or even label GMOs could be vulnerable to a successful U.S. WTO challenge because the WTO SPS and TBT Agreements contain the same backwards logic. If a country's regulations on GMOs are based on food safety concerns, the SPS Agreement would require the importing countries to prove that GMOs are un-safe, rather than requiring exporting countries to prove scientifically that GMOs are safe.[67] If a country regulates GMOs as an environmental precaution, the TBT rules would require a showing of an environmental threat and proof that the measures constitute the least trade-restrictive option to deal with a legitimate threat.[68]

Given the threat that existing WTO rules could pose to important GMO regulations, the outcome of the September 1999 Biosafety Protocol talks will be critical to safeguarding governments' ability to regulate GMOs to avoid harm to the public or the environment. Specifically, the needed outcome is the converse of the U.S. proposal. The Biosafety Protocol must limit any application of WTO SPS and TBT rules that would restrict nations' GMO safeguards.[69]

Absent specific language in the Biosafety Protocol to this effect (called a hold harmless clause), there is no guarantee that measures taken by countries under a possible Biosafety Protocol would be WTO-consistent. As described in Chapter 1, domestic implementation of obligations under Multilateral Environmental Agreements (MEAs) can conflict with WTO rules. Indeed, two laws implementing U.S. obligations under MEAs already have been ruled GATT/WTO-illegal.

The rapid adoption of a strong Biosafety Protocol with an explicit WTO hold-harmless clause (giving the protocol supremacy to the extent it conflicts with WTO) is vital because so little conclusive research has been conducted on the long-term effects of GMOs on the environment, biological diversity and human health. The existence of this type of emerging technology is a perfect example of why nations use the "Precautionary Principle" (which requires a manufacturer to demonstrate a product's safety before the product is allowed on the market) when developing cutting edge domestic and international public health and environmental protection standards *(See* Chapter 1 and 2). Absent precautionary measures in this instance, GMOs will proliferate from farms to stores to kitchen tables and will be hard to contain should problems arise in the future.

New EU Directive On GMOs Could Face WTO Challenge By U.S.

At a marathon meeting of European environmental ministers in June 1999, the EU stopped short of declaring a moratorium on GMO approvals despite French and Greek calls for a ban.[70] However, important changes were made to the EU Directive on Deliberate Release of Genetically Modified Organisms.[71] The directive was changed to include a mandatory labeling scheme, tougher risk assessment of all GMOs and a time limit of 10 years on the approval of GMO products. EU officials concede that its practical effect is a *de facto* ban.[72] This could lead to a show-down in the WTO between the EU and the U.S.[73] The new U.S. ambassador to the EU, Richard Morningstar, used his first policy statement in August 1999 to warn that EU GMO hostility was "on the verge of breaching WTO rules."[74]

U.S. Industry Pushing for New Biotechnology Rights and Protections at Seattle

Despite the growing global consensus in favor of GMO regulation, the U.S. industry and the Clinton administration are seeking to strengthen the existing WTO constraints on government action in this area. The "built-in" agenda for the Seattle Ministerial (items agreed to at past negotiations) includes a revision of the Agreement on Agriculture.[75] Thus, issues of food safety and GMOs are sure to surface in Seattle.

The EU has called for the Seattle Ministerial's agricultural agenda to address concerns of food safety and the so-called "multifunctional" role of agriculture.[76] (The notion of "multifunctionality" was introduced to the WTO agriculture debate by the EU and the developing world and calls for consideration of all facets of agricultural policy – crop dependency, environmental protection, development and living standards.)[77]

Meanwhile, the U.S. and Canada argue that food safety concerns are adequately addressed already under WTO rules. The Clinton administration is rejecting consumer and health groups' calls to reopen the WTO Agriculture Agreement text to rebalance it in favor of health and safety.[78] These two countries – home to giant biotechnology companies such as Monsanto and DuPont/Pioneer – also have announced that they will push to *add* trade of biotechnology products to the Seattle agenda. The issue may come as an addition to an existing agreements or as a new stand-alone agreement on biotechnology. A concrete goal for both countries is to reduce the approval process time in other WTO Member countries on imports containing GMOs.[79]

Developing countries will be pressing for concessions that would lengthen, rather than shorten, the time for GMO approvals. India has proposed a revision of the SPS Agreement generally to provide more time for developing countries to bring domestic measures into compliance with WTO rules.[80]

——————— CHAPTER **3** ENDNOTES ———————

[1] Matthew Stilwell and Brennan Van Dyke, *An Activist's Handbook on Genetically Modified Organisms and the WTO*, Center for International Environmental Law, Washington D.C., Mar. 1999, at 2.

[2] *Id.* at 5.

[3] *Id.* at 3.

[4] WTO, Agreement on Sanitary and Phytosanitary Measures, at Article 5.2.

[5] WTO, Agreement on Technical Barriers to Trade, at Article 2.2.

[6] "U.S. Considering Filing WTO Complaint Over E.U. Barriers to GMO Trade, USTR," *Daily Report for Executives*, Jun. 25, 1999.

[7] "Member States Reject Application for Two Genetically Modified Cotton Seeds," *International Environment Reporter*, Feb. 17, 1999, at 138.

[8] "Motivated to Modify Foods," *New Straits Times*, Mar. 10, 1999, at A4.

[9] U.S. Consumer's Choice Council, Letter to The Honorable Frank Loy, Undersecretary for Global Affairs, U.S. Department of State, Feb. 9, 1999.

[10] R. Jorgensen and B. Andersen, "Spontaneous Hybridization Between Oilseed Rape and Weed: A Risk of Growing Genetically Engineered Modified Oilseed Rape," *American Journal of Botany* 81 at 1620-1626, 1995; B. Hileman, "Views Differ Sharply Over Benefits, Risks of Agricultural Biotechnology," *Chemical and Engineering Microbiology*, Aug. 21, 1995.

[11] Charles Clover and George Jones, "Government Stifled Report on GM Risks," *The Daily Telegraph*, Feb. 17, 1999. *See also* report by the U.K. House of Commons Science and Technology Committee, May 12, 1999, published at www.parliament.the-stationery-office.co.uk/pa/cm199899/cmselect/cmsctech/286/28602.htm, on file with Public Citizen.

[12] James Meikle and Paul Brown, "Friend in Need. . .The Ladybird, an Agricultural Ally Whose Breeding Potential May Be Reduced by GM Crops," *The Guardian* (London), Mar. 4, 1999.

[13] U.S. Consumer's Choice Council, Letter to the Honorable Frank Loy, Under Secretary for Global Affairs, U.S. Department of State, Feb. 9, 1999, on file with Public Citizen.

[14] John Carey, "Imperiled Monarchs Alter The Biotech Landscape," *Business Week*, Jun. 7, 1999.

[15] *Id.*

[16] *Id.*

[17] "Top Scientist Backs Calls for GM Safety Screen," *The Guardian* (London), Mar. 9, 1999.

[18] "Biotech: The Pendulum Swings Back," *Environment and Health Weekly*, No. 649, May 6, 1999.

[19] "Royal Society Dismisses 'Flawed' GM Food Research," *The Guardian* (London), May 18, 1999.

[20] "Hot Potato," *The Guardian* (London), May 19, 1999.

[21] *Id.*

[22] "UN Talks on Genetically Modified Trade Protocol Collapse," *European Chemical News - CBNB*, Mar. 24, 1999.

[23] Chee Yoke Ling, "U.S. Behind Collapse of Cartagena Biosafety Talks," *Third World Resurgence*, No. 104/105, Apr./May 1999.

[24] Chee Yoke Ling, "An International Biosafety Protocol: The Fight is Still On," *Third World Resurgence*, No. 93, May 1998.

[25] *Id.*; *see also* Lavanya Rajamani, "The Cartegena Protocol - A Battle Over Trade or Biosafety?" *Third World Resurgence*, No. 104/105, Apr./May 1999.

[26] Ricardo Maldonado, "Biotech Industry Discusses Trade," *Associated Press*, Feb. 22, 1999.

[27] The U.S. is not a party to the Convention on Biological Diversity, so had no vote at the negotiations. However, it was still entitled to participate in the negotiations, and essentially "voted" through the Miami-group initiative. Chee Yoke Ling, "U.S. behind collapse of Cartagena biosafety talks," *Third World Resurgence*, No. 104/105, Apr./May 1999.

[28] Chee Yoke Ling: "U.S. Behind Collapse of Cartagena Biosafety Talks," *Third World Resurgence*, No. 104/105, Apr./May 1999.

[29] Andrew Pollack, "U.S. and Allies Block Threat on Genetically Altered Goods," *The New York Times*, Feb. 24, 1999.

[30] Chee Yoke Ling, "U.S. Behind Collapse of Cartagena Biosafety Talks," *Third World Resurgence*, No. 104/105, Apr./May 1999.

[31] *Id.*

[32] Sean Poulter, "Blank Out Labels, Says U.S.," *UK Daily Mail*, Feb. 11, 1999.

[33] Andrew Pollack, "U.S. and Allies Block Threat on Genetically Altered Goods," *The New York Times*, Feb. 24, 1999.

[34] *See* The U.S. Codex Alimentarius Commission U.S. Delegate's Report on the 27th Session of the Codex Committee on Food Labeling, on file with Public Citizen.

[35] Transatlantic Consumer Dialogue, "Many More Countries Endorse Mandatory Labeling of GE Food at International Food Standards Negotiations," Press Release, April 29, 1999.

[36] Brian Willams, "Firm Stance on Labeling Genetically Engineered Food Continues to Spark Debate," *The Columbus Dispatch*, Feb. 2, 1997, *cited in* comments on GMO-labeling to the Japanese Ministry of Agriculture submitted by the International Association of Consumer Food Organizations, Oct. 9, 1998, on file with Public Citizen.

[37] European Commission Directorate General XII, European Opinions on Modern Biotechnology, *EUROBAROMETER*, 46.1,1997, *cited in* "Summary of Consumer Surveys Related to Labeling of Foods Produced Using Biotechnology," *Consumer Polity Institute*, on file with Public Citizen.

[38] Proposed Draft Recommendations for the Labeling of Foods Obtained Through Biotechnology (Alinorm 99/22, Appendix VIII), CX/FL 99/6, Government Comments at Step 3 from the U.K and the U.S., *Codex Alimentarius Commission*, June 1999, on file with Public Citizen.

[39] *Id.*

[40] WTO, Agreement on Trade Related Aspects of Intellectual Property Rights, Article 25.

[41] Chee Yoke Ling, "U.S. Behind Collapse of Cartagena Biosafety Talks," *Third World Resurgence*, No. 104/105, Apr./May 1999.

[42] Lavanya Rajamani, "The Cartagena Protocol - A Battle Over Trade or Biosafety?" *Third World Resurgence* No. 104/105, Apr./May 1999.

[43] "EU Accuses US, Others of 'Extreme' Positions That Will Block Biosafety Protocol," *International Environment Reporter*, Feb. 17, 1999, at 136.

[44] *Id.*

[45] Lavanya Rajamani: "The Cartagena Protocol - A Battle Over Trade or Biosafety?" *Third World Resurgence* No. 104/105, Apr./May 1999.

[46] *Id.*

[47] Gurdial Singh Nijar: Biosafety Protocol Talks to Resume in September," *South-North Development Monitor*, Jul. 4, 1999.

[48] "A Biotech Warrior Stresses Subtlety," *St. Louis Post-Dispatch*, Jun. 6, 1999.

[49] *Id.*

[50] National Press Club Newsmaker Luncheon with Agriculture Secretary Dan Glickman, *Federal News Service*, Jul. 13, 1999, on file with Public Citizen.

[51] *Id.*

[52] *Id.*

[53] Proposed Draft Recommendations for the Labeling of Foods Obtained Through Biotechnology (Alinorm 99/22, Appendix VIII), CX/FL 99/6, Government Comments at Step 3 from the U.K and the U.S., *Codex Alimentarius Commission*, Jun. 1999, on file with Public Citizen.

[54] 35 U.S.C. Secs. 101-103.

[55] Proposed Draft Recommendations for the Labeling of Foods Obtained Through Biotechnology (Alinorm 99/22, Appendix VIII), CX/FL 99/6, Government Comments at Step 3 from the U.K and the U.S., *Codex Alimentarius Commission*, Jun. 1999, on file with Public Citizen.

[56] Michael Wehr, Office of Constituent Operations, Center for Food Safety and Applied Nutrition, Personal Communication with Marianne Mollmann, Public Citizen, Aug. 10, 1999. Of course, the two methods are entirely different and result in different products. Genetic engineering allows the transfer of genes between totally unrelated organisms, even across natural species barriers, resulting in gene combinations that never would occur naturally. For example, soil bacterium genes have been introduced into soya plants to make them herbicide-resistant, and "anti-freezing" genes from arctic sea flounder have been transplanted into tomatoes, strawberries and potatoes to make them frost-resistant. Crossbreeding, by contrast, is the hybridization of two varieties or breeds within the same species. *See* Dr. Michael Antoniou, "Genetic Engineering and Traditional Breeding Methods: A Technical Perspective," *Living Earth*, Issue 197, Jan.-Mar. 1998, on file with Public Citizen.

[57] USTR, *1999 National Trade Estimate Report on Foreign Trade Barriers* (1999) at 115.

[58] *Id.* at 111.

[59] EEC/90/220, quoted in "E.U. Environment Ministers Strengthen De Facto Ban On GMOs Pending New Law," *International Trade Reporter, Volume 16, Number 26,* June 30, 1999.

[60] Frederick Noronha, "India's High Court Stops Field Trials of Biotech Cotton," *Environment News Service*, Feb. 23, 1999.

[61] "Australian, New Zealand Health Ministers Recommend Labeling of Genetically Modified Foods," *World Food Chemical News*, Jan. 6, 1999, at 1.

[62] USTR, *1999 National Trade Estimate Report on Foreign Trade Barriers*, (1999), at 16.

[63] *Id.*, at 112.

[64] *Id.*, at 225.

[65] "Member States Reject Application for Two Genetically Modified Cotton Seeds," *International Environment Reporter*, Feb. 17, 1999, at 138.

[66] Diane Johnson, "France's Fickle Appetite," *The New York Times*, Aug. 2, 1999.

[67] Agreement on Sanitary and Phytosanity Measures, Article 5.2.

[68] Agreement on Technical Barriers to Trade, Article 2.2.

[69] Both the SPS and TBT Agreements require WTO Members to base domestic standards on international ones. Agreement on Sanitary and Phytosanity Measures, Article 3; Agreement on Technical Barriers to Trade, Article 9.

[70] Stephen Bates, "Tougher E.U. Controls Mean Moratorium On GM Crops," *The Guardian (London)*, June 26, 1999.

[71] EEC/90/220, quoted in "E.U. Environment Ministers Strengthen De Facto Ban On GMOs Pending New Law", *International Trade Reporter, Volume 16, Number 26,* June 30, 1999.

[72] Stephen Bates, "Tougher E.U. Controls Mean Moratorium On GM Crops," *The Guardian (London)*, June 26, 1999.

[73] "U.S. Considering Filing WTO Complaint Over E.U. Barriers to GMO Trade, USTR Says," *Daily Report for Executives,* June 25, 1999.

[74] "U.S. Warns EU of Trade War Over GM Food," *Reuters*, August 12, 1999.

[75] WTO Agreement on Agriculture, Article 20.

[76] "Member Positions Emerge For Next Round," BRIDGES Weekly Trade News Digest, Vol. 3, Number 31, Aug. 9, 1999.

[77] *See* "WTO Agriculture Committee Addresses Developing Country Concerns", *BRIDGES Weekly Trade Digest,* Vol. 3 Number 25, June 28, 1999

[78] "G-8 Urges Environment Considerations In Millennium Round," *BRIDGES*, Vol. 3 Number 24, June 21, 1999.

[79] Inside U.S. Trade, Vol. 17, No. 18, May 7, 1999 at 28.

[80] "India to Push for Reform Not Expansion of WTO Agreements," *BRIDGES, V*ol. 3, Number 23, June 14, 1999.

In this chapter ...

CASES:

- **Guatemala Implementation of UNICEF Baby Formula Marketing Code:** Guatemala implemented the UNICEF Code, which bans infant formula packaging with labels depicting healthy, fat babies to ensure that illiterate mothers do not associate formula with healthy infants and stop breast-feeding. Gerber, whose trademarked logo includes a pudgy baby, refused to comply and threatened GATT action. Guatemala, faced with the prospect of a costly, lengthy fight before a secretive tribunal in Switzerland, backed down and now exempts imported baby food products from its law.

- **South African Medicines Law:** To increase affordable access to vital medicines, especially the AIDS treatments available in developed countries, then-President Nelson Mandela created the Medicines Law, which promotes parallel importing and compulsory licensing of pharmaceuticals to create competition and lower prices. Although these policies are permitted by the WTO intellectual property rules, the U.S. pharmaceutical industry trade group and its South African branch have continually threatened the Medicines Law with WTO action. The Clinton administration prioritized getting rid of the law, and a State Department memo described in this book outlines the efforts of Vice President Gore, whose presidential campaign has been disrupted by AIDS activists outraged by his role.

- **India Required to Change Patent Laws in Threat to Food Security:** India's patent laws have excluded seeds, plants and other items with medicinal or food uses to ensure broad access. WTO rules effective in 2005 require India to protect monopoly intellectual property rights, including for these items. The U.S. challenged India's patent registration system, and the WTO agreed that India must change its underlying patent law.

- **Thailand Traditional Medicine, Anti Bio-Piracy:** The U.S. has questioned Thailand as to the WTO-consistency of its proposed law that would allow traditional healers to register traditional medicines with the government — and thereby protect them from being patented by foreign companies.

- **Israeli Generic Medicine Law:** The U.S. has claimed that the Israeli law that allows producers to gear up to be prepared to *sell* generic versions of drugs immediately after their patents expire violates WTO rules.

- **Thai Medicine Access Policy:** The U.S. used trade threats to pressure Thailand to disband its Pharmaceutical Review Board encouraging compulsory licensing, including of vital AIDS treatment drugs, to keep down prices.

CONCEPTS:

Agreement on Trade Related Aspects of Intellectual Property: One of the most controversial Uruguay Round Agreements. In contrast to other WTO rules, it explicitly *limits* trade by establishing monopoly marketing rights for intellectual property owners. The TRIPs Agreement includes trademarks, patents and copyrights, and covers a remarkable list of items: seeds, microorganisms such as cell lines and genes, genetically modified animals and more.

Food Security, Seeds & Terminator Technology: Because the TRIPs Agreement permits patenting of seeds, farmers whose ancestors may have created a seed variety must pay annual royalty fees to use that seed if a corporation obtains a patent on it. Some companies are genetically engineering seeds so that they produce sterile seeds that cannot be saved and replanted, yet billions of subsistence farmers' very survival depends on saving and replanting seeds.

Bio-Piracy: This refers to a foreign corporation's "prospecting" in developing countries for indigenous knowledge, new medicinal plants or seed varieties, which it can get patented and therefore "own" all rights to market. Examples described in this chapter include: India's Neem tree and Basmati rice, and Thailand's Plao Noi and Jasmine rice.

U.S. Patent Extension Required by WTO: To comply with the TRIPs Agreement, the U.S. had to extend its 17-year monopoly patent to 20 years. This change has resulted in U.S. consumers facing billions in higher medicine costs.

WTO Intellectual Property Rights For Corporations Threaten Food Security and Access to Medicines

Intellectual Property Rights, or IPRs, bestow ownership rights and legal protections on ideas, artistic creations (such as novels, music and films), technological innovations and marketing tools (logos and trademarks, for instance). The idea underlying the creation of property rights for intellectual output is to promote and reward innovations in the fields of art, science, technology and industry. For instance, when a company invents a product, it can be awarded a patent giving it the exclusive right to market the product for a certain amount of time, thus ensuring it can profit on the investments made to develop it. The WTO Agreement on Trade Related Aspects of Intellectual Property (TRIPs) establishes enforceable global property rights and requires all 134 WTO Members to enact domestic legislation to enforce these new rights.

Patenting Life: What the WTO TRIPs Agreement Allows

Are WTO Members legally obligated under the TRIPs Agreement to grant and protect patents on life forms? The answer is: almost. And if the biotech industry and Clinton administration have their way at the Seattle WTO Ministerial, the answer will be "yes" in the future.

The TRIPs Agreement nominally allows countries to ban patenting of plants, animals and what it terms "essentially biological processes for the production of plants or animals."[1] However, it requires that WTO Member countries protect non-biological and microbiological processes for the production of plants and animals, meaning that plants and animals are patentable if they are cloned or genetically altered.[2] The TRIPs Agreement also requires countries to protect property claims on microorganisms.[3] These include human and animal cell lines, genes and umbilical cord cells.[4] Indeed, the only area explicitly excluded from the TRIPs Agreement protection is medical treatment (like surgical techniques).[5]

The TRIPs Agreement thus has tremendous implications for food security and public health and the environment.

Effectively, the TRIPs Agreement establishes new global protection for the trademarks, copyrights and patents of multinational corporations.

Before the TRIPs Agreement set into motion the international "harmonization" of intellectual property and competition laws, countries had the freedom to decide individually how to balance the interest of industry in profiting from innovation with the competing interest in ensuring that society as a whole can enjoy the fruits of innovation. Moreover, since industrial innovation is often a direct result of public investment in research and development,[6] many nations' domestic intellectual property laws often gave substantial weight to the public claim on new technologies, especially as pertains to access to medicine.

By 2005, the TRIPs Agreement will, with limited exceptions, sharply restrict the maneuvering room of national policymakers by imposing *uniform* global IPR protections on 134 WTO Member countries.[7] While countries are given limited flexibility in narrowly prescribed areas to develop their own approaches to intellectual property policy, for the most part the TRIPs Agreement sets out a single definition of what qualifies as intellectual property and a single set of rules governing governments' obligations to protect it.[8]

Further, the level of IPR protection required by the TRIPs Agreement is extremely high – higher than most WTO Members had in place before implementing the Uruguay Round Agreements. For instance, under the TRIPs Agreement, even the U.S. had to extend its law governing patent duration – from 17 years to the 20 years WTO requires.[9]

The TRIPs Agreement is also broader in its scope of coverage than any previous global intellectual property rules. The TRIPs Agreement has a definition of IPRs that extends mandatory global patent rights beyond the typically covered industrial innovations. It includes pharmaceuticals, agricultural chemicals, plant varieties and seed germplasms, including those resulting from generations of plant breeding and traditional remedies.[10] It also requires countries to protect property claims on microorganisms. These include human and animal cell lines, genes and umbilical cord cells.[11] Many countries had excluded such areas from coverage in their domestic intellectual property laws.[12] The only area excluded from intellectual property protection under the TRIPs Agreement is medical treatment (diagnostic, therapeutic and surgical techniques), although pharmaceuticals are covered.[13]

WTO Double Standard: What Does IPR Protectionism Have to Do With "Free" Trade?

The addition of intellectual property rules to the Uruguay Round Agreements at U.S. insistence was highly controversial. First, an international regime of intellectual property rules already existed within the World Intellectual Property Organization (WIPO), an international body created specifically for that purpose.[14] Second, while the purpose of the WTO is, ostensibly, to liberalize trade, IPR protections restrict trade by design. Once a corporation is granted a patent for a product or process, it is given a monopoly on the manufacture and pricing of that innovation for a set number of years. The 20-year monopoly granted under WTO TRIPs rules undercuts price competition and consumer choice. To critics, this contradiction suggested

Global Uniformity Required

Harmonization is the term given to the process of replacing diverse national standards with uniform global standards. The WTO SPS and TBT Agreements on food and product standards have been criticized as inevitably leading to weakened national standards. Neither agreement requires that countries adopt minimum standards of protection for the public and the environment, but they do limit when national standards can be stronger than international ones. The harmonization of intellectual property and competition laws achieved by the TRIPs Agreement, however, is an exception to the WTO's bias towards downward harmonization of standards. From the corporate perspective, the TRIPs Agreement harmonizes upward by requiring countries to adopt very high standards in most areas of intellectual property protection.

that the Uruguay Round – notwithstanding the claims of its proponents – was not based on a principled commitment to "free trade" as a universal good but was instead designed to advance whatever trade rules corporations happened to find expedient.

Environmentalists and advocates for workers logically have asked why, if it is acceptable to limit trade on behalf of corporate property rights in almost every sphere, limitations could not also be included to protect workers and the environment?

Distracting attention from the ideological inconsistency of including trade restrictive IPRs in an agreement allegedly aimed at trade liberalization required a semantic sleight of hand. By putting the clause "trade related" as a prefix to "intellectual property," the proponents of globalizing monopoly-style IPR protections simply fabricated a connection to get strong WTO enforcement of new trade restrictions.

Combining the WTO's extensive new IPR protections with its powerful dispute resolution mechanism means corporations have a weighty new tool: the threat of WTO-approved sanctions against countries that adopt public health or pharmaceutical policies the industry opposes. As described below, industry has wasted no time leveraging the possibility of WTO-imposed sanctions to attack such public interest policies. Often industry has obtained government backing for the threats. Particularly in the U.S., trade officials have been remarkably aggressive in using the WTO to advance the agenda of the pharmaceutical industry, even attacking laws in areas where the WTO TRIPs Agreement rules do not apply.

The WTO TRIPs Agreement:
Developing Country Access to Food and Medicine

The TRIPs Agreement has created a firestorm of protest in the developing world. Many developing countries have traditionally excluded food and medicine from their IPR laws in order to ensure that these basic necessities are accessible and affordable and not subject to private monopoly control.[15] Under the TRIPs Agreement, however, what was once in the public domain – food and medicine – must now be privatized through global patent law. From the perspective of many in the developing world, where food shortages and disease threaten the population on an ongoing basis, WTO TRIPs protections for corporate property rights outrageously undermine the ability of governments to respond generally to basic public needs and specifically to public health crises. In addition, as the location of most of the world's biodiversity, developing countries also fear widespread "biopiracy" of indigenous plants and other wildlife. Already biotechnology corporations send out "prospectors" to collect medicinal plants and indigenous knowledge about their uses. The TRIPs Agreement gives these corporations the ability to obtain worldwide patents on these resources and thus exclusive ownership and marketing rights.

> ## U.N. Criticizes WTO Intellectual Property Rules
>
> The United Nations Development Program (UNDP) criticizes the TRIPs Agreement in its 1999 Human Development Report as undermining food security and public health in developing nations. The UNDP reports that TRIPs rules make it much more costly for poor and developing countries to procure seeds for crops and make medicine more accessible to the public.

The United Nations Development Program (UNDP) criticizes the TRIPs Agreement in its 1999 Human Development Report as undermining food security and public health in developing nations. The UNDP reports that WTO TRIPs rules make it much more costly for poor and developing countries to procure seeds for crops and make medicines more accessible to the public.[16] UNDP recommends that the rules be revised.[17]

Critics of the TRIPs Agreement see few benefits for the developing world to offset the Agreement's costs. The protection of intellectual property rights aids the industrial world disproportionately. Corporations or individuals in industrialized countries currently hold 97% of all patents worldwide; in 1995 more than half of global royalties and licensing fees were paid to the U.S.[18] Even within developing countries themselves, 80% of the patents granted belong to residents of industrial countries.[19]

Critics in the developing world also point out, correctly, that the now industrialized countries did not themselves adopt such stringent IPR protections when they were in the process of developing (and therefore were net importers of) intellectual property and technology.[20]

The threat of possible WTO challenges is extremely worrisome for developing countries, given their limited resources to defend such cases at the Geneva-based WTO and their comparatively lesser capacity to withstand economic retaliation. Under WTO rules, countries that win WTO cases can impose cross-sectoral sanctions. This means that pursuant to a WTO dispute panel ruling in its favor on a TRIPs Agreement issue, an industrialized country could impose economic sanctions against the developing country's commodities or manufactured goods.[21] Indeed, as is described below in the Guatemala baby milk case, the *threat* of the costs of mounting a WTO defense and/or sanctions alone often serves to force a developing country to change its IPR laws or drop proposals to which industry and government in the industrialized world are hostile.

The TRIPs Agreement does allow for some narrow public interest limits on intellectual property rights protection. For instance, as described below, the TRIPs Agreement does allow governments to engage in parallel importing and compulsory licensing (although this has not stopped the United States from using WTO threats to try to thwart a South African law that would use these mechanisms to make desperately needed AIDS drugs more affordable. However, these provisions are much more clear-cut in some areas than in others.

TRIPs Agreement rules about what sort of IPR protections countries must provide for plant varieties are vague. The text technically allows countries to create their own *sui generis* regimes (and thus does not exclusively require patent rules in this area), but it is entirely unclear what alternative regime would pass WTO muster. For instance, will countries be allowed to take the measures necessary to protect against bio-piracy's plundering and commodification of indigenous flora and fauna? U.S. threats against a Thai policy promoting the registry of traditional medicines suggest not.

In addition, the TRIPs Agreement fails to set a high standard for what counts as a "technological innovation" – thus allowing corporations to seek and receive patents on processes that have been used by indigenous groups for generations.

Indian Parliament Coerced Into WTO TRIPs Implementation

The Indian Parliament refused to implement the TRIPs Agreement and implemented only the other aspects of the Uruguay Round. The Prime Minister of India then issued an executive decree that enacted the TRIPs rules on pharmaceutical and agricultural chemical patents in late 1994. The executive decree had to be upheld by both houses of Parliament, which twice refused to amend Indian patent law. India's Patent Act bans patents for substances "intended for use, or capable of being used, as food or as medicine or drug."[22] Section 15(2) of the Patents Act states that the patent office "shall refuse" an application in respect to a substance that is not patentable.[23]

The Indian government then developed an administrative procedure for keeping track of patent applications until it was required to implement the TRIPs Agreement in 2005.[24] The U.S. challenged India's actions at the WTO.[25] In September 1997, a WTO panel ruled that India is required to establish *statutory* procedures for receiving applications for patents on pharmaceutical and agricultural chemicals immediately so that, upon its full implementation of the TRIPs Agreement, patents can be back-dated to the date of filing.[26] The panel ruled that India's administrative patent tracking procedure does not trump Indian law, which prohibits the patenting of agricultural chemicals and pharmaceuticals, and thus does not give corporations a reasonable expectation that their patent applications — submitted while it was still illegal to patent — will be reviewed and accepted as required once the new rules go into effect in 2005.[27] In March 1999, the Indian Parliament satisfied the WTO's demand and approved the TRIPs Agreement implementing legislation amending the Patents Act.[28]

The WTO TRIPs Rules Endanger Food Security

Despite improved agricultural techniques, much of the world's population continues to suffer from malnutrition. While the volume of food now produced could feed the world, food and seed distribution and access problems leave many hungry.[29] During the 1980s, the proportion and number of families lacking access to basic nutrition increased in Latin America and sub-Saharan Africa.[30] In sub-Saharan Africa, nearly 7 million people are currently in need of emergency food assistance.[31] On a worldwide basis, 72 of the United Nation's World Food Program's in-country projects have been operating for five years or more, suggesting that lack of food is a structural as well as an acute problem.[32]

Food security has not improved in the 1990s. The per capita protein intake for the developing world fell 3.3% between 1970 and 1996, and over the same period it fell 5.7% in sub-Saharan Africa.[33] Caloric intake in sub-Saharan Africa has declined from 2,226 in 1970 to 2,205 in 1996 – a 9% decline.[34] According to U.S. Department of Agriculture Recommended Dietary Allowance figures from 1989, adults between 25 and 50 years old should consume 2,550 calories a day.[35]

Despite enormous growth in food trade, only 15% of the world's food supply is traded.[36] A large share of the world's population relies on subsistence farming for its food supply. Subsistence farmers are able to grow crops year after year only by saving seeds. In fact, 1.4 billion rural people worldwide rely on farm-saved seeds for both food and livelihood.[37]

> **"Terminator" seeds are genetically engineered so the crops they produce have sterile seeds, and thus farmers must purchase new seeds each year.**

The TRIPs Agreement further undermines precarious worldwide food security by exacerbating food and seed access and distribution problems. For instance, Article 27.3(b) requires that WTO Members protect agribusiness ownership over plant varieties, including seeds. This requirement provides dramatic new tools to consolidate the power of large seed and biotechnology manufacturers by shifting ownership and control of seed stocks away from farmers.

When corporations patent seeds, local farmers must pay annual fees to use the seed type, even if the seed was the product of breeding conducted over generations by the very ancestors of the farmers themselves. So far, patents have been awarded on varieties of soybeans, corn and canola.[38] Subsistence farmers can ill-afford to pay the cost of purchasing seed each year. On the other hand, the TRIPs Agreement contains no protections for indigenous communities that have been planting and crossbreeding strains for centuries to develop that perfectly adapted variety that a bio-prospector can collect and have patented to some distant corporation.

Corporations also have turned to gene technology to effectively control the "use" of "their" property by literally eliminating the ability of farmers to save seeds. Monsanto already requires farmers who purchase genetically modified seeds to agree not to save seeds for next year's crop, and it posts signs threatening investigations and legal actions against farmers breaking the contract.[39]

The next logical step in the companies' control is already under way. Monsanto has applied for and received patents for seeds that *cannot* reproduce,[40] eliminating the need for expensive investigations and legal battles. The sterile seeds, dubbed "terminator seeds" by food security groups, can be activated to grow only by use of a chemical, and the seeds that the crop produces will never germinate.[41]

The main target market for these seeds seems to be the developing world, where market concentration, combined with terminator technology, could create a stranglehold on local farmers.[42] There are concerns that the terminator crops could accidentally pollinate non-terminator crops, potentially destroying the fertility of other seeds from plants of the same variety planted nearby.[43] The uproar this new technology has sparked in the U.S and across the world caused Monsanto to put the development on hold for now, but it still holds the patent.[44]

Many developing countries have taken steps to ban terminator technology. The Indian government has, for example, introduced a complete ban on the entry of terminator genes and technology into India – as the technology poses a grave threat to subsistence farmers.[45] However, under WTO Agreements relating to food and product safety (the SPS and TBT Agreements), it is likely that the Indian law could face a challenge in the future.

The ability to patent crop varieties is also promoting corporate consolidation in the food and agriculture sectors as agribusiness corporations merge. For instance, in North America, just four companies now control almost 60% of the seed market.[46] As described by the president of the U.S. National Farmers Union to a congressional committee, the result is a de facto monopoly in which new companies are restricted from entering the market.[47] This concentration of the market into the hands of a few multinational corporations increases the likelihood of cartels and price increases for food, exacerbating rather than addressing food insecurity in the developing world.

The development of terminator technology also reflects the rapid consolidation of the agriculture, chemical and biotechnology industries. Most seed companies now are either aligned with, or have been acquired by, biotechnology and pesticide giants such as Monsanto, DuPont or Dow Chemical.[48] The percentage of the seed market owned by bio-tech companies developing terminator technology is constantly growing, and the five dominant bio-tech companies – Monsanto, AstraZeneca, Novartis, DuPont/Pioneer and Avantis – each have their own versions of terminator patents.[49]

Finally, monopoly ownership over crop varieties as encouraged by the TRIPs Agreement has also been linked to the spread of "mono-culture agriculture." Aggressive marketing of the products protected by intellectual property rights can lead to the spread of the same variety of crop or livestock worldwide and to the displacement of hundreds of local varieties of crops and breeds of livestock.[50] The planting of only one variety of a crop on a massive scale poses tremendous risk to food security and the environment. First, mono-cropping stamps out the diverse crop and animal varieties that are useful to maintaining balanced ecosystems. The end product – the so-called "mono-culture" – is a dangerously unstable ecosystem that has lost its diversity and hence its resistance against pests, diseases and environmental stresses. The deadly Irish potato famine resulted in part from mono-cropping. The potato blight was able to move from field to field throughout the country because of reliance on one variety of potato, the lumper. In 1970, a corn blight epidemic ravaged at least 15% of the U.S. corn crop due to genetic uniformity.[51] The homogeneity of the corn plant variety made the entire crop vulnerable to the same fungus.

Governments have taken steps to protect from the disappearance of biological diversity and the resulting impacts on food security. The Convention on Biological Diversity urges parties to cooperate to ensure that intellectual property rights "are supportive of and do not run counter to" the objectives of the convention: namely, the conservation and sustainable use of biodiversity and the equitable sharing of its benefits.[52] Yet, the TRIPs Agreement's guarantees of corporate ownership of seeds and plant varieties limit the ability of nations to implement the principles of the Convention.

WTO TRIPs Agreement Facilitates Bio-Piracy of Developing Country Resources

Many WTO Members in the developing world are turning to other fora to make policy that protects communities and subsistence farmers from the trend towards agribusiness monopolization of the food supply.

However the WTO TRIPs Agreement's terms undermine the principles and enforcement of these Agreements. There are two main international Agreements covering the issue. The 1992 Convention on Biological Diversity obligates parties to "respect, preserve and maintain knowledge, innovations and practices of indigenous and local communities" relevant to biodiversity.[53] The Convention acknowledges that communities and subsistence farmers were responsible for the development of important agricultural crops and that they safeguarded the tremendous biodiversity that agribusiness now uses as its

Once the TRIPs Agreement is fully phased in, developing country WTO Members will have the obligation to enforce seed companies' patent rights, by either uprooting "illegal" crops or collecting fees from subsistence farmers. Failure to do so would leave the country susceptible to WTO trade sanctions.[55]

source material. The second agreement, the "Principles of Farmer's Rights," was adopted under the United Nations' Food and Agriculture Organization (FAO) in 1987 in order to devise legal and financial instruments to support farming communities in the ongoing development and conservation of the germ plasm and technologies their ancestors cultivated collectively over many generations.[54]

Yet, the TRIPs Agreement provisions conflict with these agreements' attempts to prevent "bio-piracy" from developing countries of indigenous seeds, herbs and traditional processes for obtaining medicinal or pesticidal benefits from local flora and fauna. One version of bio-piracy is corporate patent appropriation of plant varieties that rural and indigenous communities have been cultivating for hundreds or even thousands of years. Companies merely must claim that they have altered them to earn the right to patent the plant, even if that alteration does not change the plant in any meaningful way.[56] Since patent examiners often do not have access to facilities to test the alleged "new trait," the patent is often granted and validity of the claim is left to civil litigation, which is too costly for indigenous communities to undertake.[57]

Once the TRIPs Agreement is fully phased in, developing country WTO Members will have the obligation to enforce seed companies' patent rights by either uprooting "illegal" crops or collecting the fees from subsistence farmers. Failure to do so would leave the country in violation of its TRIPs obligations and susceptible to trade sanctions.[58]

Indeed, patent rights for hundreds of indigenous species already may have been siphoned off into state or regional agricultural centers and even into the hands of private companies. A collaborative study by the Rural Advancement Foundation International and Heritage Seed Curators Australia found nearly 150 cases of research institutions and businesses applying for patents or licenses for naturally occurring plant varieties.[59] The study found that an agreement between the Consultative Group on International Agriculture Research and the UN Food and Agricultural Organization, which had placed germ plasm from more than 500,000 plant varieties "in trust," was not being followed. Instead, plant varieties, some of which had been farmed for generations, were being included in intellectual property claims in countries that had signed the trust agreement.[60]

Corporate Bio-Piracy Of Basmati Rice

The Texas-based firm RiceTec was granted a patent for "Basmati" rice in 1997, even though in its patent application RiceTec admits that India and Pakistan have grown Basmati for generations.[61] This patent was revealed in a recent report to have been inappropriately licensed from the public trust.[62] RiceTec altered the traditional Indian rice very slightly . Granting a U.S. patent for a product native to India drew heavy protests in New Dehli, since Basmati is an important export crop with more than half a million tons sent to Europe, America and the Middle East each year.[63] A coalition of eminent Indian civil society groups sent a letter to the U.S. ambassador to India challenging the premise of the U.S. intellectual property position, stating: "The truth is that the U.S. is pirating the intellectual property of the farmers, healers, tribals, fisherfolk of India and other developing countries."[64] Under the TRIPs Agreement, India is required to enforce the American company's patent right over Indian farmers.

The Neem Tree Example

The first famous example of bio-piracy involves patents on certain products derived from the neem tree, which is native to India. The indigenous population in India has always revered the tree for its medicinal value and use as a bio-pesticide.[65] Nicknamed "the village pharmacy," for centuries people in India have used products derived from the tree for cleaning teeth and treating conditions ranging from acne to ulcers.[66] While the indigenous population had always noted and utilized the tree's properties, it was not until the 1970s that Western scientists displayed interest in its qualities.[67]

Since 1971, when a U.S. importer observed the tree's pharmaceutical properties, multinational corporations from the U.S. and Japan have sought and been granted numerous patents on various products extracted from the neem tree.[68] The U.S.-incorporated W.R. Grace Company has already started manufacturing and commercializing its products by establishing a base in India.[69] Grace's justification for its patent is that its modernized extraction processes constitute a genuine innovation.[70] It matters little that the so-called innovation was based on traditional knowledge and that neem-based bio-pesticides and medicines have been produced by indigenous populations, many using complex processes for centuries.

More than 200 nongovernmental organizations from 35 nations have challenged the W.R. Grace Company in the U.S. Patent and Trademark Office against the patent granting it the exclusive use of a pesticidal extract from neem seed.[71] The challenge is grounded in the argument that the pesticidal extract in question has long been known to and used by the Indian people.[72] Therefore, the knowledge was available to the Indians at the time of patenting and therefore the patented product was "obvious" and not the product of innovation. The W.R. Grace Company is expected to defend its right to patent the traditional pesticide – and to emphasize India's obligation to protect its patent – under the TRIPs Agreement.[73] Not only are corporations using TRIPs rules to consolidate control over seed varieties and indigenous knowledge, but countries that attempt to counter this trend can face TRIPs threats.

Threat 1: U.S. Charges Thai Anti Bio-Piracy Policy Violates WTO

In 1997, legislation was introduced in the Thai parliament that was designed to protect traditional medicines by granting them legal protections available to other forms of unique knowledge. The legislation would allow Thai traditional healers to register their traditional

"Plao Noi" a Thai plant that has been used to treat ulcers,[74] was patented by a Japanese company, and Thais lost all rights to market it.[75]

medicines so that, in the event that a biotechnology or pharmaceutical company sought a patent on the substance or process, the company would have to negotiate with the traditional healer.[76]

The impetus behind the legislation is a history of pharmaceutical raids on various plants and insects. Several years ago "Plao Noi," a Thai plant used to cure ulcers,[77] was patented by a Japanese company, and Thais lost all rights to market it.[78] Thailand is also currently trying to protect its right to market its jasmine rice against a U.S. rice product called "Jasmati" that officials say misleads consumers into thinking it was the same as Thai fragrant rice.[79] Most recently, a British University refused to turn over to Thailand 200 strains of marine fungi taken from the wild in Thailand years ago for pharmaceutical industry-sponsored research.[80] The fungi strains are one of the most endangered collections in the world given their size and genetic importance. Experts say the disputed strains may be worth billions of baht – millions of dollars — if the pharmaceutical industry discovers potential in them for curing diseases like cancer or AIDS.[81]

In response to the Thai traditional medicine registration legislation, the U.S. State Department sent a letter in April 1997 to the Royal Thai Government (RTG) warning that "Washington believes that such a registration system could constitute a possible violation of the TRIPs Agreement and hamper medical research into these compounds."[82] The State Department letter requests a copy of the draft legislation and official responses to eleven questions, beginning with the ques-

---

Study Finds Patents Too Expensive for Poor Countries Whose Biodiversity Is at Risk

The Gaia Foundation, a U.K.-based environmental group, was approached by a Namibian nongovernmental organization seeking assistance on patenting a local plant with medicinal properties in order to prevent bio-piracy by multinational pharmaceutical companies. After researching the costs involved in patenting the plant, the Gaia Foundation concluded that patenting was prohibitively expensive for poor communities.[83]

Poor communities wishing to patent indigenous plant life would have to secure patents in any number of developed countries. Thus farmers and indigenous peoples would incur huge costs in applying, securing and maintaining patents. According to the report, ten patents covering a single invention in 52 countries would cost almost $500,000.[84] The report also identified the additional cost of enforcing a patent in civil courts, where the costs of litigation fall solely on the patent holder as opposed to the state. "It is clear from these figures that there is no way a community in Namibia could possibly afford to jump on the patent bandwagon. The costs involved make patents the domain of the rich and powerful."[85]

tion: "What is the relationship of the proposal to the granting of patent protection in Thailand?" and ending with the question: "Does the RTG envision a contractual system to handle relationships between Thai healers and foreign researchers in the future?"[86]

On June 30, 1997, more than 200 non-governmental organizations and individuals from dozens of countries around the world signed a letter to U.S. Secretary of State Madeline Albright expressing "concern at the manner in which the United States government is intervening in the domestic affairs of numerous other nations regarding their intellectual property laws."[87] Acknowledging the need for governments to conform with international agreements to which they subscribe, the signatories pointed out to Secretary Albright that it is neither "the United States' responsibility nor its right to interfere with their national democratic processes for doing so."[88]

To date, the Thai government has not heeded the U.S. threat, and the legislation is currently making its way through Parliament.

U.S. consumers are "conservatively estimated" to face $6 billion in higher drug prices due to windfall patent extensions under WTO.[90]

The TRIPs Agreement, Pharmaceuticals and Health

The TRIPs Agreement requires WTO Member countries to have in place 20-year IPR protections for pharmaceuticals by 2005.[89] Patents give pharmaceutical companies the exclusive right to market a particular medication. While the pharmaceutical industry is expected to benefit by increasing its profit margin, consumer groups around the world – and most developing country governments – are concerned that the TRIPs Agreement will impose significant burdens on governments trying to increase public access to medicine.

The U.S. already had stringent IPR protections before the Uruguay Round, yet entry into the WTO required the U.S. to extend patents from 17-year terms to the WTO's 20-year standard. This change has resulted in considerably higher prices in the U.S. for medications that otherwise would have been available as generics. The delay in a generic version of just one drug, ranitidine HCI, will result in additional expenses of $1 billion for U.S. consumers by 2009.[91] A 1995 study on the overall impact of the TRIPs Agreement on consumers found that the U.S. public would be "conservatively estimated" to pay $6 billion in higher drug prices due to windfall drug patent extensions under WTO.[92] The study also found that the TRIPs Agreement would have a significant, negative impact on U.S. healthcare cost containment efforts. The increased direct cost to federal and state government health programs such as Medicaid and Medicare will total nearly $1.25 billion due to patent extension required under the TRIPs Agreement.[93]

For the industrialized countries, the TRIPs Agreement was a key first step in establishing global, enforceable intellectual property rights for pharmaceuticals.[94] However, the TRIPs Agreement does contain several important caveats – such as permitting compulsory licensing and parallel importing — that were designed to allow governments to modify some patent holders' rights in the name of promoting public welfare.

Compulsory licensing allows governments to suspend exclusive marketing rights so that others (such as a generic drug company) can also produce a drug by paying a royalty to the patentholder.[95] Compulsory licensing provides an inventor with a return on investment while also stimulating competition and benefiting the public with lower prices.

All industrialized countries, including the U.S., issue compulsory licenses for a variety of innovations.[96] For instance, in the U.S., the Clean Air Act provides for compulsory licensing of patents related to air pollution control technology. U.S. antitrust authorities often seek compulsory licenses as remedies for problems of monopoly or anti-competitive practices.[97] National Public Radio (NPR) was granted compulsory licenses for noncommercial educational broadcasting use of the repertoires of the American Society of Composers, Authors and Publishers (ASCAP).[98]

The second practice allowed by the TRIPs Agreement is parallel importing.[107] Parallel importing is the practice of importing goods through wholesalers or other third-party intermediaries from countries where goods are cheaper, rather than buying directly from the manufacturer. Parallel importers find the national markets where goods are cheapest and import them into countries with higher prices. While a boon for consumers,

After U.S. Trade Threats Thailand Drops Medicine Access, Pricing Policy

After seven years of U.S. pressure and threats, Thailand finally amended its 1992 Patent Law. Among other things, the amendments disband Thailand's Pharmaceutical Review Board (PRB).[99] The PRB had the authority to control pharmaceutical prices in Thailand.[100] This PRB role was considered a critical public health tool since there are no Thai equivalents to the public health insurance programs, such as Medicaid, that are available to some people in developed countries.[101] The PRB had successfully lowered prices for such life-extending medications as flucanozole, which is used to treat a fatal form of meningitis contracted by one in five AIDS sufferers in Thailand.[102] Flucanozole is marketed by Pfizer, which, until the PRB issued a compulsory license allowing three local companies to make the drug, charged $14 for a daily dose.[103] The price is now $1 for a daily dose.[104] Likewise, the PRB forced down the monthly cost of the AIDS drug zidovudine from a prohibitive $324 in 1992 to just $87 in 1995.[105] Although compulsory licensing is allowed under the TRIPs Agreement, the U.S. justified its relentless campaign against the Thai law on the basis that it was not in compliance with the TRIPs Agreement and, indeed, that the existence of the Pharmaceutical Review Board itself was WTO-inconsistent.[106]

parallel imports are opposed by some manufacturers who seek to engage in significant price discrimination by geographic area.[108] For example, a commonly used antibiotic, Amoxicillin, costs 50 cents a tablet in South Africa compared to 30 cents in New York and only 4 cents in Zimbabwe.[109]

Parallel importing is used in rich and poor countries alike. The U.S. does not currently allow parallel imports for drugs, but does for many other products.[110] In Europe, parallel importing is commonly used in the pharmaceutical industry so smaller nations can take advantage of larger economies' scale of production by importing from more populated neighbors.

The fact that compulsory licensing and parallel importing are allowed in the TRIPs Agreement has not prevented the U.S. government and the pharmaceutical industry from threatening WTO challenges as a means to discourage poor countries from adopting these policies to make medicine more accessible and affordable. Indeed, even the few publicly known industry threats demonstrate that trade associations have taken it upon themselves to threaten countries with WTO challenges. So far, the U.S. government has yet to initiate a formal WTO challenge to compulsory licensing or parallel importing, although numerous countries have been threatened with action.

Industry and the U.S. government often demand levels of intellectual property protection that far exceed the TRIPs Agreement (and U.S.) standards. In fact, the Clinton administration acknowledged this in a State Department report on its effort to force South Africa to repeal its progressive medicines access law: "On the parallel import issue ... U.S. attorneys note that under the terms of the TRIPs Agreement, disputes related to parallel importation are not subject to WTO dispute settlement procedure."[111] Therefore, launching formal WTO challenges

---

World Health Organization: WTO Limits Access to Medicines in Poor Nations

In a resolution to the Fifty-First World Health Assembly, the WHO Executive Board stated that:

"Concerned about the situation in which one third of the world's population has no guaranteed access to essential drugs, in which new world trade Agreements may have a negative impact on local manufacturing capacity and the access to and prices of pharmaceuticals in developing countries ..." nations must "ensure that public health rather than commercial interests have primacy in pharmaceutical and health policies and to review their options under the [WTO] Agreement on Trade Related Aspects of Intellectual Property Rights to safeguard access to essential drugs." [112]

In addition, the WHO report requested that the health body's director-general assist WTO Member states to "analyze the pharmaceutical and public health implications of Agreements overseen by the World Trade Organization and to develop appropriate policies and regulatory measures." [113]

would not be in the interest of either the U.S. or the pharmaceutical industry, since such challenges would not likely be successful and would render TRIPs threats ineffective in the future.

Already, however, there are several prominent instances where threats of TRIPs actions have been enough to discourage the adoption of public health measures. For instance, industry pressure led Guatemala to drop initiatives advanced by world health bodies like the United Nations Children's Fund (UNICEF) and the World Health Organization (WHO). The following cases outline efforts on behalf of the pharmaceutical and agricultural industry to use the threat of challenges and sanctions under the TRIPs Agreement to force nations to change their laws.

Threat 2: U.S., Gerber Trade Threats Pressure Guatemala to Weaken Infant Formula Law

In an attempt to reduce its infant mortality rate, Guatemala passed a law and issued regulations in 1983 designed to encourage new mothers to breast feed their infants and to fully understand the health threats to their babies of using infant formula as a substitute for breast milk. The law, which implemented the terms of the WHO Code on Marketing of Breast-Milk Substitutes, included prohibitions on the use of words like "humanized breastmilk" or "equivalent to breastmilk."[114] To be accessible to illiterate people, the WHO Code and Guatemala's regulations also included prohibitions against visual depictions of infants that "idealize the use of bottle feeding."[115]

One infant formula producer, Gerber Food® (Gerber), bridled at the Guatemalan law and its regulations because the company's trademarked logo includes the picture of a pudgy infant, the "Gerber Baby." Shortly before the Uruguay Round's effective date, a Gerber vice president wrote to Guatemala's president, implicitly threatening some form of trade sanctions.[116] The dispute pit a nation trying to protect its most vulnerable citizens, its newborns, against a transnational food producer (motto: "Babies are our business"[117]) insistent not only on selling infant formula but in marketing its products in a manner that Guatemalan law deemed misleading.

According to UNICEF, 1.5 million infants die each year because their mothers are induced to replace breast feeding with artificial breast milk substitutes.[118] UNICEF reports that the major cause of death is fatal infant diarrhea caused by mothers in poor countries mixing the infant formula with unclean water.[119] UNICEF attributes the fact that only 44% of infants in the developing world (even less in the industrialized countries) are breast-fed to the relentless promotion of breast milk substitutes.[120]

A global citizens movement in the 1970s, including a boycott against the infant formula giant Nestle, resulted in political pressure to establish public health rules on infant formula marketing.[121] The World Health Organization and UNICEF drafted the Code of Marketing of Breast Milk Substitutes to help protect the lives of infants by promoting breast-feeding over artificial formulas.[122] The Code also applies to baby food when it is marketed or otherwise represented to be suitable for use as a partial or total replacement of breast milk.[123]

In 1983, Guatemala enacted a law covering the marketing of breast milk substitutes based on the WHO Code, implementing it by a presidential decree that incorporated the WHO Code's ban on the use of packaging that would induce illiterate parents to associate formula with healthy, fat babies, including pictures on labels for baby food for children under the age of two. The law and regulation also require that milk substitute producers clearly state the superiority of breast-feeding on their labels, and prohibit both the free distribution of samples without approval of the Guatemalan Health Ministry and the direct marketing of the product by sales personnel.[124]

With the prominent exception of U.S.-incorporated Gerber, all of Guatemala's domestic and foreign suppliers of infant formula and other breast milk substitutes made the necessary changes to their packaging to comply with the Guatemalan law.[125] Guatemalan infant mortality rates dropped significantly after the law passed, and UNICEF held up Guatemala as a model of the Code's success in its literature.[126]

U.S. Plans to Challenge EU Country-of-Origin Labeling at WTO

The U.S. has announced it will challenge EU country-of-origin labeling requirements for agricultural and food products as a violation of the TRIPs Agreement.[127] The U.S. claims that the EU's procedures for country-of-origin labeling violate the trademarks of U.S. corporations, which are protected forms of intellectual property under the WTO TRIPs Agreement.[128]

Gerber was potentially in violation of the labeling law on many fronts. It allegedly marketed the formula directly to new mothers in hospitals and provided free samples to doctors and day care centers, but most importantly it refused to remove the "Gerber Baby" from its label or state the superiority of breast-feeding over formula.[129] The Guatemalan Ministry of Health made numerous attempts to negotiate with Gerber to seek compliance with the labeling law.[130] In autumn 1992, Gerber submitted its formula packaging to the Guatemalan Food & Drug Registration and Control Division (like the FDA in the U.S.) for approval. The FDRC requested that Gerber remove the baby image and add the words "Breastmilk is the best for baby."[131] Gerber resisted changing its labeling through the regulatory process. It asked for a four-month extension to make changes; it filed an injunction against the Ministry of Health's attempt to require labeling changes; and it asked for permission to continue importing its products to Guatemala while the regulatory enforcement process continued.[132] In November of 1993, the Guatemalan Administrative Tribunal ruled in favor of the Minister of Health[133] – five years after the labeling regulations went into effect and ten years after the law was enacted.

Instead of complying, Gerber opened a new line of attack on the grounds that the health rule violated international trademark rights and agreements. In December 1993, Gerber filed a statement with the U.S. trade representative encouraging the suspension of Guatemala's General System of Preferences (GSP) benefits because the labeling law was a "*de facto* expropriation of Gerber's Trademark."[134] Ultimately, Gerber withdrew its GSP certification challenge, but at the same time it continued to threaten Guatemala on other trade-related fronts.

Gerber threatened the Guatemalan government with a challenge under the WTO because of trademark infringement.[135] The letter includes an explicit threat: "Upon the favorable and permanent resolution of this matter, we will withdraw all complaints before the … GATT." Though Guatemala prohibited the use of the "Gerber Baby" to sell infant formula, Guatemala was prepared to respect and protect this trademark logo from potential competitors.[136] Although Gerber cannot itself launch a WTO challenge, it raised the specter of a challenge to intimidate the Guatemalan government and defend its "rights before the CBI, GATT and in the Congress of the United States of America."[137]

According to Gerber's letter to the president of Guatemala, the "Gerber Baby" is an integral part of its trademark,[138] and as such, the Uruguay Round TRIPs Agreement would provide Gerber with new trademark protections. By 1995, Gerber's threats of WTO action, taken seriously by the Guatemalan government at home and at its Washington embassy, succeeded. Guatemala changed the law so that imported baby food products would be exempt from Guatemala's stringent infant food labeling policy.[139]

Threats of WTO action have a particularly high likelihood of success when wielded against developing countries like Guatemala, which often lack the financial and technical means with which to successfully defend policies attacked in WTO tribunals in Geneva, Switzerland.

Unfortunately, Guatemala had no in-house expertise on the question of the WTO legality of its implementation of the WHO/UNICEF Code.[140] WTO practice would have made it difficult for Guatemala to call Gerber's bluff and fight the case in the WTO. Nothing in the Uruguay Round Agreements formally prevents a party to a WTO case from hiring outside legal counsel with expertise in international commercial law. However, the informal practice is that if a party to a WTO panel hearing objects to the other party's delegation, the WTO panel decides if the objection is valid.[141] Thus, the deck in trade disputes is further stacked against poor countries, many of whom cannot afford permanent staff dedicated to defending possible legal challenges under WTO Agreements.[142] The WTO practice of allowing rich adversaries to object to the delegations of poor countries undermines poor countries' meaningful participation in the WTO – and makes threats of WTO challenges enormously powerful tools to forestall the adoption of public health safeguards by poor countries that need them the most.

Indeed, it is highly possible that the Guatemalan law would have withstood a U.S. challenge at the WTO, because the TRIPs Agreement contains a public health exception to intellectual property protections. Article 8 of the TRIPs Agreement allows WTO Members to "adopt measures necessary to protect public health and nutrition [and to take] appropriate measures … needed to prevent the abuse of intellectual property rights by right holders … provided that such measures are consistent with the provisions of this Agreement."[143] Article 8 "exceptions" are on their face weak and even tautological, as they require that deviations from the TRIPs Agreement comply with the TRIPs Agreement.[144] However, it is difficult to conceive of a situation where such an exception would more likely apply, since a public health crisis (an epidemic of marketing-induced infant mortality) had been identified and international efforts to address the crisis had been codified by the United Nations through its Code on the Marketing of Breast Milk Substitutes. Indeed, by concentrating on the marketing practices of infant formula manufacturers, the WHO/UNICEF Code and the consumer campaigns are at the very least tacitly operating on the assumption that the manufacturers are, in the language of the TRIPs Agreement, "abusing their intellectual property rights" at the expense of babies' lives.

Further, TRIPs Agreement provisions on trademarks primarily set rules governing competition among corporations and require WTO Members to protect trademark holders from infringement by competitors.[145] The TRIPs Agreement does not directly address the issue of trademark "infringement" by a WTO Member in the interest of public health.

However, TRIPs Agreement Article 20 prevents governments from "unjustifiably encumber[ing the use of a trademark] by special requirements, such as … use in a manner detrimental to its capability to distinguish the goods or services of one undertaking from those of other undertakings."[146] This is the provision that would most likely be used in a challenge to legislation implementing the WHO/UNICEF infant marketing code, and it forms the core of Gerber's threats. Gerber argued that a ban on its identifying logo effectively was an expropriation of its intellectual property.[147]

Indeed, Gerber's basic right to a certain level of treatment is the product of TRIPs provisions that confer absolute rights to intellectual property holders. This is a departure from the nondiscrimination-focused provisions of the original GATT, which require countries only to provide treatment to foreign products equal to or no less favorable than that provided to products made domestically. Thus, it did not matter that the substance and implementation of the Guatemalan law were both nondiscriminatory – that is, that the law applied equally to domestic and foreign formula and baby food companies. Under the TRIPs Agreement, corporations like Gerber have a right to a certain standard of treatment. These absolute rights could serve to shield transnational companies like Gerber from compliance with nondiscriminatory public health laws.

The pharmaceutical industry, both in the U.S. and Europe, appears to have learned a lesson from the Gerber experience in Guatemala. It has launched a campaign of TRIPs Agreement threats against countries that are trying to make medicine more affordable and accessible, even when the actions countries take are explicitly WTO-legal, as the following case describes.

WTO Trumps World Health Organization Code?

Even though 104 of the WTO's 134 Members have ratified the WHO/UNICEF Breast Milk Substitute Marketing Code,[148] the international agreement and countries' implementations of it are exposed to challenge under WTO rules. Absent a "hold harmless" clause, newer international commitments take precedence over older ones, meaning WTO trumps the WHO Code. The TRIPs Agreement constitutes an effective weapon for industry and governments acting on their behalf to undermine international efforts to improve public health in the developing world.

Threat 3: Pharmaceutical Industry Threatens South African WTO Challenge Over Medicine Law

[USTR did not] pursue unthinkingly all of the international IPR concerns of the so-called innovator pharmaceutical industry. We have been balanced in our approach to the protection of pharmaceutical products. The relevant provisions of the TRIPs Agreement reflects this problem:

TRIPs specifically sets out a considerable number of conditions under which compulsory licensing may be utilized for use by those countries wishing to impose limits on intellectual property protection within its own borders.

TRIPs contains no transition period phasing-out the use of these compulsory licensing provisions, they may be relied upon for the indefinite future.[149]

— Former U.S. Trade Representative Mickey Kantor

The international pharmaceutical industry, with assistance from the Clinton administration, has fought to reverse the effort by former South African President Nelson Mandela to make health care and medicines more accessible for South Africans. The South African Medicines Law was enacted in 1997 but has not yet been fully implemented.[152] When it is,[153] it would encourage the use of generic drugs, prohibit pharmaceutical companies from paying doctors bounties for prescribing their products (already illegal in the U.S. under anti-kickback laws) and institute parallel importing as a means to control pharmaceuticals costs.[154] South Africa's Medicines Law would also allow the government to require compulsory licensing – so that competing producers (for instance, drug companies) could obtain licenses to produce drugs in exchange for royalty payments to a drug's developer with cost and profit built in. Under Article 31 of the TRIPs Agreement, compulsory licensing is legal if royalties are paid to the patent holder.[155]

The South African pharmaceutical industry group is composed of subsidiaries of large foreign pharmaceutical corporations and is closely linked with PhRMA, the U.S. Pharmaceutical Research and Manufacturing Association.[156] Thus, the South

U.S. Industry's WTO Threat To Israeli Generics Law

The U.S. drug trade association, Pharmaceutical Research and Manufacturers of America (PhRMA), threatened Israel with a WTO challenge over proposed legislation concerning generic drugs.[150] The Israeli legislative proposal would allow domestic drug companies to produce generic versions of drugs for research and development before their patents expire. The goal of the legislation is to make less expensive pharmaceuticals available to consumers promptly after a monopoly patent expires, rather than effectively extending the term of monopoly control by forbidding generic producers from gearing up for future production until after the patent expires.

"We're looking at the option in terms of international treaties, like the WTO TRIPs Agreement," said Thomas Bombelles, PhRMA's assistant vice president for international affairs.[151]

African and U.S. pharmaceutical industries are presenting a united front in opposition to the South African law with the head of the South African Pharmaceutical Manufacturers' Association (PMA) threatening the South African government with a WTO challenge.[157]

Mirryena Deeb, chief executive of PMA, said in a September 1997 press conference in Johannesburg that the trade association's members had consulted with their parent companies and were prepared to take their complaint to the WTO if South Africa didn't change the proposal. "If they don't alter it we will have no choice," she said. "[T]he issue is being pursued with a mind to going to the WTO." [158]

Several weeks later, U.S. Ambassador to South Africa James Joseph sent a letter to a South African parliamentary committee, urging the government to eliminate the parallel import provisions of the proposed health bill. "The U.S. government," the letter said, "is gravely concerned over the public policy implications of a law which could infringe on intellectual property rights."[159] Joseph's letter claimed that Switzerland, France and the European Union had made similar requests.[160] The Clinton administration even raised the industry complaint during President Clinton's state visit to South Africa in March 1998

"NAFTA for Africa" Bill:
End-Run Around Compulsory Licensing, Parallel Importing

In 1999, provisions of the controversial African Growth and Opportunity Act (AGOA), dubbed "NAFTA for Africa" by the U.S. press, brought a new constituency into the national trade debate. The HIV/AIDS community strongly opposed the bill because to be eligible for narrow new trade benefits, African countries were forced to comply with the U.S.'s radical conception of intellectual property rights. By creating a legal basis beyond the WTO TRIPs Agreement to pressure African countries, this AGOA provision would have given the U.S. leverage to discourage the adoption of parallel importing and compulsory licensing by African countries worried about losing trade benefits.[161]

HIV/AIDS activists in the U.S. and Europe actively opposed the "NAFTA for Africa" bill but endorsed a competing "HOPE for Africa" proposal sponsored by Rep. Jesse Jackson Jr., an Illinois Democrat.[162] Unlike AGOA, the HOPE measure increased funding for HIV/AIDS prevention and treatment, and prohibited the U.S. from pressuring African governments to eliminate TRIPs-compliant laws that make pharmaceuticals more available and affordable to the public.[163]

Although a massive corporate coalition, including oil companies, and the Clinton administration, was pushing the AGOA, there was little popular support for the bill. A national coalition of African American religious leaders and hundreds of African civic organizations called on Congress to reject AGOA. In April 1999, hundreds of HOPE supporters joined Rep. Jackson in downtown Washington, D.C., to condemn "NAFTA for Africa's" potential to worsen the HIV/AIDS epidemic in Africa and to call upon the pharmaceutical industry to lift its opposition to parallel importing and compulsory licensing.[164] In July, after ACT-UP was refused a meeting with one of AGOA's leading sponsors, Democratic Rep. Charles Rangel, activists confronted him at his home in Harlem, New York. Rangel's neighbors were perplexed that the congressman would support the pharmaceutical industry over the plight of HIV/AIDS patients in Africa.[165]

and during subsequent meetings between Vice President Gore and Vice President Mbeki in early 1999.[166] The U.S. Trade Representative suspended some of South Africa's GSP benefits (Generalized System of Preferences) and has placed them on the so-called Section 301 "watch list."[167]

The U.S. and others are making this TRIPs Agreement threat despite the fact that both compulsory licensing and parallel importing are commonly used and legal under the TRIPs Agreement.[168] Many nations not only allow parallel imports, but some national antitrust authorities, including the European Community and Japan, actively take steps to prevent manufacturers from discouraging or impeding parallel imports.[169]

State Department Memo Details U.S. Vice President Gore's Role in Attacking South Africa Medicines Law

In a February 1999 report to a member of Congress, the State Department details the efforts undertaken by Vice President Gore in his role on the U.S.-South Africa Binational Commission to undermine South Africa's Medicines Law.[170] According to the report, in August 1998, Gore made the South African legislation "a central focus" of discussions held with then-South African Deputy President Mbeki.[171] Indeed, the next Binational Commission meeting held in February 1999 was used by Gore to again raise the issue of repealing the South African Medicines law with Mbeki.[172]

In response to protests by HIV/AIDS community activists at Gore's presidential campaign stops in June 1999, a "senior Gore advisor" defended Gore's role in pressuring South Africa to eliminate the Medicines Law, which would increase the availability of pharmaceuticals, including AIDs medicines: "Obviously the Vice President's got to stick up for the commercial interests of U.S. companies."[173] However, repeated demonstrations at subsequent Gore campaign stops have pressured the Vice President to moderate his stance somewhat.

In a June 25, 1999, letter to Rep. James Clyburn (D-SC), the chair of the Congressional Black Caucus, Gore states: "I support South Africa's efforts to enhance health care for its people – including efforts to engage in compulsory licensing and parallel importing of pharmaceuticals – so long as they are done in a way consistent with international Agreements."[174] His statement represents a *rhetorical* shift but, unless it is accompanied by an actual *change* in U.S. policy toward the law, not much more. In fact, his statement is logically inconsistent, since parallel licensing is completely legal – in any legislative form – under the WTO TRIPs Agreement. Indeed, the phrasing of Gore's statement echoes the doublespeak of GATT provisions that limit how governments can take action to safeguard human health: Governments are free to protect the public or set their own environmental standards *as long as* the actions are consistent with the GATT itself. Whether the Clinton-Gore administration will change its stance toward South Africa's medicine access policies remains to be seen.

In addition, such practices have not adversely affected the pharmaceutical industry's profit margin. The pharmaceutical industry routinely records profits much higher than the health care industry average. Between 1996 and 1998, the 35 health care companies listed in the Standard & Poor's 500, an index of the largest U.S. corporations, increased their profits by 6.3% on average. But the top ten pharmaceutical companies increased their profits an average of 17.5% — and six of these firms made the Standard & Poors' top 50.[175] The CEOs of these top six firms took home $212.8 million in salaries, bonuses and stock options over the same three-year period — about $11.8 million a year on average.[176] The enormous profitability and executive compensation in the pharmaceutical industry that has occurred while practices like compulsory licensing and parallel importing have been in place make a strong case that these policies provide a more than reasonable return on investment in exchange for needed access to medicines.

U.S. Worried About "Rollback" of WTO TRIPs Agreement in Seattle

The TRIPs Agreement currently includes a phase-in period for developing countries. The phase-in period means that whereas the Agreement went into effect in 1995 for industrialized countries, the developing world was given a five-year grace period. This period is now over, and several developing countries have circulated so-called "non-papers" in the WTO suggesting an extension of the phase-in period.[177]

Article 27.3(b) of the TRIPs Agreement – dealing with the patenting of life forms – causes the most concern. As it stands, Article 27.3(b) calls for protection of intellectual property over plant varieties either by patent or by any other "effective" system.[178] The end of the phase-in period essentially means that this Article must take effect now for all WTO Members. Nongovernmental organizations from both developed and developing countries have, however, called for a moratorium on the full implementation of this Article "until a substantial review ... is conducted."[179] Indeed, the Uruguay Round Agreements include an obligation to review Article 27.3(b) in 1999, before the phase-in period for developing countries runs out,[180] though there is disagreement as to whether the review should include substantial revision or merely focus on the status of implementation.[181]

In addition to this very specific concern about the patenting of life forms, the African Group has presented to the WTO a list of proposals regarding the TRIPs Agreement, all designed to allow developing countries to participate more effectively in WTO work connected to the TRIPs Agreement and to ensure the protection of indigenous knowledge under the Agreement.[182]

These and other initiatives have led the U.S. to back away from its earlier demand that the intellectual property topic should be central to the Seattle Ministerial, with a view to tightening the existing TRIPs requirements. Now the U.S. is fearful that new negotiations could lead to "backsliding" in the current WTO TRIPs Agreement.[183] Thus, the U.S. is calling for freestanding bio-tech talks and prefers to deal with the issue of genetically modified organisms in the context of the WTO Agreement on Agriculture, so as to avoid issues of indigenous knowledge and community rights. The mandatory review of Article 27.3(b) of the TRIPs Agreement could mean that the U.S. will still have to address these concerns in Seattle, but if the U.S. has its way, the review will be reduced to a "meaningless exchange of information about implementation."[184]

State Department Documents Clinton Administration's Fight Against South Africa's AIDS Medicine Access Law

The Clinton administration's efforts to force South Africa to "repeal, suspend, or terminate" its Medicines Law is proudly detailed in a State Department report to the U.S. House Committee on International Relations. [185]

- The representation of U.S. industry views at a South African parliamentary hearing in June of 1997 by U.S. Ambassador James Joseph did not yield the desired result.

- In July of 1997, then-Secretary of Commerce Richard Daley took up the matter with his South African counterpart. This led to a revision of South Africa's proposed legislation, addressing some of the U.S. industry concern. The U.S. was still not satisfied and engaged in a "full court press" in late 1997 to persuade South Africa to suspend the law entirely. [186]

- In the beginning of 1998, U.S. Trade Representative for Africa, Rosa Whitaker, went to South Africa to make the case for U.S. industry, [187] and Daley met with the South African health minister. [188]

- In August 1998, Vice President Gore spearheaded the "Vice President's Plan for a Negotiated Solution" between the two governments. [189] The U.S. would restore South Africa's suspended Generalized System of Preferences benefits "as progress was made in [the] negotiations." [190]

- South Africa then asked the U.S. government to use its influence to end the U.S. pharmaceutical industry's South African Supreme Court challenge against the Medicines Law, so as to give legislators breathing room to redraft the law to make the terms of its implementation clearer. The U.S. decided that the legal challenge strengthened its negotiating position and told South Africa that it had no power to interfere. [191]

- With the administration still strongly pressuring South Africa, the national AIDS activist group ACT-UP disrupted five of Vice President Gore's campaign events in June 1999. [192] After public health advocates had tried unsuccessfully for years to persuade the Clinton administration to stop attacking South African parallel importing and compulsory licensing, the ACT-UP protests finally attracted significant media coverage to the issue: "While the news media did not find the deaths of now two million people a year in the world compelling, the disruption of five campaign stops did get some attention," noted Robert Weissman, editor of the *Multinational Monitor*. [193]

- After a series of meetings between administration policy staff and the activists, Gore issued a statement denying that the U.S. was pressuring South Africa and also promising support for AIDS prevention and treatment in South Africa. Gore's statement was quickly dismissed by AIDS and public health advocates as vague and as not committing the administration to any real policy change.

—————————— CHAPTER **4** ENDNOTES ——————————

[1] WTO, Agreement on Trade Related Aspects of Intellectual Property (WTO "TRIPs Agreement") at Article 27.3(b).

[2] *Id.*

[3] *Id.*

[4] Patents have been granted to Human Genome Sciences, a U.S.-based company for human genes. *See* U.S. 5,597,709, WO 9520398, EP74158. It has filed patent applications covering over 1 million partial human gene sequences. Another U.S. company, Biocyte, has received patents on human umbilical cord blood cells. Any doctor wishing to use them in surgery must pay royalties. *See* U.S. Patent and Trademark Office, Washington, D.C. for information.

[5] WTO, TRIPs Agreement at Article 27.3(a).

[6] Ralph Nader and James Love, "Federally Funded Pharmaceutical Inventions," testimony in U.S. Senate, Special Committee on Aging, *The Federal Government's Investment in New Drug Research and Development: Are We Getting Our Money's Worth?*, Serial No. 103-1, Washington, D.C.: U.S. Government Printing Office, Feb. 24, 1993.

[7] WTO, TRIPs Agreement at Article 65 and Article 66.

[8] The WTO TRIPs Agreement also allows countries that choose to do so to adopt a *sui generis* system, that is, to devise their own legal form of intellectual property protection – and not necessarily rely on patenting *per se* – for plant varieties. Article 27.3(b). However, the TRIPs Agreement does not clarify what other type of IPR regimes would be permitted, and a country's IPR laws can always be challenged under the WTO dispute system. It is thus doubtful whether the *sui generis* system is a viable instrument for allowing countries flexibility in balancing IPRs with public interest concerns.

[9] 35 U.S.C. 154(a)(2).

[10] The WTO TRIPs Agreement Article 27.1 reads, "[P]atents shall be available for any inventions, whether products or processes, in all fields of technology, provided they are new, involve an inventive step and are capable of industrial application." Article 27.3(b) reads, "Members shall provide for the protection of plant varieties either by patents or by an effective *sui generis* system or by any combination thereof."

[11] WTO, TRIPs Agreement at Article 27.3(b).

[12] India, Pakistan, Argentina and Egypt, for example, had to change the coverage of their intellectual property laws to comply with the TRIPs, as did the U.S.

[13] WTO, TRIPs Agreement at Article 27.3(a).

[14] WIPO is a specialized U.N. agency, responsible for promoting state cooperation in the protection of intellectual property and charged with the administration of various multilateral treaties dealing with this subject. Some of these treaties may contain enforcement provisions, but WIPO itself is a promoter and administrator rather than enforcer of intellectual property rights.

[15] For instance, India and Argentina.

[16] United Nations Development Programme (UNDP), *Human Development Report 1999*, Geneva (1999) at 68.

[17] "UNDP Report Criticizes WTO TRIPS and CTE," *BRIDGES Weekly Trade News Digest*, vol. 3, no. 28, Jul. 19, 1999.

[18] United Nations Development Programme (UNDP), *Human Development Report 1999*, Geneva (1999) at 68.

[19] *Id.*

[20] Laudeline Auriol and Francis Pham, "What Pattern in Patents?" *OECD Observer*, Dec. 1992 at 15.

[21] *See* Chapter 8 on Dispute Resolution for more on cross-sectoral sanctions.

[22] WTO, India - Patent Protection for Pharmaceuticals and Agricultural Chemical Products (WT/DS50/R), Report of the Panel, Sep. 5, 1997, at Para. 7.1.

[23] WTO, India - Patent Protection for Pharmaceutical and Agricultural Chemical Products (WT/DS50/R), Report of the Panel, Sep. 5, 1997, Annex I at 69.

[24] All WTO countries were required to implement most aspects of the Uruguay Round as a "single understanding." However, certain agreements had phased in application dates for developing countries. These include inter alia, the TRIPs and TRIMs.

[25] WTO, India - Patent Protection for Pharmaceutical and Agricultural Chemical Products (WT/DS50), Complaint by the U.S.

[26] WTO, India - Patent Protection for Pharmaceutical and Agricultural Chemical Products (WT/DS50/R), Report of the Panel, Sep. 5, 1997, at Paras. 6.10-6.12

[27] *Id.* at Paras. 7.26-7.28.

[28] "India's New Patent Law 'By Year-End,'" *Marketletter* (London), Jul. 26, 1999.

[29] *See* Amartya Sen, *Poverty and Famine, An Essay in Entitlement and Deprivation*, Oxford: Clarendon Press (1981).

[30] *See* Peter Uvin, *The State of World Hunger,* Part of Series of Annual Reports on hunger from the Alan Shawn Feinstein World Hunger Program, Brown University, Providence (1993) at 13.

[31] U.N. Food and Agriculture Organization, *Food supply situation and crop prospects in Sub-Saharan Africa*, Global Information and Early Warning System on Food and Agriculture, Annual FAO Report No. 2, Rome, Aug. 1999.

[32] *United Nation's World Food Programme Statistics 1998*, "Active Projects/Operations in 1998," Rome: World Food Programme (1998) at Table 8.

[33] UNDP, *Human Development Report 1999*, Geneva (1999), Table 20 (Food Security and Nutrition) at 214.

[34] *Id.*

[35] National Academy of Sciences, *Recommended Daily Allowances*, 10th Ed. (1989).

[36] R. Gommes, "Climatic Risk Management," *U.N. Food and Agriculture Organization*, FAO Research Extension Division, May 28, 1999.

[37] UNDP, *Human Development Report 1999*, Geneva (1999) at 68.

[38] Martha L. Crouch, *How the Terminator Terminates: An Explanation for the Non-Scientist of a Remarkable Patent for Killing Second Generation Seeds of Crop Plants*, Edmunds Institute (1998) at 1.

[39] Tom Bearden, "High-Tech Crops," *Newshour with Jim Lehrer*, Aug. 12, 1999.

[40] U.S. Patent 5,723,765: Control of Plant Gene Expression, by Delta and Pine Land Company, Mar. 1998. Delta and Pine was subsequently purchased by Monsanto.

[41] Martha L. Crouch, *How the Terminator Terminates: An Explanation for the Non-Scientist of a Remarkable Patent for Killing Second Generation Seeds of Crop Plants,* Edmunds Institute, 1998, at 6.

[42] Matthew Townsend, "Meet the Company that Would Privatise Nature Itself," *The Melbourne Age*, Dec. 15, 1998; Louise Jury, "UN Aid Agencies Slam Monsanto's Campaign," *London Independent*, Jul. 25, 1998.

[43] Martha L. Crouch, *How the Terminator Terminates: An Explanation for the Non-Scientist of a Remarkable Patent for Killing Second Generation Seeds of Crop Plants*, Edmunds Institute (1998) at 7.

[44] "Monsanto Will Wait for Studies on Disputed New Gene Technology," *St. Louis Post Dispatch*, Apr. 23, 1999.

[45] Lavanya Rajamani, "The Cartagena Protocol - A Battle Over Trade or Biosafety?" *Third World Resurgence,* No. 104/5, Apr./May 1999.

[46] Dr. William Heffernan, *Consolidation in the Food and Agriculture System*, University of Missouri-Colombia, Feb. 5 1999, at 5.

[47] Leland Swenson, President of the National Farmers Union, "Agricultural Concentration," Testimony to the House Agriculture Committee, Feb. 11, 1999.

[48] Dr. William Heffernan, *Consolidation in the Food and Agriculture System*, University of Missouri-Colombia, Feb. 5 1999, at 5.

[49] "Traitor Technology: The Terminator's Wider Implications," *Rural Advancement Foundation International Communique,* Jan./Feb. 1999, on file with Public Citizen.

[50] Vandana Shiva, *Biopiracy: The Plunder of Nature and Knowledge,* Boston: South End Press (1997) at 88.

[51] *Id* at 89.

[52] 1992 Convention on Biological Diversity at Article 16(5).

[53] *Id.* at 8(j).

[54] Resolution 5/89, "Farmers' Rights," Report of the Conference of FAO, Twenty-Fifth Session, Rome, International Undertaking on Plant Genetic Resources, Nov. 11-29, 1989. At Annex to the FAO International Undertaking on Plant Genetic Resources.

[55] WTO, TRIPs Agreement at Article 64.1.

[56] WTO, TRIPs Agreement at Article 27.3(c).

[57] Rural Advancement Foundation International, "Basmati Rice Patent," *Geno-Type*, Apr. 1, 1998.

[58] WTO, TRIPs Agreement at Article 64.1 .

[59] "Plant Breeders Wrongs," Report by Rural Advancement Foundation International and Heritage Seed Curators Australia, Aug. 1998, at 4.

[60] *Id.* at 19.

[61] U.S. Patent No. 5663484, Description 2.3, Sep. 2, 1997.

[62] "Plant Breeders Wrongs," Rural Advancement Foundation International and Heritage Seed Curators Australia, Aug. 1998, case no. HSCA/RAFI-136/137/138 (Basmati rice).

[63] Prangtip Daorueng, "Farmers Protest Copycat 'Jasmine' Rice," *InterPress Service*, May 13, 1998.

[64] Letter to U.S. Ambassador to India, Apr. 3, 1998, signed by Research Foundation for Science, Technology and Ecology; Bharatiya Kisan Union; NAVDANYA; Forum on Biotechnology and Food Security; Kisan Trust; Swashdi Science Movement; and others, on file at Public Citizen.

[65] Vandana Shiva, *Biopiracy, The Plunder of Nature and Knowledge*, Boston: South End Press (1997) at 69.

[66] John F. Burns, "Tradition in India vs. A Patent in the U.S.," *New York Times*, Sep. 15, 1995.

[67] Joris Kocken and Gerda van Roozendaal, "The Neem Tree Debate," *Biotechnology and Development Monitor*, Mar. 1997 at 8-11.

[68] *Id.*

[69] *Id.*

[70] *Id.*

[71] "Global Attack on U.S. Firm's Neem Patent," *India Abroad, Ethnic News Watch*, Sep. 22, 1995.

[72] *Id.*

[73] *Id.*

[74] "Thailand: Tussle Over Fungi Strains Brings Painful Lessons," *InterPress Service*, Sep. 4, 1998.

[75] *Id.*

[76] *See,* Thai Network on Biodiversity and Community Rights, "Rationale and Background to the Draft Thai Traditional Medicine and Local Knowledge Protection and Promotion Act as approved in principle by the cabinet on Jul. 15, 1997," on file with Public Citizen.

[77] "Thailand: Tussle Over Fungi Strains Brings Painful Lessons," *InterPress Service*, Sep. 4, 1998.

[78] *Id.*

[79] Arindam Mukherjee, "Say No To Kasmati," *Outlook*, Jun. 25, 1997, and "Farmers Protest Copycat 'Jasmine' Rice," *InterPress Service*, May 13, 1998.

[80] "Thailand: Tussle Over Fungi Strains Brings Painful Lessons," *InterPress Service*, Sep. 4, 1998.

[81] *Id.*

[82] Letter from the U.S. State Department to the Royal Thai Government, Apr. 21, 1997, on file with Public Citizen.

[83] Gaia Foundation, "WIPO's Mission Impossible," Published by Genetic Resources Action International (GRAIN) in its quarterly newsletter, *Seedling,* Barcelona, Spain, Sep. 1998, at 10.

[84] *Id.*

[85] *Id.*

[86] Letter from the U.S. State Department to the Royal Thai Government, Apr. 21, 1997, on file with Public Citizen.

[87] Kristin Dawkins, "U.S. Unilateralism: A Threat to Global Sustainability?" *BRIDGES Weekly Trade News Digest,* Vol. 1, No. 4, Oct. 1997, at 11.

[88] *Id.*

[89] WTO, TRIPs Agreement at Article 33.

[90] Stephen W. Schondelmeyer, *Economic Impact of GATT Patent Extension on Currently Marketed Drugs,* PRIME Institute, College of Pharmacy, University of Minnesota, Mar. 1995, at 6.

[91] *Id.* at Table 1.

[92] *Id.* at 6.

[93] *Id* at 7.

[94] The U.S. had announced its goal to strengthen the TRIPs Agreement in subsequent GATT negotiations. However, its position seems to be wavering as it fears that developing country opposition to the TRIPs Agreement could lead to a "roll-back" of existing TRIPs positions. *See* "U.S. Wants TRIPS Off Seattle Agenda," *Washington Trade Daily*, Aug. 5, 1999.

[95] WTO, TRIPs Agreement at Article 31(h).

[96] 42 U.S.C., Ch. 85, Sec. 7408

[97] Consumer Project on Technology, *Frequently asked questions about compulsory licenses,* Jan. 20, 1999.

[98] *Id.*

[99] USTR, *1999 National Trade Estimates Report,* (1999), at 403; *see also* U.S. Trade Representative *National Trade Estimate Reports* from 1995-1999. (These reports detail a campaign begun by the Pharmaceutical Manufacturers Association in 1991 to prevent Thailand from adopting a patents law that would increase patent protection for pharmaceuticals for 20 years, but also create a Pharmaceutical Review Board that would ensure that the public had access to necessary medications.)

[100] Aphaluck Bhatiasevi, "Patents Law: Groups Urge Review of Amendments," *Bangkok Post,* Aug. 17, 1999.

[101] *Id.*

[102] Sarah Boseley, "U.S. Attempts to Stop Developing Countries Producing Cheap AIDS Drugs Have Become a Political Time Bomb," *The Guardian (London),* Aug. 11, 1999.

[103] *Id.*

[104] *Id.*

[105] *Id.*

[106] USTR, *1997 National Trade Estimates*, (1997) at 365. ("Thailand is in the process of amending its patent law to comply with the WTO Agreement on Trade-Related Aspects of Intellectual Property Rights (TRIPs). The Thai legislature is expected in 1997 to consider a bill abolishing the Pharmaceutical Review Board.")

[107] WTO, TRIPs Agreement at Article 6: "For the purposes of dispute settlement under this Agreement . . . nothing in this Agreement shall be used to address the issue of the exhaustion of intellectual property rights." (This provision means that the TRIPs Agreement is silent – and WTO Members are free to decide for themselves – on when the rights of a manufacturer over its intellectual property have been exhausted. The premise of parallel importing policies is that, having already sold its product, the manufacturer has exhausted its rights over it, and cannot claim an intellectual property violation.)

[108] D.A. Malueg and M. Schwartz, "Parallel Imports, Demand Dispersion and International Price Discrimination," U.S. Department of Justice -- Antitrust Division, 1993, *cited* in James Love, "The Comments of the Consumer Project on Technology to the Portfolio Committee on Health Parliament, Cape Town Medicines and Related Substances Control Amendment Bill and South African Reform of Pharmaceutical Policies," Oct. 6, 1997.

[109] Donald G. McNeil, "South Africa's Bitter Pill for World's Drug Makers," *The New York Times*, Mar. 29, 1998.

[110] Consumer Project on Technology, "Health Care and IP: Parallel Imports," on file with Public Citizen. Legislation to create parallel importing regimes in the U.S. for pharmaceuticals is working its way through Congress. 106th Congress, H.R. 1885, co-sponsored by Reps. Ann Emerson (R-MO), Marion Berry (D-AS) and Bernie Sanders (I-VT) would allow pharmacies, wholesalers and distributors to buy U.S. manufactured drugs at lower prices and then pass along the savings to consumers.

[111] Barbara Larkin, legislative assistant to the U.S. secretary of state, Reports sent to Rep. Sam Gejdenson (D-CT), House of Representatives Committee on International Relations, Feb. 5, 1999, at 3. on file with Public Citizen.

[112] World Health Organization Executive Board, Revised Drug Strategy, Conference Paper No. 18, Jan. 27, 1998.

[113] *Id.*

[114] Guatemalan Presidential Decree 66-83, Jun. 7, 1988, Article 13: Labeling.

[115] Guatemalan Government Agreement No. 841-87, Sep. 30, 1987, Article 12.

[116] Frank T. Kelly, Gerber's Vice President for Latin America, Letter to the President of Guatemala, Jun. 16, 1994, on file with Public Citizen.

[117] Gerber Letterhead, c. 1994.

[118] UNICEF data, *cited in* The Right Reverend Simon Barrington-Ward, "Putting Babies Before Business," *The Progress of Nations* (1997).

[119] The Right Reverend Simon Barrington-Ward, "Putting babies before business," *The Progress of Nations* (1997).

[120] *Id.*

[121] Edith Butler, "Nestle Practices Are Still Suspect, New Boycott Target, Taster's Choice Coffee," *WomenWise*, Mar. 31, 1983. (Infant Formula Action Committee – INFACT — was formed to combat Nestle's practices in 1977 and was instrumental in getting the WHO rules implemented. *See* Formula Promotion Hearing in U.S. Senate Sub-Committee on Health and Scientific Research), May 23, 1978. (Nestle admitted that its product required "clean water, good sanitation, adequate family income and a literate parent" and could not be used safely "in areas where water is contaminated, sewage runs through the streets, poverty is severe and illiteracy is high.")

[122] WHO, International Code of Marketing Breast-Milk Substitutes, 1981, Introduction.

[123] *Id.* at Article 9.3.

[124] *See* Law on the Marketing of Breastmilk Substitutes, Guatemalan Presidential Decree 68-83, Jun. 7, 1988, and Rules for the Marketing of Breastmilk Substitutes, Guatemalan Government Agreement No. 841-87, Sep. 30, 1987, Article 12 a)-b) (baby images), Article 11a (labeling), and Articles 8a and 9 (unapproved donations and direct marketing).

[125] Nutrition League Table, UNICEF, "Protecting Breast-Milk from Unethical Marketing," *The Progress of Nations* (1997).

[126] *Id.*

[127] Keith Koffler, "Administration to Bring Seven Trade Complaints to WTO," *Congress Daily*, May 3, 1999.

[128] *Id.*

[129] Guatemalan Ministry of Health, Memo Related to Gerber's Alleged Violations of Guatemalan Presidential Decree 68-83, Nov. 17, 1993, and Guatemalan Government Agreement No. 84-87, on file with Public Citizen.

[130] Frank T. Kelly, Gerber's Vice President for Latin America, Letter to the President of Guatemala, Jun. 16, 1994, on file with Public Citizen. The letter states, "We would like to thank you for all the efforts made in solving the commercial problem which originated from the misunderstanding among the Guatemalan Department of Health Services, the Office for Food Control" at 1.

[131] "Chronology of the Gerber Case in Guatemala," Ministry of Health Guatemala, Nov. 1993 on file with Public Citizen.

[132] *Id.*

[133] *Id.*

[134] Gerber Products Company's Post-Hearing Statement Regarding the Status of Guatemala as a Beneficiary Developing Country Under the Generalized System of Preferences (GSP) to the GSP Subcommittee of the Office of the USTR, Dec. 8, 1993, at 7.

[135] Frank T. Kelly, Gerber's Vice President for Latin America, Letter to the President of Guatemala, Jun. 16, 1994, on file with Public Citizen.

[136] Mario Permuth, Attorney Representing Guatemalan Ministry of Health, Letter to Dr. Gustavo Hernandez Polanco, Minister of Public Health, Feb. 16, 1994, on file with Public Citizen.

[137] Frank T. Kelly, Gerber's Vice President for Latin America, Letter to the President of Guatemala, Jun. 16, 1994, at 2.

[138] *Id.*

[139] "Gerber Uses Threat of GATT Sanctions to Gain Exemption from Guatemalan Infant Health Law," *Corporate Crime Reporter*, Vol. 10, No. 14, Apr. 8, 1996.

[140] Mario Permuth, Letter to President Bill Clinton, Dec. 12, 1993, on file with Public Citizen. (In the letter, Mario Permuth identifies himself as "the Attorney hired by UNICEF to help support the Guatemalan Ministry of Health.")

[141] Personal communication between Darci Andresen, Public Citizen, and WTO staff, Aug. 17, 1999. (In the EU-U.S. Banana dispute, the parties succeeded in blocking the Caribbean Island nations' private counsel third-party submissions, arguing that the WTO was a government-only body and that private counsel therefore had no access.)

[142] *See* Chapter 5 on developing countries and Chapter 8 on dispute resolution for more on this issue.

[143] WTO, TRIPs Agreement at Articles 8.1-8.2 (Principles).

[144] TRIPs Agreement, Article 8 is untested. However, GATT Article XX that allow exceptions to GATT market access provisions when human health or environmental protection/conservation is at stake have never been successfully used despite repeated attempts.

[145] TRIPs Agreement Articles 15.1-15.5 define trademarks; Articles 16.1-3 and Article 21 require WTO Members to protect trademarks from infringement by competitors; Article 17 lays out limited "fair use" exceptions to trademark protection; Article 18 stipulates the length of time that governments must protect trademarks; and Article 19 lays out rules for registering trademarks.

[146] WTO, TRIPs Agreement at Article 20 (Other Requirements).

[147] Frank T. Kelly, Gerber's Vice President for Latin America, Letter to the President of Guatemala, Jun. 16, 1994.

[148] *See* "Protecting Breast-Milk from Unethical Marketing," *The Progress of Nations*, UNICEF 1997; *see also* WTO Membership information found at www.wto.org, on file with Public Citizen.

[149] U.S. Trade Representative Michael Kantor, Letter to Alfred B. Engelberg, patent attorney and public health advocate, Feb. 1, 1996, acknowledging that compulsory licensing – where exclusive rights to market a drug are suspended so that generic companies can market it more cheaply and stimulate competition necessary to lower the price across the board – is WTO TRIPs legal.

[150] David Rosenberg, "U.S. Drug Makers May Turn to WTO Over Israeli Law," *Reuters*, Nov. 26, 1998.

[151] *Id.*

[152] South Africa (1997), Medicines and Related Substances Control Amendment Bill (B72-97).

[153] Esme du Plessis, "The Battle Over Making Medicine Affordable," *Euromoney Publications*, (1998).

[154] Paul Harris, "South Africa: Drug Industry Threatens to Take S. Africa to WTO," *Reuters*, Sep. 8, 1997.

[155] WTO, TRIPs Agreement at Article 31: "Where the law of a Member allows for other use of the subject matter of a patent without the authorization of the right holder, including use by the government or third parties authorized by the government, the following provisions shall be respected . . . (h) the right holder shall be paid adequate remuneration in the circumstances of each case, taking into account the economic value of the authorization . . .."

[156] PhRMA claims a membership of 45 multinational pharmaceutical companies, including Novartis, Bristol-Myers Squibb, Amgen, DuPont, Glaxo Wellcome, Johnson & Johnson, Eli Lilly, Merck, Pfizer, Rhone-Poulenc and Smithkline Beecham.

[157] Paul Harris, "South Africa: Drug Industry Threatens to Take S. Africa to WTO," *Reuters*, Sep. 8, 1997.

[158] *Id.*

[159] "U.S. Urges S. Africa to Change Draft Medicine Bill," *Reuters*, Oct. 6, 1997.

[160] Barbara Larkin, legislative assistant to the secretary of state, Report sent to Rep. Sam Gejdenson (D-CT), House of Representatives Committee on International Relations, at 4. The Medicines Law, the U.S. Embassy in Pretoria "approached the Swiss and EU member embassies in South Africa to suggest a joint effort to protest the provisions . ..." As a result of this effort, French President Chirac raised the issue during his July 1998 state visit to South Africa and the Swiss and German presidents raised the issue privately with South African Vice President Mbeki.

[161] 106th Congress, H.R. 434, Section 4 (a)(3), as reported to the House of Representatives, Jul. 16, 1999.

[162] Kai Wright, "Expanding Foreign Interests: U.S. AIDS Activists Develop Global Perspective on Epidemic," *Washington Blade*, Apr. 30, 1999, at 12.

[163] 106th Congress, H.R. 772, Title III, Section 301 and Title VI, Section 601.

[164] Lisa Richwine, "U.S. Protest Targets African Access to AIDS Drugs," *Reuters*, Apr. 22, 1999.

[165] Personal communication with Bob Lederer, ACT-UP Co-Founder, with Michelle Sforza, Research Director, Public Citizen's Global Trade Watch, Aug. 25, 1999.

[166] "South Africa's Bitter Pill for World's Drug Makers," *The New York Times*, Mar. 29, 1998.

[167] USTR, "USTR Announces Results of Special 301 Annual Review," Press Release 99-41, Apr. 30, 1999. Section 301 is a provision of U.S. trade law that empowers the U.S. to impose sanctions on countries that restrict market access of U.S. imports and that violate the IPRs of U.S. investors. If an investigation reveals that South Africa is causing adverse damage to U.S. IPR interests, under Section 301 the U.S. could impose trade sanctions. The WTO-consistency of unilateral economic sanctions under Section 301 is in doubt, however. (See Chapter 9 on WTO Dispute Resolution).

[168] WTO, TRIPs Agreement at Article VI.

[169] James Love, "The Comments of the Consumer Project on Technology to the Portfolio Committee on Health Parliament, Cape Town Medicines and Related Substances Control Amendment Bill and South African Reform of Pharmaceutical Policies," Oct. 6, 1997.

[170] Barbara Larkin, legislative assistant to the secretary of state, Report sent to Rep. Sam Gejdenson (D-CT), House of Representatives Committee on International Relations, Feb. 5, 1999, at 6.

[171] *Id.* at 7.

[172] Charles R. Babcock and Ceci Connolly, "AIDS Activists Dog Gore a Second Day; Role in Drug Dispute with S. Africa is Hit," *The Washington Post*, Jun. 18, 1999.

[173] *Id.*

[174] Vice President Al Gore, Letter to The Honorable James E. Clyburn, Chair of the Congressional Black Caucus, Jun. 25, 1999, on the affordability of AIDS medicines in South Africa.

[175] "Business Week's Industry Rankings," *Business Week*, Mar. 29, 1999, at 152. [The top six firms in their S&P rankings are Shering-Plough (10); Warner-Lambert (12); Merck (16); Eli-Lilly (25); Bristol-Meyers Squibb (42); and Amgen (45)].

[176] "Executive Compensation Scoreboard," *Business Week*, Apr. 19, 1999, at 96.

[177] "U.S. Wants TRIPS Off Seattle Agenda," *Washington Trade Daily*, Aug. 5, 1999.

[178] WTO, TRIPs Agreement at Article 27.3(b).

[179] "Calls for Moratorium on TRIPS Biodiversity Clause," *BRIDGES Weekly Trade News Digest*, Apr. 26, 1999.

[180] WTO, TRIPs Agreement at Article 27.3(b).

[181] "Calls for Moratorium on TRIPS Biodiversity Clause," *BRIDGES Weekly Trade News Digest*, Apr. 26, 1999.

[182] "Preparations for the 1999 Ministerial Conference - The TRIPS Agreement - Communication from Kenya on behalf of the African Group," WTO Document No. WT/GC/W/302, Aug. 6, 1999.

[183] "U.S. Wants TRIPS Off Seattle Agenda," *Washington Trade Daily*, Aug. 5, 1999.

[184] "Calls for Moratorium on TRIPS Biodiversity Clause," *BRIDGES Weekly Trade News Digest*, Apr. 26, 1999.

[185] Barbara Larkin, legislative assistant to the secretary of state, Report sent to Rep. Sam Gejdenson (D-CT), House of Representatives Committee on International Relations, Feb. 5, 1999, at introduction.

[186] *Id.* at 3.

[187] *Id.* at 4.

[188] *Id.* at 4-5.

[189] *Id.* at 6.

[190] *Id.* at 7.

[191] *Id.* at 9.

[192] See e.g. B. Drummond Ayres Jr., "Gore Is Followed by AIDS Protesters," *The New York Times*, July 2, 1999.

[193] Personal Communication between Robert Weissman, editor of the *Multinational Monitor*, Aug. 23, 1999 and Marianne Mollmann, Public Citizen.

In this chapter ...

CASES:

• **Small Caribbean Banana Farmers:** The non-banana exporting U.S. successfully attacked Europe's preferential treatment of bananas from former EU colonies (all islands together represent 8% of the EU market share) on behalf of the giant Chiquita (which has 50% of the EU market share alone) after Chiquita's CEO gave a series of major campaign contributions to both Democrats and Republicans. The WTO ruled that an exception that the EU had negotiated for its Lome Convention development treaty did not cover provisions that set aside a small portion of the EU market at lower tariffs for bananas from former European Caribbean colonies. The U.S. has implemented trade sanctions against the EU for not fully implementing the ruling yet. The EU has said it will comply, which will doom the Caribbean's small independent farmers and help the three huge banana businesses (Chiquita, Dole and Del Monte) that already have two-thirds of the world market for bananas grown on their huge Latin American plantations staffed by underpaid workers.

CONCEPTS:

Wage Inequality Increases Between and Within Countries: UNCTAD found that in developing countries that have undertaken rapid trade liberalization, wage inequality increases, most often in the context of declining industrial employment of unskilled workers and large absolute falls in the real wages. The income gap between the fifth of the world's people living in the richest countries and the fifth in the poorest was 74-to-1 in 1997, up from 60-to-1 in 1990 and 30-to-1 in 1960. By 1997, the richest 20% captured 86% of world income, with the poorest 20% capturing 1%.

Share of Trade Declines for Lesser Developed Countries (LDCs) Under WTO: The 47 poorest countries have seen their export earnings drop between 2.6% and 5% each year of the Uruguay Round. Meanwhile, food import prices have increased.

Developing Country Growth: Rather than the boost in growth promised by promoters of the Uruguay Round, in the past four and a half years, economic growth in the developing world has slowed. Indeed, in most countries the period under the Uruguay Round has brought dramatic reversals in fortune. In Asia, Latin America and Africa, the standard of living has declined. Latin America is foundering, mired in its deepest economic slump since the debt crisis of the 1980s. East Asia is paralyzed by an economic crisis caused in part by the very investment and financial service sector deregulations that the WTO intensifies and spreads to other nations. While the U.S. press has announced that the crisis is over, in South Korea and Indonesia, where the crisis has quadrupled unemployment and precipitated a 200% increase in absolute poverty, the effects have rolled back decades of economic progress.

Tariff Escalation: Developing countries did not have much leverage at WTO negotiations. As a result, the rules contain several built-in disadvantages for developing country interests. One is the design of tariff rates so that raw commodities have the lowest tariff rates and value-added goods have increasingly high tariffs. The result of this policy is to ensure rich countries a constant cheap supply of natural resources. For developing countries, the promotion of "rip and ship" natural resource exploitation is a dead-end, low earnings route that limits economic diversification. Yet, with tariff escalation, it is cheaper to make furniture in a rich country using imported tropical wood than to ship finished furniture from a developing country that grows the wood.

GSP, Lomé Programs Undermined: The WTO continues the GATT tradition of waiving MFN requirements and allowing special lower tariffs for developing countries. However, given the general tariffs cuts provided by the Uruguay Round, the relative benefit of the GSP or Lomé tariff rates have been reduced — and in some instances will disappear as WTO tariff schedules zero-out tariffs in certain commodities. Also, the EU is renegotiating the entire Lomé Convention, in part because some Lomé provisions do not comply with WTO rules. The EU is using the WTO compliance issue to move the Lomé Convention away from a development model and toward a reciprocal free trade agreement model similar to NAFTA.

5 The WTO and Developing Countries

At the conclusion of the Uruguay Round negotiations in 1994, developing countries were promised they would experience major gains as industrialized countries lowered and eventually eliminated tariffs on such items as textiles and apparel[1] and cut agricultural subsidies that enabled them to dominate world commodity markets. Uruguay Round proponents also promised that the WTO would level the playing field so that powerful economies, such as the United States, could not threaten unilateral sanctions to obtain commercial benefits while refusing access to its markets for products from developing countries.

Yet contrary to this rosy scenario, after nearly five years of the WTO, the share of the pie for most of the world's population living in developing countries got smaller, and that smaller portion was divided even less equally among individuals. First, under the Uruguay Round the share of trade among the poorest countries has decreased rather than increased.[3] Second, while the world's largest corporations have generated record earnings,[4] income inequality has increased between and within countries since the WTO's implementation.

> **In almost all developing countries that have undertaken rapid trade liberalization, wage inequality has increased, most often in the context of declining industrial employment of unskilled workers and large absolute falls in their real wages, on the order of 20-30% in Latin American countries."[2]**
>
> — United Nations

Share of Trade Declines For Developing Nations Under Uruguay Round

The full impact of the Uruguay Round Agreements on developing countries can be gauged only after full implementation. Several key agreements – the Agreement on Trade Related Aspects of Intellectual Property Rights (TRIPs), the Agreement on Agriculture (AoA) and the General Agreement on Trade in Services (GATS) – have 10- to 15-year phase-in periods for developing countries for certain provisions. However, some general trends already have emerged during the nearly five years since implementation began.

According to the United Nations Commission on Trade and Development (UNCTAD), the share of world exports and imports has fallen sharply in the Least Developed Countries (LDCs) since the Uruguay Round. [7] According to UNCTAD, as a result of the implementation of the Uruguay Round accords, the world's poorest nations — the 47 least developed countries — will lose an estimated $163 billion to $265 billion in export earnings while paying $145 million to $292 million more for food imports.[8]

UNCTAD concludes that LDCs continue to be marginalized in world trade not because of any resistance to openness but because of their inability to expand productive capacity.[9] For instance, the removal of tariff barriers to manufactured goods in poor countries forces nascent industry to compete with vastly more productive foreign manufacturers, thus stunting industrial development.

For the LDCs especially, UNCTAD recommends that they eschew rapid and additional liberalization of trade in favor of a managed approach. "A gradual approach to trade liberalization is desirable in view of the existing weaknesses in supply. The case for infant industry protection and industrial policies to promote learning and develop skills in domestic firms is no less relevant today … than it has been for all successful late developers in this century."[10]

Thus, UNCTAD has diagnosed the LDCs' inability to enjoy the potential benefits of trade liberalization. The diagnosis: that LDCs are denied the traditional economic development tools used so successfully by the fastest growing economies of the past two decades, the so-called "Asian Tigers" of South Korea, Indonesia, Malaysia and China. These countries have "kept a heavy role for government in the economy: Industrial policy, planning, state control over the financial system and other interventions enabled these countries to benefit from expanding access to foreign markets."[11] Indeed, the extent to which the Asian Tigers abandoned managed trade and investment policy – especially in the area of financial services regulation – corresponds rather

Africa Loses Under WTO

In 1994, an OECD study predicted that the Uruguay Round could worsen Africa's terms of trade by a further 0.2% by 2002.[5] UNCTAD has since reported that agricultural price liberalization under the Uruguay Round Agriculture Agreement has failed to boost incomes of farmers in Africa. Instead the benefits of liberalization have been reaped mainly by traders.[6]

neatly to the extent to which they were destabilized by the financial crisis of 1997 and 1998. "East Asia became vulnerable to external financial shocks in part because it attempted to reform its financial markets in the 1990's in a market-oriented manner. These reforms lead to a dramatic increase in the number of banks and their linkages to the international economy, which in turn, increased the exposure of these economies to international financial shocks mainly through the remarkable buildup of short term debts."[12]

Yet the Uruguay Round Agreements transformed core components of economic development policy into trade law violations. For instance, the TRIMs Agreement specifically prohibits infant industry protection when it is linked to regulation of foreign investment.[14] Hence, a developing country cannot require that a foreign investor export products to generate foreign currency or to shield domestic producers from competition for the local market.

WTO TRIMs Agreement Cases

Japan v. Canada: Japan argues that Canadian rules under the U.S.-Canada Auto Pact impose value-added domestic content requirements and sales requirements on foreign manufacturers. A panel was established in February 1999.

EC v. India: the EU argues that import licenses for the auto sector may be granted only to local joint venture manufacturers that have signed a Memorandum of Understanding with the Indian government, which requires them to comply with certain local content and export balancing requirements that would violate the TRIMs Agreement.

Japan, EC, U.S. v. Brazil: The complainants allege that Brazilian rules relating to investment in the automotive sector violate the TRIMs Agreement. Consultations have been pending since August 1996.

U.S. v. Philippines: U.S. argues that Philippine tariff-rate quotas on pork and poultry adversely affect foreign investors. In March 1998, the parties settled.

— *Source: WTO* [13]

Likewise, the TRIPs Agreement inhibits flow of technology to developing countries, which used to be a benefit of foreign investment. The present industrial countries did not have patent and intellectual property protections as strict as those now in place while they were industrializing,[15] which allowed them to import technology design from abroad.

Promise of Rising Living Standards Based on Non-Existent Growth

To obtain the rising wages and living standards promised in the WTO's preamble, economies must grow. Indeed, according to UNCTAD, the world economy must grow by at least 3% per year to ameliorate unemployment in Europe and poverty in developing countries.[16] However, notwithstanding the exaggerated promises of WTO-led

WTO's Plan for Developing Nations

The Uruguay Round Agreements function as an engine to drive corporate economic globalization. As a result, vast segments of developing nation economies and populations are catapulted into the existing global market. This strategy has alarming consequences for the 75% of the world's population still living on the land and depending on small-scale agriculture for their livelihoods.[22] A WTO goal is to rapidly transform such rural developing country subsistence economies into cash-driven market economies. For efficiency, rural villages and whole countries are to eschew independence in food production or other basic needs. Rather, all should produce for world markets to obtain cash to purchase food and other needed items. This vision has been attacked for its social and cultural implications.[23] What has received little attention is that if the Uruguay Round pacts are fully implemented and the efficiency rates in production or food imports of western high-input farming are imposed on developing countries, 2 billion of the 3.1 billion people now living on the land would no longer be "needed" to participate in the agricultural sector.[24] According to neoliberal economic theory, these rural people displaced from their communities and livelihoods would be more efficiently employed in other economic sectors. In reality, they would join an urban workforce in the developing world whose constant oversupply will keep down labor costs.

economic growth, between 1995 and 1998, the 3% target was reached just once, in 1996.[17]

UNCTAD reports that growth in the developing world needs to reach 6% per year to close the income gap with industrialized nations.[18] Proponents of the WTO argued that the only way to obtain such growth was to "modernize" by adopting the package of Uruguay Round policies that liberalized trade, deregulated service sectors and protected investors. Yet for most developing countries, similar deregulation of their economies over the past two decades under the orders of the International Monetary Fund (IMF) has coincided with sharp *declines* in their rates of growth.[19]

For instance, real per capita income in Mexico increased by 3.9% annually in the 1960s and 3.2% in the 1970s. However, since the 1980's, when Mexico joined the GATT and came under the IMF's structural adjustment policies, per capita income in Mexico has stagnated.[20] For Latin America as a whole, the economy grew by 5.6% per capita from 1980 to 1997, compared to a 73% per capita increase from 1960 to 1980.[21]

Meanwhile, Asia has been plunged into economic crisis by the same investment and financial services liberalization policies that the Uruguay Round accelerates with the WTO's Trade Related Investment Measures (TRIMs), General Agreement on Trade in Services (GATS), and the Financial Services Agreement (FSA.) According to the Council of Economic Advisors' 1999 Economic Report of the President, "In most countries, significant liberalization of international capital transactions and the progressive elimination of capital controls preceded the crisis. ... East Asian economies had embarked on financial liberalization, both domestic and international, over the course of the 1990s."[25] Countries such as Thailand, Korea and Indonesia, which year after year enjoyed annual growth rates of 8-10%, maintained full employment and made progress in eradicating poverty, suffered severe economic contraction.[26] The crisis, which the financial press declared over even though people in Asia saw it deepening monthly, increased absolute poverty and unemployment in some countries by as much as 200%.[27]

Meanwhile, the increased integration of nation's economies, which the Uruguay Round is designed to dramatically intensify, meant that the Asian crisis spilled over into Latin America and Africa, harming countries in these regions that depend on trade with Southeast Asia for their growth. African countries depend on East Asia for 25-35% of their total export earnings.[28] African growth is expected to slow to 1% in 1999.[29] And about 10% of Latin America's total merchandise exports go to Asia, where they must compete with cheaper Asian goods for the OECD market, which comprises 60% of total Latin American exports. Latin America is foundering, mired in its deepest economic slump since the debt crisis of the 1980s.[30]

In fact, those countries experiencing the highest rates of growth over the past five years have not adopted Uruguay Round-style deregulation policies or exposed their countries to speculation in the market. For instance, the economy in China – whose government strictly controls investment and currency flows, has import controls on many industrial and agricultural products, and provides extensive protections to domestic industry[31] – has grown an average of 8% per year in the 1990s (and an average of 10% per year during the past twenty years).[32] Unlike other Asian countries that have been pressured to deregulate their markets as a condition to receive IMF loans, China does not have a freely convertible currency. Thus China largely weathered the "Asia" crisis without significant damage.

Increasing Income Inequality Within and Between Countries

While the economic growth promised by WTO proponents has not materialized, in the nearly five years of the WTO, an unwelcome economic development has intensified: income inequality between and within countries. This outcome has given credence to the warnings of WTO critics in developing countries. They had argued that under the Uruguay Round's "corporate managed trade" rules, the winners would be the giant multinational corporations that generally are incorporated in the developed countries.

According to the United Nations Development Program (UNDP), the differential in per capita incomes between the countries with the poorest 20 percent of the world's population and the richest 20 percent is widening as globalization picks up pace. The income gap between the fifth of the world's people living in the richest countries and the fifth in the poorest was 74-to-1 in 1997, up from 60-to-1 in 1990 and 30-to-1 in 1960.[33] By 1997, the richest 20% captured 86% of world income, with the poorest 20% capturing a mere 1%.[34] Indeed, in 1998 a quarter of the world's population lived in extreme poverty, a number that is projected to continue to grow.[35]

UNCTAD has noted that the growing polarization among countries has been accompanied by increasing income inequality within countries.[36] A report by UNCTAD found that, "In almost all developing countries that have undertaken rapid trade liberalization, wage inequality has increased, most often in the context of declining industrial employment of unskilled workers and large absolute falls in their real wages, on the order of 20-30% in Latin American countries."[37] In an in-depth analysis of the relationship between trade liberalization and rising wage inequality focusing on the 1985 Mexican trade reform required for Mexico's 1996 entry into GATT, the National Bureau of Economic Research concluded that wage inequality in Mexico rose after the reform, countering the "logic" that all members of society will benefit if a country opens its markets by deregulating its economy and relying on its comparative advantage – in Mexico's case, low-wage labor – in world markets.[38]

Uruguay Round Agreements Include Provisions Especially Threatening to Developing Countries

Some development experts in the industrialized world admitted as early as 1993 that the trade and investment liberalization policies of the Uruguay Round Agreements would hurt many developing countries. In a report buried by WTO boosters in the developed world, OECD reported that Sub-Sahara Africa in particular had the most

Developing Nations Dragged Into Uruguay Round Negotiations

Many developing countries were virtually dragged into the Uruguay Round negotiations largely against their will and better judgment.[39] The Uruguay Round was launched at U.S. initiative with the support of most major industrial nations. "It really was about global production and production capacities"[40] and not "technical issues like tariff and non-tariff measures ... thus the main negotiations were a trilateral affair involving the U.S., the European Economic Community (EEC) and Japan" writes long term GATT analyst Chakravarthi Raghavan in his book *Recolonialization: GATT, the Uruguay Round and the Third World*.[41]

As a result of many handicaps ranging from lack of technical expertise to the limited financial and human resources available for the examination of international commercial issues, most of the developing country negotiators remained "uncertain" about the probable consequences and economic costs their countries would have to bear upon implementation.[42] As a result of this lack of information, and the inherent power imbalance, many negotiators from developing countries reacted to proposals during negotiations with a view to minimizing the negative effects and containing the damage, rather than negotiating to maximize their economic benefits.[43]

to lose under the Uruguay Round Agreements.[44] The organization was a supporter of the Uruguay Round, making this warning especially compelling.

The OECD forecast was echoed by the U.S. Congressional Research Service (CRS), which predicted in 1995 that there would be both winners and losers from Uruguay Round implementation.[45] According to CRS, the Uruguay Round's big losers would be the least developed countries (LDCs) and African, Caribbean and Pacific countries (ACP).[46] Indeed, prominent economists, including scholars from developing countries, where popular opposition to the Uruguay Round was often stronger than in industrialized countries, largely predicted what is now coming to pass.[47]

These outcomes are being caused by several specific concepts and provisions in the Uruguay Round package:

Systematic Tariff Escalation Promotes "Rip and Ship" Natural Resources Use

Uruguay Round tariff schedules provide for the escalation of tariff rates as value is added to a product. Thus, the lowest rate is for a raw commodity; the tariff rate increases with processing and manufacturing.

This Uruguay Round feature is one reason developing country WTO critics say the Uruguay Round promotes economic "recolonization" of developing countries that only recently gained political independence. Tariff escalation creates an incentive for "rip and ship" natural resource exploitation in poor countries. In addition to its environmental threat, tariff escalation strongly favors countries with developed manufacturing sectors by increasing access to cheap raw natural resources and discouraging least developing countries from further industrialization, because tariff rates increase as value is added to products through manufacturing. Thus, furniture produced in a developing country from that country's tropical wood and exported for sale in a developed country faces a relatively high tariff. Raw tropical timber logs shipped into the rich country face relatively lower tariffs, and when the furniture is produced in the rich country from that wood, it faces no additional tariff mark-up.

Many developing countries have considered the potential for vertical diversi-

NAFTA, Mexico and Hunger

Mexico had used subsidies and import quotas to manage the supply and thus the prices of its main staple, corn. NAFTA opened Mexico's corn market to U.S. imports, providing a large quota. Mexico ended its subsidies for Mexican growers, reasoning that it would import cheaper U.S. corn.[52] Within a year, Mexican production of corn and other basic grains fell by half and millions of peasants were displaced.[53] When the U.S. experienced a corn shortage in 1996, Mexico was thrown into a food crisis,[54] resulting in the malnourishment of one out of five Mexican children.[55]

137

fication into processed agricultural products. Such diversification offers real opportunity to develop endogenous capacity and is thus far more profitable than the export of raw commodities. Unfortunately, moves in that direction tend to be restricted by tariff escalation, i.e., Uruguay Round tariff levels for processed goods are higher than for primary commodities, reducing poor countries' competitiveness in finished goods and thus posing a disincentive to invest in this processing capacity. [48]

Under the Uruguay Round tariff schedule, by 2000, tariffs are to be eliminated in many product categories that currently represent a substantial export income for the world's poorest countries.[49] These include coffee, tea, cocoa beans, metal ores, cotton, gold, diamonds and fresh vegetables.[50] This would lower world prices for the commodities and further lower the export earnings of countries that specialize in them. "[Primary commodities] are important sources of foreign exchange, but they are risky because of the shift in world prices," notes a West African agriculture expert.[51]

Falling Commodity Prices Undermine Food Security

Primary commodity prices already have fallen by 25% since 1995, the year the WTO went into effect, and now are at historic lows. [56] Compounding the problem of lower export earnings caused by plunging commodity prices is the fact that least developed countries have become net importers of food and therefore must have a steady stream of foreign exchange simply to finance the *imports* needed to feed the population.[57]

The Uruguay Round Agriculture Agreement prohibited numerous internal support programs and import controls that developing countries typically use to protect small producers and encourage self-sufficiency in food production[58] while permitting continuing export subsidies.[59] With small local producers no longer shielded from the subsidized agricultural commodities

Developing Countries at the WTO: Destiny Without Representation

According to a recent report, the African nation of Sierra Leone has faced numerous obstacles to participating in WTO proceedings and committees. Given severe financial limitations, the country has been forced to rely on Geneva-based NGOs to comprise its delegation at the WTO.[62] Sierra Leone, like most Least Developed Countries (LDCs), cannot afford a large, full-time staff in Geneva to keep it apprised of the myriad WTO committees that address issues of concern to LDCs. Yet outside representatives of governments often are excluded from WTO activities. This predicament was expressed succinctly by the ambassador of Tanzania: "In a country like mine where so many people are starving, it is very hard to think about spending money for the GATT."[63] Yet under the expansive Uruguay Round agreements policies decided at the WTO can and are affecting LDC's fate.

of the U.S. and particularly the EU, the Uruguay Round creates increased dependency on imported staples like wheat and corn.[60] However, the lack of consistent streams of foreign exchange – compounded by reliance on the export of primary commodities that are falling in price – to purchase imported food is increasing the likelihood of food shortages and subsequent starvation in the least developed countries.

Vital WTO Decisions Still Made Without Developing Country Input at WTO

Developing countries – the least developed countries in particular – do not have the bargaining leverage or the technical staff to shape trade rules in their favor in the WTO. Indeed, these countries have been and continue to be excluded from decision-making forums and forced to rubber-stamp proposals for the WTO agenda after they have been hammered out between the so-called Quad countries – the U.S., EU, Japan and Canada – and the larger developing countries such as India and Brazil.[61]

Uruguay Round Undermines Existing LDC Trade Preferences

The Uruguay Round allows industrialized countries to maintain programs to benefit LDCs, such as the Generalized System of Preferences (GSP) programs used in the U.S. and the EU. These programs provide preferential tariffs to the poorest countries. The programs are safeguarded by granting waivers insofar as they clash with Most Favored Nation (MFN) obligations.[64] Notwithstanding these waivers, Uruguay Round tariff reductions lowered the values of such programs as compared to regular post-Uruguay Round tariff levels.

In addition, many of the EU's Lomé Convention preferences for the 70 underdeveloped, mostly former colonies in Africa, the Caribbean and Pacific Islands (ACP) are in danger of elimination altogether. The Lomé treaty provides a variety of trade

Brazil Challenges EU "Coffee-Not-Cocaine" Trade Preference

Other EU policies aimed at promoting trade with developing countries are also under WTO attack. In December 1998, Brazil submitted a complaint alleging that the EU's preferential treatment of coffee from Central and South American countries that engage in anti-narcotics efforts violates GATT Article I, guaranteeing most favored nation treatment.[65] Impoverished peasants often are pushed into narcotics cultivation by economic necessity. The EU's Generalized System of Preferences (GSP) encourages the at-risk peasants to grow legal crops and rewards farmers who participate in narcotics control programs with duty-free access to the EU market.[66] The EU preferences apply to products originating in the Andean Group and Central American Common Market, where for many countries, narcotics are a substantial source of income.[67]

benefits that go beyond the GSP program including setting aside small portions of the EU market for certain ACP products. A successful WTO challenge leveled by the U.S. against the Lomé treaty preferences for ACP bananas has provided an impetus for negotiations to dismantle the Lome's development approach.[68] "Right now, the Lomé Convention is not WTO compatible because of the trade preferences ACP countries get, and our major trading partners are watching these negotiations very closely. We cannot carry on with the status quo. We must make a change because of WTO rules," said the EU's chief Lomé negotiator.[69]

Renegotiations of the Lomé Convention's trade regime – Lomé V – currently are under way. However, instead of granting an extension of the non-reciprocal Lomé scheme as has been customary during past extensions, the EU is determined to substitute it with reciprocal trade agreements individually negotiated between the various regions in the ACP and the EU, similar to the North American Free Trade Agreement. The EU cites WTO compatibility as one of the reasons for this change in negotiating mandate.

The ACP countries remain highly skeptical about the proposed new trade regime and the EU's motivations.[70] First, the reciprocal nature of the deals forces the ACP governments' vulnerable markets to open to subsidized European agricultural products,[71] increasing the possibility that already tenuous food security in such countries will be undermined. Second, the individually negotiated deals pit the various ACP regions in competition against each other.[72] And third, the ACP countries argue that establishing free trade agreements between economically disparate countries tends to divert trade rather than create it.[73] Indeed, the EU and South Africa recently concluded a free trade agreement, which UNCTAD reports is likely to benefit the EU more than South Africa because it excludes nearly half of South Africa's agricultural exports but includes subsidized EU agricultural exports.[74]

The following case describes the impact of WTO rules on the ability of developing countries to pursue economic development strategies that nurture local business and empower local workers and communities.

> ## Bananagate?
>
> That governments with no economic stake, if the price were right, might be willing to do the bidding of multinational firms has aroused suspicions that the WTO dispute resolution system can be used on a *"rent-a-nation"* basis.[75]
>
> The Clinton administration filed a WTO complaint on bananas – a crop the U.S. does not grow for export – days after the U.S.-based multinational Chiquita gave $500,000 to the Democratic Party.[76] Then, in response to an EU plan to implement the WTO's eventual ruling against the banana regime, GOP Senate leaders introduced the "Uruguay Round Agreements Compliance Act of 1998," which imposed tariffs on the EU for not fully complying with the WTO.[77] This move came one month after Chiquita CEO Carl Lindner donated $350,000 – this time to the Republican Party.[78]

Case 1: U.S. Attacks Caribbean Bananas for Chiquita

The Lomé Convention between the EU and its former colonies in Africa, the Caribbean and the Pacific (ACP countries) establishes preferential tariffs and sets aside some portion of the EU market for the ACP countries for a set list of products.[79] This regime is considered indispensable for the economic and political stability of the ACP countries.[80] The EU negotiated a waiver for the Lomé Convention for Uruguay Round Most Favored Nation (MFN) tariff requirements. However, in 1996, the U.S. government, on behalf of the U.S corporation Chiquita Brands International (Chiquita), challenged the EU, claiming that the Lomé banana regime violated its WTO obligations.

Background: The U.S. itself does not produce a single banana for trade. Chiquita employs more than 85% of its 37,000-person workforce in Latin America on extensive plantations in Colombia, Costa Rica, Honduras and Panama.[81] Chiquita has 50% of the EU banana market.[82] All of the Caribbean Island producers combined have 8% of the EU market[83] and 3% of the world market. [84] Three giant multinational companies – Chiquita, Del Monte and Dole – control two-thirds of the global market.[85]

> **"T**he trading arrangements of the Lomé Convention are not about diverting trade but providing opportunities [for countries] that otherwise would have little or no possibility of participating in the global trading system. "[87]
>
> — Kenny Anthony,
> Prime Minister of St. Lucia

While most of the world's bananas are grown on large Latin and Central American plantations that rely on cheap farm labor,[86] Eastern Caribbean banana producers, in contrast, tend to be small-scale farmers who own and work small plots of mountainous land and whose production costs are therefore higher. According to the prime minister of St. Lucia, "The trading arrangements of the Lomé Convention are not about diverting trade but providing opportunities [for countries] that otherwise would have little or no possibility of participating in the global trading system."[87]

Bananas are central to the economic and political stability of several small Caribbean island nations, where mountainous terrain and limited arable land make cultivation of other legal cash crops literally impossible. The ACP countries most dependent upon the Lomé Convention banana regimes include the Windward Islands nations of St. Lucia, Dominica, St. Vincent and the Grenadines, where banana production accounts for between 63% and 91% of export earnings.[88] Also, 33% of Dominica's workforce and 70% of St. Vincent's population are involved in the production and marketing of bananas.[89] In 1990, banana exports to the EU represented 94% of all banana exports from the ACP countries.[90] A St. Lucia small banana farmer noted, "[Only tourism] can bring in a regular dollar like banana [but] tourism brings in the top dollar. It stays on the top and doesn't come down to us. Banana money comes from the ground and goes up."[91]

The WTO Challenge: The U.S. claimed that the EU's policy of setting aside a specific small portion of its market for bananas exported by ACP countries was unjustifiably discriminatory under WTO rules.[92] The EU argued that paragraph 1 of its WTO Lomé waiver – stating that the MFN principle would be waived "to the extent necessary" for the EU to comply with its Lomé Convention obligations – implicitly included the quota guarantee, as any other interpretation essentially would render the Lomé Convention waiver meaningless. This argument however, was not accepted by the WTO panel.[93] It also ruled that the Lomé waiver failed to cover General Agreement on Services (GATS) rules relating to the allocation of import licenses for distributors and marketers of goods. The EU appealed.

In September 1997, the WTO Appellate Body handed down its ruling, affirming and clarifying the original panel's ruling that the Lomé waiver did not allow the EU to favor ACP bananas by providing them with a 7% guaranteed market access license at a guaranteed tariff rate that is lower than those imposed on other producers.[94] According to the panel, despite the EU's Lomé Convention waiver, the special tariff quotas enjoyed by ACP countries had to be eliminated or provided to all. This effectively eliminated the Lomé benefit and forced ACP countries to compete against multinational, large-plantation producers such as Chiquita.

> ## WTO to Caribbean Banana-Producing Nations: Your Future Is Not Your Business
>
> Representatives of the governments of St. Lucia and St. Vincent, whose preferential access to the EU banana market was under attack by the U.S in its challenge to the EU's Caribbean banana regime, were not allowed to participate in the arguments and hearings on the case. Both St. Lucia and St. Vincent, whose futures were most at stake in the case, were forced to hire outside counsel to represent them in the case because they lacked GATT/WTO experts in their trade ministries. However, arguing that the WTO is a governments-only body, the WTO dispute panel ejected the outside counsel hired from the proceedings, leaving the island nations' interests completely unrepresented.[100]

In 1998, the EU issued a proposal to address the panel's ruling. It agreed to remedy other policies that the panel ruled against but stood firm on the quota issue, proposing to maintain the two-tier tariff quota regime for ACP and non-ACP banana producers.[95] According to St. Lucia Trade Minister Earle Hunteley, "The simple tariff would leave us wide open to fruit from cheaper sources, thus making it even more difficult to compete."[96]

In response to the EU's proposals, the Republican Senate leadership introduced the Uruguay Round Agreements Compliance Act of 1998, which imposed tariffs on the EU for not fully complying with the WTO's banana ruling.[97] This move came one month after Chiquita donated $350,000 to the Republican National Committee and the House and Senate campaign committees.[98] At the last minute, the GOP leadership agreed to pull the bill after the Clinton administration promised to take action to sanction the EU.

In February 1999, the administration announced that it would impose tariffs against a wide range European-made goods in retaliation for the EU's failure to comply with the WTO. Products subject to the sanctions included goat cheese, cashmere, biscuits, candles and chandeliers. The list added up to an annual value of $520 million, which is what the U.S. banana marketers claimed to lose because of the Lomé Convention.[99] A WTO panel rejected the U.S. tabulation of damages and reduced the amount to $190 million, but approved and legitimated the tariffs, which took effect in March 1999.[101]

The EU argued that the U.S. could not impose retaliatory tariffs without a WTO panel ruling saying that the EU's new proposals didn't comply with the previous WTO dispute body report. In response to a complaint by Ecuador (one of several Latin American countries the U.S. pressured into signing on to the original U.S. brief) against the EU's proposed remedy, a WTO panel held in April of 1999 that the new EU regime did not comply with its earlier ruling.[102] The EU has announced it would have no choice but to rescind the ACP preferences.[103]

> **"Will Dominica or St. Vincent and the Grenadines be the first democracies to be put out of business by a WTO ruling?"[104]**
>
> — Douglas W. Payne, consultant, Freedom House

Pursuit of Banana Case Was Against U.S. Interests: While the elimination of the EU's preferential regime for ACP bananas will do nothing to advance U.S. economic interests, it will undermine U.S. security and drug interdiction goals for the region.

The fallout from the WTO ruling could be seriously damaging to both the islands directly involved *and* the U.S. Replacing the European banana regime with direct aid payments to support governments or farmers would obviously lead to the end of an important way of life in the Caribbean. The end of the banana "middle class" in the Caribbean will destabilize the economic foundation of the region, leaving thousands of people with no means of independent livelihoods. Economic destabilization in the region in the past has led to social upheaval. Considering that this economic destabilization is permanent (unlike past weather- or blight-caused damage to the banana economies), it threatens to undermine the strong democratic traditions of these countries and their traditions of human and labor rights. Given the standard of living of these island nations – almost all of whom are democracies with voter turnout double U.S. rates – the potential threat to the well-being of the Caribbean people is enormous.

Indeed, from a purely economic perspective, the U.S. WTO attack undermines broad U.S. interests. First, the U.S. is the main beneficiary of the worldwide Caribbean tourism boom, which relies on countries' safety and stability. Second, the Caribbean is one of the few regions in the world with whom the U.S. has a trade surplus.[105] The Caribbean sells bananas to Europe and uses the hard currency to buy U.S. exports – to the tune of $37.2 billion worth of U.S. goods and services

Banana Index:
U.S. Challenge to Caribbean Banana Trade

Number of bananas the United States exports each year	0[109]
Percent of workforce of Dominica involved in banana trade	33[110]
Percent of St. Lucia's population involved in banana trade	16[111]
World market share of independent Caribbean banana producers	3%[112]
EU market share of U.S.-based Dole, in 1993, before EU preferential treatment for ACP bananas	11%[113]
EU market share of Dole in 1998, five years after EU's banana preferences started	15%[114]
EU market share of Chiquita	50%[115]
Independent Caribbean banana producers market share with EU countries	8%[116]
Amount Chiquita pays workers for a 12- to 18-hour work day	$6[117]
Amount of money Carl Lindner, Chiquita Brands Int'l CEO, contributed to the Democratic Party two days after the Clinton administration filed at WTO on EU banana policy in 1996	$500,000[118]
Amount of money Carl Lindner gave the GOP in 1998, before GOP leaders pushed a "WTO Enforcement Act" to punish EU for ACP banana rules	$350,000[119]
Percent of export earnings the banana industry brings to Dominica and St. Lucia	Over 50[120]
Percent of Europeans that would pay more for "fair trade" bananas from the Caribbean, if made available in ships alongside "standard" bananas	74[121]

between 1992 and 1996 alone.[106] Third, the U.S. has invested considerable public resources into trying to stop the flow of illegal drugs through the Caribbean from South America into the U.S.

There is widespread acknowledgment that a direct effect of the elimination of the Caribbean banana economy would be a surge in illegal drug cultivation and trafficking. A 1996 article in *The Washington Post* quotes Marine General John Sheehan, commander of U.S. forces in the Atlantic and the Caribbean: Caribbean island nations "are dependent on a single crop – bananas. People need to provide for their families" and will resort to drug dealing or illegal migration if driven to it.[107] South American drug cartels, which have already worked their way into the Caribbean, encounter less resistance from displaced farmers who see no economic alternative to the drug trade. Indeed, Caribbean governments, outraged over the U.S.'s pursuit of the case against the banana regime, have withdrawn from cooperative narcotics efforts with the U.S.[108] Finally, another effect of the banana economy's demise will be a surge of unauthorized immigration to the U.S. because so many people in the Caribbean will be thrown out of work.

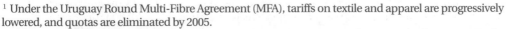

CHAPTER **5** ENDNOTES

[1] Under the Uruguay Round Multi-Fibre Agreement (MFA), tariffs on textile and apparel are progressively lowered, and quotas are eliminated by 2005.

[2] UNCTAD, *1997 Trade and Development Report: Overview*, Geneva: United Nations Conference on Trade and Development (1997), at 6.

[3] UNCTAD, *The Least Developed Countries 1998 Report: Overview*, Geneva: United Nations Conference on Trade and Development (1998), at 3.

[4] *See* "Corporate Profits Year-by-Year," *Associated Press*, Mar. 31, 1999, citing U.S. Department of Commerce, Bureau of Economic Analysis data, Mar. 26, 1999, showing corporate profitability increases of 10.3% in 1997, the fifth consecutive year of double-digit increases.

[5] Ian Goldin and Dominique van der Mensbrugghe, *Trade Liberalisation: What's at Stake, OECD Policy Brief No. 5*, Paris: OECD Development Centre (1994), at 25.

[6] UNCTAD, *Trade and Development Report, 1997: Overview*, Geneva: United Nations Conference on Trade and Development (1997), at 7.

[7] UNCTAD, *Least Developed Countries Report, 1998: Overview*, Geneva: United Nations Conference on Trade and Development (1998), at 3.

[8] Charkravathi Raghavan, "LDCs to Lose $3 Billion in Uruguay Round," *North-South Development Monitor (SUNS)* 3620, on file with Public Citizen.

[9] UNCTAD, *Trade and Development Report, 1998: Overview*, Geneva: United Nations Conference on Trade and Development (1998), at 14-15.

[10] *Id.*

[11] Mark Weisbrot, *Globalization: A Primer*, Washington, D.C.: Preamble Center (1999) at 13.

[12] Steven Radelet and Jeffrey Sachs, "The East Asian Financial Crisis: Diagnosis, Remedies, Prospects," Cambridge: Harvard Institution for International Development, Apr. 20, 1998, at 13. Indonesia, Korea and Thailand had all implemented financial deregulation packages that led to a tremendous expansion in the banking sector, and a rapid growth in the number of financial institutions that could borrow and lend in foreign currencies.

[13] *See* WTO, "State of Play of Disputes," found at www.wto.org/dispute/bulletin.htm, on file with Public Citizen.

[14] WTO, Agreement on Trade-Related Investment Measures (TRIMs), Article 2, read together with Article 5 and the Annex (illustrative list).

[15] Laudeline Auriol & Francois Pham, "What Pattern in Patents," *OECD Observer 179*, Dec. 1992/Jan. 1993, at 15.

[16] UNCTAD, *Trade and Development Report, 1998: Overview*, Geneva: United Nations Conference on Trade and Development (1998) at 2.

[17] *Id.*

[18] *Id.*

[19] Mark Weisbrot, *Globalization: A Primer*, Washington, D.C.: Preamble Center (1999) at 10.

[20] Mark Weisbrot, "Globalization for Whom?" *Cornell International Law Journal*, 1998 Symposium Issue, vol. 31, no. 3, at 4.

[21] Mark Weisbrot, *Globalization: A Primer*, Washington, D.C.: Preamble Center (1999) at 13; *see also* UNDP, *1998 Human Development Report* and UNDP, *1999 Human Development Report* data.

[22] Brian Tomlinson, *A Call to End Global Poverty: Renewing Canadian Aid Policy and Practice Recommendations*, Ottawa: Canadian Council for International Cooperation, Mar. 1999, at 12.

[23] *See, e.g.*, Martin Khor, "A Greater Need for the United Nations in a Liberalizing, Globalizing World," *UN 50th Anniversary Issue, Cooperation South*, Oct. 1995.

[24] Sir James Goldsmith, "GATT and Global Free Trade," in *The Trap*, New York: Carroll and Graf Publishers (1993) at 39.

[25] Council of Economic Advisors, *1999 Economic Report of the President*, Washington, D.C.: U.S. Government Printing Office (GPO) (1999) at 226. Financial Services Agreement (FSA) is designed to further deregulate the financial services sectors of WTO members.

[26] Steven Radelet and Jeffrey Sachs, *The East Asian Financial Crisis: Diagnosis, Remedies, Prospects*, Cambridge: Harvard Institute for International Development, Apr. 20, 1998, at 14-17.

[27] *See* International Labor Organization, "Asian Labor Market Woes Deepening," Press Release ILO/98/42, Dec.

2, 1998.

[28] UNCTAD, *Trade and Development Report, 1998: Overview*, Geneva: United Nations Conference on Trade and Development (1998) at 4.

[29] Christopher Wren, "Sub-Saharan Africa: Growth in Peril," *The New York Times*, Oct. 20, 1998.

[30] Anthony Faiola, "Deep Recession Envelops Latin America," *The Washington Post*, Aug. 5, 1999, at 1.

[31] Mark Weisbrot, *Globalization: A Primer*, Washington, D.C.: Preamble Center (1999) at 13.

[32] *See* International Monetary Fund, *World Economic Outlook* Database: Real Gross Domestic Product, Apr. 1999, on file with Public Citizen, *see also* www.imf.org/external/pubs/ft/weo/1999/01/data/index.htm, at Table 1.2.

[33] United Nations Development Program (UNDP), *Human Development Report 1999*, Geneva: UNDP (1999) at 3.

[34] *Id.*

[35] UNCTAD, *Least Developed Countries 1998 Report: Overview*, Geneva: United Nations Conference on Trade and Development (1998) at 3.

[36] *Id.*

[37] UNCTAD, *1997 Trade and Development Report: Overview*, Geneva: United Nations Conference on Trade and Development (1997) at 6.

[38] *See* Harrison and Hanson, "Who Gains from Trade Reform? Some Remaining Puzzles," National Bureau of Economic Research Working Paper W6915, Jan. 1999.

[39] Chakravarthi Raghavan, *Recolonization: GATT, The Uruguay Round and the Third World*, Penang: Third World Network (1990) at 32.

[40] *Id.* at 36.

[41] *Id.* at 37.

[42] Vinod Rege, "Developing Countries and Negotiations in the WTO," *Third World Economics No. 191*, Aug. 16-31, 1998, at 3.

[43] *Id.* at 4.

[44] *See* Ian Goldin, Odin Knudsen and Dominique van der Mensbrugghe, *Trade Liberalization: Global Economic Implications*, Paris: OECD and Washington: World Bank (1993).

[45] Susan B. Epstein, "GATT: The Uruguay Round Agreement and Developing Countries," *CRS Report for Congress*, Washington, D.C.: Congressional Research Service, Feb. 9, 1995, at summary.

[46] *Id.*

[47] *See* Martin Khor Kok Peng, "The End of the Uruguay Round and Third World Interests," *Third World Network Briefing Paper*, Feb. 1994, on file with Public Citizen.

[48] Chakravarthi Raghavan, "Third World Exports Still Face Major Tariff Barriers," SUNS 4087, at 4.

[49] *See* Jane Kennan & Christopher Stevens, *From Lomé to the GSP: Implications for the ACP Losing Lomé Trade Preferences*, Oxford: Institute of Development Studies, Research Paper for Oxfam Great Britain, Nov. 1997.

[50] *See id.*

[51] "West Africa: Focus on Indigenous Peoples, Crop Diversification," *BRIDGES Weekly Trade News Digest*, vol. 2, no. 34, Sep. 7, 1998.

[52] "Mexico's Average Workers Left Behind Amid Recent Economic Gains," *The Dallas Morning News*, May 26, 1999.

[53] Kristen Dawkins, *Gene Wars*, New York: Seven Stories Press (1997), at 12.

[54] *Id.*

[55] Government of Mexico, National Nutrition Institute, 1997, cited in *Id.* According to the Mexican Institute of Social Security, since NAFTA 158,000 Mexican children die each year before reaching 5 years from illnesses related to malnutrition. *See* Steven Suppan and Karen Lehman, *Food Security and Agricultural Trade under NAFTA*, Minneapolis: Institute for Agriculture and Trade Policy, Jul. 11, 1997, at 4.

[56] Government of Mexico, National Nutrition Institute, 1997, cited in Kristen Dawkins, *Gene Wars*, New York: Seven Stories Press (1997), at 12.

[57] Alison Matiland, "Agriculture Accord Could Leave Poor Worst Off," *Financial Times*, Apr. 14, 1994.

[58] WTO, Agreement on Agriculture (AoA) at Part IV. The AoA requires developing countries to remove non-tariff import controls, converting them to tariffs and then eventually removing them.

[59] *Id.* at Part V. The standstill on agricultural subsidies means no new subsidies can be applied by governments. Developing countries – particularly the least developed countries – that due to budgetary constraints have not afforded domestic support and export subsidies in the past are therefore prohibited from adopting them now or in the future, making it even more difficult for them to compete with cheap agricultural imports from the rich countries that had agriculture subsidy programs in place at the time of the Uruguay Round Agreements' implementation.

[60] *Id.*

[61] Chakravarthi Raghavan, *Recolonization: GATT, The Uruguay Round and the Third World*, Penang: Third World Network (1990) at 32.

[62] *See* Beatrice Chaytor & Michael Hindley, *A Case Study of Sierra Leone's Participation at the WTO*, London: Cameron & May (1997).

[63] *See* C. Christopher Parlin, "WTO Dispute Settlement: Are Sufficient Resources Being Devoted to Enable the System to Function Effectively?" 32 *The International Lawyer* 863, Fall 1998.

[64] The waiver – contained in a 1979 Decision on Differential and More Favourable Treatment, Reciprocity and Fuller Participation of Developing Countries (BISD S/103), (known as the 1979 Enabling Clause) — allows countries to waive MFN obligations to provide preferential tariff treatment to products of LDCs "without being required to extend the same tariffs to the products of any other Member… provided [such treatment is] on a generalized, non-reciprocal and non-discriminatory basis … [and provided it does] not raise barriers or create undue difficulties for the trade of any other Member." Under GATT Article I on MFN, WTO members must treat all WTO members the same; the WTO waiver for development programs allows industrialized and larger developing countries to provide preferential access to their markets to goods produced in LDCs.

[65] WTO, European Communities - Measures Affecting Differential and Favorable Treatment of Coffee, (WT/DS154/1), Report of the Panel (unpublished), Dec. 7, 1998, alleging that Council Regulation (EC) No. 1256/96 is inconsistent with the Enabling Clause as well as with Article I, GATT 1994.

[66] Council Regulation (EC) No. 2820/98, Dec. 21, 1998, at Preamble and Articles 7 and 22.

[67] The EU noted continued disappointment over the U.S. persistence in the banana dispute. EU Trade Commissioner Sir Leon Brittan said, "I really do not see why it is in the interest of the United States that poor countries in the Caribbean and elsewhere, which are not able to do anything other than grow bananas, should be driven into more dangerous economic activity such as drug trafficking." "EU-US Banana War Heats Up," *Bridges Weekly Trade News Digest*, vol. 2, no. 44, Nov. 16, 1998.

[68] "EU Commission, Lomé Countries Fail to Progress on New Trade Pact," *BNA Daily Report for Executives*, Aug. 11, 1999.

[69] *Id.*

[70] *See* Henri-Bernard Solignac Lecomte, "Lomé V et le commerce ACP-UE : quels enjeux pour les pays de la Francophonie?" *European Centre for Development Policy Management Report*, no. 9, Apr. 1999.

[71] "Lomé Talks Slowed By Disagreement Over Regional Agreements," *BRIDGES Weekly Trade News Digest*, vol. 3, no. 20, May 24, 1999.

[72] "Caribbean Leaders Prepare for Lomé," *BRIDGES Weekly Trade News Digest*, vol. 2, no. 32, Aug. 24, 1998.

[73] "Lomé Talks Slowed By Disagreement Over Regional Agreements," *BRIDGES Weekly Trade News Digest*, vol. 2, no. 20, May 24, 1999.

[74] Lorenza Jachia and Ethel Teljeur, *Free Trade Between South Africa and the European Union: A Quantitative Analysis*, Geneva: United Nations Conference on Trade and Development, May 1999.

[75] *See* Michael Weisskopf, "The Busy Back-Door Men," *Time*, Mar. 31, 1997, at 40, and Brook Larmer, "Brawl Over Bananas," *Newsweek*, Apr. 28, 1997, at 44.

[76] Steven Bates, "Billion Dollar Banana Split," *The Guardian* (London), Mar. 6, 1999.

[77] 105th Congress H.R. 4761, Sponsor: Rep. Phil Crane (R-IL), introduced Oct. 9, 1998.

[78] Donations of Carl Lindner, CEO of Chiquita Brands International for Election Cycle 1998, retrieved from The Center for Responsive Politics' contributor database at www.crp.org, on file with Public Citizen.

[79] For example, bananas, coffee, cocoa, beef, veal, sugar and rum. ACP countries heavily dependent on banana trade are, *inter alia*, Dominica, St. Lucia, St. Vincent and the Grenadines.

[80] The Lomé Convention has been instrumental in boosting the growth of vulnerable states. *See* "Vulnerable ACP States," *Lomé 2000*, no. 7, Feb. 1998, at 2.

[81] Chiquita Brand International Form 10-K, Annual Report Pursuant to Section 13 or 15(d) of the Securities Exchange Act of 1934, For the Fiscal Year Ended 1998, at 11, found at the Securities and Exchange Commission EDGAR database at www.sec.gov, on file with Public Citizen.

[82] John Tomlinson, MEP (Member of European Parliament), "Going Bananas?," *EU Development Issues*, Autumn 1997, at 1.

[83] Richard Bernal, "Banana Trade Vital to Caribbean," *Journal of Commerce*, Feb. 3, 1999.

[84] *Id.*

[85] Brook Larmer, "Brawl Over Bananas," *Newsweek*, Apr. 28, 1997, at 44.

[86] Mike Gallagher & Cameron McWhirter, "Violence and Drugs: Armed Soldiers Evict Residents in Chiquita Plan to Eliminate Union," *Cincinnati Enquirer*, May 3, 1998.

[87] Prime Minister Kenny Anthony of St. Lucia, *quoted in*, "Go Easy on Us in Trade, Islands Plead, Give Us

Time to Adapt, Decrease Dependence on Bananas, They Say," *The Miami Herald*, Dec. 11, 1997.

[88] John Tomlinson, MEP (Member of European Parliament), "Going Bananas?" *EU Development Issues*, Autumn 1997, at 1.

[89] Claire Godfrey, *The Importance of Europe's Banana Market to the Caribbean*, Oxford: Oxfam UK (Mar. 1998) at 2.

[90] WTO, European Communities - Regime for the Importation, Sale and Distribution of Bananas (WT/DS27/R), Report of the Panel, May 22, 1997, at para. 426, data submitted by the FAO.

[91] Gary Younge, "Green Gold Loses Out to Dollar Bananas," *The Guardian* (London), Apr. 20, 1999.

[92] WTO, European Communities - Regime for the Importation, Sale and Distribution of Bananas (WT/DS27/R), Report of the Panel, May 22, 1997, at Para. 144.

[93] WTO, European Communities - Regime for the Importation, Sale and Distribution of Bananas (WT/DS27/AB/R), Report of the Appellate Body, Sep. 9, 1997, at Para. 183.

[94] *Id.* at Paras. 255(e) and 255(i).

[95] RAPID (The Spokesman's Service of the European Commission), "The Commission Proposes to Modify the EU's Banana Regime", Press Release, Jan. 14, 1998.

[96] James Canute, "Caribbean, U.S. Officials Go Bananas After Ruling," *Journal of Commerce*, Feb. 26, 1998.

[97] 105th Congress H.R. 4761, Sponsor: Rep. Phil Crane (R-IL), introduced Oct. 9, 1998.

[98] Donations of Carl Lindner, CEO of Chiquita Brands International for Election Cycle 1998, retrieved from The Center for Responsive Politics' contributor database at www.crp.org, on file with Public Citizen.

[99] Stephen Bates, "Billion Dollar Banana Split," *The Guardian* (London), Mar. 6, 1999.

[100] Jessica Pearlman, "Participation by Private Counsel in World Trade Organization Dispute Settlement Proceedings," *Law and Policy in International Business*, No. 2, Vol. 30, Jan. 1, 1999, at 399.

[101] U.S. Mission to the EU "WTO Authorizes U.S. to Retaliate in Banana Dispute," Press Release, Apr. 20, 1999.

[102] WTO, European Communities - Regime for the Importation, Sale and Distribution of Bananas, Recourse to Article 21.5 by the European Communities (WT/DS27/RW/ECU), Report of the Panel, Apr. 12, 1999, at Para. 7.1.

[103] Summary of the EU's 73rd Council Meeting, General Affairs, Luxembourg, Apr. 26, 1999, at 8, on file with Public Citizen.

[104] Douglas W. Payne, "Progress, and Pitfalls, In Latin America," *The Miami Herald*, Jan. 7, 1996, at 1C.

[105] U. S. Department of Commerce, International Trade Administration, "U.S. Trade by Commodity with Caribbean," 1992-1996, found on ITA database at www.ita.doc.gov, on file with Public Citizen. The U.S. had a trade surplus of $5.1 billion with the region between 1992 and 1996.

[106] *Id.*

[107] Thomas W. Lippman, "An Appeal for Banana Peace: General Suggests U.S. Trade Fight May Undercut Caribbean Drug Battle," *The Washington Post*, Jun. 6, 1996.

[108] "Caricom Fires Warning Shot Against U.S. in Banana War," *BRIDGES Weekly Trade News Digest*, vol. 3, no. 9, Mar. 8, 1999.

[109] Brook Larmer, "Brawl Over Bananas," *Newsweek*, Apr. 28, 1997, at 44.

[110] Claire Godfrey, *The Importance of Europe's Banana Market to the Caribbean*, Oxford: Oxfam UK (Mar. 1998) at 2.

[111] John Tomlinson, MEP (Member of European Parliament), "Going Bananas?," *EU Development Issues*, Autumn 1997, at 2.

[112] Richard Bernal, "Banana Trade Vital to Caribbean," *Journal of Commerce*, Feb. 3, 1999.

[113] Claire Godfrey, *The Importance of Europe's Banana Market to the Caribbean*, Oxford: Oxfam UK (Mar. 1998) at 5.

[114] *Id.*.

[115] John Tomlinson, MEP (Member of European Parliament), "Going Bananas?," *EU Development Issues*, Autumn 1997, at 2.

[116] Richard Bernal, "Banana Trade Vital to Caribbean," *Journal of Commerce*, Feb. 3, 1999.

[117] John Nolan, "Workers Seek Better Pay, Conditions," *Associated Press*, Nov. 6, 1998.

[118] Steven Bates, "Billion Dollar Banana Split," *The Guardian* (London), Mar. 6, 1999.

[119] Donations of Carl Lindner, CEO of Chiquita Brands International for Election Cycle 1998, retrieved from the Center for Responsive Politics' contributor database at www.crp.org, on file with Public Citizen.

[120] John Tomlinson, MEP (Member of European Parliament), "Going Bananas?," *EU Development Issues*, Autumn 1997, at 2.

[121] "Europeans Would Pay More for Fair Trade Bananas," *InterPress Service*, Dec. 18, 1997, citing EU Executive Commission poll.

In this chapter ...

CASES:

- **Japanese Megastores**: Japan changed its law promoting mom-and-pop neighborhood retail stores after the U.S. challenged it at the WTO. The law had required economic, traffic, environmental and other impacts to be assessed before a mega-retailer could open a facility.

- **Beer II**: This 1992 GATT ruling set two important precedents. First, it requires national governments to take all constitutionally available measures to force state and local governments to meet GATT rules. Second, it declares that tax laws designed to promote small business conflict with GATT rules to the extent that they discriminate against foreign big business.

- **Canadian Magazines**: The U.S. successfully challenged Canada's excise tax on "split-run" magazines (those with U.S. editorial content and Canadian ads) at the WTO. The law levied a special tax on such publications after Canada concluded that huge U.S. publishing conglomerates were underpricing ads in their split-run publications in a way that threatened smaller independent Canadian publishers. Canada changed the policy to satisfy U.S. demands.

CONCEPTS:

Clinton Administration Promises on Wages and Trade Deficit: While it is too early to measure some WTO effects, the results are in regarding two specific promises. The promise that Uruguay Round implementation would increase U.S. family income by $1,700 *each* year has failed to come true for *any* year since the Uruguay Round was implemented. The promise that the U.S. trade deficit would drop by $60 billion in 10 years, thus creating new jobs, can come true only if the currently *growing* trade deficit were to suddenly decline by $20 billion annually for the next six years.

WTO Agreement on Trade Related Investment Measures: The WTO TRIMs Agreement makes foreign investment more profitable by prohibiting performance requirements and requiring MFN and national treatment.

WTO Agreement on Trade in Services: The WTO calls the GATS Agreement the world's first multilateral agreement on investment since it covers not just cross-border trade in services, but every possible means of supplying a service, including the right to set up a commercial presence in an export market. Before the Uruguay Round, GATT rules applied only to trade in goods. Services include banking, insurance, utilities, telecommunications, transport, etc.

Financial Services Agreement: This specific, top-down sectoral agreement was negotiated after the Uruguay Round's completion and eliminates many restrictions on mergers and acquisitions. It also constrains countries' ability to regulate the financial services sector in other ways. Many of the FSA's requirements, which cover banking and insurance, are the same as those imposed by the IMF on Asian countries that have been implicated in the Asian financial meltdown.

Relocation of High-Tech and Service Sector Jobs: This chapter debunks the myth that these types of jobs will always be around even as manufacturing jobs disappear. Rather, a trend is emerging of relocating certain high-wage jobs (such as computer programming and accounting) and lower-wage, back-office jobs (such as data entry and medical record keeping) to developing countries to cut costs. A Ph.D. computer programmer in India is paid $9,000 a year.

GATS and TRIMs Agreements and Merger Mania: The major trend that has accompanied these new WTO agreements is consolidation in many service sectors through international mergers and acquisitions, which now account for 60% of foreign direct investment. These consolidations typically lead to cuts in "redundant" jobs and also to consumer concerns about competition and access to services.

Developed Country Wages: U.S. workers' real median wages remain more than 4% lower than in 1973. The Labor Department lists low-wage service jobs (retail clerks, janitors, cashiers, waiters) as top categories for future growth.

6 Developed Country Economies Under WTO: Mergers, Service Jobs and Low Wages

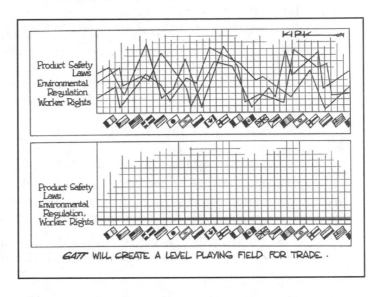

GATT WILL CREATE A LEVEL PLAYING FIELD FOR TRADE .

Uruguay Round proponents in the United States and in other developed countries sold the controversial GATT expansion and the establishment of the WTO to the public by promising concrete economic benefits from the deal. For instance, the Clinton administration promised that each American family would gain $1,700 in annual income from the Uruguay Round,[1] another promise to which the WTO has not measured up. Large multinational firms, small businesses, farmers and workers were all promised to win under the Uruguay Round.

U.S. and European governments continually touted one finding of an Organization for Economic Cooperation and Development (OECD) study, written with the World Bank, that concluded that world income would grow by $213 billion per year if the Uruguay Round were implemented.[2] Critical analysis of this aspect of the report revealed a small detail: The gains occurred only in the tenth year of WTO as measured against the implementation year. Given the background growth-rate forecast for the world over ten years, the seemingly huge Uruguay Round "boost" was actually less than 0.7% per year.[3] This revelation received no U.S. media coverage.

The debate over the Uruguay Round's probable impacts on U.S. employment and economic growth revolved around competing views of the role of the services sector in the U.S. economy. Proponents of the Uruguay Round emphasized that the U.S.'s economic future lay with the service and high-technology sectors.[4] Manufacturing jobs, on the other hand, were cast as quaint vestiges of the past, now more appropriately shifted to developing countries where wages are low, allowing such countries to exercise a comparative advantage in supplying cheap workers for labor-intensive jobs.

Thus, the U.S. strategy at the Uruguay Round was to obtain its goals in the high-tech and service sectors – foreign investor rights and protections, and intellectual

The WTO Agreement on Trade-Related Investment Measures

Past trade agreements set rules for moving goods around the world. The Uruguay Round included an Agreement on Trade Related Investment Measures (TRIMs), which set rules for moving goods and services production around the world.

During Uruguay Round negotiations, the U.S. sought expansive NAFTA-style investor rights and protections. Opposition by developing countries resulted in a slightly narrower approach. However, the developed countries succeeded in ensuring that "their" corporations would be treated favorably in other countries. Given that most developed countries have fewer rules shaping investment, the most significant changes were required of developing countries. The effect was to shift investment policies away from domestic economic development and toward ensuring investor rights.

For instance, the TRIMs Agreement makes foreign investment more profitable by banning policies traditionally used by developing countries to shape foreign investment so that it benefits the country's development. Under the TRIMs Agreement, forbidden policies include:

- requiring foreign corporations to purchase materials locally (to promote capital accumulation, economic diversification);

- requiring foreign corporations to balance imports with exports (to maintain a healthy balance of payments);

- restrictions on foreign corporations' access to foreign exchange to purchase imported inputs (to increase foreign currency reserves); and

- requiring foreign corporations to export their products (so as not to compete with local firms for market share).

The biggest effect of the TRIMs Agreement in developed countries has been to promote the frenzy of service sector mega-mergers. This is the case for two reasons: First, the WTO's Financial Services Agreement and Telecommunications Agreement explicitly eliminated developed country regulations on foreign ownership and mergers in these sectors. Second, by guaranteeing a right to sell services across borders, the GATS Agreement eliminated the need to operate service providers in each market.

Investment is a controversial issue for the WTO's Seattle Ministerial. The OECD negotiations that began in 1995, shortly after completion of the Uruguay Round, to establish a Multilateral Agreement on Investment (MAI) were a backdoor attempt to impose worldwide the NAFTA-style investor rights that had been kept out of the WTO.[5] After a global citizens' campaign exposed and stopped the MAI talks, the EU and Japan began pushing to add the MAI to the WTO starting with the Seattle Ministerial. This has led to the transformation of international campaigns against the MAI into WTO Ministerial-focused campaigns.

property rights guarantees – in exchange for concessions in certain industries (textiles and apparel) and for weakening manufacturing trade remedies (anti-dumping and Section 301 laws). The U.S. was not able to forge agreements as favorable to U.S. corporate interests in some sectors as it was able to in North American Free Trade Agreement (NAFTA) negotiations. However, in the WTO General Agreement on Trade in Services (GATS), the Agreement on Trade Related Investment Measures (TRIMs) and the Agreement on Trade Related Aspects of Intellectual Property (TRIPs), the U.S. succeeded in establishing new enforceable commercial rights for multinational companies in numerous WTO Member country markets.

Meanwhile, critics of the Uruguay Round pointed out that, first, the very purpose of the GATS, TRIMs and TRIPs Agreements was to protect U.S. investment *overseas*. In other words, many of the Uruguay Round Agreements paved the way for the export of U.S. jobs to lower wage countries. This included service sector and high-tech jobs, meaning the transformation of the traditional service sector job – linked to the local economy and community and thus relatively secure – into yet another mobile aspect of the global economy. A new trend of shifting even high-paying service sector jobs – engineering, computer programming and accounting – overseas is increasing. Also, the new Uruguay Round Agreements have helped foster the frenzy of global mergers. Given the practice of cutting "redundant" jobs after mergers, this trend has led to soaring stock values and job losses.

Second, Uruguay Round critics – and others – have general critiques of the realities of the service economy relative to its myths. With some notable exceptions in the information sectors most susceptible to being shipped overseas, such as computer programming, U.S. government data conclusively show that service sector jobs on average are lower-paying than those in the manufacturing sector.[6] They also do not typically include the permanence or the unionization rate and thus the benefits (health insurance, pensions) available in the manufacturing sector.[7] Currently, the largest employer in the world is the temporary work agency called "Manpower Inc.," which brokered 1.4 million temporary jobs in 1997.[8] Meanwhile, the U.S. Department of Labor projects that low-wage service jobs such as cashiers, waitresses, janitors and retail clerks are the professions with the greatest expected future growth in the U.S.[9]

In contrast, corporations generally have benefited richly from the new rights and protections in the global services and investment sectors. In 1994, U.S. companies' direct investment abroad was $613 billion. By 1998, it had increased by more than 50% to $980.5 billion.[10] This coincided with a trend in double-digit profits; corporate profits rose 10.3% in 1997, the fifth consecutive year of double-digit increases.[11] This increase pushed the before-tax profit rate to 8.5%, the highest level since the mid-1960s. The after-tax rate rose to 6.4%, the highest rate in the post-World War II period.[12]

The promises that the service sector economy and the GATS Agreement would be a boon to workers in the industrialized countries have not been realized, in part because they were based on a series of myths and faulty premises.

Common Myths About the Service Sector and High-Tech Economy

A 1996 Yankolovich Partners study found that U.S. service providers' expansions overseas are creating lots of jobs, just not for Americans. The study surveyed 250 multinational corporations and found that nearly half of them were "seriously considering" relocating company-wide or regional responsibilities for non-manufacturing functions outside the U.S.[13]

The WTO General Agreement on Trade in Services

The General Agreement on Trade in Services (GATS) was designed to open markets for trade in services in a similar manner as GATT did for trade in goods.

Services were brought within GATT rules after intense lobbying by the U.S.[14], the world's largest exporter of services.[15] The U.S. wanted the GATS Agreement to establish new rights of "establishment" in every WTO Member country, meaning that countries must permit mergers, acquisitions or new service start-ups in their markets by foreign companies.

Developing countries, on the other hand, were intensely opposed to service sector liberalization.[16] They predicted that giant multinational service providers from industrialized countries would overwhelm fledgling domestic competitors if they had a new right to set up shop without government supervision.[17]

Generally the GATS Agreement applies to all service industries, but according to what is called a "bottom-up" approach. This means that only the service sectors that countries agree to include are covered.

However, there are four specific economic sectors explicitly addressed in the GATS Agreement. These are financial services, telecommunications, maritime transport and air transport. Agreements were completed to deregulate financial services (Financial Services Agreement) and telecommunications (Telecommunications Agreement).[18] These agreements are top-down, in the sense that they set rules with which all WTO Members must comply, including the right of foreign ownership in these sectors.

The GATS Agreement requires WTO Members to allow companies from other countries to:

- establish a "commercial presence" (set up subsidiaries or acquire or merge with local companies);

- provide services from one country to another (e.g., international telephone calls, data processing); and

- travel between countries to supply services (e.g., lawyers, consultants).

Myth 1: High-Tech and Professional Service Jobs Will Always Be Around

Amid the press coverage of massive U.S. manufacturing job losses[19] and merger-related layoffs, the steady movement of high-tech and other service sector jobs overseas has not received much notice.

Two types of service jobs are being moved away: high-wage professional jobs that are mobile, such as those relating to computer programming or actuarial work, and low-wage jobs that can be separated from corporate centers.

For instance, Owens Corning moved higher-end professional jobs in finance, procurement, business support and even college recruiting functions overseas.[20] SwissAir shifted a large portion of its accounting department to India,[21] while a Washington, D.C., suburban hospital transferred its medical records typing and filing via modem to Bangalore, India (the salary in the U.S. is $25,000 per year, compared to $3,000 per year in India).[22]

The maquiladora region along the U.S.-Mexican border, originally intended to allow tariff-free product assembly for re-export, no longer consists only of manufacturing plants only. Supermarket chains are now cheaply employing the well-educated and using the conveniently close Mexican labor market to enter computer data from coupons.[23] The trend to transfer such "back office" operations, from insurance actuaries to airline reservations (American Airlines is the largest private employer in Barbados), has led governments in Ireland, the Philippines, Barbados and other nations to form development corporations to U.S. service providers to relocate to their countries.[24]

Meanwhile, the trend of sending "white-collar" jobs overseas also is occurring in high-technology sectors. The companies that created Silicon Valley, such as Advanced Micro Devices and Hewlett-Packard, have been shifting employment to low-wage countries.[25] For instance, many U.S. technology companies now contract with computer programmers in Bangalore, India, where workers holding Ph.Ds in computer science are paid $9,000 annually.[26] Another example is IBM's hard disk drive business, which started in the U.S. and Western Europe but was shifted to cheaper labor markets since it took off.[27] According to *The Wall Street Journal*, "IBM plans to establish this new site as a joint venture with an undetermined Asian partner and use non-IBM employees so that it will be easier ... to move to an even lower-cost region when warranted. Moving from higher-cost regions in Asia cuts in half the cost of assembling the disk drive."[28]

> **T**he GATS is "the world's first multilateral agreement on investment" since it covers "not just cross-border trade but every possible means of supplying a service, including the right to set up a commercial presence in the export market."[29]
>
> — World Trade Organization

Myth 2: Mega-Mergers Benefit Both Employers *and* Employees

The primary trend that has accompanied the implementation of the GATS Agreement has been a tidal wave of global mergers between existing service providers. The WTO describes the GATS Agreement as "the world's first multilateral agreement on investment" since it covers "not just cross-border trade but every possible means of supplying a service, including the right to set up a commercial presence in the export market."[30] Commercial presence means that corporate service providers have a new right to enter WTO Member markets and compete against and acquire domestic companies.

The new corporate right to a "commercial presence" in other WTO Member countries under the GATS Agreement fosters increased consolidation in numerous service sectors. Indeed, 1998 is considered the year of the "mega-merger," witnessing more than 12,500 deals totaling more than $1.6 trillion — an all-time record for mergers and acquisitions.[32]

Most of these mergers were in the financial and telecommunications sectors – the two sectors that so far have undergone the most WTO deregulation – and many were cross-border in nature.[33]

Indeed, the very nature of corporate foreign investment is changing, with cross-border mergers and acquisitions comprising 60% of total foreign direct investment (FDI), a greater percentage of FDI than at any time during the 1990s.[34]

Global mergers represented nearly three-fifths of total foreign direct investment inflows in 1997, increasing by 50% over 1996.[31]

Mergers and acquisitions, like most consolidations, typically lead to layoffs.[35] The widespread firings of workers made redundant by mergers is a major factor in the soaring stock prices of the resulting mega-companies.[36] Personnel cuts show up in balance sheets as savings, boosting net worth. The rash of mergers in numerous sectors is a significant factor exacerbating the fact that some one billion workers – one third of the world's labor force – remain unemployed or underemployed.[37]

Myth 3: Free Trade Raises Living Standards

According to standard economic theory, efficiency gains from increased trade (i.e., cheaper imports for consumers) should allow all nations to gain from freer trade. The theory predicts, however, there will be "winners and losers" within each country. In the U.S. over the last quarter century, the losers have included the majority of the U.S. labor force.[44]

Imports as a percentage of U.S. GDP have more than doubled since 1973, the year economists use to refer to the onset of globalization in its current form.[46] Yet the real median wage of the U.S. worker has fallen since 1973 and, after more than nine years of economic growth, has just reached its pre-recession 1989 level. The U.S. worker's real median wage still remains more than 4% lower than in 1973.[47]

This contrasts sharply to the period before 1973, when the wages of the typical U.S. worker rose 79% between 1946 and 1973.[48]

In the U.S., workers' median real wages are more than 4% lower than in 1973.[45]

While wages have been stagnating, corporate profits have been soaring. In the United States, the share of national income going to corporate profits has increased by 3.2 percentage points since the last business cycle peak.[49]

Increased trade continues to harm U.S. workers. Economists have found that in the economic sectors experiencing the largest import growth, imports are destroying better-than-average jobs.[50] Further, jobs created through exports are typically not as high-paying as those destroyed by import competition. Increased import shares over the past 15 years have displaced almost twice as many high-paying, high-skilled jobs as increased export shares have created.[51] Industries facing fast-growing import competition pay wages that are up to 4.5% higher than those paid in sectors with rapidly growing exports.[52]

Loan Guarantees for U.S. Steel Sector Threatened As An Illegal Subsidy Under WTO

Legislation aimed at granting the U.S. steel sector limited relief from a historically high surge of imports and 35,000 lost jobs triggered by the Asian financial crisis has been targeted by the EU as a WTO-illegal subsidy.[38] With the IMF pushing countries to export their way to "recovery," and massive currency devaluations in East Asia, Russia and Brazil making imports cheaper,[39] Congress passed the Emergency Steel Loan and Guarantee Act in 1999. The bill, which provides $270 million to guarantee $1 billion in loans to steel companies,[40] was the weaker alternative to a bill that would have imposed quotas on steel imports to shield steel jobs from the repercussions of the Asian financial crisis.[41] The U.S. steel industry is the most efficient in the world, having been dramatically restructured in the 1980s.

The EU's ambassador to the U.S. wrote: "We recognize the serious pressures that have arisen in the steel sector and understand the need for both Congress and the administration to consider the problems confronting the domestic steel industry. We do, however, urge you to ensure that the U.S. does not respond to the temporary pressures facing one sector of the U.S. economy by signing into law new trade-distorting measures, which could well, in our view, be contrary to your WTO obligations."[42] The EU claimed that the loan guarantees violate the WTO Agreement on Subsidies and Countervailing Measures because they increased the relative creditworthiness of the U.S. steel industry on the world market.[43] Ironically, the weaker bill had been developed only because the Clinton administration strenuously opposed quotas and other unilateral action, informing union leaders that these options were no longer available because they were WTO-illegal.

More Broken WTO Promises: U.S. Income Gains Fail to Materialize, Deficit Up

While a comprehensive economic impact assessment of the Uruguay Round cannot be undertaken until all of the disciplines have been fully phased in, the Clinton administration made two key short-term promises that can be evaluated now – nearly five years after implementation of the Uruguay Round Agreements.

- The administration promised that the Uruguay Round would reduce the 1993 $115.6 billion U.S. trade deficit by $60 billion over 10 years, thus creating jobs through increased exports.[53]

- The administration promised an increase in family income of $1,700 per year if the Uruguay Round were approved.[54]

TRADE DEFICIT: The U.S. trade deficit has climbed steadily since the WTO's inauguration, from $98 billion in 1994 and 1995 to $164 billion in 1998.[55] In order for the administration's predictions to be borne out in the long term, the deficit would have to decrease by $21 billion per year for the next six years. Yet the U.S. trade deficit further ballooned to $218 billion by mid-1999[56] and was predicted to be at yet another all-time record high at the end of 1999.

MEDIAN INCOME: Median family income did not increase by the promised $1,700 during *any* year since the Uruguay Round Agreements went into effect.[57] The small gains in income that have occurred over the past few years are more attributable to the Federal Reserve's loosening of monetary policy than to trade.[58] Indeed, the increasingly bloated U.S. trade deficit means that employment in those higher-wage industries battered by import competition (such as manufacturing) has fallen. Applying the Clinton administration formula for calculating employment effects of trade, 858,000 U.S. jobs have been lost due to trade since 1994.[59] The impact of the loss of good manufacturing jobs is not canceled out by the service sector jobs the U.S. economy is creating at a rapid pace. The U.S. Department of Labor reports that jobs now being created do not generally pay as well as those being lost, as the former are primarily located in the lower-paying service sector and the latter were in the higher-paying manufacturing sector.[60] Indeed, workers who lose their jobs due to trade are twice as likely to be forced to accept lower-paying employment than to find a job that pays the same or more than the one they lost.[61] Finally, gains in family-wide income are higher than in personal real median income, representing in part the need for more family members to enter the workforce to maintain the standard of living achievable in the past by fewer workers per family.

The Uruguay Round Agreements have not benefited all businesses. Both in what it promotes and what it prohibits, the WTO has undermined some key small business interests.

WTO Undermines Small Business Promotion in Industrialized Countries

One reason the WTO has developed a reputation of favoring large multinational corporations over small, local producers is that the WTO's rules are more suited to use by large, multinational enterprises. For instance, many of the Uruguay Round's new provisions target opportunities typically outside the range of small businesses – operating a foreign country's telecommunication system, chartering banks in foreign countries, relocating factories, acquiring foreign firms or marketing a product worldwide, which requires global intellectual property protections. In addition, there have been several cases where GATT or WTO tribunals have explicitly ruled against small business interests.

The first case involved a 1992 GATT ruling in a case in which Canada challenged numerous U.S. states' alcohol licensing and distribution laws as well as U.S. federal excise tax policy that provided a tax break for small breweries.[62] In the case, known as "Beer II," the GATT panel ruled that the U.S. could not favor its small producers over large U.S. producers because this would have a discriminatory effect on large foreign breweries.[63] It also ruled that federalism — specifically applied to the alcohol distribution and licensing procedures required by many states — was too onerous and therefore was impermissible under GATT rules because it had the effect of making imported beer more costly.[64]

The principal complaints of Canada were that the U.S. had increased the excise tax on beer but had left unchanged the existing lower rate for the first 60,000 barrels produced by small U.S. breweries with annual production not exceeding $2 million.[65] Canada also complained that different states' excise tax differentials or credits based on annual production were inconsistent with GATT rules and that many states' alcoholic beverages distribution requirements imposed greater burdens on imported beers.[66]

The U.S. argued that the lower excise tax rate for small U.S. beer producers was an allowable subsidy under GATT rules to spur economic growth for small businesses.[67] The state distribution and licensing procedures that Canada objected to, on the other hand, the U.S. argued, were put in place under state discretion inherent in the U.S. system of federalism to promote social welfare — for instance, to ensure that there was adequate regulation in the sale and distribution and consumption of alcoholic beverages.[68] The panel disagreed on both points.[69]

One of the ruling's key implications is that governments cannot use tax policy — an archetypal government function — to spur economic growth by subsidizing small-scale producers. This bias was highlighted in the Beer II case, especially regarding laws in Minnesota, Oregon, Michigan, Wisconsin, Ohio and Pennsylvania. The GATT ruling condemned these states for offering excise tax breaks to local beer producers even though these tax breaks did not discriminate against out-of-state producers and merely targeted all micro-producers that were operating within the state.[70] One recent WTO example demonstrates the Uruguay Round's impact on government policy aimed at promoting small business.

Case 1: WTO Undermines Policies Promoting Small Businesses Over Megastores

Japan's Large-Scale Retail Law required extensive public hearings and economic, traffic, environmental and other impact assessments before a large retailer could open for business.[71] The goal of the law was to promote the establishment of and maintain small shops, such as neighborhood-owned and -operated retail shops. By pre-empting unfair competition by large corporations whose higher social costs in traffic and environmental damage would otherwise go uncounted, the law sought to balance the playing field for the small shops. The laws' requirements applied equally to domestic and foreign investors and service providers, and established a comprehensive screening process for all retailers over a certain size.

The United States Trade Representative (USTR) mounted a two-pronged assault on the law. First, the U.S. challenged it during the WTO Kodak film case, arguing that it created obstacles to imports.[72] The U.S. contended that since large-scale retailers are more likely to sell imported goods than local shopkeepers, the law served to disrupt trade.[73]

The WTO dispute panel ruled that because there was nothing in the Large Scale Retail law that prevented small shops from retailing imported goods, the U.S. had not proven its case.[74]

Second, the U.S. had also registered a WTO complaint against the pro mom-and-pop store law under the General Agreement on Trade in Services (GATS), contending that its procedural requirements – hearings and impact assessments – created a barrier to the market access of foreign retailers and increased the leverage of smaller merchants over larger competitors.[75]

All of the USTR's evidence in the WTO case was anecdotal; it asserted that small companies used the law to limit the operations of larger retailers, that is, to delay opening dates, to restrict their business hours, etc.[76] It also claimed that the law enabled small merchants to "extract promises" that the large retailers would not compete against them in certain narrowly defined areas.[77]

Consultations between the U.S. and Japan began in 1996 and continued past the resolution of the Kodak case in 1998. By May 1998, Japan acquiesced to U.S. demands that it abolish its Large-Scale Retail Law, passing legislation that transformed the Large-Scale Retail law into a zoning law.[78] It's new name is the Large-Scale Retail Store Location Law, and it provides only for environmental and traffic impact assessments for large-scale retail locations.[79] It will no longer take into consideration the economic impact of competition from large retailers on local businesses. The WTO threat resulted in a policy change that sacrifices small business owners so that mega-corporations such as Wal-Mart and its Japanese equivalents have an easier time dominating the market.

The WTO GATS Agreement:
Mergers, Competition and Consumer Issues

The recent growth in the occurrence and scale of global service sector mergers raises a number of red flags for consumers, workers and small businesses in both the industrialized and developing worlds.

Mergers, Acquisitions and Anti-Competitive Practices

Part of the liberal economic philosophy is the promotion of "specialization" and "economy of scale." Ironically, the far end of an economy of scale is monopoly – the least efficient state. When mega-companies are empowered by trade rules guaranteeing market access in limitless economic sectors, they establish global monopolies, wielding their power to establish cartels, fix prices and engage in other anti-competitive business practices. Such an eventuality not only denies the served communities the benefits of competition but serves the opposite purpose — that of driving out small competitors and restricting entry into the market.

The WTO contains no provisions to regulate competition for the benefit of consumers and entrepreneurs. Indeed, U.S. companies now use globalization as a way to weaken domestic antitrust policy. U.S. corporations are pressing regulators to reinterpret U.S. antitrust policy in light of the increasingly global nature of their operations. According to Albert A. Foer, president of the American Antitrust Institute, "The line of argument is that such corporations are not primarily competing domestically, but globally, and that antitrust regulations should be interpreted more leniently to take into account the essentially transnational character of competition."[80]

The transnational nature of competition has suited the small handful of large entertainment conglomerates in the U.S., which have established market share all over the world. Yet global consolidation of the entertainment industry creates a unique set of problems: Nations often seek to regulate foreign entry into the so-called "cultural industries" of movies, television, radio and publishing to preserve cultural diversity and identity. When a domestic movie house, record company, television station or publisher goes out of business due to competition with an entertainment conglomerate, not only jobs are lost. Products that reflect local heritage, tradition and culture also disappear from the market.

Therefore, proposals to have the GATS Agreement cover cultural industries was very controversial, pitting the U.S. against the French and Canadians who wanted to protect their film and audiovisual industries from complete dominance by Hollywood competitors.[81] In the end, a compromise was reached allowing some application of GATS rules to the cultural industries. First, MFN (nondiscrimination among products from different foreign countries) is the only GATS principle that was generally applied to culture.[82] Second, while the GATS Agreement does not contain any general "exception" carving out the so-called cultural industries, it does allow countries to withhold specific commitments on audiovisual services.[83] This U.S. concession was viewed as the "sacrifice" of Hollywood interests in the name of closing a Uruguay Round deal.

Because the GATS Agreement does not provide for a general exception of cultural industries from its requirements, this sector (like all other services) will always be on the table for future liberalization under the GATS Agreement's built-in negotiating agenda. Also, even with the existing GATS rules, WTO Member countries have a variety of avenues for challenging other countries' laws. For instance, the WTO recently ruled against Canada when the U.S. challenged its policies restricting the entry of certain foreign magazines. The U.S. built its case around GATT provisions requiring the non-discriminatory treatment of goods (i.e., magazines).

Case 2: The WTO Says "No" to Cultural Diversity — Canadian Magazines

Recently liberalized trade in services already has had an impact on the cultural industries. Recent press reports in the U.S. indicate that the Hollywood movie industry is relocating service jobs, in such areas as producing, sound and set design, to Canada.[84] This is particularly ironic given that Canada is extraordinarily protective of its own cultural industries sector and takes great pains to guard against the more typical trend of U.S. dominance in television, movies and publishing.[85]

Critics of the World Trade Organization both within government and outside it often have focused on the role of U.S. entertainment-sector exports in homogenizing culture worldwide and promoting the value of consumerism. The WTO's recent ruling against Canada's effective ban on so-called "split-run magazines" sent the warning that a nation's culture cannot be exempted from the principles of so-called "free trade." Under WTO rules, the interest in preserving domestic and indigenous cultural forms has been eclipsed by the right of entertainment conglomerates to sell their products worldwide. Indeed, Canada's market for foreign magazines was far from closed when the U.S. initiated its challenge of Canadian cultural policy on behalf of Time Warner, Inc.[86] Half of the English-language magazines in Canada and four-fifths of those sold in newsstands are from abroad.[87] However, in 1997, the WTO ruled that Canada could not maintain any nationality-based regulation of its magazine market.

Since 1965, Canada had levied a tariff on split-run magazines.[88] Split-run magazines are special editions that contain foreign editorial content but sell space to

> *In a letter to the USTR's Section 301 Committee, the U.S. Chamber of Commerce condemned all foreign governments acting to "protect [their markets] from American cultural dominance."* [89]

domestic advertisers or aim advertising at the domestic market. Canada enacted the tax law to protect smaller Canadian-owned publications from losing advertising revenue to larger magazines from the U.S.[90] The government was concerned that Canadian-owned magazines would not survive competition with U.S.-based publishing conglomerates.

In 1995, Canada amended the 1965 law to impose an 80% excise tax on split-run magazines.[91] Canada took this action in response to the evasion by *Sports Illustrated* of the split-run tariff. Earlier that year, Time Warner began to beam its magazine via satellite into Canada to avoid the tariff.[92]

In 1996, the U.S. launched a WTO challenge against Canadian magazine import policies.[93] The U.S. challenged the 80% excise tax, as well as the 1965 tariffs on split-run magazines and Canada's policy of imposing higher postal rates for imported magazines.[94]

Canada defended the excise tax, arguing that *Sports Illustrated's* advertising revenues from its U.S. edition more than covered the publication costs of the Canadian edition. *The New York Times* reports that *Sports Illustrated* was thus able to sell advertising in the local edition to Canadian companies at rock bottom rates,[95] threatening smaller Canadian publishers. To Canada, Time Warner's underpricing of advertising services amounted to a "dumping" offense (selling goods below the cost of their production in order to dominate the market).[96]

From the Canadian perspective, at issue was the disappearance of Canadian journalism itself. As Canadian publishing houses lost advertising revenue and began to go out of business, the number of magazines with local Canadian content would be whittled down. In its place would be U.S. journalism, effecting a cultural imperialism over Canada.

Indeed, the U.S. industry conceptualized the magazine case in terms of a crusade for American culture. In a letter to the USTR's Section 301 Committee, the U.S. Chamber of Commerce condemned all foreign governments acting to "protect [their markets] from American cultural dominance."[97]

In March 1997, a WTO panel found the Canadian measures to be in violation of GATT rules forbidding discrimination and import restrictions.[98] This decision later was upheld by the Appellate Body.[99]

Instead of allowing unrestricted import of magazines with American copy and Canadian ads as the U.S. had hoped, the Canadian government proceeded to propose legislation that focused on regulating sales of "advertising services."[100] This was meant to move the disputed legislation into the area covered by the more permissive GATS Agreement, thereby complying with the letter of the 1997 WTO ruling, yet maintaining the effect of protecting domestic industry and culture.[101]

Since the GATS Agreement is a bottom-up agreement, Canada can choose those services to which it extends nondiscriminatory treatment. It was thus able to exclude advertising and maintain restrictions on the foreign sale of advertising services.

The U.S. was infuriated by Canada's maneuver and threatened $4 billion worth of import sanctions as well as the suspension of favorable tariffs accorded to Canada under NAFTA.[102] Finally, in May 1999, Canada was pressured into abandoning the new legislation. Canada cut a deal with the U.S. that allows U.S. publishers to sell 18% of their advertising space to Canadian clients if a "substantial" level of Canadian content is maintained in the publication.[103] "Substantial," however, is not defined in detail in the deal, which has been described as a "sell-out" of the Canadian publishing industry.[104] In a concession to domestic publishers, the Canadian government has promised to set up a "multimillion-dollar" fund to support the Canadian industry, but U.S. publishers are already claiming that they too should qualify for these new subsidies.[105]

Financial Services Sector Consolidation & Market Volatility

Economic research indicates that increasing mergers in the financial services sector, accompanied by liberalization of capital transfers, contributes to volatility in financial markets.[106] The 1997 WTO Financial Services Agreement promoted access to new markets for the world's largest banking and finance multinationals by establishing a right of commercial presence either via acquisition, merger or start-up. Yet, such financial institutions helped provoke the Asian financial crisis, which caused widespread economic hardship abroad and undermined the stability of U.S. mutual funds and other pension instruments domestically.

The Bank for International Settlements (BIS) reports that the volume of foreign exchange trading grew by 26% between 1995 and 1998, reaching a volume of $1.5 trillion per day.[107] The majority of such trading is conducted by the financial services industry[108] and is no longer performed primarily for the purposes of facilitating trade or foreign investment, but is predominately speculative (i.e., conducted for the purpose of profiting from slight fluctuations in currency values).[109] Economists have attributed the devaluation of the Thai baht in 1997 — the first event in the Asian financial crisis — to this practice.[110]

Consumers' Basic Access to Services

The GATS and TRIMs Agreements require "national treatment" for investors in all WTO Member countries. This means foreign corporations will have the same rights to bid on privatizing public services as community cooperatives or domestically owned companies.[111] As countries, especially in the developing world, increasingly succumb to International Monetary Fund pressure and privatize public assets, these become subject to GATS Agreement rules requiring the service sector to open itself up to foreign competition. The threat to community access to

Canada May Challenge U.S. Food Stamps in WTO

Canadian agricultural officials recently hinted that Canada will raise the issue of whether U.S. food stamp and school lunch programs constitute agricultural subsidies under WTO rules. Asked whether Canadian trade negotiators would be likely to take up the position of a Canadian dairy group that says these social insurance programs should be considered domestic agricultural subsidies, the Canadian official stated, "Part of the discussion [in Seattle] will have to be a definition of what constitutes a domestic subsidy," and some of those programs "certainly" will fall within that definition.[112]

basic services is likely to increase as utilities such as electricity, telephone service, water and gas are privatized and then under the GATS Agreement are acquired by or merged into foreign corporations.

Privatization in the utilities sector is one of the defining characteristics of globalization.[113] It also is the first step in the eventual trade in such services.

If the trend toward privatization of essential public services continues and such services are steadily liberalized under GATS Agreement rules, many consumers could lose access to those services. For instance, in the U.S., electricity and telephone services for rural customers – which are more expensive to provide than for urban customers – are subsidized to prevent geographical discrimination in pricing and to ensure that all citizens have equal access.[114] In the absence of utility regulation, corporations could control prices and access, depriving many economically or geographically disadvantaged con-

Health Care Services Targeted By Industry for "Seattle Round"

The U.S. health care industry seeks to use the WTO Seattle Ministerial to press for further global liberalization, privatization and what it calls "pro-competitive regulatory reform"[118] in the health sector. Worse, the U.S. government officially has come out in support of liberalization of the health care "sector."[119]

In a paper calling for wide and "flexible" (i.e., open) negotiations on health care in Seattle, the industry complains that public ownership and regulation of health care has made it difficult for private U.S. health care providers to penetrate foreign markets.[120] According to the health industry, OECD country regulations are particularly excessive, whereas "existing regulations are by and large not a problem in emerging markets."[121] Consequently, the industry wishes the U.S. delegation to push for deregulation in developed countries and privatization in the developing world.

Yet, deregulation of the health sector is bound to leave consumers increasingly unprotected, as the industry is also keen to get rid of restrictions regarding the licensing of health care professionals, as well as certain privacy and confidentiality regulations.[122] Many of these are agenda items that have failed repeatedly when pushed in the U.S. Congress.

sumers of basic services. This is a reality in many developing countries where water has been privatized. In Pakistan, for instance, slum dwellers pay 83 times the price for water from private vendors than do wealthy families hooked up to public water systems.[115] In Indonesia, the poor who buy from water vendors pay 60 times more; in Peru 20, times more.[116]

In addition, in the financial services sector, deregulation and liberalization encourage consolidation of financial services into the hands of a few multinational corporations that have no links to the places in which they operate. Large multinational banks can effectively bar entire communities from capital markets.[117]

Services Agenda for the Seattle Ministerial

Despite these warning signs, the U.S. supports further service sector deregulation and liberalization, even in the health care and education sectors under the GATS Agreement.[123] If the precedent already set in the financial services industry is repeated in the health care industry, far from strengthening the capacities of various countries to provide health services to all, the merging of health services providers would create large and monopolistic entities that span the globe and literally hold the power of death and life. The trend toward consolidation is already emerging in the health care and pharmaceuticals industries. Health services, for example, placed second in the number of merger and acquisition deals in 1997; 640 mergers took place within the U.S. alone.[124] In the U.S., the trend toward mergers and acquisitions in health services – with huge for-profit hospital chains and managed care providers – has led to decreased access to health care and a resulting backlash in Congress, which is currently considering "Patient's Bill of Rights" legislation to protect consumers from the excesses and dangers of market-based health care delivery.[125] The further liberalization and deregulation of services in a proposed WTO "Seattle Round" is therefore a highly contentious issue. As the most insistent supporter of service liberalization, the U.S. is pressing for the launch of new GATS Agreement negotiations in such diverse areas as finance, telecommunications, distribution, audio-visual services, construction, tourism, education, health and government procurement.[126] By putting all service sectors on the table at once, including health and education, objecting countries are put in the weak position of having to ask for exemptions for services they want protected and potentially having to "trade off" different sectors in a final agreement. Developing countries are wary of any further liberalization of services[127] and are interested in protecting tourism, maritime transport and construction from foreign investment.[128]

—————— CHAPTER ENDNOTES ——————

[1] Lloyd Bentsen, "The Uruguay Round Now," *The Washington Post*, Sep. 13, 1994.

[2] *See* Ian Goldin, Odin Knudsen and Dominique van der Mensbrugghe, *Trade Liberalization: Global Economic Implications*, Washington, D.C.: World Bank (1993), at 13.

[3] Samuel Brittan, "Where GATT's $200b really Comes From," *Financial Times*, Oct. 4, 1993.

[4] Bart Ziegler, "IBM Is Overhauling Disk Drive Business, Cutting Jobs, Shifting Production to Asia," *The Wall Street Journal*, Aug. 5, 1994.

[5] NAFTA's investment Chapter 11 established a list of new rights countries owe to foreign investors and corporations, such as a guarantee that foreign investors will be compensated for any government action – even if non-discriminatory – that undermines expected future profitability. *See* NAFTA at Sec. 1110.

[6] Bureau of Labor Statistics, *National Employment Hours and Earnings: Manufacturing and Services*, Jul. 1999. Historically, manufacturing wages have driven wages in the rest of the economy.

[7] *See* "Contingent Worker Safety: A Full-Time Job in a Part-Time World," *Occupational Hazards*, Oct. 1997, at 2, citing Occupational Safety and Health Administration data.

[8] "Manpower Inc. Is Shaken Up in Power Struggle," *International Herald Tribune*, Jul. 7, 1998.

[9] George Silvestri, "Occupational Employment Projections to 2006," *Monthly Labor Review*, Nov. 1997, at 58.

[10] U.S. Department of Commerce, Bureau of Economic Analysis, "U.S. Direct Investment Abroad: Country Detail for Selected Items 1994-1998," found at www.bea.doc.gov/bea/di/dia-ctry.htm, on file with Public Citizen.

[11] "Corporate Profits Year-by-Year," *Associated Press*, Mar. 31, 1999, citing U.S. Department of Commerce data.

[12] Lawrence Mishel, Jared Bernstein and John Schmitt, *The State of Working America,1998-1999*, New York: M.E. Sharpe (1999) at 110.

[13] Fred R. Bleakley, "US Firms Shift More Office Jobs Abroad," *Wall Street Journal*, Apr. 22, 1996.

[14] John Madeley, *Trade and the Poor: The Impact of International Trade on Developing Countries*, 2nd Ed., Intermediate Technology Publications (1996), at 71-72. "At the GATT Ministerial meeting in 1982, the U.S government proposed that services be included in trade liberalization schemes, and vigorously campaigned on the issue throughout the 1980s . ... The U.S even proposed that the words 'and services' simply be added every time that the word 'goods' appeared in a GATT document. ... Since 1985, the USA has refused to be involved in any trade negotiations that did not include services. Ironically, by 1992, when the USA realized that some developing countries stood to do very well by selling services to the American market, it argued in the UR negotiations that it should be exempt from around three-quarters of tradable services." *Id.*

[15] "International Trade Statistics - Leading Exporters and Importers in World Trade in Commercial Services, 1997," *World Trade Organization Annual Report* (1997), at Table 1.7.

[16] Chakravarthi Raghavan, "Not So Fool-Proof: GATS Safeguards and Prudential Rights, *Third World Economics*, No. 175, December 1997, at 3.

[17] Indeed, years of participation in International Monetary Fund (IMF) structural adjustment programs had led to the mass privatization and selling-off of domestic utilities, banks and telecommunications companies. *See inter alia* various "Letters of Intent" between the IMF and borrower countries available at www.imf.org/external/np/loi/mempub.htm; on file with Public Citizen.

[18] The WTO Agreement on Telecommunications, setting out rules for access to telecommunications systems, was completed in February 1997, and went into effect in 1998. The WTO Agreement on Financial Services was completed in 1998 and went into effect in January 1999, although most countries have not implemented their commitments. Maritime transport negotiations have been deferred until 2000.

[19] *See* Bureau of Labor Statistics, "National Employment, Hours, and Earnings," on file with Public Citizen.

[20] Fred R. Bleakley, "US Firms Shift More Office Jobs Abroad," *The Wall Street Journal*, Apr. 22, 1996.

[21] Sir James Goldsmith, *The Trap*, New York: Carrol & Graf Publishers, Inc., (1995), at 31.

[22] Mike Mills, "In the Modem World, White Collar Jobs Go Overseas," *The Washington Post*, Sep. 17, 1996, at 1.

[23] Augusta Dwyer, *On the Line, Life on the U.S.-Mexican Border*, London: Monthly Review Press (1995),

at 6-7.

24 Mike Mills, "In the Modem World, White Collar Jobs Go Overseas," *The Washington Post*, Sep. 17, 1996, at 1.

25 "US Multinationals Take 'Brain Work' to Plants Overseas," *The Wall Street Journal Europe*, Sep. 30, 1994.

26 Mike Mills, "In the Modem World, White Collar Jobs Go Overseas," *The Washington Post*, Sep. 17, 1996, at 1.

27 Sir James Goldsmith, *The Trap*, New York: Carrol & Graf Publishers, Inc., (1995), at 29.

28 "IBM Is Overhauling Disk Drive Business, Cutting Jobs, Shifting Production to Asia," *The Wall Street Journal*, Aug. 5, 1994.

29 WTO, "General Agreement on Trade in Services: The Design and Underlying Principles of the GATS," (undated), found at www.wto.int/wto/services/services.htm, on file with Public Citizen.

30 *Id.*

31 World Bank, *World Investment Report 1998: Trends and Determinants* (1999) at 19.

32 Jeremy Kahn, "The World's Largest Corporations," *Fortune*, vol. 140, no. 3, Aug. 2, 1999, at 45.

33 *Id.* Some mergers in 1998 include the $42 billion merger of Worldcom and MCI, the acquisition by insurance giant Travelers, soon after acquiring Salomon Smith Barney – of Citibank to form Citigroup in a $73 billion deal; and First Union's purchase of CoreStates for $17 billion. *See* also James Aley and Matt Siegel, "The Fallout From Merger Mania," *Fortune*, vol. 137, no. 4, at 26.

34 World Bank, *World Investment Report 1998: Trends and Determinants* (1999) at 19.

35 *See* European Foundation for the Improvement of Living and Working Conditions, "Mergers in Banking Cause Serious Concerns About Employment," Jun. 1998; *see also* "Keeping Layoffs to a Minimum," *Business Times*, Apr. 11, 1998.

36 *See* Institute of Policy Studies, "Workplace America's 50 Largest Layoff Announcements of 1996," Mar. 24, 1997; *see also* Stephan Frank, "J.P. Morgan Plans to Fire 700 Staffers Amid Surging Costs, Crimped Earnings," *The Wall Street Journal*, Feb. 24, 1998, at B15.

37 ILO, *World Employment Report 1998-1999* data, *cited in* ILO, *World of Work*, no. 27, Dec. 1998.

38 The WTO Agreement on Subsidies and Countervailing Measures sets out rules and prohibitions concerning the use of subsidies and measures governments use to offset subsidies given to industries or enterprises by other WTO members, like anti-dumping remedies.

39 United Steel Workers President George Becker, Testimony Before the Senate Committee on Finance, Mar. 23, 1999, at 1, on file with Public Citizen.

40 106th Congress, H.R. 1664 was sponsored by Rep. Bill Young; S. 544 was sponsored by Sen. Ted Stevens.

41 106th Congress, H.R. 975 was overwhelmingly passed in the House of Representatives, but was defeated in the Senate. President Clinton had vowed to veto it if it had passed both the House and Senate.

42 Rossella Brevetti, "EC Weighs in Against U.S. Program For Steel Loans, Hints at WTO Case," *Daily Report for Executives*, Aug. 11, 1999.

43 The WTO Agreement on Subsidies and Countervailing Measures defines a loan guarantee as a subsidy under Article 1.1(a)(1)(i). Under Article 6, WTO members are prohibited from using subsidies to "cover operating losses sustained by an industry," (6.1(b)) or "operating losses sustained by an enterprise." (6.1(c)). Under the Agreement on Subsidies and Countervailing Measures, such subsidies constitute "serious prejudice to the interests of [other WTO] member[s]." (Article 5(c)).

44 Lawrence Mishel, Jared Bernstein and John Schmitt, *The State of Working America,1998-1999*, New York: M.E. Sharpe (1999) at 131.

45 Economic Policy Institute, *Hourly Wage Decile Cutoffs, for All Workers, from the CPS ORG, 1973-98* (1999), using Census Bureau Data.

46 *See* President's Council of Economic Advisors, *1999 Economic Report of the President,* Washington, D.C.: U.S. Government Printing Office (1999), at Table B-1 (Appendix b); U.S. Department of Commerce, Bureau of Economic Analysis (BEA), "Gross Domestic Product: Second Quarter 1999," News Release, Jul. 29, 1999; and BEA, National Income and Product Accounts, Summary, found at www.bea.doc.gov/, on file with Public Citizen. According to the *1999 Economic Report of the President*, 1973 marks the onset of the age of globalization, as the oil shock of the early 1970s led to third world debt and subsequent bank lending and foreign direct investment to finance growing external trade balances. *Id.* at 221.

47 Economic Policy Institute, *Hourly Wage Decile Cutoffs, for All Workers, from the CPS ORG, 1973-98 (1998 Dollars)* (1999), using Census Bureau Data.

48 Lawrence Mishel, Jared Bernstein and John Schmitt, *The State of Working America,1998-1999*, New

York: M.E. Sharpe (1999) at 127.

[49] Mark Weisbrot, "Globalization for Whom?," *Cornell International Law Journal*, 1998 Symposium Issue, vol. 31, no. 3, citing Economic Policy Institute analysis of NIPA data, at 8.

[50] *See* Robert E. Scott, Thea Lee and John Schmitt, "Trading Away Good Jobs," Economic Policy Institute, Oct. 1997, at 2.

[51] *Id.* at 5.

[52] *Id.* at 11.

[53] Lloyd Bentsen, "The Uruguay Round — Now," *The Washington Post*, Sep. 13, 1994, at A21.

[54] *Id.* Bentsen states, "We have estimated that this agreement will increase America's income by about $1700 per family per year."

[55] U.S. Department of Commerce, International Trade Administration data available at www.ita.doc.gov, on file with Public Citizen.

[56] *Id.*

[57] Economic Policy Institute, "Median Family Income 1947-1997 (1997 Dollars)" ; EPI calculations using U.S. Bureau of Census data.

[58] This U.S. Federal Reserve has adjusted its policy on the Non-accelerating Inflation Rate of Unemployment, which it had previously believed to be 6-61/4%. It has, in the last four years, allowed U.S. unemployment to fall to a 30-year low of 4.3% (currently). (See Bureau of Labor Statistics (BLS) "Employment, Wages and Earnings" data at www.bls.gov; on file with Public Citizen.)

[59] Lester Davis, "U.S. Jobs supported by Merchandise Exports to Mexico," U.S. Department of Commerce Economic and Statistics Administration, 1995.

[60] *See* "NAFTA at 5, Promises & Realities," *Chicago Tribune*, Nov. 29, 1998.

[61] *Id.*

[62] *See* WTO, United States - Measures Affecting Alcoholic and Malt Beverages (DS/23/2), Complaint by Canada, Apr. 12, 1991.

[63] WTO, United States - Measures Affecting Alcoholic and Malt Beverages (DS23/R-39s/206), Report of the Panel, Feb. 2, 1992, at Paras. 5.2-5.12.

[64] *Id.* at Paras. 5.12 and 5.48.

[65] *Id.* at Paras. 2.7 and 3.6.

[66] *Id.* at Paras. 2.10-2.11 and 3.7-3.8.

[67] *Id.* at Para. 3.21.

[68] *Id.* at Para. 3.59.

[69] *Id.* at Para. 5.12.

[70] *Id.* at Para. 6.2.

[71] Japan, Large-Scale Retail Store Law (1974) (Daitenho).

[72] *See* WTO, Japan - Measures Affecting Consumer Photographic Film and Paper (WT/DS44), Complaint by the United States, Jun. 13, 1996.

[73] WTO, Japan - Measures Affecting Consumer Photographic Film and Paper (WT/DS44/R), Report of the Panel, Mar. 31, 1998, at Para 10.212.

[74] *Id.* at Paras. 10.225-10.226.

[75] *See* WTO, Japan - Measures Affecting Distribution Services (WT/DS45), Complaint by the United States, Jun. 13, 1996.

[76] WTO, Japan - Measures Affecting Consumer Photographic Film and Paper (WT/DS44/R), Report of the Panel, Mar. 31, 1998, at Para. 6.6, note 5.

[77] *Id* at Para. 6.8.

[78] *See* Japan, Large-Scale Retail Store Location Law (1974) (Daitenho); *see also* U.S. Department of Commerce, "Access to Japan's Photographic Film and Paper Market: Report on Japan's Implementation of Its WTO Representations," Jun. 9, 1999.

[79] U.S. Department of Commerce, "Access to Japan's Photographic Film and Paper Market: Report on Japan's Implementation of Its WTO Representations," Jun. 9, 1999.

[80] Interview of Albert Foer, President of the American Antitrust Institute, by Darci Andresen, Public Citizen's Global Trade Watch Staff, Aug. 8, 1999, on file with Public Citizen.

[81] I. Bernier, "Cultural Goods and Services in International Trade Law," Seminar paper prepared for the Centre for Trade Policy and Law, Carleton University, Ottawa, Oct. 1997, at 2.

[82] *Id.* at 6.

[83] *Id.* at 7.

[84] Andrew Pollack, "Hollywood Jobs Lost to Cheap (and Chilly) Climes," *The New York Times*, May 10, 1999.

[85] Canada has implemented a cultural policy designed to preserve Canadian ownership in the cultural industries. *See* Laura Eggertson, "Cultural 'Assault' by U.S. Feared," *Globe and Mail*, Jan. 18, 1997.

[86] John Urgquhart and Bhushan Bahree, "WTO Orders Canada to Drop Magazine Rule," *The New York Times*, Jul. 1, 1997.

[87] Drew Fagan and Laura Eggertson, "Canada Loses Magazine Case," *The Globe and Mail*, Jan. 17, 1997.

[88] Canadian Tariff Code 9958.

[89] U.S. Chamber of Commerce, Letter to Staff Assistant Sybia Harrison, Section 301 Committee, Office of the U.S. Trade Representative, Apr. 12, 1996, on file with Public Citizen.

[90] Drew Fagan and Laura Eggertson, "Canada Loses Magazine Case," *The Globe and Mail*, Jan. 17, 1997.

[91] R.S.C. 1985, c. 41 (3rd Suppl.) as amended to 30 April 1996, s.114, Sch. VII, Item 9958, (1996 Customs Tariff: Departmental Consolidation) Ottawa: Minister of Supply & Services Canada, 1996.

[92] Drew Fagan and Laura Eggertson, "Canada Loses Magazine Case," *The Globe and Mail*, Jan. 17, 1997.

[93] *See* WTO, Canada - Certain Measures Concerning Periodicals (WT/DS31), Complaint by the United States, Mar. 11, 1996.

[94] *Id.*

[95] Anthony DePalma, "World Trade Body Opposes Canadian Magazine Tariffs," *The New York Times*, Jan. 19, 1997.

[96] *Id.*

[97] U.S. Chamber of Commerce, Letter to Staff Assistant Sybia Harrison, Section 301 Committee, Office of the U.S. Trade Representative, Apr. 12, 1996, on file with Public Citizen.

[98] WTO, Canada - Certain Measures Concerning Periodicals (WT/DS31/R), Report of the Panel, Mar. 14, 1999, at Paras. 5.5, 5.11, 5.30, and 5.39.

[99] *See* WTO, Canada - Certain Measures Concerning Periodicals (WT/DS31/AB/R), Report of the Appellate Body, Jun. 30, 1999.

[100] Edward Alden, "Canada Faces $4bn Sanctions Threat as U.S. Opens New Front in Fight to Make WTO Judgments Stick," *Financial Times*, Jan. 19, 1999

[101] *Id.*

[102] *Id.*

[103] Mark Bourrie, "Trade: Canada Backs Down on Periodicals Law," *InterPress Service*, May 31, 1999.

[104] *Id.*

[105] *Id.*

[106] *See* John Eatwell, *International Capital Liberalization, The Impact on World Development*, CEPA, Working Paper Series I, Working Paper No. 1, Center for Economic Policy Analysis, Aug. 1996 (Revised Oct. 1996).

[107] BIS, "Triennial Survey of 43 Foreign Exchange Markets: Preliminary Results," Oct. 1998. In comparison, the global volume of exports of goods and services for all of 1997 was $6.6 trillion. *Cited in* President's Council of Economic Advisors, *1999 Economic Report of the President* (1999), at 224.

[108] BIS reports that 80% of trades in the foreign exchange markets were made by financial services companies. *Id.*

[109] John Eatwell, *International Capital Liberalization, The Impact on World Development*, CEPA, Working Paper Series I, Working Paper No. 1, Center for Economic Policy Analysis, Aug. 1996 (Revised Oct. 1996), at 2.

[110] *See* Mark Weisbrot, "Globalization for Whom?," *Cornell International Law Journal*, 1998 Symposium Issue, vol. 31, no. 3, at 13.

[111] Government business - including the business of selling off public sectors to private enterprises - must follow GATT Article 1 rules on MFN.

[112] Jerry Hagstrom, "Canadian Official Raises Concern Over Meat Labels," *National Journal's Congress Daily*, Apr. 20, 1999.

[113] *See* Mary Shirley, "Trends in Privatization," *Economic Reform Today*, no. 1, 1998.

[114] Long distance telephone rates subsidize the more expensive costs of providing telephone service in rural areas so that these costs are not passed onto rural consumers. Similarly, electricity in rural areas is kept affordable by regulating utility rates. For instance, Kansas state law prohibits utility companies from charging consumers different rates based on where they live (66 Kan. Stat. Ann. Sec. 109 (1998), and Virginia state law imposes a cap on electricity rates (56 Vir. Code Sec 582(D) (1999)).

[115] World Bank, UN World Commission on Water for the 21st Century data, *cited in* "Precious Gallons," *The Washington Post*, Aug. 21, 1999.

[116] *Id.*

[117] In the U.S., several federal banking laws prohibit consolidation of banking, insurance and securities operations (the Glass-Steagall Act and the Bank Holding Company Act) while requiring that lenders provide credit to all the neighborhoods where they operate (the Community Reinvestment Act). These laws are currently threatened by deregulatory legislation (Rep. Jim Leach, Financial Services Act, H.R. 10, Jan. 6, 1999) which would allow cross-sector mergers, thus threatening pro-community regulations such as the Community Reinvestment Act as banks shift assets away from deposit accounts and into securities and insurance accounts.

[118] *See* Coalition of Service Industries' response to Federal Notice of Aug. 19, 1998 (Solicitation of Public Comment Regarding U.S. Preparations for the WTO's Ministerial Meeting, Fourth Quarter 1), FR Doc. 98-22279, on file with Public Citizen.

[119] "Barshefsky Reveals U.S. Push to Broaden WTO Services Talk," *Inside US Trade*, Jun. 4, 1999.

[120] *See* Coalition of Service Industries' response to Federal Notice of Aug. 19, 1998 (Solicitation of Public Comment Regarding U.S. Preparations for the WTO's Ministerial Meeting, Fourth Quarter 1), FR Doc. 98-22279, on file with Public Citizen.

[121] *Id.*

[122] *Id.*

[123] "Barshefsky Reveals U.S. Push to Broaden WTO Services Talk," *Inside US Trade*, Jun. 4, 1999.

[124] James Aley and Matt Siegel, "The Fallout From Merger Mania," *Fortune*, vol. 137, no. 4, at 27.

[125] S. 1256, the Patients' Bill of Rights Act of 1999, was introduced by Sen. Tom Daschle in June 1999.

[126] *See* U.S. Trade Representative, "Preparation for the WTO 1999 Ministerial, Communication from the United States of America, Further Negotiations as Mandated by the General Agreement on Trade in Services," 1999.

[127] *See* Position taken, *inter alia*, in statement circulated at World Trade Organization by Venezuelan Minister of Trade and Industry, Geneva, May 18, 1998, WT/MIN(98)/ST/53; *see also* "EU Says Freer Services Good for Developing Countries," *BRIDGES Weekly Trade News Digest*, vol. 3, no. 25, Jun. 28, 1999.

[128] *See id.*

In this chapter ...

CASES:

- **French Asbestos Ban Attacked:** Canada has filed a WTO case claiming that France's decision to join eight other EU countries in banning asbestos, a known carcinogen, violates trade rules. Canada, a leading asbestos producer, says the French ban fails WTO requirements that policies be the least trade restrictive alternative *and* based on international standards. Those standards, influenced by industry, call for the "controlled use" of asbestos, not the banning of it. A decision in what will be the WTO's most prominent worker safety case is not expected soon. However, if the WTO panel interprets the rules strictly (rather than with a political view toward avoiding damage to the WTO's credibility), the French ban could be declared an illegal trade barrier.

- **Massachusetts Procurement Policy on Burma:** The EU and Japan challenged this state's preferential purchasing law, which penalizes companies doing business with Burma's military dictatorship. This policy of economically starving the ruling junta, based on the South Africa anti-apartheid strategy model, has been called for by Burmese democracy leaders. However, WTO procurement rules forbid the consideration of non-commercial factors, such as human rights, in government purchasing decisions. They also require that all countries be treated the same regardless of their conduct (MFN treatment). The WTO case has been temporarily suspended while a domestic court challenge is pursued by a U.S. corporate front group called "USA*Engage."

- **Maryland Nigeria Procurement Bill:** At the height of the WTO challenge against the Massachusetts law, the state of Maryland was on the verge of passing preferential procurement rules punishing Nigeria's military dictatorship. The Clinton administration dispatched State Department staff to the state capitol to lobby against the measures. State Department testimony focused on how the measure would violate WTO rules and thus draw a challenge. The law, which had been expected to pass handily, lost by one vote.

CONCEPTS:

Agreement on Government Procurement: This agreement covers the multi-trillion dollar government purchasing of goods and services. It requires national treatment (thus, no domestic preferences), MFN treatment and bans the consideration of non-commercial factors (such as human rights, the environment and labor rights) in government purchasing decisions.

ILO, Not WTO Is Proper Venue for Labor Rights Issues: The Clinton administration and other WTO Member nations signed a 1996 Singapore Ministerial Declaration explicitly banishing the labor rights issue from the WTO and dispatching it to the ILO, a body without enforcement capacity. The Declaration also specifically endorses the use of low wages to give developed countries a comparative advantage and decries "protectionist" uses of labor rights measures to undermine that "advantage."

Clinton Administration's Duplicity on Labor Rights at WTO: While often talking the talk on labor rights for the WTO, the Clinton administration has been walking backwards toward 19th century Dickensian labor exploitation. President Clinton has employed a "charm strategy" of high-profile speeches endorsing labor rights, while simultaneously pushing actual trade policies — a "NAFTA for Africa" bill and the FTAA NAFTA expansion negotiations — that exclude labor rights. The administration scaled back its labor agenda for the Seattle Ministerial.

Bans on Goods Made With Child Labor Violate WTO Rules: WTO rules do not allow countries to distinguish between products based on *how* they are manufactured. Thus, U.S. laws banning imports of child labor-made products would violate GATT rules. This fact makes the high-profile Clinton signing of the recent ILO Treaty on exploitative child labor a profile in cynicism, as enforcement of that treaty through laws banning commerce in child-labor-made goods would be WTO-illegal.

Migration for Service Providers, but Not Political Refugees: The WTO services agreement includes commitments by countries to exempt service providers from some immigration restrictions, which would keep out people interested in entering the U.S. for many important non-commercial reasons — such as to avoid political persecution at home.

Human and Labor Rights
Under the WTO

The International Labour Organization (ILO) is the competent body to set and deal with [internationally recognized labor] standards, and we affirm our support for its work in promoting them. We believe that economic growth and development fostered by increased trade and further trade liberaliza-

"It's the World Trade Organization. Something about noncompliance with GATT."

tion contribute to the promotion of these standards. We reject the use of labour standards for protectionist purposes, and agree that the comparative advantage of countries, particularly low-wage developing countries, must in no way be put into question.[1]

— WTO Singapore Ministerial Declaration, December 1996
Signed by the Clinton administration and 131 other governments

The Uruguay Round Agreements, when taken as a whole, create a system of global commerce best suited to large multinational corporations with the resources to move production around the world and to provide goods and/or services to numerous markets simultaneously. This design is exemplified by the degree of privileges and protections provided in the Uruguay Round Agreements for corporations versus those offered to communities or individual workers. For instance, new corporate property rights are created and protected by the Agreement on Trade Related Aspects of Intellectual Property (TRIPs), the Agreement on Trade Related Investment Measures

(TRIMs) and the General Agreement on Trade in Services (GATS).[3] However, the rights of workers are completely ignored, except to the extent that government policies promoting workers' rights are considered barriers to trade and therefore are subject to challenge under WTO rules. Indeed, the 1996 WTO Singapore Ministerial Declaration contains language inviting challenges to laws that seek to enforce labor rights: "We reject the use of labour standards for protectionist purposes, and agree that the comparative advantage of countries, particularly low-wage developing countries, must in *no way* be put into question."[4]

> **A** *Congressional Research Service study has confirmed that U.S. proposals to ban imports of goods produced with child labor would violate GATT.[2]*

Similarly, differential treatment of countries based on their human rights records is explicitly forbidden. Thus, the sort of sanctions requested by South African leaders in the struggle against aparthied would have run afoul of the current WTO rules. Already one U.S. state's selective purchasing law against the Burmese military dictatorship has been challenged under WTO rules.

The threat these WTO principles pose to effective protection of human and labor rights cannot be overestimated. When there are no ground rules for corporations concerning labor or human rights, a brutal "race to the bottom" in wages and working conditions is triggered. The country that can offer the cheapest production costs "wins" by merit of production being moved there, but people working in that country — under horrific conditions and paid starvation wages – lose, as do the people in the competing countries.[5]

Opposition to the Uruguay Round among labor, development and human rights groups was not based solely on its expected negative impact on wages and employment. Enforceable GATT/WTO rules were perceived as and now have proved to be a threat to advocating and enforcing international human rights law, including workers' rights. First, the WTO rules generally prohibit distinguishing among non- product-related Production and Processing Methods (PPMs).[6] PPMs are defined as distinctions between products based not on their physical characteristics or end uses, but on the way the way they are produced. This makes it nearly impossible for citizens and consumers to hold corporations and governments accountable to human rights standards. Second, under the Most Favored Nation rule, one WTO country cannot treat other WTO countries differently. That means that the treatment provided any WTO Member country must be provided to all WTO Member countries, regardless of their labor or human rights records. Third, the WTO Agreement on Government Procurement (AGP) prohibits noncommercial considerations in governments' purchasing decisions. These provisions make procurement rules giving environmental or social preferences or banning the purchase of goods produced in violation of ILO labor or U.N. human rights conventions — a violation of WTO rules. Finally, the WTO dispute settlement body can be used to challenge worker safety safeguards as technical barriers to trade.

Taken together, these WTO rules set up formidable barriers to traditional methods of promoting labor and human rights around the world. Any effort to prohibit or discourage even the most abusive forms of child labor can be subject to chal-

Clinton: Talking the Talk on Labor Rights, but Walking Backwards

The Clinton administration has played a duplicitous game on trade and labor rights. After pledging to prioritize the modest goal of ensuring the formation of a WTO labor rights working group at the 1996 Singapore WTO Ministerial, the U.S. ultimately signed onto a Singapore Ministerial Declaration explicitly banishing the labor rights issue from the WTO to the International Labor Organization (ILO).

By agreeing that the ILO, not the WTO, was the appropriate forum for countries to work together on labor rights issues, the Clinton administration made a critical decision. Many of the world's labor unions urged the WTO governments to agree to make binding labor rights part of the WTO. Business interests have long argued that the ILO is the only proper place for labor rights issues to be discussed. The business groups prefer the ILO because its rules, unlike those of the WTO, are not enforceable. The Clinton administration chose the industry position, adding injury to insult by signing a Singapore Ministerial Declaration that many view as having undermined the current status of labor rights at the WTO.

The ILO's rules operate like the rules of Multilateral Environmental Agreements (MEAs). Countries sign onto ILO conventions and are supposed to enforce the rules domestically. This is in sharp contrast to the WTO, where the failure of one country to follow the mutually agreed-upon rules can be challenged by another WTO Member country in WTO dispute panels, which are empowered to authorize trade sanctions for violations. There is no similar enforcement at the ILO.

To make matters worse, absent specific changes in GATT/WTO rules, countries' enforcement of ILO obligations, such as banning products made with child labor, would violate current WTO rules. Thus, although President Clinton recently and vigorously promoted a new ILO convention on exploitative child labor, WTO countries seeking to enforce it by keeping child labor products out of their markets would be violating WTO rules.

Clinton used his 1999 University of Chicago graduation speech to call for the signing of the new ILO agreement against the most exploitative forms of child labor.[7] Clinton then traveled to Geneva, Switzerland, amidst much public relations hoopla to sign the proposal. The new ILO treaty has been harshly criticized by both labor and child advocates for its compromised language; it does not forbid all child labor – only the most "exploitative" forms such as prostitution and slavery. The language also was watered down to cut out language opposing children serving in the military. However, second and most cynically, under current WTO rules, enforcement of even the compromised language likely would be WTO-illegal. The treaty calls for countries to make distinctions based on how goods are made (i.e., are they made with exploited child labor?). Under WTO rules, countries are not allowed to make distinctions about what goods they allow in their markets based on how a good is made (*See* Chapter 1 for more on production and processing methods). Thus, while the U.S. could (and does) ban child labor, under WTO rules it could not ban sale in the U.S. of products made in *other* countries in violation of the new ILO treaty.

lenge on any one of these grounds. Indeed, a Congressional Research Service study has confirmed that U.S. proposals to ban imports of goods produced with child labor would violate GATT.[8]

Workers and labor unions in industrialized and developing countries opposed the adoption of the Uruguay Round Agreements in 1994. They knew that absent a more balanced approach between the interests of industry and workers, the WTO merely would accelerate the process of corporate-dominated globalization that began in the 1970s. In addition, Uruguay Round agriculture rules would push millions of subsistence farm families in the developing world off their land and into cities to seek jobs. The new migrants would flood labor markets, and wages would plummet from already unlivable levels.

Meanwhile, new Uruguay Round investor protections would make relocation of manufacturing from higher-wage regions to low-wage regions less risky for corporations and would guarantee market access back into rich countries for the finished goods. Imports produced at poverty-level wages, with child labor and in unsafe conditions, could be priced to maximize profit margins while slightly undercutting domestic-made goods. Thus, the low production costs would not be passed on to consumers, but domestic producers meeting labor and environmental standards would be pushed out of business. Alternatively, wages in industrialized countries would be pushed downward as domestic industries cut labor costs to compete, until ultimately the companies relocated overseas, simply unable to compete with $1-a-day average wages in China[9] or $3-$4 a day in Mexico.[10] At the same time, the living standards of workers in the developing world would not be improved.

After nearly five years of the Uruguay Round, aspects of this scenario already are coming to pass. Developing countries are pitted against each other in a race to the bottom in wages and nonenforcement of environmental and labor rules spurred by the increasing freedom of corporations to relocate to where production is cheapest. Since there is no floor of minimum conduct required to obtain Uruguay Round market access benefits, there is no market incentive for countries to meet even basic standards. Indeed, companies can punish countries trying to promote worker rights or environmental standards simply by relocating with impunity.

No Labor Rights at WTO

Of particular concern to development experts and labor unions in the developing world is the WTO's provisions abolishing trade-related investment measures that are used by governments to encourage the development of the domestic industrial base and thus create and sustain jobs. Instead, the WTO Trade Related Investment Measures (TRIMs) rules encourage the spread of export processing zones (EPZs), where global manufacturing firms import most of their

Gains in U.S. national income during the Uruguay Round years have been captured by profit – and not by wages.[11]

— United Nations Commission on Trade and Development

components from overseas subsidiaries and pay production workers starvation wages to assemble the products for export for sale in rich markets. The ILO has noted that the number of EPZs is likely to grow throughout the world, particularly in developing countries, and is urging governments to ensure labor protection and basic union rights, since these often are waived in the EPZs.[12] While workers in these assembly plants are paid a pittance, major global corporations sell the products for top dollar. For instance, a pair of Nike sneakers costing well in excess of $100 is made by workers making pennies an hour.[13] Meanwhile, the U.S. manufacturing workers fired by relocating companies generally face lower wages in their next jobs.[14] In the Americas, similar export zones provide rich data to examine the prudence of spreading the EPZ model globally. For instance, in the EPZs on the U.S.-Mexican border – the so-called maquiladora plants – workers are not paid nearly enough to live on.[15] In the maquila zones, a basic market basket composed of food, gas, rent, electricity, transportation, water and refrigerator costs totaled $54 per week in 1998.[16] The average net weekly pay for maquila workers is $55.77. This leaves $1.77 per week to spend on education, clothing, medical attention and other necessities.[17] Even with a special, if toothless, labor side agreement to NAFTA, labor rights enforcement in Mexico has been abysmal in nearly six years since NAFTA's implementation, and Mexico's wages have not kept up with productivity gains.[18]

The low-wage EPZ scenario is promoted by a com-

GATS Immigration Rules: Ensuring Lower Wages in the U.S. and Abroad?

The General Agreement on Trade in Services (GATS) contains an Annex on Movement of Natural Persons Supplying Services Under the Agreement. This Annex is designed to let service providers move more freely from one country to another[19] and prohibits signatories from implementing border-control regulations that will "nullify and impair" other provisions of GATS.[20]

In contrast, human rights concerns – for example, with regard to refugees – have never led to the same kind of required border opening. Lawyers working on behalf of migrant workers and human rights activists often ask why managers have WTO-guaranteed rights to move freely across borders while workers, political refugees or persons persecuted because of their beliefs do not. The latest trend under the WTO services agreement is to require countries to recognize the professional licenses of other countries – for lawyers, engineers, nurses and others. Indeed, U.S. Trade Representative Charlene Barshefsky cites "the [recognition of] accreditation or licensing granted by [other countries'] regulatory standards in the services field" as an important goal for EU-U.S. Transatlantic Economic Partnership negotiations, and underlines the importance of this kind of regional initiative as "models for what we might hope to achieve worldwide"[21] – that is, under the auspices of the WTO.

The Annex on migration covers "all categories of natural persons,"[22] but in practice, the people most likely to take advantage of this provision are managers moving from developed to developing countries to oversee newly expatriated service divisions. Indeed, experience from globalization of manufacturing shows that top management positions rarely are filled by local workers, essentially minimizing the transfer of knowledge needed to make the developing world less dependent upon foreign direct investment.[23]

bination of WTO rules that forbid the sorts of countermeasures governments would need to take to ensure both labor rights protections and more diversified production. For example, the WTO TRIMs Agreement forbids developing country governments from requiring that a certain portion of inputs be procured domestically. Doing so would create more jobs besides those needed to simply assemble products to export to rich countries. Also, countries' attempts to enforce labor rights – such as workers' rights to organize unions and bargain for better wages and conditions – are usually "rewarded" by companies' relocation to less pro-worker countries. The obvious answer to this race to the bottom would be to deny the deluxe market access privileges otherwise conferred by the Uruguay Round Agreements to goods and services produced in violation of internationally agreed basic rules concerning work conditions, the right to organize, and such. While such a policy would not inherently raise wages in poorer countries, it would remove corporate incentives to pressure countries to *deny* the labor rights necessary for workers to fight for improvements. The bottom line would be altered: If a product cannot be sold in the desired market, it does not matter how cheaply it can be produced.

The prospects for rectifying the WTO's bias against workers *vis-a-vis* multinational corporations through any reform of the WTO are slim. In 1994, during the Uruguay Round negotiations, the U.S. and France had suggested that a "social clause" should be included in the WTO.[24] (Different countries and organizations mean different things when they use the term "social clause," ranging from useless NAFTA-style side agreements to provisions included in the core text of agreements that would have authority equal to all other WTO rules.) The International Labor Organization (ILO) had also said it favors a WTO social clause, issuing a report arguing that compliance with the most basic labor rights should be included among the obligations attached to membership in the WTO.[25]

Many nongovernmental organizations most involved with globalization issues view the notion of a WTO "social clause" as useless and politically damaging at best, and as a dangerous distraction from the WTO's real problems, at worst.[26] The basic argument of these groups is that absent actually changing or eliminating the numerous core WTO principles and rules that undermine the public interest, adding pro-labor or other language is like putting a bandage over gangrene. The same damage will continue unabated, but it might draw less attention in the short term.

At the very least, the U.S. had pledged in 1994 "not [to] approve the Marakesh Ministerial Declaration establishing the WTO unless it contains a reference to early consideration of the relationship of the trading system and internationally recognized labor standards,"[27] either through a WTO study on labor issues or through the creation of a WTO working group on labor. Working groups are the lowest level formal WTO grouping. They conduct studies and discussions but do not conduct negotiations or other activities that could lead to binding changes to WTO rules.

However, the U.S. approved the Marakesh Declaration in 1995 without a single reference to labor rights, much less the establishment of a labor working group.[28] At the Marakesh WTO Ministerial, the Clinton administration did successfully push for the establishment of a WTO working group on the environment *(See* Chapter 1 for more on the WTO Committee on Trade and Environment).

The Clinton Administration's "Charm" Strategy on Trade

The Clinton administration has launched a new political strategy after a series of humiliating defeats for its corporate-managed trade policy, including congressional rejection of Fast Track trade authority (twice), the defeat of a Latin American NAFTA expansion known as "CBI" and the demise of the Multilateral Agreement on Investment (MAI) negotiations.

Instead of getting the message that the time was overdue for a new, more balanced approach to trade that the public could support, the administration instead decided to try to repackage its business-as-usual policies. Realizing that it could no longer simply ram unpopular trade proposals through Congress, it launched a "Charm Initiative."

First, President Clinton gave a speech at the 1998 Geneva WTO Ministerial calling for new pro-labor, pro-environment approach to trade within the WTO.[29] Ironically, all of the specific policies he called for were those the administration was already obligated to have obtained under the requirements of the 1995 Uruguay Round implementing legislation, such as greater openness of WTO procedures and a WTO working group on labor rights. However, the administration made no new push on this long-overdue set of improvements after the speech. Indeed, shortly thereafter, the administration explicitly agreed to remove labor, human rights and the environment from the agenda of a proposed NAFTA expansion now being negotiated called the Free Trade Area of the Americas (FTAA).

Then, in his January 1999 State of the Union address, President Clinton again called for a new approach – this time one that would put a "human face on the global economy."[30] Unfortunately, while Clinton was talking the talk, the Clinton administration was walking the global economy backwards toward the expansion of 19th century Dickensian labor exploitation. First, the administration launched a major campaign to push the "NAFTA-for-Africa" bill through House passage despite broad opposition by African and U.S. labor unions and many Democratic members of Congress because it failed to include labor rights provisions. Then, the administration scaled back its already weak position regarding labor standards at the WTO. The U.S. July, 1999 submission to the WTO only calls for better WTO-ILO cooperation.[31] The administration also has established new venues, such as new "civil society" committees for non-governmental organizations (NGO) to be heard on trade issues as part of the Charm Strategy. These committees have consumed many NGO and labor union resources and much time but have resulted in no policy modifications.

During the next WTO Ministerial in Singapore in 1996, the U.S. made additional proposals concerning labor rights at the WTO. It proposed a WTO study on labor issues and the creation of a Labor Working Group.[33] The motivation for the Clinton administration's apparent push for labor rights was exposed as being largely inspired by domestic political calculations.[34] U.S. trade officials admitted that the Clinton administration's motivation was to show the U.S. labor movement that it was trying hard to include workers' rights on the WTO agenda.[35] That way, when the U.S. ceded the labor issues in favor of higher-priority commercial goals, U.S. union leaders would be less likely to attack the outcome.[36]

> ## *Still No WTO Working Group on Labor*
>
> At the 1996 Singapore Ministerial, the U.S. pressed for the inclusion of workers' rights into the WTO agenda. The objective was to have core labor rights at least studied by the WTO through the establishment of a "Working Group." Working Groups are formed to research the implications of subjecting new areas to WTO negotiations. A working group on labor was considered the most modest possible concession that would postpone any real commitment on the subject for years.[32] Yet not even that was achieved.

The Singapore Ministerial Declaration, which the U.S. signed, not only failed to include the U.S labor goals but has been interpreted by some as undermining the *status quo ante* by explicitly relegating labor issues to the ILO[37] — a body with weak enforcement capacity (unlike the WTO). The Singapore Ministerial Declaration also made it clear that the WTO was not an appropriate forum to consider labor issues, unless, of course, a country's labor laws were challenged at the WTO as alleged protectionist barriers to trade.[38] Some international and national labor federations declared the Singapore Ministerial Declaration to be progress on labor rights. They argued that merely getting the WTO to recognize labor rights as an issue, even as it was banished from WTO consideration, was a positive development. The U.S.'s inability to secure even the emptiest of commitments on labor among WTO trade partners during the Singapore Ministerial contrasted unfavorably with its ability to force through an equally controversial proposal on information technology. The resulting Information Technology Agreement was signed at the end of the Singapore Ministerial.

By 1999, the Clinton administration was again talking the WTO labor rights talk, albeit a much watered-down version. In its submission to the WTO on U.S. priorities for the Seattle Ministerial, the U.S. called for future WTO talks to give high priority to "the relationship between trade and labor."[39] However, the explicit U.S. goal in this regard is feeble: to encourage ILO participation in the WTO as an observer. The second U.S. proposal is to seek to persuade more WTO Members to commit to internationally recognized core labor standards, although how it will accomplish this is difficult to envision and not described in the proposal. The U.S. itself has ratified only one of the ILO conventions defining core labor standards, and its credibility on this issue in the eyes of other countries is lacking. The third proposal is the vague call for the creation of a future work program to address trade issues relating to labor standards.

This is by far the weakest attempt by the U.S. yet to pursue labor issues at the WTO. First, the U.S. has stopped pushing for "hold harmless" language that would protect countries' labor laws – including laws that implement or enforce international labor standards developed under the auspices of the ILO – from WTO scrutiny as illegal barriers to trade. Second, the labor issue is not among the list of items on which the U.S. called for negotiations to be launched after Seattle. Instead it is on a list of items on which some "forward program" should be established.[40] However, unlike other issues the U.S. added to what it calls a "forward work program," it again relegated labor to a weak work group. In contrast, the door was left open for WTO negotiations in other controversial areas on the forward program list that are not trade issues *per se*, such as investment and competition policy. The U.S. has claimed it would consider all suggestions for negotiations on these latter issues with an eye to what can realistically be accomplished in three years.[41] This is a classic example of the Clinton administration's smoke-and-mirrors treatment of labor issues in trade negotiations: claim credit for highlighting labor rights but continue to advocate relegating the subject to a work group in contrast to, for example, the possible launch of highly controversial global investment talks in the WTO.

Indeed, many labor unions in the U.S. are weary of the Clinton administration's broken promises and oppose the start of any new WTO talks after Seattle. For instance, the International Brotherhood of Teamsters and the United Steelworkers of America are working with hundreds of consumer, environmental, religious, farm, food security, development and human rights organizations worldwide demanding *"No New Round, Turnaround."* The Teamsters and the Steelworkers have joined nearly one thousand nongovernmental organizations worldwide in a call for negotiators to assess the damage that the WTO has already done and initiate concrete steps to rectify it.

WTO Challenges Threaten
Basic Labor and Human Rights

The following WTO cases demonstrate that labor and human rights concerns about the WTO were well-founded. As regards labor issues, instead of "lifting all boats," the WTO has failed to deliver on its proponents' promises of rising living standards *(See* Chapter 5 regarding developing countries and Chapter 6 on developed countries*).* Indeed, WTO rules make it much easier for footloose corporations to continuously relocate to seek the cheapest wages and most lax working conditions. The WTO now also is being used as an aggressive tool to attack strong occupational safeguards as described below in the case of Canada's WTO challenge of the new French asbestos ban. In addition, WTO rules have been used — both in a challenge and as threats — to discourage governments from using their purchasing power to send a powerful message to vicious dictatorships that a lack of human rights will cost the regime.

Case 1: Canada Attacks French Asbestos Ban at WTO

Asbestos is a proven carcinogen for humans.[42] As early as 1927, scientists have known that asbestos causes lung cancer, mesothelioma (cancer of the tissues lining the chest and abdomen) and asbestosis (a deadly lung inflammation) in people who come into contact with the substance.[43] Often the diseases do not manifest themselves for 20 years after exposure. A study by the French Institute National de la Santé et de la Recherche Médicale (INSERM) found that construction workers and people in the general public who incidentally came into contact with white asbestos products were most at risk for asbestos-related illness.[44]

Industry Ties to International Standard-Setting Organizations

The legitimacy of international standards has become an issue of great concern given that the WTO's TBT Agreement requires use by WTO Member countries of such standards except for extremely limited circumstances. The chemical industry has exerted especially strong influence at the International Program on Chemical Safety (IPCS), a program located at the World Health Organization in Geneva and jointly sponsored by WHO, ILO and the United Nations Environment Program.[45] A 1993 article in the medical journal *The Lancet* reports that chemical manufacturers ICI, Hoechst and DuPont wrote the first drafts of IPCS reports on chlorofluorocarbon refrigerants and the fungicide benomyl.[46] Scientists from the U.S. National Institute for Occupational Safety and Health (NIOSH) criticized the IPCS's failure to modify statements in the report to reflect opposing views within its expert panel. The *Lancet* article describes undisclosed conflicts of interest by corporate consultants on expert task groups assigned to write IPCS documents, as well as the fact that industry "observers" usually present at IPCS task group meetings were rarely offset by representatives of public health and safety organizations.[47] Indeed, in 1993, U.S. government scientists found that the IPCS environmental health criteria document on methylene chloride was based on material drafted by officials from manufacturers of the chemical.[48] NIOSH decided to cease all participation in IPCS activities until IPCS established an objective process to develop criteria documents.[49]

According to asbestos experts in the public health arena, the asbestos industry uses two front groups to represent itself to the ILO, WHO and other international worker safety standard-setting fora. For instance, the International Fiber Safety Group and the International Commission of Occupational Health (ICOH) have tried to influence ILO policy on asbestos under the guise that they are composed of impartial health experts, when in fact they are spin-offs of the Asbestos Institute, formed for the purpose of gathering support for the asbestos industry.[50]

Each year, France alone loses at least 2,000 people to asbestos-related cancer.[51] A British study concluded that asbestos exposure will lead to 500,000 deaths in the EU by 2020.[52] In 1996, France joined Germany, Austria, Denmark, the Netherlands, Finland, Italy, Sweden and Belgium to ban all forms of asbestos.[53]

The French law bans asbestos and any product containing it, unless the use of asbestos substitutes would pose a graver public health risk.[54] The ban applies to domestic production as well as to the import of asbestos.

Canada, the second-largest exporter of asbestos in the world,[55] challenged the French ban in the WTO in 1998 as a violation of the WTO Technical Barriers to Trade (TBT) Agreement and therefore of GATT Articles III and XI banning quantitative restrictions on imports and forbidding discriminatory trade measures.[56] Canada claims that under WTO rules, countries can regulate but not ban asbestos. Canada has also claimed that even if the ban does not violate any specific WTO provisions, the French ban requires Canada to be compensated because it impairs trade benefits Canada expected from the Uruguay Round for asbestos.[57]

The U.S. filed a third-party submission in support of the French ban.[58] The WTO has begun to hear arguments on the case.[59] In addition, Canada already has begun to threaten the EU with a WTO challenge over its July 1999 continent-wide ban of the substance.[60]

The TBT Agreement sets limits on the measures that governments can take in the interest of environmental and public health protection. The TBT Agreement requires that technical standards for products be no more trade restrictive than is necessary to achieve a social, environmental, consumer or public health objective permitted by the TBT Agreement, and that such standards be based on international ones where these exist or even where their completion is imminent.[61] Canada argues that France has violated these TBT Agreement provisions by banning asbestos.

Least Trade Restrictive Rule: Canada claims that less trade-restrictive measures are available to protect workers from the ill effects of asbestos. Indeed, Canada asserts that chrysotile asbestos is less harmful than other types of asbestos and that "it can be used without incurring any detectable risk."[62] It therefore argues that an alternative form of regulation exists that will satisfy the French objective to safeguard public health – that of "controlled use."[63]

In its complaint to the WTO, Canada also points to international standards that support the "controlled use" form of regulating asbestos. "Controlled use" involves setting standards for worker protection in all circumstances where workers may encounter asbestos, from manufacturing and handling to use. The ILO has set worker safety guidelines relating to asbestos.[64] However, public health advocates point out that the ILO is subject to tremendous pressure by, and influence from, the asbestos industry.[65] The International Fiber Safety Group has tried to influence ILO policy under the guise that the group is composed of impartial health experts, when in fact it is a spin-off of the Asbestos Institute, formed for the purpose of gathering support for the asbestos industry.[66] Similarly, the International Commission of Occupational Health (ICOH) also has been accused of being a front for the asbestos industry: "When we looked at where the WHO and [the] ILO were getting their information, we found that most of it was coming from the International Commission on Occupational Health ... a group made up of virtually all consultants to the Asbestos Institute of Canada," reported asbestos expert Barry Castleman quoting Joseph LeDou, Editor-in-Chief of the *International Journal of Occupational and Environmental Health.*[67]

International Standards Must Be Used: Canada also cites as the presumptive legal standard for regulating asbetos the International Organization on Standardization (ISO) guidelines for working with chrysotile asbestos.[68] Unlike the ILO and WHO, the ISO is formally an industry group *(See Chapter 2 for more information on ISO).* In addition, the ISO's mandate for standard-setting does not include the promotion of public health and safety at all. Notwithstanding the industry membership and funding and the narrow focus of the ISO, the WTO dispute panel in the case against France has consulted the organization to provide a list of experts to advise it on technical issues relating to asbestos regulation.[69] Selection of experts from an industry standardization group with no expertise in public health issues almost ensures that WTO deliberations will be skewed against the public health and in favor of standards designed to increase trade.

In its submission, Canada also relied on the testimony of scientists allegedly affiliated with the asbestos industry to undermine the risk assessment conducted by France and to bolster its claim that chrysotile asbestos is safe.[70] It attached to its submission a study by Dr. Graham Gibbs.[71] Dr. Gibbs was dismissed from the room while the International Program on Chemical Safety was writing the concluding sections of its report on asbestos, because he was seen by the panel as representing the asbestos industry.[72] Another study appended to Canada's complaint is by Dr. Jacques Dunnigan.[73] He is the former director for health and environment for the Asbestos Institute, the trade association for the asbestos industry.[74]

Indeed, the TBT Agreement makes no distinction among international standard-setting organizations. It contains no conflict-of-interest rules for technical experts that WTO may call on or relating to the membership or composition of international standard-setting bodies. Yet, based on the existence of these international standards, Canada argues that France is obligated under WTO law to import asbestos:

> Canada is not challenging the right of the Members of the World Trade Organization to take necessary measures to protect the health and safety of their populations. That right, however, must be exercised with respect for the obligations that a Member bears under the WTO agreements. *In that respect, France could not adopt a total ban on asbestos, with no distinction between fibers and products, without scientific proof of the health risk posed by modern products containing chrysotile.*[75] [emphasis added]

Discrimination in Favor of Asbestos Substitutes: Canada also claims that by banning asbestos, France is treating asbestos less favorably than the products that would be used as asbestos substitutes in France.[76] Of course, there are always competing products that benefit from health bans of another product. Canada is arguing that the incidental benefits that accrue to producers of competing products constitute a trade violation. Indeed, Canada is pushing for a definition of "like products" that includes substitute products. Such a definition would be so general as to prevent countries from banning *any* products on health grounds, since all their substitutes would be "like products."

Canada additionally claims that the health effects of substitute fibers and cement products are unknown.[77] It is in essence claiming that France is discriminating against asbestos by replacing the use of chrysotile with substitutes whose health risks are unknown. Canada wants the TBT Agreement to be read in a way that would compel any domestic regulatory action that would negatively affect commerce in a given product to be tested against the hypothetical risks engendered by the use of likely alternative products.

"Nullification and Impairment": Finally, Canada alleges that the French asbestos ban "nullifies and impairs" benefits accruing to it as a result of tariff concessions granted by the EU during the Uruguay Round, because the ban would have the effect of disrupting the conditions of competition between domestic substitute products and chrysotile asbestos.[78] Canada is thus arguing that it has a right to trade in dangerous substances if those substances were legal at the time it entered into a trade agreement with France. This poses problems for goods for which trade concessions were granted but whose adverse health impacts were unknown at the time of the concession. Indeed, Canada does not need to prove any specific violations of WTO provisions to maintain a nullification and impairment claim *(See* Chapter 8*)*. If upheld by the dispute panel, this argument could render any worker safety or public health law that is otherwise WTO-consistent to be a compensable violation.

Clearly, the asbestos case raises many issues, including how much discretion each country will have to decide how to regulate hazardous substances. However, many people view the prospects of a WTO ruling against an asbestos ban mainly as a massive blow against the universally recognized right to a safe workplace.[79] According to the World Health Organization, there are already 160 million cases a year of occupational disease worldwide.[80] This epidemic points to a broad problem of lax enforcement — or no enforcement at all — of occupational health and safety laws. If the WTO were to rule against a public health ban of a proven carcinogen present in numerous countries, the future of many laws aimed at ensuring a safe workplace is put at risk.

According to the ILO, the majority of the 160 million victims of occupational disease reside in the developing world.[81] Seven of Canada's top ten asbestos markets are developing countries. With a dwindling asbestos market in rich countries, Canada wants to ensure it doesn't lose markets in Africa, South America and Asia, where asbestos use is on the rise.[82] Indeed, there are reports that Canada has targeted France among all EU members that have implemented asbestos bans because it fears the French ban will influence its former colonies, particularly Morocco, Tunisia and Algeria – all of which are Canadian clients – to do the same.[83]

As the world's poorer nations industrialize, asbestos often is the most effective and cheapest way to make materials needed for water pipelines, power plants, factories, schools and prisons. Yet worker safeguards in these countries are often substandard or non-existent.[84] Asbestos-related deaths in the developing world are expected to reach one million in the next 30 years.[85] Of the top ten countries to which Canada exports, only one has ratified an international resolution on the safe handling of asbestos first proposed in 1986.[86]

The Uruguay Round Agreement Preamble promises that the new international trade rules will raise the living standards of working people all over the world.[87] Its rules, on the other hand, allow a nondiscriminatory occupational safety law, which has been embraced by many WTO Members, to be attacked as a trade violation. In this case, some observers predict the politics of the WTO may trump its legal rules. Given the public backlash against the WTO's recent anti-environmental rulings, as well as the well-known health risks posed by asbestos, the WTO might not risk a ruling that places Canada's right to peddle asbestos above the right of France to protect workers and the public – even if the WTO's backwards rules could be interpreted to support such an outcome.

> **" I think it's important to continue to defend the [Massachusetts Burma] law. It's legislation that was passed and signed by our governor. It's really about the state's right to choose who it does business with. "**[88]
>
> — Thomas F. Reilly,
> Massachusetts Attorney General

Case 2: WTO Challenge of Law Targeting Burmese Military Dictatorship's Human Rights Abuses

There is abundant evidence before the Commission showing the pervasive use of forced labor imposed on the civilian population throughout Myanmar by the authorities and the military for portering, the construction, maintenance and servicing of military camps, other work in support of the military, work on agriculture, logging and other production projects undertaken by the authorities or the military, *sometimes for the profit of private individuals*. ... none of which comes under any of the exceptions of the Convention. ... Forced labor in Myanmar is widely performed by women, children, and elderly persons as well as persons otherwise unfit for work. ... All of the information and evidence before the Commission shows utter disregard by the authorities for the safety and health as well as the basic needs of the people performing forced or compulsory labor. [*emphasis added*] [89]

— ILO Report, *Forced Labor in Myanmar*

The serious human rights violations and the deliberate suppression of democracy perpetrated by the military junta ruling Burma (which the junta has renamed Myanmar) since it came to power in 1988 are well known throughout the world. The International Labor Organization recently issued a scathing report on the human rights violations of the Burmese dictatorship.[90] Burma's pro-democracy movement, led by Nobel Peace Prize holder Aung San Suu Kyi, has called for South Africa-style foreign divestment from Burma to financially starve the military dictatorship.[91] Some two dozen U.S. municipal and county governments, and the state government of Massachusetts[96] have acted on this request and terminated purchasing contracts with companies doing business in Burma.[97] The selective purchasing laws are designed to ensure that public money is not

Agreement on Government Procurement: Governments Must Follow WTO Rules When Acting As Market Participants

The selective purchasing law against Burma passed by the Massachusetts state legislature in 1996 was challenged by the EU and Japan in the summer of 1997. These countries argue that the state's policy violates the WTO 1994 Agreement on Government Procurement (AGP).[92]

The AGP was negotiated during the Uruguay Round with the backing of developed countries eyeing the enormous global market in government procurement. The developed countries wanted procurement to be one of the agreements to which all WTO Members would be bound. However, many developing countries that use procurement policy as a development tool strenuously objected. The compromise was an AGP that applies only to countries or subfederal (state or local) entities that sign on. The AGP, unlike all other Uruguay Round Agreements, does not automatically apply to all WTO Members. The U.S. and 26 other mostly industrialized countries have signed the agreement.

The AGP requires "national treatment" for all goods and services a government purchases, meaning signatory governments cannot give preference to local companies.[93] The AGP also bans even nondiscriminatory performance requirements. This means that governments are not allowed to take into account any factors in awarding public contracts other than the ability of the company to fulfill the terms of the contract. Environmental, human rights or labor practices cannot be considered even if these criteria would apply to both domestic and foreign bidders.[94] The AGP also requires most favored nation treatment, meaning that governments cannot treat foreign companies differently based on their human rights, labor rights or environmental records at home or overseas. It was the combination of the last two rules that undergirded the WTO attack on Massachusetts' selective purchasing law relating to Burma. The WTO procurement agreement thus eliminates a powerful and effective tool for citizens who wish to make both governments and corporations accountable to taxpayers.

Developed countries now seek to expand the AGP rules to all WTO countries. A first step is a U.S.-EU proposal for the Seattle Ministerial to require all WTO countries to list all of their procurement activities with the WTO. The global government procurement market is worth trillions of dollars annually.[95]

used to indirectly support a regime whose conduct taxpayers find repugnant. A goal of such policies is to create incentives to encourage transnational corporations to divest from Burma. The selective purchasing laws are based on the effective divestiture and selective purchasing initiatives that animated the anti-apartheid movement in the U.S. in the 1980s and which are widely credited for helping to facilitate the successful transition to democracy in South Africa.

The attack on the Massachusetts' selective purchasing law was two-pronged. While Japan and the EU pressed their case in the WTO, a front group for multinational corporations called USA*Engage[98] challenged the measure in Massachusetts state court as a violation of the U.S. Constitution.

In the U.S. court challenge, USA*Engage claimed that the Massachusetts law interfered with the executive branch's exclusive authority to conduct foreign policy.[99] Massachusetts claimed that it was exercising its constitutionally valid right as an economic actor to make choices about its purchases, including its international commercial activity.[100]

On November 4, 1998, the Massachusetts state court ruled in favor of USA*Engage,[101] holding that municipalities and states may not interfere in foreign policy when it has a "great potential for disruption or embarrassment."[102] An appellate court upheld the ruling in June 1999.[103] The important case is now headed for the U.S. Supreme Court.

Meanwhile, the EU and Japan suspended their WTO challenge pending the outcome of the domestic case.[104] Should Massachusetts' appeal to the Supreme Court prevail, the EU and Japan would likely reopen the WTO challenge. This potential case will be monitored as an important test of the WTO's encroachment into areas of democratic policymaking regarding the advancement of human rights around the world.

However, the EU-Japan WTO challenge has already claimed a casualty. The Clinton administration, concerned about another WTO suit and the bad press it would generate, launched a successful campaign against a similar Maryland human rights proposal. The Clinton administration dispatched State Department Deputy Assistant Secretary David Marchick to testify before a Maryland legislative committee that was considering selective purchasing legislation targeting Nigeria at the very time the Burma WTO case was coming to a head.[105] The law, which was expected to pass, would have barred Maryland from signing any contracts with the Nigerian regime or with companies doing business there.[106] "All state and local sanctions are perceived to violate the rules, they can cause counterproductive disagreements. ... [W]e would like to work with you to ensure that *we don't expose ourselves to a potential WTO challenge,*" said the Clinton administration representative.[107] State Department lobbying convinced the Maryland legislature, which rejected the Nigeria legislation by a single vote.[108]

The continuation of the EU-Japan challenge at the WTO also would serve as a test case concerning the WTO's treatment of decisions taken by the International Labor Organization. The ILO found that the Burmese military dictatorship was systematically violating the basic human rights of Burmese citizens and non-Burmese minorities.[109] It ordered the Burmese dicatorship to reform its laws and practices regarding labor rights. If the case goes forward, a ruling against the Massachusetts law will also be the first example of the WTO's explicit disregard for the ILO's position in the area of competency – an area that the WTO has decreed is solely the ILO's.

———————— CHAPTER ENDNOTES ————————

[1] WTO, *Singapore Ministerial Declaration* (WT/MIN(96)/DEC), Dec. 13, 1996, at 4, on file with Public Citizen.

[2] Congressional Research Service, Memorandum to Sen. Tom Harkin (D-IA) "Whether Legislation Authorizing Restrictions on the Importation of Goods Produced by Child Labor is Consistent with the GATT," Jul. 15, 1993.

[3] The WTO TRIPs Agreement establishes a set of binding property protections that are enforceable through the WTO. These rules require WTO members to confer exclusive ownership rights over inventions by awarding and protecting patents, copyrights and trademarks. The TRIPs rules thus actually limit trade, undermining competition between firms and keeping consumer prices artificially high. In addition, the General Agreement on Trade in Services (GATS) and the Agreement on Trade-Related Investment Measures (TRIMs) confer a new right on foreign corporations to establish commercial presence in most industries to compete with local businesses and to conclude mergers and acquisitions that cause industry consolidation and resulting monopoly behavior, especially in the developing world where domestic industry is in its infancy and cannot compete.

[4] WTO, *Singapore Ministerial Declaration* (WT/MIN(96)/DEC), Dec. 13, 1996, at 4, on file with Public Citizen (emphasis added).

[5] One prominent example of race-to-the-bottom employment is Nike, which first manufactured its sneakers in Taiwan and South Korea. When workers attempted to organize for better wages in the 1970s, Nike pulled out and began production in Indonesia, the People's Republic of China and Vietnam. *See* Global Exchange, *Nike Chronology*, Nov. 1997. Other examples include the numerous U.S.-based manufacturing firms that have relocated to Mexico under NAFTA, or that have threatened to relocate to Mexico under NAFTA to discourage unionization and to depress wages. *See* Kate Bronfenbrenner, Final Report: The Effects of Plant Closing or Threat of Plant Closing on the Right of Workers to Organize, Submitted to the Labor Secretariat of the North American Commission for Labor Cooperation, Sep. 30, 1996; *see also* Public Citizen's Global Trade Watch database containing U.S. Department of Labor data on companies that have used NAFTA to shift employment to Mexico, where the U.S. Bureau of Labor Statistics has determined that manufacturing wages are less than 10% of those in the U.S., at www.citizen.org/pctrade/taa97acs/KEYTAA.html.

[6] See Chapter 1 for more information on production and processing methods.

[7] *See* President William J. Clinton's remarks at the University of Chicago convocation ceremonies, Chicago, IL, Jun. 12, 1999, on file with Public Citizen.

[8] Congressional Research Service, Memorandum to Sen. Tom Harkin (D-IA) on "Whether Legislation Authorizing Restrictions on the Importation of Goods Produced by Child Labor is Consistent with the GATT," Jul. 15, 1993.

[9] Charles Kernaghan, "Made in China: Behind the Label," Special Report, New York: National Labor Committee (1998), *cited in* Robert E. Scott, "China Can Wait: WTO Accession Deal Must Include Enforceable Labor Rights, Real Commercial Benefits," Economic Policy Institute, Briefing Paper, May 1999, at 2, on file with Public Citizen.

[10] George Kouros, "Workers' Health Is on the Line, Occupational Health and Safety in the Maquiladoras," *Borderlines 47*, vol. 6, no. 6, Aug. 1998.

[11] United Nations Conference on Trade and Development (UNCTAD), *Trade and Development Report 1997*, Document UNCTAD/TDR/17, Overview, at 4.

[12] The ILO has gathered significant data on labor rights abuses in EPZs worldwide and is urging governments to ensure the fulfillment of their international and domestic obligations with regard to labor rights. *See* International Labor Organization, "ILO Meeting Calls for Improved Social and Labour Conditions in Export Processing Zones and End to Restrictions On Trade Union Rights," Press Release, ILO/98/35, Oct. 2, 1998.

[13] Nike's internal documents showed in Nov. 1997 that Vietnamese workers were being paid nineteen cents or less per hour. *See* Global Exchange, *Nike Chronology*, Nov. 1997.

[14] "[T]he most difficult issues confronting these [laid-off] workers…[is] the prospect of earning lower wages in their new jobs. Two studies have concluded that…government programs [for displaced workers] had no positive effect on workers' wages." Karen Brandon and Stephen Franklin, "Free Trade's Growing Pains," *Chicago Tribune*, Nov. 29, 1998, at 1-14.

[15] George Kouros, "Workers' Health Is on the Line, Occupational Health and Safety in the Maquiladoras," *Borderlines 47*, vol. 6, no. 6, Aug. 1998.

[16] Data compiled by Coalition for Justice in the Maquiladoras, Oct. 1998, on file with Public Citizen.

[17] *Id.*

[18] *See, inter alia*, Han Young submission to the U.S. National Administrative Office (NAO), established through NAFTA, Bureau of International Labor Affairs, Public Report and Review of NAO Submission No. 9702, Apr. 28, 1998. The productivity of Mexican workers has risen 36.4% since NAFTA went into effect. *See* INEGI, "Manufacturing Industry Productivity, Various Countries January 1993-September 1998," Sep. 1998.

[19] WTO, General Agreement on Trade in Services (GATS), Annex on Movement of National Persons Supplying Services Under The Agreement at Article 3.

[20] *Id.* at Article 4.

[21] U.S. Trade Representative Charlene Barshefsky, "Services in the Trading System," Speech to the World Services Conference, Washington, DC, Jun. 1, 1999, at 13, on file with Public Citizen.

[22] WTO, GATS Agreement, Annex on Movement of National Persons Supplying Services Under The Agreement at Article 3.

[23] *See* John Madeley, *Trade and the Poor*, 2nd Edition, Intermediate Technology Publications (1996) at 74.

[24] George Graham, "Pressure for Social Clause in GATT Deal," *Financial Times*, Mar. 16, 1994.

[25] John Zarocostas, "UN Agency Suggests WTO Social Standards," *Journal of Commerce*, Nov. 9, 1994. The "core labor rights" are Right to Freedom of Association, Right to Collective Bargaining, Freedom from Slavery, Freedom from Discrimination in the Workplace, and Freedom from Child Labor.

[26] Chakravarthi Ragavan, "Barking Up the Wrong Tree: Trade and Social Clause Links," *SUNS*, 1996.

[27] "U.S. Waves Flag for Workers' Rights," *Financial Times*, Mar. 30, 1994.

[28] *Id.*

[29] President William J. Clinton, Statement at the Geneva WTO Ministerial Meeting, Geneva, Switzerland, May 20, 1998.

[30] President William J. Clinton, 1999 State of the Union Address, Washington, DC, Jan. 19, 1999.

[31] *See* Deputy U.S. Trade Representative Susan Esserman, Statement by the U.S. Delegation to the WTO General Council Session, Geneva, Switzerland, Jul. 29, 1999.

[32] Sandra Sugawara, "WTO Trade Ministers Making Scant Progress," *The Washington Post*, Dec. 12, 1996.

[33] *See* Sandra Sugawara, "25 Nations Endorse Ending Many High-Tech Tariffs," *The Washington Post*, Dec. 13 1996; and "World Trade Overload," *The Economist*, Aug. 3, 1996.

[34] "Agenda for the WTO," *Financial Times*, Editorial, Nov. 12, 1996.

[35] Helene Cooper, "White House Seeks to Link Labor Rights, World Trade to Gain Union Support," *The Wall Street Journal*, Dec. 10, 1996.

[36] *Id.*

[37] WTO, *Singapore Ministerial Declaration* (WT/MIN(96)/DEC), Dec. 13, 1996, at Para. 4.

[38] *Id.*

[39] *See* Deputy U.S. Trade Representative Susan Esserman, Statement by the U.S. Delegation to the WTO General Council Session, Geneva, Switzerland, Jul. 29, 1999.

[40] *Id.*

[41] *Id.*

[42] U.S. Environmental Protection Agency, "The Asbestos Informer," EPA 340/1-90-020, Dec. 1990, at 6.

[43] Debora MacKenzie, "In Safe Hands?," *New Scientist*, Apr. 3, 1999.

[44] European Communities, "EU Backs French Asbestos Ban in Face of Canadian WTO Panel," Press Release, Oct. 22, 1998.

[45] Barry Castleman, "Corporate Junk Science: Corporate Influence at International Science Organizations," *Multinational Monitor*, Jan./Feb. 1998, at 2.

[46] Andrew Watterson, "Chemical Hazards and Public Confidence," *The Lancet*, Vol. 342, Jul. 17, 1993, at 131-132.

[47] *Id.*

[48] Barry Castleman, "Corporate Junk Science: Corporate Influence at International Science Organizations," *Multinational Monitor*, Jan./Feb. 1998, at 2.

[49] *Id.*

[50] "Battling over Asbestos in the Third World," *Environmental Health Perspectives*, vol. 105, no. 11, Nov. 1997, quoting Barry Castleman, asbestos expert and consultant, and Joseph Le Dou, Editor-in-Chief of the *International Journal of Occupational and Environmental Health*.

[51] Debora MacKenzie, "In Safe Hands?," *New Scientist*, Apr. 3, 1999.

[52] Bill Schiller, "Why Canada Pushes Killer Asbestos," *Toronto Star*, Mar. 29, 1999.

[53] French Decree 96-1133, Dec. 24, 1996, on prohibition of asbestos (J.O. dated Dec. 26, 1996), on file with Public Citizen.

[54] *Id.* at Articles 1 and 2.

[55] Bill Schiller, "Why Canada Pushes Killer Asbestos," *Toronto Star News,* Mar. 20, 1999.

[56] European Communities - Measures Affecting the Prohibition of Asbestos and Asbestos Products (WT/DS135), Complaint by Canada, May 28, 1998.

[57] European Communities, "EU Backs French Asbestos Ban in Face of Canadian WTO Panel," Press Release, Oct. 22, 1998.

[58] United States, European Communities - Measures Affecting the Prohibition of Asbestos and Asbestos Products, Third Party Written Submission of the United States, May 28, 1999, available at the EPA Asbestos Ombudsman and EPA Public Information Center, and on file with Public Citizen.

[59] The Dispute Settlement Board established a panel at its meeting on Nov. 25, 1998.

[60] A spokesperson for the Canadian government said that Canada believes the ban convenes World Trade Organization rules. *See* "EU Confirms White Asbestos Ban," *ENDS Daily*, Jul. 29, 1999.

[61] WTO, TBT Agreement at Articles 2.2 and 2.4.

[62] WTO, European Communities – Measures Concerning Asbestos and Products Containing It, Canadian First Draft, Apr. 26, 1999, at 1. The Canadian government echoes the arguments of the Canadian asbestos industry that "white" or chrysotile asbestos is safe when managed properly, but the older "blue" and "brown" forms of asbestos are responsible for worker deaths. The U.S. Occupational Safety and Health Administration (OSHA), disputes this claim, finding that "chrysotile exposure should be treated the same as other forms of asbestos" and that it may be an even more potent carcinogen. *See* Debora MacKenzie, "In Safe Hands?," *New Scientist*, Apr. 3, 1999.

[63] WTO, European Communities – Measures Concerning Asbestos and Products Containing It, Canadian First Draft, Apr. 26, 1999, at 3.

[64] *See* International Labor Conference, Agreement Concerning Safety in the Use of Asbestos (Agreement 162), Jun. 24, 1986; *see also* International Labor Conference, Recommendation Concerning Safety in the Use of Asbestos (Recommendation 172), Jun. 24, 1986.

[65] *See* Barry Castleman, "Corporate Junk Science: Corporate Influence at International Science Organizations," *Multinational Monitor*, Jan./Feb. 1998.

[66] "Battling over Asbestos in the Third World," *Environmental Health Perspectives*, vol. 105, no. 11, Nov. 1997, quoting Barry Castleman, asbestos expert and consultant.

[67] *Id.*, quoting Joseph Le Dou, Editor-in-Chief of the *International Journal of Occupational and Environmental Health*.

[68] International Organization on Standardization, Standard ISO-7337, 1984.

[69] Personal communication, Aug. 21, 1999, between anonymous asbestos expert and Michelle Sforza, Research Director, Public Citizen.

[70] *See* Barry Castleman, "Corporate Junk Science: Corporate Influence at International Science Organizations," *Multinational Monitor*, Jan./Feb. 1998.

[71] WTO, European Communities – Measures Concerning Asbestos and Products Containing It, Canadian First Draft, Apr. 26, 1999, at Exhibit 46.

[72] Barry Castleman, "Corporate Junk Science: Corporate Influence at International Science Organizations," *Multinational Monitor*, Jan./Feb. 1998, at 2.

[73] WTO, European Communities – Measures Concerning Asbestos and Products Containing It, Canadian First Draft, Apr. 26, 1999, at Exhibit 47.

[74] Barry Castleman, "Corporate Junk Science: Corporate Influence at International Science Organizations," *Multinational Monitor*, Jan./Feb. 1998, at 2.

[75] WTO, European Communities – Measures Concerning Asbestos and Products Containing It, Canadian First Draft, Apr. 26, 1999, at 2-3 (emphasis added).

[76] *Id.* at 65.

[77] *Id.* at 2.

[78] *Id.* at 76.

[79] The right to safe working conditions is covered by the 1981 Occupational Safety and Health and the Working Environment Convention (C155, International Labor Organization); 1966 International Covenant on Economic Social and Cultural Rights, Article 7; 1988 Additional Protocol to the American Convention on Human Rights in the Area of Economic, Social, and Cultural Rights, Article 7; and 1961 European Social Charter, Article 3.

[80] World Health Organization, *World Health Report 1997*, Executive Summary, Geneva (1998).

[81] Bill Schiller, "Why Canada Pushes Killer Asbestos," *Toronto Star*, Mar. 29, 1999.

[82] *See id.; see also* Dennis Cauchon, "The Asbestos Epidemic - A Global Crisis," *USA Today*, Aug. 2, 1999.

[83] Bill Schiller, "Why Canada Pushes Killer Asbestos," *Toronto Star*, Mar. 29, 1999.

[84] Dennis Cauchon, "The Asbestos Epidemic - A Global Crisis," *USA Today*, Aug. 2, 1999.

[85] *Id.*

[86] Bill Schiller, "Why Canada Pushes Killer Asbestos," *Toronto Star*, Mar. 29, 1999.

[87] Agreement Establishing the World Trade Organization, Preamble: "The Parties to this Agreement, recogniz[e] that their relations in the field of trade and economics endeavour should be conducted with a view to raising standards of living . . . ."

[88] "State Attorney General Seeks Review of Burma Trade Ruling," *Associated Press*, Jul. 13, 1999.

[89] International Labor Organization, *Forced Labour in Myanmar*, Jul. 21, 1998 (emphasis added).

[90] *See id.*

[91] "Burmese leader in exile welcomes limited U.S. sanctions," *Agence France Presse*, Sep. 24, 1996.

[92] *See* WT/DS88/1, filed Jun. 20, 1997 by the European Community, and WT/DS95/1, filed Jul. 18, 1997, by Japan.

[93] 1994 Agreement on Government Procurement (AGP) at Article III (National Treatment and Non-discrimination).

[94] *Id.* at Article IV (Rules of Origin).

[95] *See* Martin Khor, "Government Spending Under WTO Scrutiny?," *Third World Network Features*, Feb. 1999.

[96] Act of June 25th, 1996, Chapter 130, 1, 1996, Mass. Acts. 210, codified at Mass. Gen. L. ch. 7. 22G-22M.

[97] Jim Lobe, "Government Opts Out of Court Case on Globalization," *InterPress Service*, Mar. 11, 1999. Most recently, the Los Angeles City Council voted unanimously in Dec. 1997 to ban companies that do business in Burma from bidding for any city contracts.

[98] Prominent USA*Engage members are: AT&T, Boeing, BP, Calix, Chase Manhattan Bank, Coca-Cola, Dow Chemical, Ericsson, GTE Corporation, IBM, Intel, Monsanto, Siemens, and Union Carbide. For a full list, *see* http://usaengage.org/background/members.html, on file with Public Citizen.

[99] "[T]he Constitution vests full and exclusive authority for regulating affairs with other nations in the national government, and . . . the Commonwealth's enactment and enforcement of the Massachusetts Burma Law is entirely inconsistent with this principle." Plaintiff's Opposition to the Commonwealth's Motion for Summary Judgment and Reply in Support of Its Motion for Summary Judgment, Civil Action No. 98-CV-10757 (JLT), Aug. 13, 1998.

[100] "In imposing a price preference for firms that do not do business with Burma, the Commonwealth of Massachusetts is acting as a market participant. It is exercising the power and discretion that any private actor would enjoy as a matter of contract and property rights — the power to decide 'with whom it will deal.'" Defendants' Memorandum in Support of Their Motion for Summary Judgment, Civil Action No. 98-CV-10757 (JLT), Jul. 27, 1997.

[101] *See* Civil Action No. 97 12042 (JLT), U.S. District Court, District of Massachusetts.

[102] *Id.* at Para. 2.

[103] *See* Civil Action No. 98-2304, U.S. Court of Appeals for the First Circuit.

[104] "EU Suspends WTO Panel on Massachusetts Burma Law," *United Press International*, Feb. 8, 1999.

[105] State Department Deputy Assistant Secretary David Marchick, Testimony before the Maryland House of Delegates' Committee on Commerce and Government Matters, Annapolis, MD, Mar. 25, 1998, on file with Public Citizen.

[106] "African Trade-Offs," *The Nation*, Editorial, Apr. 6, 1998.

[107] State Department Deputy Assistant Secretary David Marchick, Testimony before the Maryland House of Delegates' Committee on Commerce and Government Matters, Annapolis, MD, Mar. 25, 1998, on file with Public Citizen (emphasis added).

[108] Maryland House Bill 1273 on Floor Mar. 25, 1998, Senate Bill 354 on Floor Mar. 31, 1998 (emphasis added); *see also, inter alia*, Ken Silverstein, "Nigeria Deception," *Multinational Monitor*, Jan./Feb. 1998, vol. 19, nos. 1 and 2; and *Human Rights Watch World Report 1999*.

[109] International Labor Organization, *Forced Labour in Myanmar*, Jul. 21, 1998.

In this chapter ...

CASES:

- **U.S. Trade Law Section 301 and the Kodak case:** The Clinton administration promised Congress and industry that Section 301, a unilateral trade sanctions mechanism established in U.S. law, would remain effective under the WTO. As was apparent in the WTO text, this was a bald-faced lie. Indeed, when the U.S. tried to use Section 301 against Japan in a dispute over access to the photographic film market, Japan threatened to formally challenge Section 301 at the WTO. The U.S. backed down and instead filed the Kodak case with the WTO, which it lost on all points because the conduct it opposed is not covered by WTO rules. Now the EU has formally challenged the continuing existence of Section 301 on the U.S. law books as a WTO violation.

CONCEPTS:

Challenging Countries Win at WTO: In only three out of 22 completed WTO cases has a defending country won a case. This makes clear that countries that can afford to bring challenges are the main beneficiaries of the system. Poor countries — and challenged health and environmental laws — have been the consistent losers. Ironically, two of the three anomalous cases included failed U.S. challenges regarding access to the Japanese photographic film market and EU tariff reclassification regarding computer equipment.

U.S. Has Lost Every WTO Challenge Against U.S. Laws: The WTO has labeled as illegal U.S. policies ranging from anti-dumping laws and corporate tax rules to sea turtle protections and clean air rules.

WTO Tribunals Are Secretive and Without Due Process Protections: The WTO's powerful dispute resolution system is missing even basic due process protections. For instance, among this chapter's revelations is a potential conflict of interest with a well-known WTO panelist's involvement in the WTO case on the Helms-Burton Cuba policy. Even WTO-booster former USTR Mickey Kantor has expressed concerns about the WTO's secrecy.

WTO Judges Biased, Not Well-Informed on Diverse Issues: The criteria under which WTO dispute resolution panelists are chosen ensures that panelists will have an interest in maintaining the status quo trade system. Also, panelists' knowledge is often limited to commercial policy, even though they must rule on health, environmental and other issues. This chapter discusses the choice of an avowed critic of labor rights protections in trade pacts to serve as a panelist in a case in which labor issues were involved.

Amicus Briefs Still Allowed Only if Countries Approve: Although a recent WTO Appellate Body reversed a lower panel's explicit ban on submission of outside briefs, the body ruled that interested private parties can submit briefs *only* if they convince a government to make those briefs part of its formal submission.

Non-Violation Claims: The WTO allows challenges to nations' laws that do *not* actually violate WTO rules but that could undermine a benefit another country reasonably expected from the agreement. This is one basis of Canada's claim against France's asbestos ban. Canada says that even if France's ban does not violate any specific WTO rules, Canada should be compensated because it expected to enjoy improved tariff rates and market access for its asbestos under the Uruguay Round of GATT.

WTO Rules and Enforcement Apply to State and Local Law: The EU and Japan challenge against the state of Massachusetts' Burma human rights law demonstrates that WTO rules apply to all levels of government. However, this principle is also explicitly included in the rules of several of the WTO Agreements. When state and local laws are challenged, only the U.S. federal government has a right under WTO procedures to be present — raising the possibility that a national government opposed to a state law would be its only defender behind closed doors in Geneva.

8 The WTO's Unprecedented Dispute Resolution System

The WTO contains the strongest enforcement procedures of any international agreement now in force. Indeed, one of the most dramatic changes made to the global trade system by the Uruguay Round negotiations was the transformation of the consensus-based GATT contract into the binding tribunal system of the World Trade Organization. Countries that signed onto the GATT were called "Contracting Parties" and legally were bound to the GATT rules only to the extent they agreed in each instance. The WTO is a free-standing organization with "legal personality" (the same political status of the United Nations) and with self-executing enforcement, meaning that the WTO contains binding dispute mechanisms to enforce its trade rules. Countries in the WTO are called Members, are bound to all WTO terms and can stave off a WTO enforcement action only if all other WTO Members unanimously agree.

The GATT contained the typical sovereignty safeguards found in almost every international agreement; consensus was required to bind any country to an obligation. Thus, while countries could challenge other GATT contracting party countries laws before dispute panels, adoption of the ruling and approval of sanctions for noncompliance required a consensus decision of all GATT countries, including the losing country. In order to maintain the legitimacy of the GATT system, countries rarely objected to rulings against them, although the option existed as a sort of emergency brake. This was the mechanism the U.S. and Mexico used to stop final adoption of the 1991 ruling against the U.S. dolphin law.

Unlike the GATT before it, WTO panel rulings are automatically binding and do not require unanimous consent to be adopted. Nor do WTO trade sanctions need consensus approval. Indeed, the WTO is unique among all other international agreements in that consensus is required to *stop* action. Once a WTO tribunal has declared a country's law WTO-illegal, the country must change its law or face trade sanctions. Even more alarming, it is the official position of the U.S. government that such sanctions or negotiated compensation are only interim measures and that WTO rules require countries to amend their domestic laws.[1]

The WTO's binding dispute resolution procedure and the Uruguay Round's expansive new rules encroaching into areas traditionally considered the realm of domestic policy effectively shift many decisions regarding public health and safety and environmental and social concerns from democratically elected domestic bodies to WTO tribunals meeting behind closed doors in Geneva, Switzerland.

WTO rules promote selection of panelists for these dispute tribunals who have a predetermined trade perspective and a stake in the existing trade model and rules. The enforcement system is an integral part of the WTO, the inherent purpose of which is "expanding . . . trade in goods and services."[2] It is therefore not surprising that WTO panelists consistently have issued interpretations that lean toward furthering trade liberalization whenever that goal conflicts with other policy goals.

Indeed, the WTO system gives trade-motivated tribunal members the power to reverse the preferences of national governments. Such an infringement on democratic, accountable governance itself raises many inherent problems. However, the WTO's system additionally fails to provide safeguards for ensuring an open decision-making process or a full airing of all the issues involved, especially by those who would be most affected by the decisions, namely the citizenry of the countries involved in the dispute. Many national policies are aimed at noneconomic goals such as environmental or public health protection or labor rights guarantees. While such policymaking inherently takes into account economic considerations, once such laws are subject to a WTO panel's review they will be judged exclusively by narrow, specific WTO-set economic standards.

Given the power of the WTO dispute resolution system, its processes and procedures demand close scrutiny.

The WTO Record: Public Interest Big Loser Under WTO Dispute Resolution

The WTO's powerful and enforceable dispute resolution system was to be all things for all WTO Members. U.S. WTO proponents promised that it would enable the U.S., which has the most open markets in the world, to enforce the obligations assumed by the rest of the world during the Uruguay Round negotiations. By the same token, proponents in other countries promised that it would protect the rest of the world from U.S. unilateralism and give nations at various stages of development more equal access to remedies for trade law violations.

After almost five years of WTO panel rulings, however, the reality is quite different. The bottom line is that countries that can afford to launch WTO challenges generally are winning. To date, WTO tribunals have almost always sided with a challenging country and ruled against the targeted law. In only three out of 22 completed WTO cases did the respondents win. As of July 1999, the U.S. had lost every completed case brought against it, with the WTO labeling as illegal U.S. policies ranging from sea turtle protection and clean air regulations to anti-dumping duties.[3] The U.S. – which has brought more complaints than any other country – was a claimant or co-claimant in nine of the 22 cases.[4] Interestingly, the U.S. was also the loser in two of three unusual cases where the plaintiff lost on the merits, the Kodak case and the EU computer case.

Developed countries have the resources to take advantage of the WTO's pattern of ruling in favor of the challenger. Many developing countries not only cannot afford to bring cases but also cannot afford the costs of a WTO defense. Indeed, an alarming trend under the WTO is that developing countries – faced with the enormous expertise and resources involved in mounting a WTO defense in Geneva – are changing laws merely after the threat of a WTO challenge from wealthy countries.

Finally, when viewed outside the context of competition between countries, the real loser at the WTO is the public interest. *After an in-depth analysis of the decisions reached by WTO dispute resolution panels, this book concludes that no democratically achieved environmental, health, food safety or environmental law challenged at the WTO has ever been upheld. All have been declared barriers to trade.*

WTO Tribunals:
Secret Proceedings, Lack of Due Process

The design and operation of the WTO's dispute resolution system is established in the Uruguay Round Dispute Resolution Understanding (DSU). The DSU provides only one specific operating rule – that all panel activities and documents are confidential.[7] Under this WTO rule, dispute panels operate in secret, documents are restricted to the countries in the dispute, due process and citizen participation are absent and no outside appeal is available. The WTO's lower panel and Appellate Body meet in closed sessions[8] and the proceedings are confidential.[9] All documents are also kept confidential unless a government voluntarily releases its own submissions to the public.[10] The closed nature of the dispute process prevents domestic proponents of health, environmental or other policies that are being challenged from obtaining sufficient information about the proceedings to provide input. This is in sharp contrast to domestic courts and even to other international arbitration systems (for instance the International Court of Justice) that also pit nation against nation. The International Court of Justice deliberates in public and employs strict due process criteria.[11] The WTO's closed operations also stand in sharp contrast to the promises of then-U.S. Trade Representative

Former U.S. Trade Representative Mickey Kantor on Secrecy, Then and Now

Lobbying for WTO passage: "The Uruguay Round Agreements provide for increased transparency in the dispute settlement process."[5]

After the WTO was approved: "He said he strongly supported the idea of making the WTO more accessible to most Americans and noted that he has been pushing WTO Members to agree to end rules keeping most WTO proceedings secret. He reported that important progress was made in the last few weeks on this point, and said he would be glad to brief the *committee behind closed doors.*"[6]

Mickey Kantor, who said in 1994 that "the Uruguay Round Agreements provide for increased transparency in the dispute settlement process."[12]

WTO disputes are heard by tribunals composed of three panelists (unless the disputing countries opt for five-member panels).[13] The WTO secretariat nominates panel members for each dispute, and the disputing parties may oppose nominations only for "compelling reasons."[14] The only recourse after a panel ruling is to appeal to the WTO Appellate Body. To date, the Appellate Body, composed of seven panelists, has reversed only one case *(See information about U.S. losing an appeal to EU on computers later in this chapter).*

Bureaucrats with Trade Expertise Judge Environmental, Public Health, Worker Rights and Economic Development Policies

Qualifications for serving on WTO dispute panels include past service on GATT panels, past representation of a country before a trade institution or tribunal, past service as a senior trade policy official of a WTO Member country, and teaching experience in or publishing on international trade law or policy.[15] These qualifications promote the selection of panelists with a stake in the existing trade system and rules. They also winnow out potential panelists who do not share an institutionally derived philosophy about international commerce and the role of the GATT system that supports the status quo.

These qualifications also serve to narrowly limit the panelists' areas of expertise to international commercial policy. Given the Uruguay Round's 700-plus pages of nontariff rules, most trade disputes now arise between national legislation enacted to protect broader public interests such as the environment, animal and human health, economic development and workplace health and safety, and WTO constraints on such policies. The record shows that WTO panelists have needed more than just trade law expertise, as the outcome of several cases has turned on the interpretation of environmental treaties or general rules of international law.[16] The outcomes have not always been consistent with conventional interpretations, and WTO panels have been criticized in international law journals for their excessively narrow interpretations of general rules of international law.[17]

> **T**he selection criteria for WTO panelists ensure that they have a set trade perspective and a stake in the existing system and rules. The criteria also act to keep the WTO roster predominantly male. The Member Roster of WTO Dispute Panelists contains 159 names. Of those, 147 are men (92.5%) and 12 are women (7.5%).

WTO Banana Case Panelist:
Avowed Critic of Enforceable Green, Labor Policy

The over-use of trade measures to pursue environmental or labor market objectives has *"an important, indirect negative effect ... namely the potential erosion of the rules-based multilateral trading system."*[18]

"Environmental and labor concerns can provide a convenient additional excuse for raising trade barriers."[19]

These are quotes from articles written by Kym Anderson, a trade expert appearing on the WTO roster of panelists. Anderson is an economist who has published extensively on international trade and development issues, advised the Australian minister for foreign affairs and trade,[20] and generally fulfills to a "T" the WTO criteria for dispute panel eligibility. Anderson's ideological bias against environmental and labor protection in the global economy also confirms concerns of the public interest community that the WTO's dispute resolution system empowers biased judges.

Anderson served on the WTO panel for the U.S. challenge to the EU Lome Treaty preferences for Caribbean bananas.[21] The case had an important labor policy component. At issue was an EU policy giving preference to bananas grown in the Caribbean on small, family-owned plots, as compared to bananas from vast Latin American plantations owned by U.S.-based agribusiness corporations notorious for terrible labor conditions.[22] An explicit purpose of the EU policy was to ensure some market for the Caribbean's more costly, but preferable mode of banana production.

In 1997, the WTO panel ruled against the Caribbean banana preferences, and this ruling was later upheld by the WTO Appellate Body. If the EU caves to U.S. punitive tariffs now in effect as a result of the WTO panel ruling, the elimination of the EU's preferences for Caribbean bananas would undermine economies and democracies built on small-scale banana cultivation. This likely will result in a banana production system in which Caribbean growers who once owned their own small tracts and earned a decent living will be replaced by a handful of giant corporations employing low-wage workers on massive Central American plantations.

In fact, there are no mechanisms for ensuring that individuals serving as panelists have any expertise in the subject of the dispute before them. This is particularly worrisome in disputes concerning health and environmental measures, as the DSU does not even require panelists to consult with experts. A panel may, but is not required to, call on outside experts.[23] One very basic safeguard for minimally ensuring accurate legal analysis would be the selection of panelists with broader competencies.

Conflict of Interest Standards at the WTO: "Don't Ask, Don't Tell"

As established in the Uruguay Round Agreements, the WTO dispute resolution system lacked any mechanism guaranteeing that panelists do not have potential conflicts of interest in serving on a panel. In 1996, the WTO adopted the Rules of Conduct for the Understanding on Rules and Procedures Governing the Settlement of Disputes.[24] The document recognizes that confidence in the DSU panels is linked closely to the integrity and impartiality of its panelists.[25] The provisions designed to achieve this, however, are so weak that they are pointless, as made clear in the case described below about the appointment of an International Chamber of Commerce representative who serves on the board of Nestle to judge the WTO challenge of the Helms-Burton sanctions against certain foreign investors in Cuba, where Nestle has a plant.

Under the Rules of Conduct, discovery of the panelists' backgrounds is based on self-disclosure, leaving it up to the individual panelist to decide which aspects of his or her past should be known.[26] The rules stipulate that the disclosure "shall not extend to the identification of matters [of insignificant] relevance;" that it must "take into account the need to respect the personal privacy" of the panelists; and that it must not be "so administratively burdensome as to make it impracticable for otherwise qualified persons to serve on the panels."[27] In other words, if the person fulfills the criteria set out in the original DSU, it is up to him or her to disclose whether a conflict exists. Further, if full disclosure is deemed burdensome by the panelist, it is waived, and the panelist still can qualify without disclosing potential conflicts of interest. This process is a far cry from the procedures used in U.S. domestic jurisdictions to ensure the integrity and independence of judges. The WTO has been called a global Supreme Court of Commerce, but U.S. Supreme Court judges must pass Senate scrutiny after their presidential appointment to make it to the bench, and U.S. federal judges are bound by a strict set of conflict-of-interest rules.

The lack of meaningful WTO conflict-of-interest rules has, on at least one occasion, led to the selection of a panelist with a potential conflict of interest. This example highlights why such serious questions about the efficacy and fairness of the WTO's dispute resolution system are continually raised. Former GATT-head Arthur Dunkel was selected by WTO Director-General Renato Ruggiero to serve on the dispute panel ruling on the merits of an EU challenge of the U.S. Cuban Liberty and Democratic Solidarity Act (also known as Helms-Burton).[28] At the time, Dunkel served on the board of Nestle S.A., which operates a production company in Cuba. He also chaired a key International Chamber of Commerce committee that produced a paper harshly critical of the U.S. law. (See box on following page for more information.)

Contrary to the majority of court hearings, whether international or domestic, where the judges sign their opinions by name, opinions expressed in the final WTO panel reports by individual panelists remain anonymous.[29] This practice removes yet another important way for the public to monitor the relationship between the panelists' background and their work on the panels. The example of the selection of Dunkel, a well-known figure whose career has been dedicated to advocating on

Example of WTO Tribunalist's Potential Conflict of Interest

Arthur Dunkel, a well-known figure in trade circles, had both a potential conflict of interest relating to his role on the board of directors of Nestle, S.A., and an obvious prejudicial bias relating to his role chairing a policy committee of the International Chamber of Commerce (ICC). Dunkel serves as the chair of the ICC's Commission on International Trade and Investment Policy, a body that has strongly opposed the U.S. Cuban Liberty and Democratic Solidarity Act, also known as the Helms-Burton Act. [30] The law sanctions foreign companies benefiting from investment in assets illegally seized from U.S. nationals during the Cuban revolution. It includes U.S. visa restrictions for the executives of such companies.

The ICC, an organization founded to promote the industry perspective on international trade and investment, is a harsh public critic of the U.S. law. According to its June 19, 1996, position paper: "The ICC believes that the Helms-Burton Act, which threatens to distort international trade and investment and to cause considerable commercial disruption to companies from countries which are trading partners of the U.S., is in clear contradiction of the fundamental principles of the World Trade Organization and may contain elements which are incompatible with U.S. obligations under the WTO."[31] Dunkel chairs the committee that defines and determines the ICC's positions on trade issues.[32]

Dunkel also served as a member of the board of directors of Nestle, S.A., from 1994 to 1999.[33] Nestle has operated a production company in Cuba since 1930,[34] and thus has an interest in the outcome of this case and in the status of U.S. commercial policy regarding Cuba.

The WTO's director general appointed Dunkel as a panelist to judge the legality of the Helms-Burton Law when it was challenged by the EU. The USTR says it was unaware of Dunkel's role chairing the ICC committee until Public Citizen notified it in 1998 — two years after the WTO panel was constituted. [35] Dunkel's role on the board of a company with a possible economic stake in the case's outcome was never raised either. This oversight — or lack thereof — does not inspire confidence in either the WTO's "conflict-of-interest safeguards" or in the zeal of the Clinton administration's defense of U.S. laws before the WTO.

The Clinton administration has been hostile toward the Helms-Burton Law,[30] raising the troubling issue of whether governments can be trusted to defend laws, especially those to which they are hostile, in closed fora such as the WTO. Given that the trade agenda of governments is shaped primarily by multinational corporations (for instance, the U.S. trade advisory committees that shape U.S. negotiating positions on trade issues have hundreds of representatives from business and only a handful from the public interest community), the willingness of governments to strongly defend environmental, public health, development and other policies opposed by their constituents in industry is suspect.

behalf of industry, who was chosen after the establishment of "conflict-of-interest rules," at a minimum shows strong contempt by the WTO for judicial independence.

Adding Insult to Injury: WTO Limits Citizens' Ability to Rectify Panel's Shortcomings

The lack of competence on health, environment and other matters among tribunal members could have been rectified to some extent by requiring the participation by *ad hoc* independent experts on panels or by requiring panels to consider third-party submissions from parties with a demonstrated interest in the case (*amici curiae* or *amicus briefs*). The WTO's dispute resolution system does neither.

WTO panels are allowed, but not required, to seek information and technical advice from outside individuals and expert bodies.[37] However, the names of such experts are kept secret until the panel issues its report on the case,[38] making it impossible to prevent conflicts of interest among the technical experts.

Technical experts and panelists can second-guess policies crafted by elected government representatives while having no understanding or appreciation of that government's domestic law and policy objectives. Panelists are bound only by the Uruguay Round rules and may have connections to parties with an economic interest in the dispute. In contrast, citizens of WTO Member countries whose laws are challenged cannot serve on expert review groups.[39] This can prevent participation by those most knowledgeable about the reasons for and the operation of the domestic measures in question.

Even though the WTO recently lifted its absolute ban on *amicus* briefs, interested parties who wish to provide input in the form of *amicus* briefs face an array of obstacles. During the beef hormone case, U.S. public interest groups strenuously opposed the U.S. government attack on a nondiscriminatory European health law. The groups' perspective was totally excluded from the U.S brief. The groups attempted to submit an *amicus* brief in favor of the European ban. At the time, the WTO explicitly forbade such briefs from members of the public, arguing that the WTO is a governments-only body.

In 1998, the WTO changed its policy, allowing *amicus* briefs if they constitute part of a government's formal submission in a case.[40] The change occurred as dicta in an Appellate Body ruling in the shrimp-turtle case, in

Eliminating Impure Thoughts

So intense was the WTO's opposition to submissions of *amicus* briefs to WTO tribunals from public interest groups that the WTO staff went to the expense of returning – by registered mail from Switzerland – one such submission from Washington D.C.-based Public Citizen and several other health and consumer groups. The groups sent a brief and scientific data to the WTO contradicting the U.S. position in the Beef Hormone case. The material was sent back with a letter scolding Public Citizen and noting that WTO dispute resolution rules ban outside submissions.

which the lower panel in the case had ruled that accepting information from non-governmental sources that had not been requested would be "incompatible with the provisions of the DSU as currently applied."[41] The rationale of the lower panel ruling was that access to the WTO dispute settlement system is reserved for WTO Members — i.e., countries represented by their governments.[42] The Appellate Body noted that the government system was preserved by giving the countries the ultimate discretion concerning submissions from outside parties.

The Clinton administration praised the change as major progress. However, the new policy's effect is very limited. Governments always were able to include the contents of outside briefs or other materials in official submissions if they chose to do so. What remains unchanged is that if a public interest or advocacy organization disagrees with the position of its government in a WTO case, it is unlikely that the information would be considered by a WTO panelist, because the government would not submit it.

Most international organizations and their arbitration systems are less exclusive than the WTO concerning what information they receive from outside organizations and those who are not parties to cases. The International Court of Justice (ICJ), for example, may request information from public international organizations and is required to review any information presented to it by such organizations.[43] The European Court of Justice allows the European Commission, member states, the European Council, and in limited cases citizens and organizations to intervene as *amici curiae*.[44]

However, a major difference between the WTO dispute panels and other international arbitration systems is that in these other systems, the need for expert advice and public interest safeguards is lessened by a more careful selection of the judges themselves. The ICJ, for example, requires its judges to possess competence in international law and be of high moral standard.[45] Thus, the ICJ is unlikely to deal with matters its judges are not equipped to rule on, whereas the very narrow qualifications of WTO panelists heightens the possibility that a dispute involves subjects about which the panelists have little knowledge. In addition, the European Court of Justice employs a unique system of advocates general to represent the public interest.[46] In contrast, the powerful WTO Dispute Settlement Understanding makes an unprecedented move away from public interest safeguards in international arbitration.

Winner Takes All: No Outside Appeal Allowed, Cross-Sectoral Sanctions Permitted

WTO panels establish specific deadlines by which a losing country must implement the panel's decision.[47] If this deadline is not met, the winning party may request negotiations to determine mutually acceptable compensation.[48] If compensation is not sought or not agreed to, the winning party may request WTO authorization to impose trade sanctions.[49] Once requested, sanctions are disallowed only if there is unanimous consensus against sanctions, requiring the winning country to also agree to drop its sanctions request.[50]

And unlike GATT, WTO sanctions may be applied "cross-sectorally," meaning that a country can retaliate against the key exports of the noncompliant party and not simply against similar products in the same sector.[51] This places an especially large burden on developing countries that have not diversified their exports and could thus be more easily pressured by threats of retaliation from a developed country against a single major export.

For a government that loses a case, there is no appeals process outside of the WTO's Appellate Body. The DSU merely provides that those persons serving on the Appellate Body are to be "persons of recognized authority with demonstrated expertise in law, international trade and the subject matter of the covered Agreements generally."[52] Again, there are no provisions for environmental, consumer law or labor experts to serve on the panel. Unlike members of lower panels who are called to serve in particular cases, the appeal panelists are part of a seven-person standing WTO body, meaning that they are on the permanent WTO payroll.[53] This is a startling conflict in its own right, given that every case requires a determination of whether domestic law or the Appellate Body tribunalists' employer's rules take precedence.

Two of the Appellate Body's most dramatic actions have involved the U.S. The first one came after a lower panel ruling in the shrimp-turtle case that was so fanatical in its anti-environmental tone that it created a backlash among even WTO boosters – including *The New York Times* editorial entitled, "The Sea Turtles Warning."[54] In a move seen by some as a political mission to save the WTO from itself,[55] the Appellate Body narrowed the lower panel ruling and reversed its most offensive extraneous pronouncements, although it maintained the outcome, which required the U.S. to change or eliminate certain provisions of its Endangered Species Act.

The second unusual Appellate Body ruling involved the only time in the history of WTO dispute resolution that the Appellate Body has reversed a full panel ruling. This case involved tariffs imposed by the EU on U.S.-manufactured computers. In February 1998, a WTO dispute panel ruled in favor of the U.S. in its complaint that the EU was violating the GATT by reclassifying computer equipment to impose higher tariffs.[56] U.S. Trade Representative Charlene Barshefsky gloated that the victory involved the largest case, in dollar terms, that the U.S. had brought before the WTO.[57] Said Barshefsky, "These products are made in the U.S.A with leading-edge American technology. The EU tariffs affect billions of dollars in U.S. exports."[58]

But in June 1998, the WTO Appellate Body reversed the earlier decision.[59] Incredibly, the USTR then reversed its earlier proclamations that the ruling would effect "billions of dollars in U.S. exports," now claiming that "under the Information Technology Agreement (ITA), tariffs … will go to zero on January 1, 2000, no matter where LAN [computer] equipment is classified. Consequently, this decision will have a limited economic impact."[60]

In stark contrast, computer industry officials viewed the Appellate Body ruling as a serious setback that would allow European competitors to establish market share in an industry where U.S. manufacturers have captured 50% of the market. "We thought the original decision was a significant victory for U.S. exporters and established an important precedent that switching classifications was a violation of world trade rules," one computer industry official said. "We are very upset that the decision has been overruled."[61]

WTO's Frivolous "Non-Violation" Clause

The WTO dispute resolution rules also include very broad and vague provisions that can be used by any WTO Member to challenge another Member country's laws. Called "Nullification and Impairment," these provisions allow challenges on the grounds that "any benefit accruing to it [a WTO Member country] directly or indirectly" under WTO rules is "being nullified or impaired or the attainment of any objective of that Agreement is being impeded … whether or not it conflicts with the provisions of that Agreement."[62]

WTO Nullification and Impairment challenges do not require an actual breach of a legal obligation contained in any of the WTO's underlying agreements. All that must be alleged is that the actions of one country have impaired the benefits expected to be attained by another country from the Uruguay Agreements overall.

Challenges made under these premises are called "nonviolation" challenges. They can be particularly effective in threatening countries that seek to enact general laws to protect the environment and workers. For instance, Canada included such a claim in its pending challenge against France's ban on asbestos.[63]

Canada is arguing that even if the WTO panel finds no actual violation of the WTO Technical Barriers to Trade (TBT) Agreement, France's asbestos ban constitutes a violation under the Nullification and Impairment provisions. Canada alleges that the French ban impaired benefits that otherwise would accrue to Canada as a result of tariff concessions granted by the EU during the Uruguay Round. Canada's point is that France's asbestos ban enhances the relative position of domestic substitute products that compete with chrysotile asbestos.[64]

On the other hand, as a WTO ruling in a U.S. challenge against Japanese marketing practices made clear, the Nullification and Impairment provisions are not useful when attempting to force changes in economic policies or practices not covered by the Uruguay Round rules. The U.S. claimed that the Japanese government had a duty to act against informal, nongovernmental commercial practices – such as informal relationships based on exclusive distribution commitments or shopkeepers' anti-import sentiments – to *ensure* that U.S. producers achieved actual gains from market access improvement agreed in the Uruguay Round. The U.S. claimed that failure by the Japanese government to take action impaired expected U.S. gains. The U.S. claim of a nonviolation impairment in the case, dubbed the Kodak-Fuji Case, was rejected,[65] deflating the vaunted promises of then-U.S. Trade Representative Mickey Kantor and other Clinton administration officials that these provisions could be used to open new markets – such as in Japan, where market barriers involve activity not covered by GATT-WTO rules.

You Can't Have It Both Ways:
Unilateral Trade Sanctions Are WTO-Illegal

Section 301 of the U.S. Trade Act of 1974, as amended in 1979, permits the U.S. trade representative to investigate and sanction countries whose trade practices are deemed "unfair" to U.S. interests.[66] The language of Section 301 calls for the U.S. government to take unilateral action in trade disputes by allowing the president to "suspend, withdraw, or prevent" the application of benefits of trade agreement concessions and to "impose duties or other import restrictions" if the president determines it to be appropriate to do so. Section 301 also requires the trade representative to identify, investigate and prioritize foreign countries deemed to be engaged in unfair trading practices. Those countries are then subject to Section 301 sanctions. "Under Section 301, foreign negotiators were confronted with the stark prospect of either opening their markets to U.S. exports or facing U.S. trade sanctions. Time and again, the U.S. threat succeeded," noted one trade commentator.[67]

During the Uruguay Round debate in Congress, members of Congress and U.S. industry expressed concern that WTO rules would forbid the application of Section 301. Even as Japan and other countries promoted the WTO to their public and parliaments on the basis that the WTO would end the use of Section 301, Kantor and a score of other administration representatives promised repeatedly that nothing in the WTO would limit U.S. use of the law.[68]

Yet, the whole logic of the WTO dispute mechanism is to compel countries – particularly those that have such a large internal market that their threats of unilateral re-

Section 301, Meet Your Master: The Kodak Case

In 1995, Eastman Kodak Co. filed a request with the U.S. trade representative's office, requesting Section 301 action on a claim that the Japanese government and Fuji Photo Film Co. had conspired to keep Kodak film out of Japanese retail stores.[69] Kodak claimed that Fuji maintained its 70% share of the Japanese film market (compared to Kodak's 10% share) through an unfair system of cooperation with film wholesalers, camera shops and government bureaucrats. After investigating Kodak's claim, the USTR threatened Section 301 sanctions against Japan.[70] The Japanese government responded that it would no longer be bullied by the threat of unilateral U.S. sanctions and refused to even talk to U.S. negotiators.[71] Japan announced it would challenge Section 301 at the WTO. The USTR, realizing it would lose such a WTO case, dropped its Section 301 threats and brought a WTO case against Japan based on Kodak's claim.[72] Japanese officials were overjoyed. One Japanese official called the USTR's decision "a good thing" and was described as "visibly struggling to contain his delight."[73] Fuji officials called the move "a positive development." Forcing the U.S. to drop a Section 301 threat was generally considered a significant procedural victory for Japan.[74] Ultimately, the WTO panel ruled in favor of Japan on each and every point in the U.S.'s complaint.[75] This ruling is one of only two completed WTO cases in which the party initiating the challenge did not win.

taliation are intimidating – to forego unilateral trade sanctions in favor of the WTO dispute resolution. A series of events in 1998 relating to the U.S.-based Eastman Kodak Company illustrated this point. Kodak was concerned that the Japanese had conspired to keep Kodak film out of Japanese stores to boost sales of Japanese-made Fuji film. The U.S. government threatened to take unilateral Section 301 action but backed off and tried to pursue the case at the WTO after Japan threatened to challenge U.S. Section 301 use at the WTO, a case the U.S. knew Japan would win.[76] *The Washington Times* reported, "The administration is considering its options [including a Section 301 investigation.] But unilateral sanctions in almost all cases would violate WTO rules."[77]

The U.S. then brought the matter before the WTO, which ruled that the activities that were resulting in Kodak film receiving less favorable placement in Japanese stores were not covered by WTO disciplines.[78] The WTO also ruled that the nonviolation impairment claim the U.S. made was unfounded.[79] Thus, there simply was no remedy available – either unilaterally or via the WTO.

Section 301 actions, insofar as they are unilateral, violate U.S. commitments under the GATT/WTO on two levels. First, the U.S. cannot impose sanctions by removing trade benefits in any sector covered by WTO tariff schedules. Second, a WTO dispute panel must rule that a country has violated GATT/WTO obligations; the U.S. alone cannot make this determination. This means that if the U.S. were to raise tariffs on a WTO Member nation even in retaliation for activity *not* covered in GATT/WTO rules, the other country could challenge the action in the WTO. According to trade experts, such a challenge most likely would succeed because at issue would be the elimination of tariff benefits granted under the WTO.[80]

Indeed, despite assurances of no conflicts, the U.S. in 1994 amended Section 301 to try to move it into compliance with the WTO Dispute Settlement Understanding. "Super 301 has been weakened, downgraded and largely declawed," noted a trade expert involved with writing the law.[81] Even so, insofar as Section 301[b] seeks to preserve the authority of the U.S. to engage in unilateral retaliation, it is still WTO-illegal.[82]

Now the U.S. attempt to avoid a formal WTO ruling against Section 301 is being foiled. Such a ruling is anticipated in a new case filed by the EU. The EU argues that the U.S., in retaining the *possibility* of imposing unilateral trade sanctions, has violated what it dubbed the "Marrakesh deal."[83] The EU's understanding of this "deal" was that the U.S obtained the practical certainty of the adoption of WTO rulings and thus automatic WTO sanctions against countries violating WTO rules in exchange for the complete abandonment by the U.S. of unilateral action.[84] This interpretation was not the "deal" the Clinton administration sold to Congress. "The Uruguay Round will not impair the effective enforcement of U.S. trade laws, especially Section 301,"[85] pledged Kantor. Nevertheless, when the WTO rules on the EU challenge, the U.S. might find that it cannot have it both ways: In signing the Uruguay Round Agreements, including the enforceable dispute resolution, it gained international backing for trade sanctions but lost the ability to choose when to impose them.

WTO Rules Trump State and Local Laws

The first indication that the GATT regime could broadly preempt state and local laws and preferences came in 1992, when a GATT panel upheld complaints by Canada and declared a preferential federal excise tax plan for small U.S. brewers and numerous tax rules and distribution practices in 41 states and Puerto Rico to be inconsistent with GATT rules.[86]

It was clear that GATT rules applied to some degree to subfederal (state and local) policy. GATT Article XXIV-12 says, "Each contracting party shall take such reasonable measures as may be available to it to ensure observance of the provisions of this Agreement by the regional and local governments and authorities within its territories." What was not clear prior to this ruling was the extent of this obligation.

In defending the various state laws regulating alcoholic beverages, the U.S. had argued that GATT Article XXIV-12 required an effort by federal governments to get subfederal entities to meet GATT rules. In the case, which was dubbed "Beer II," the U.S. argued that it had taken all reasonable measures and that this state activity was outside of its direct control.

A GATT dispute panel made a controversial interpretation of Article XXIV-12, holding that a country has not satisfied the provision unless it has exercised all powers against its subfederal entities that are constitutionally available to it.[87] Thus, the U.S. federal government was held responsible as the GATT contracting party for its states' laws unless it could show that it had tried every possible way to change the states, such as pre-empting legislation, suing subfederal entities and/or pressuring them for changes by cutting off benefits such as highway funds.

Moreover, the GATT panel in Beer II ruled on the question of the relative legal effect of GATT versus U.S. state law: "GATT law is part of federal law in the United States and as such is superior to GATT-inconsistent state law."[88] This ruling was all the more difficult to fathom because the state tax breaks that the GATT had ruled against would have passed very onerous constitutional muster had they been challenged under the Commerce Clause of the U.S. Constitution as burdening interstate commerce.

The Uruguay Round Agreements then added even more explicit language binding states and cities to WTO rules. For instance, in making clear that all of the terms of the Agreement on Technical Barriers to Trade apply to states and localities, the agreement explicitly requires that "Members are fully responsible under this Agreement for the observance of all provisions ... Members shall formulate and implement *positive measures and mechanisms* in support of the observance of the provisions ... by other than central government bodies."[89] The requirement for countries to take "positive measures" is understood to have raised the bar, requiring federal governments actively to impose WTO rules on state legislatures and local authorities, for instance through broad pre-emptive legislation in areas covered by the WTO.

Finally, as the EU and Japan's challenge against Massachusetts' preferential procurement law *(See* Chapter 7*)* shows, the WTO does not differentiate between challenges of either federal or subfederal law. In either instance, only the WTO Member — the federal government — is empowered to defend the law before the WTO's closed tribunals, raising the specter of a federal government being the sole defender of a state policy that it does not favor.

———————— CHAPTER **8** ENDNOTES ————————

[1] This position is reflected in the USTR Statement on the WTO Beef Hormone dispute. USTR, "USTR Barshefsky Committed to Resolving Beef Hormone Dispute," Press Release, Apr. 19, 1999.

[2] Agreement Establishing the WTO, Preamble, at Para. 1.

[3] *See* Overview of the State-of-Play of WTO Disputes, found at www.wto.org/dispute/bulletin.htm, on file with Public Citizen.

[4] *See id.*

[5] U.S. Trade Representative Michael Kantor, Testimony to the Senate Commerce Committee, Jun. 16, 1994, at 9, Sec. D.

[6] John Maggs, "Congress Frowns on Clinton Plan to Expand NAFTA," *Journal of Commerce*, Apr. 5, 1995 (emphasis added).

[7] WTO, Understanding on Rules and Procedures Governing the Settlement of Disputes (DSU) at Article 14 and Appendix 3, Paras. 2 and 3.

[8] *Id.* at Appendix 3, Para. 2.

[9] *Id.* at Article 14.

[10] *Id.* at Appendix 3, Para. 3.

[11] For example, the International Court of Justice, or the European Court of Justice. *See* Dinah Shelton, "Non-Governmental Organizations and Judicial Proceedings," 88 *American Journal of International Law* 611 (1993).

[12] U.S. Trade Representative Michael Kantor, Testimony to the Senate Commerce Committee, Jun. 16, 1994.

[13] WTO, DSU at Article 8.5.

[14] *Id.* at Article 3.6.

[15] *Id.* at Article 8.1.

[16] *See* Palmeter and Mavroidis, "The WTO Legal System: Sources of Law," 92 *American Journal of International Law* 398 (1998).

[17] *Id.* at 411.

[18] Kym Anderson, "The Entwining of Trade Policy with Environmental and Labour Standards," in W. Martin and L.A. Winters (eds.), *Implications of the Uruguay Round for Developing Countries*, World Bank (1995).

[19] Seminar Paper 97-04, "Environmental and Labor Standards: What role for the World Trade Organization?," University of Adelaide Centre for International Economic Studies, Mar. 1997, at 13.

[20] *Id.*

[21] *See* Chapter 5 for a discussion of the importance of the banana trade to the Caribbean Island nations.

[22] *See* Mike Gallagher and Cameron McWhirter's expose on Chiquita in the *Cincinnati Enquirer*, May 3, 1998.

[23] WTO, DSU at Article 13.

[24] WTO Document WT/DSB/RC/1 (96-5267), Dec. 11, 1996.

[25] *Id.,* Preamble at Para. 3.

[26] *Id.* at Article VI.2.

[27] *Id.* at Article VI.3.

[28] WTO, United States - The Cuban Liberty and Democratic Solidarity Act (WT/DS38), Complaint by the European Communities, May 3, 1996.

[29] WTO, DSU at Article 14.3.

[30] P.L. 104-114, also known as the "Helms-Burton Act." Title III of Helms-Burton denies entry into the U.S. of corporate executives who have acquired property from the Cuban government that had been "expropriated" from U.S. citizens during the Cuban revolution. Title IV enables U.S. citizens whose property was expropriated to sue foreign investors who later acquire it from the Cuban government.

[31] International Chamber of Commerce, *ICC Statement on the Helms-Burton Act,* Jun. 19, 1996, on file with Public Citizen.

[32] Agence France Presse, "GATT's Dunkel Urges No Hurry in China's Accession to WTO," Apr. 8, 1997.

[33] *See,* Annual report of Nestle, S.A., Nestle Management Report 1998, Directors and Officers (1999) found at www.nestle.com/mr1998/ar1998/01/index.htm on Sep. 7, 1999, on file with Public Citizen. Members of the board serve five-year terms. Dunkel was up for re-election on Jun. 3, 1999. *See Id.*

[34] *See,* Annual report of Nestle, S.A., Nestle Management Report 1998, consolidated accounts of the Nestle Group (1999) found at www.nestle.com/mr1998/consoloaccts/13/index.htm on Sep. 7, 1999, on file with Public Citizen; *see also* Nestle Worldwide North and South America, found at www.nestle.com/html/w3.html, on file with Public Citizen.

[35] Personal communication between Chris McGinn, Public Citizen and USTR staff, May 18, 1998.

[36] For instance, the Clinton Administration has never allowed its enforcement provisions to enter into force. To convince the EU to drop its WTO challenge, which it did in 1997, it regularly grants waivers from Title III to EU-based companies, and has never let Title IV enter into force.

[37] WTO, DSU at Article 13.

[38] *Id.* at Appendix 3, Para. 3.

[39] *Id.* at Article 8.3.

[40] WTO, United States - Import Prohibition of Certain Shrimp and Shrimp Products (WT/DS58/AB/R), Report of the Appellate Body, Oct. 12, 1998, at Para. 100.

[41] WTO, United States - Import Prohibition of Certain Shrimp and Shrimp Products (WT/DS58/R), Report of the Panel, May 15, 1998, at Para. 7.8.

[42] WTO, United States - Import Prohibition of Certain Shrimp and Shrimp Products, (WT/DS58/AB/R), Report of the Appellate Body, Oct. 12, 1998, at Para. 101.

[43] International Court of Justice Statute at Article 34(2).

[44] Dinah Shelton, "Non-Governmental Organizations and Judicial Proceedings," 88 *American Journal of International Law* 611 (1993) at 629.

[45] International Court of Justice Statute at Article 2.

[46] *See* Dinah Shelton, "Non-Governmental Organizations and Judicial Proceedings," 88 *American Journal of International Law* 611 (1993).

[47] WTO, DSU at Article 21.

[48] *Id.* at Article 22.2.

[49] *Id.*

[50] *Id.*

[51] *Id.* at Article 22.3.

[52] *Id.* at Article 17.3.

[53] *Id.* at Article 17.1.

[54] "The Sea Turtle's Warning," *The New York Times* (editorial), Apr. 10, 1998.

[55] *Id.*

[56] WTO, European Communities - Customs Classification of Certain Computer Equipment (WT/DS62, 67, 68), Report of the Panel, Feb. 5, 1998. European countries had reclassified the computers as telecommunications equipment, which carried tariffs that were nearly double what they would have been under the old classifications. *See* Martin Crutsinger, "U.S. Loses WTO Computer Trade Case," *Associated Press,* Jun. 5, 1998.

[57] USTR, "USTR Barshefsky Announces U.S. Victory In WTO Dispute On U.S. High-Technology Exports," Press Release, Feb. 5, 1998.

[58] *Id.*

[59] WTO, European Communities - Customs Classification of Certain Computer Equipment (WT/DS62, 67, 68), Report of the Appellate Body, Jun. 5, 1998.

[60] USTR, "USTR Responds To WTO Report On U.S. High-Technology Exports," Press Release, Jun. 5, 1998.

[61] Martin Crutsinger, "U.S. Loses WTO Computer Trade Case," *Associated Press,* Jun. 5, 1998.

[62] WTO, DSU at Article 26.2.

[63] WTO, European Communities - Measures Affecting the Prohibition of Asbestos and Asbestos Products, (WT/DS135), panel established Nov. 25, 1998. The Third Party Written Submission of the United States, submitted May 28, 1999, in the France - Canada Asbestos Case, is available at the EPA Asbestos Ombudsman and EPA Public Information Center.

[64] *See id.*

[65] WTO, Japan - Measures Affecting Consumer Photographic Film And Paper (WT/DS44/R), Report of the Panel, Mar. 31, 1998, at 403, Para. 10.106.

[66] *See* 16 U.S.C. Section 301.

[67] *See* Greg Mastel, "Section 301: Alive and Well," *Journal of Commerce,* Aug. 16, 1996.

[68] U.S. Trade Representative Michael Kantor, Testimony to the Senate Commerce Committee, Jun. 16, 1994.

[69] Richard Lawrence, "Kantor Referees the Kodak-Fuji War of Worlds," *Journal of Commerce,* Jun. 1, 1995.

[70] *See* Lorraine Woellert, "Kodak, U.S. Lose Trade Dispute," *The Washington Times,* Dec. 6, 1997.

[71] Martin Crutsinger, "U.S. Sends Film Dispute to Global Trade Panel," *The Washington Times*, Jun. 14, 1996.

[72] *See* WTO, Japan - Measures Affecting Consumer Photographic Film and Paper (WT/DS44/R), Report of the Panel, Mar. 31, 1998.

[73] Paul Blustein, "U.S. Shelving Threat of Sanctions on Japan," *Washington Post*, Jun. 12, 1996.

[74] Wendy Bounds & Helene Cooper, "U.S. to File WTO Complaint for Kodak, Handing Fuji a Procedural Victory," *The Wall Street Journal*, Jun. 12, 1996.

[75] WTO, Japan - Measures Affecting Consumer Photographic Film and Paper (WT/DS44/R), Report of the Panel, Mar. 31, 1998, at Paras. 10.106, 10.117, 10.132, 10.145, 10.155, 10.175, 10.189, and 10.203.

[76] *See* Wendy Bounds & Helene Cooper, "U.S. to File WTO Complaint for Kodak, Handing Fuji a Procedural Victory," *Wall Street Journal*, Jun. 12, 1996.

[77] Lorraine Woellert, "Kodak, U.S. Lose Trade Dispute," *The Washington Times*, Dec. 6, 1997.

[78] WTO, Japan - Measures Affecting Consumer Photographic Film and Paper (WT/DS44/R), Report of the Panel, Mar. 31, 1998, at Para. 10.155.

[79] *Id.* at Para. 10.106.

[80] *See* Greg Mastel, "Section 301: Alive and Well," *Journal of Commerce*, Aug. 16, 1996.

[81] *Id.*

[82] *See* Congressional Research Service, *Relationship of Uruguay Round Dispute Settlement Understanding to Section 301 of the Trade Act of 1974*, Mar. 22, 1994, on file with Public Citizen.

[83] "Multilateralism: The EU's Defense Against Sections 301-310 of the U.S. Trade Act," *BRIDGES Monthly*, Jun. 1999, at 8.

[84] *Id.*

[85] U.S. Trade Representative Michael Kantor, Testimony to the Senate Commerce Committee, Jun. 16, 1994.

[86] GATT, United States - Measures Affecting Alcohol and Malt Beverages (DS23/R-39s/206), Report of the Panel, Feb. 7, 1992 (known as "Beer II").

[87] *Id.* at Para 5.80.

[88] *Id.* at Para. 6.1.

[89] WTO, TBT Agreement at Article 3.5 (emphasis added).

9 Recommendations & Conclusions

In 1994, the Clinton administration painted a glowing picture of how the GATT Uruguay Round and the establishment of the WTO would affect the United States and the rest of the world on virtually all fronts: It would not erode U.S. sovereignty or undermine environmental, health or food safety protections; and it would lead to unprecedented economic growth, increased U.S. family income and the creation of thriving consumer societies that would purchase U.S. goods. In countries around the world, parliaments and the public were hearing the same promises from their trade negotiators and prime ministers.

Such promises were met with widespread skepticism. Around the globe, individual citizens and groups representing environmental, anti-hunger, consumer, small business, health, religious, worker, human rights, development, small farm and other interests were awakening to the potential threats the Uruguay Round's expansive rules could pose to hard-won public interest advances and the democratic, accountable governance that had made such progress possible. With varying levels of sophistication and organization, these groups presented a critical view of the Uruguay Round and WTO, predicting not only that the WTO's promised benefits would not come to fruition but that the WTO would do harm.

These political struggles had several common features. Most political decision-makers had no understanding of the Uruguay Round's broad provisions, much less their implications. A powerful elite consensus in favor of anything characterized as "free trade" ensured that a long line of prominent figures worldwide would announce support for the Uruguay Round despite lack of awareness of its contents. When consumer advocate Ralph Nader offered a reward to any U.S. senator who would sign an

> **The Uruguay Round and WTO have failed the most conservative of tests: Do no further harm. Instead, in key areas, conditions have deteriorated under WTO rules. That's why NGOs worldwide and some governments are calling for no further trade or investment liberalization negotiations under the auspices of the WTO until its current performance has been thoroughly reviewed and problematic aspects have been repaired or replaced.**

affidavit asserting that he or she had read the text and publicly answer ten simple questions about it, not one senator (including the clutch of prominent WTO boosters) accepted for four months. When a senator finally came forward to meet the challenge — self-proclaimed free-trade advocate and NAFTA supporter Hank Brown, a Republican from Colorado — he came out in opposition after he read the Uruguay Round Agreement and understood its implications.

Now, nearly five years later, the time for promises and speculation has passed. There is ample evidence that the rosy predictions have failed to materialize. Indeed, in many instances the opposite has occurred. The Uruguay Round and WTO have failed the most conservative of tests: do no further harm. Instead, in key areas, conditions have deteriorated under WTO rules.

WTO Fails the "First-Do-No-Harm" Test

What is truly alarming is that for many developing countries, fallout from the harshest of the WTO rules is still yet to come, because the rules have multi-year phase-ins and are not yet fully implemented. In an acknowledgment of the damage already done by WTO rules, many developing countries' governments and non-governmental organizations oppose the European call for a new and comprehensive round of WTO talks and instead have called for a "turnaround" to undo the damage wreaked by the current WTO regime.

Indeed, there are indications of serious problems in virtually every key area where the U.S. and other governments promised their citizens WTO benefits. The world has been buffeted by unprecedented global financial instability. Income inequality is increasing rapidly between and within countries. Despite efficiency and productivity gains, wages in numerous countries have failed to rise, while commodity prices are at an all-time low, causing a decrease in the standard of living for a majority of people in the world.

As critics feared, the WTO's built-in bias against public participation has made the institution a perfect venue for industry and governments to pursue agendas that would fail in open democratic forums. One WTO bureaucrat admitted this to the *Financial Times,* stating the WTO "is the place where governments collude in private against their domestic pressure groups."[1] Given this mind-set, it is not surprising – although it is completely unacceptable – that the WTO has judged a growing list of public health, environmental, food safety and development policies to be WTO-illegal trade barriers that must be eliminated or changed.

As well as being used to attack public interest policies, the WTO has consistently insulated big business and industry from social responsibility. For instance, it has enabled Chiquita Banana to "rent" the U.S. government, and thus use the WTO to undermine crucial economic development strategies — and the entire economies — of tiny, banana-producing nations in the Caribbean. This has furthered the company's goal of increasing its already dominant share of the European banana market. Similarly, the WTO has provided the Venezuelan gasoline industry a means outside U.S. policy and the domestic legal system to evade high-standard clean air regulations in the U.S. And it has assisted the U.S. Cattlemen's Association in defeating a popular European public health law banning artificial hormone-treated

---

WTO SEATTLE MINISTERIAL GOALS

PUBLIC INTEREST GOALS	VS.	CORPORATE INTEREST GOALS
No new Round, no expansion of WTO jurisdiction, and no MAI in the WTO		New Millenium Round to expand WTO
Review existing performance before considering new negotiations		Do more of same now regardless
Scale back existing WTO agreements that invade domestic policy prerogatives		Expand WTO into new areas, such as how local tax revenue can be used, education and health care
Eliminate certain topics from WTO coverage altogether, i.e., water, life forms		Commodify the common resources (water, air, oceans) and also create new forms of property (such as patenting life forms) so they can be traded
Ensure people can control the decisions that will affect their families and communities		Move decision-making to international bodies in order to set uniform global standards and reduce fragmentation of single global market

---

beef – a measure that was overwhelmingly supported by European and U.S. consumer and health groups.

Despite this compelling evidence, the EU in 1999 was leading a charge to launch an ambitious new round of negotiations to extend the WTO's constraints on government action to new issues. One EU proposal was to revive the failed Multilateral Agreement on Investment (MAI) by putting it into the WTO.[2] Japan has supported the EU initiative on launching a new round, as has the Canadian government.

The Clinton administration has never been eager for a long, drawn-out round of negotiations. First, it has been stripped both of Fast Track trade authority and congressional and public support for its extreme globalization agenda. Second, it did not want Vice President Al Gore's record of sacrificing environmental goals on the altar of globalization to be highlighted before the 2000 presidential election. The U.S. has promoted a so-called "modest" agenda, which calls for extreme agriculture and forestry liberalization, further expansion of WTO coverage and deregulation in the services sector (including health and education), and new protections for bio-technology products. These are far from the environmental-friendly policies advocated in Gore's book, *Earth in the Balance.*

Yet, any prudent proposal concerning any expansion of WTO's jurisdiction and power must be based on an honest assessment of its performance to date. This book does not purport to be a comprehensive compilation of the WTO's problems, and yet it has clearly shown that the five-year record of the WTO does not support the launch of a new comprehensive round of WTO expansion talks. Rather our review documents the urgent need for a 180-degree turnaround of badly flawed, major elements of the current GATT/WTO regime.

While groups such as Public Citizen support enforceable international commercial rules to govern the flow of goods and services, they have no tolerance for such rules being used to further undermine democratic, accountable governance or public interest safeguards. There is a growing consensus among nongovernmental organizations (NGOs) worldwide that the WTO must be pruned back to ensure:

- access to essential goods, such as food and medicines;

- access to essential services, such as safe water, sanitation and other utilities, education, transportation and health care;

- respect for basic labor and other human rights;

- product, food and workplace safety;

- a healthy environment and conservation of natural resources;

- the availability of information, such as the accurate labeling of the contents and characteristics of goods;

- choice among competitively priced goods and services;

- representation of citizen interests in decision-making; and

- an avenue of redress, including the ability to hold accountable corporations and governments that undermine core citizens' rights.

A reasonable interim step, and one that could be agreed upon at the November 1999 Seattle WTO Ministerial, is the nearly unanimous call by nongovernmental organizations worldwide for the thourough review of the WTO's performance to date rather than the launch of *further* trade or investment liberalization negotiations.

WTO rules should not be extended to cover new issues such as investment (MAI), and corporate control in existing agreements (such as the U.S. proposal to add all life forms to the definition of "property" under the existing WTO TRIPs Agreement) should not be widened. Rather, at the Seattle Ministerial, governments must agree to a comprehensive review of the outcomes and impacts of the Uruguay Round to date with an eye toward identifying which aspects should be scaled back, replaced or eliminated.

On the basis of the issues addressed in this report, the Seattle Ministerial Declaration should include the following.

Seattle Ministerial Declaration

Recommendation 1:
A Moratorium on Certain Trade Challenges

Given the troubling pattern of WTO rulings against domestic food safety, environmental and health measures, the WTO Member governments must agree in the Seattle Ministerial Declaration to impose a moratorium on WTO challenges and threats to facially nondiscriminatory environmental, health and safety measures. Challenges to domestic laws based on the level of protection a country chooses (such as France's asbestos ban) or based on countries acting under the Precautionary Principle (such as the EU ban on beef containing artificial hormone residues) must stop. A moratorium also would forestall challenges to policies treating domestic and foreign producers equally that are based on non-product related production and processing methods (such as bans on goods made with child labor) or on products harvested in environmentally destructive ways (such as the use of tuna nets that ensnare dolphins). Challenges to domestic laws that implement international commitments, such as Japan's Kyoto Protocol fuel efficiency laws and U.S. laws protecting sea turtles, also must be halted. A moratorium would restrict WTO challenges aimed at second-guessing the value choices countries make, the level of public health or environmental protection they choose, or the rules they enforce equally on domestic and foreign companies.

Recommendation 2:
An Objective Review of the Uruguay Round

The Seattle Ministerial Declaration must make a commitment to launch an objective review of the operations of the Uruguay Round Agreements, with a view toward identifying which aspects of the current agreements need to be amended or eliminated to obtain the broad benefits promised in the Uruguay Round's preamble.

Reviews of the Agreement on Sanitary and Phytosanitary Measures (SPS), Agreement on Technical Barriers to Trade (TBT), Agreement on Trade Related Aspects of Intellectual Property (TRIPs), Agreement on Agriculture, Dispute Settlement Understanding (DSU), General Agreement on Trade in Services (GATS), and Agreement on Trade Related Investment Measures (TRIMs) should be done with full consultation with public interest groups.

This objective review must include an open process with access to documents and a meaningful opportunity for NGO and citizen input at the national and international levels into determining the scale and methodology of the review. Citizens also must have an ongoing role in conducting the review.

Such a review could provide an opportunity for citizens to aid in the development of a more accountable, equitable and sustainable system of international trade and investment relations. Such changes are necessary to ensure public support for and confidence in international commercial rules.

Recommendation 3:
Ensure Access to Essential Goods and Services

Food: The basic human right to food security must be kept sovereign. An assessment of the Uruguay Round Agriculture Agreement must focus on food security, especially concerning least developed countries and poor consumers in net food-importing countries. In particular, the impact of large agrochemical and grain-trading multinational corporations must be examined with an eye toward what international antitrust measures are needed to break up the intense market concentration that now exists. Also, aspects of the TRIPs Agreement must be reviewed with a view toward changing provisions that undermine food security. This includes those provisions that permit multinational corporations to patent seeds originally developed by farmers and to require farmers to pay for the right to replant those seeds. An objective review of the current WTO rules would lead to future negotiations of a food security clause and allow governments to take measures that they deem appropriate to protect food from the effects of conflicting WTO obligations.

Medicines: The TRIPs Agreement must be reviewed with the goal of elevating public health above commercial interests and safeguarding consumer access to essential drugs. Obviously, the proposals by some developed countries to use the Seattle Ministerial Declaration to push for the expansion of TRIPs Agreement rules and to eliminate the multi-year phase-in periods applying to developing countries are unacceptable. The Seattle Ministerial Declaration also should reiterate that parallel importing and compulsory licensing are permitted under the TRIPs Agreement. This would signal the end of the Clinton administration's offensive campaign against South Africa and other countries that are attempting to make medicines, especially AIDS treatments, more affordable.

Services: A review of the General Agreement on Trade in Services (GATS) must consider how the agreement affects the right to universal access to basic services, such as health care, water, education and sanitation. A review of the agreement also should address the absence of tools to combat monopolistic international mergers and acquisitions. Finally, this review must consider a modification of GATS Article XIV (General Exceptions) to take account of measures to protect the environment, and recommendations must be developed on the relationship between services trade and the environment, and on the issue of sustainable consumption.

Recommendation 4:
Safeguard Product, Food and Workplace Safety and a Healthy Environment

Precautionary Principle: The SBS and TBT Agreements undercut the use of the Precautionary Principle in public health, safety and environmental policymaking. The Seattle Ministerial Declaration must explicitly state, in a manner that binds future WTO dispute panels, that no existing WTO rules shall be interpreted to limit the capacity of governments to establish and maintain nondiscriminatory health, environmental or food safety measures that were enacted based on the Precautionary Principle. The Seattle Ministerial Declaration must commit countries to identify and eliminate those Uruguay Round provisions that can be interpreted to undermine the right of governments to take measures under the Precautionary Principle.

Food Safety and Food Labeling: The Seattle Ministerial Declaration must commit WTO Members to an objective, open review of the Agriculture Agreement focusing on how to modify SPS Agreement rules to enable governments to establish and maintain legitimate nondiscriminatory food safety measures. Such a review must reverse rules relating to burden of proof that now require products to be proven unsafe before they can be regulated or banned. Such a review also must establish a definition of "equivalence" in the SPS Agreement that ensures that foreign regulations provide the same level of health and safety protection as domestic laws and that foreign procedural and review mechanisms are at least as strong as domestic law before they are declared equivalent. The Seattle Ministerial Declaration must clarify that measures to support informed choice by consumers, such as nutritional and informational labeling provisions that treat domestic and imported goods equally, are not inconsistent with SPS or TBT rules. The Seattle Ministerial Declaration must clarify that there is no inherent time limit on WTO Members' use of the precautionary approach to food safety under Article 5.

Product Safety and Environmental Standards: The TBT Agreement contains provisions that provide for challenges of nondiscriminatory domestic health, safety and environmental regulations simply because they are stronger than international standards. A review of this agreement must allow countries to establish their own product and worker safety, health and environmental standards as long as they are not applied in a discriminatory fashion (e.g., France should be permitted to protect its workers from asbestos).

Recommendation 5:
Control Merger Mania and Market Concentration

Anti-Competitive Practices: Some developed countries have called for the launch at the Seattle Ministerial of negotiations on WTO competition rules. Different countries calling for negotiations on "competition" may mean very different things even though they are using the same term. However, no country is calling for the sort of rules needed to deal with anti-competitive business practices and combat the growing threat of monopolistic international mergers and acquisitions. The Seattle Ministerial Declaration should instruct the existing WTO Working Group on Competition Policy to establish mechanisms to:

- control anti-competitive and restrictive business practices of transnational corporations (such as price-fixing, transfer pricing and other intra-firm practices); and

- review patterns of market concentration and the increasing number of cross-border mergers, acquisitions and alliances.

Recommendation 6:
Provide Representation and Redress

Transparency and Accountability: The WTO's accountability to the public must be increased in the wake of the Seattle Ministerial. The Seattle Ministerial Declaration should:

- adopt a presumption of openness in the interpretation of the agreement that established the WTO and the Dispute Settlement Understanding (DSU), so that documents are automatically de-restricted unless they meet clear confidentiality criteria. All documents of the dispute resolution system (including all party briefs, experts' memos, WTO legal staff memos and rulings) should be de-restricted. Dispute resolution proceedings must be opened to the public;

- establish new Dispute Settlement Understanding procedures for dispute settlement panels, including: a rewrite of the panelist qualification requirements to allow for a broader array of expertise; conflict of interest rules for the non-appellate panelists; maintenance of a public file of potential panel members; and a guarantee that after the moratorium on environmental and health challenges is lifted, cases raising health, environmental or consumer protection issues shall include panelists with relevant expertise; and

- tackle the financial, human resource and infrastructure constraints of developing country delegations in a manner chosen by the developing countries to ensure that all countries can participate equally and effectively in negotiations.

Recommendation 7:
Ensure Investment Rules Promote Financial Stability, No Clandestine MAIs

The General Agreement on Trade in Services (GATS), Agreement on Trade Related Investment Measures (TRIMs) and the 1997 Financial Services Agreement must be reviewed to consider mechanisms not included in or, in some instances, measures now forbidden by, WTO rules to ensure market stability. The review should include measures to counter currency speculation and volatile short-term investment (such as the Chilean-style capital controls now being praised by a growing number of international economists). Obviously, any MAI-style agreement will face vigorous opposition regardless of the venue in which it is pursued. The Seattle Ministerial Declaration must instruct the existing WTO Working Group on Trade and Investment to shift its focus to the examination of specific obligations that can be included in future investment rules, such as the promotion by foreign investors of the economic and social development of the host country and the protection of consumers and the environment.

Conclusion

In its short five years of existence, the WTO has had wide-ranging impacts on jobs, wages and livelihoods and on international and domestic environmental, health and food safety laws as well as on economic development, human rights and global trade and investment. These impacts have not been systematically studied nor have they been well covered in the press. As a consequence, most people around the globe lack an awareness that their lives, livelihoods, food and environment — indeed, their very futures — are being shaped by a powerful new institution.

The WTO is not just about trade and distant economic trends. Rather, it serves as the engine for a comprehensive redesign of international, national and local law, politics, cultures and values. Given how directly and personally this redesign is affecting us all, we hope this book contributes to public awareness about the WTO specifically and the important choices we face about globalization generally.

While the learning curve for many people regarding the WTO and globalization is high, the stakes of not knowing are higher.

Despite massive public relations efforts to convince us otherwise, there is nothing inevitable about the model of corporate economic globalization by which our world is now being redesigned. Rather, years of planning, lobbying and effort by the few interests who benefit from this model have led to its development and implementation.

If you learn nothing else from this book, we hope it is now clear that the WTO's hundreds of pages of rules have little to do with the 19th century philosophy of free trade. Rather, as is clear from the description of the WTO's provisions, the WTO and the Uruguay Round Agreements are only one way the rules can be designed.

This model, most accurately dubbed "corporate managed trade" is not benefiting the majority of people. Indeed, the outcomes this book describes are fundamentally undesirable and unacceptable. What is clear is that as a political matter, the tolerability and thus viability of the status quo globalization model is limited.

Obviously, there are other models that would result in a more equitable, pro-health and environment and democratically accountable design. At issue is whether the majority of people worldwide who are being ill-served by the status quo will educate and organize themselves to make the change.

CHAPTER **9** ENDNOTES

[1] Guy de Jonquieres, "Network Guerrillas," *Financial Times*, Apr. 30, 1998, at 12.

[2] The OECD negotiations on an MAI started in 1995 shortly after completion of the Uruguay Round. Despite attempts by the developed countries to establish comprehensive NAFTA-style investor rights in the WTO, developing country opposition had resulted in a compromise on the WTO TRIMs Agreement. The developed countries retreated to their OECD to attempt a backdoor imposition of the NAFTA model worldwide. Until a nearly finished draft text was liberated by NGOs in 1997, neither parliaments nor press in the OECD countries were aware of the MAI. The proposal would have literally empowered foreign investors and corporations to sue directly the U.S. federal, state, and local governments for cash damages to compensate for any government action that might undermine their profitability. The MAI talks were forced to a halt by global NGO opposition in late 1998.

Index

Buyers Up • Congress Watch • Critical Mass • Global Trade Watch • Health Research Group • Litigation Group
Joan Claybrook, President

25+ Years of Citizen Activism

Dear Friend,

It has been almost thirty years since a hardy group of enterprising young people came to the nation's capital to start an experiment in citizenship. The first "Nader's Raiders" showed special grit, integrity, and idealism that still serve us today. I am writing to ask all buyers of <u>Whose Trade Organization</u> to please help us continue this record— and nurture those values— by joining Public Citizen today.

You hold in your hands an example of the important work we do every day. Public Citizen is the only organization with the courage to write <u>Whose Trade Organization</u>. We name names and tell the real facts. Basic membership in Public Citizen is $20 and with it you'll receive our bi-monthly member publication *Public Citizen News* which will keep you abreast of all the work that Public Citizen does on behalf of citizens across the country and briefed to participate yourself. When you join Public Citizen with a gift of $35 or more you'll also get our monthly *Health Letter*, which will update you with new information on danger-ous drugs and provide you with other information important to your health and safety.

We are the only citizens group with a full time division working on trade and globaliza-tion. After seven years of organizing, research and lobbying, we led the campaign that defeated the Fast Track trade authority intended to expand NAFTA in 1998. And, we exposed the secretive Multilateral Agreement on Investment (MAI) and worked with activists around the world to defeat it.

We've helped purge cancer-producing additives from dozens of food products. Fought to ensure workplaces have fewer safety and health hazards. Many ineffective, unsafe drugs and medical devices have been forced from the market as a result of our tireless efforts. Motor vehicles are much safer because of our continuous pressure. We have helped to force government decision-making out of the smoke-filled back rooms, and we have exposed corporate attempts to short-circuit democracy, but there is so much left to do.

We need to rewrite unfair trade legislation that hurts American workers and weakens our environmental laws; remove the flood of soft money polluting our political system; stop federal give-aways to corporate fat cats; and force federal agencies to enforce the laws we already have. *But we can't do it without you!*

To retain its independence, Public Citizen does not accept government or corporate funds. Our support comes from individual members who believe there should be full-time advocates of democratic principles working on their behalf, and from foundation grants and publication sales. To remain effective, Public Citizen needs you. Please join us today. As Ralph Nader reminds us, "together we *can* make a difference."

Sincerely,

Joan Claybrook

Joan Claybrook
President

Most consumers don't have time to visit Washington, D.C., roam the halls of government and ensure their voices are heard. Public Citizen, a national nonprofit organization with 150,000 members, has tackled the task for them. After all, corporations, trade associations and other business and industry groups hire tens of thousands of lobbyists in Washington to secure tax breaks, subsidies, loan guarantees, limits on liability, cutbacks in safety standards and much more. Consumers deserve a voice too. Public Citizen speaks for you before Congress, in the courts and in the hallways of federal regulatory agencies.

Ralph Nader founded Public Citizen to empower ordinary citizens, protect their rights and give them a voice in the halls of power. We expose threats to the public health and safety, and we press for corporate accountability, clean government and public disclosure. We've won important victories for consumers in the areas of health care, injury prevention, campaign finance reform, fair trade and elimination of government handouts to wealthy corporations.

Public Citizen accepts no government or corporate grants, ensuring that we represent only citizens' interests. Our money comes entirely from our members — who believe strongly in our cause and support our work on their behalf — and from foundations and the sale of our publications.

"There can be no daily democracy without daily citizenship."
— Ralph Nader, founder of Public Citizen

1971
- Public Citizen petitions the Food and Drug Administration (FDA) to ban the use of Red Dye #2 as food coloring, citing links to cancer.

1972
- Public Citizen files a lawsuit that obligates airlines to pay damages to consumers bumped from flights.
- Public Citizen asks courts to order increased disclosure of contributions to political campaigns.

1973
- In response to Public Citizen's suit, President Nixon's firing of Special Prosecutor Archibald Cox is ruled illegal.

1974
- Public Citizen convinces Congress to override President Ford's veto and pass major improvements to the Freedom of Information Act.

1975
- Public Citizen successfully lobbies Congress for energy conservation legislation, including fuel economy requirements for cars.

1976
- FDA bans Red Dye No. 2 after Public Citizen's four-year campaign.
- A Public Citizen petition leads to FDA ban on use of cancer-causing chloroform in cough medicines and toothpaste.

1977
- Public Citizen challenges the airline industry's failure to provide adequate seating for nonsmokers.
- Public Citizen mobilizes citizens who persuade President Carter to halt the construction of the Clinch River Breeder Reactor.

1978
- Cyclamates are banned after Public Citizen raises safety concerns about the widely used artificial sweeteners.
- Congress passes Public Citizen's National Consumer Cooperative Bill, authorizing $300 million seed money for consumer cooperatives.

1979
- Public Citizen helps defeat legislation that would have raised sugar price supports, saving consumers $300 million per year.
- A Public Citizen petition leads the Environmental Protection Agency (EPA) to ban the use of DBCP, a pesticide proven to cause sterility in men.

1980
- A Public Citizen lawsuit opens the Chrysler bailout board proceedings to public.
- Public Citizen plays a critical role in the passage of Superfund law, requiring cleanup of toxic waste sites.

1981
- Public Citizen secures Toxic Shock Syndrome warning labels on tampons.
- Public Citizen helps thwart President Reagan's attempts to dismantle Clean Air Act and diminish authority of Consumer Product Safety Commission.

1982
- After extensive Public Citizen campaign, cancer-causing urea

formaldehyde is banned from home insulation.
- The arthritis drug Oraflex is withdrawn from the market after Public Citizen exposes deaths and injuries caused by the drug.

1983
- Public Citizen participates in a landmark Supreme Court decision overturning President Reagan's revocation of auto safety standard for automatic restraints.

1984
- Following AT&T divestiture, Public Citizen mounts a nation-wide "Campaign for Affordable Phones" successfully opposing rate hikes for residential customers.
- Public Citizen wins a court order forcing EPA to recall 700,000 GM cars with faulty emission controls.

1985
- FDA requires Reye's Syndrome warning label on aspirin after a four-year campaign by Public Citizen.
- Public Citizen reveals the locations of more than 250 work sites nationwide where workers have been exposed to hazardous chemicals.

1986
- Congress requires health warning labels on chewing tobacco and snuff, capping Public Citizen's two-year campaign.
- A Public Citizen suit defeats Bush administration plan to block low-income housing programs by refusing to spend appropriated funds.

1987
- Public Citizen helps persuade Congress to pass legislation restricting the time banks can hold checks after being deposited.
- After eight years of litigation by Public Citizen, the Occupational Safety and Health Administration (OSHA) imposes standards for exposure to cancer-causing ethylene oxide.

1988
- Public Citizen publishes *Worst Pills, Best Pills*, a consumer guide

to dangerous and ineffective drugs and their safer alternatives, selling 2 million copies over the next 10 years.

1989
- Public Citizen and Ralph Nader lead successful opposition to a $45,500 congressional pay raise.
- Public Citizen helps persuade California voters to shut down Rancho Seco nuclear plant.

1990
- A Public Citizen court victory forces Nuclear Regulatory Agency to require training for nuclear plant workers.

1991
- OSHA imposes a standard to protect workers from cadmium, linked to lung cancer and kidney damage, after Public Citizen wins court order.
- Public Citizen wins a landmark ruling that the Federal Election Commission (FEC) cannot restrict use of campaign finance data.

1992
- Public Citizen's four-year campaign leads the FDA to severely restrict use of silicone gel breast implants.

1993
- Public Citizen plays a leading role in opposition to the North American Free Trade Agreement (NAFTA).
- Public Citizen wins a landmark court victory that preserves the electronic records of the White House under Reagan, Bush and Clinton.

1994
- Public Citizen helps to enlist nearly 100 co-sponsors for a single-payer health care reform bill.
- Public Citizen wins consumer protections against home equity scams.

1995
- Public Citizen lawyers defend tobacco industry whistle-blowers.
- Congressional gift ban and lobbying registration reform passed after major Public Citizen campaign.

1996
- Public Citizen wins a Supreme Court decision upholding right of people injured by federal regu-lated defective medical devices to sue for compensation.
- Public Citizen wins a court ruling that class actions cannot be used to deprive future victims of their right to sue.
- Public Citizen wins release of Nixon's White House tapes, after 15 years of litigation.

1997
- Public Citizen defends con-sumer interests as the electricity industry deregulates.
- Public Citizen wins fights to prevent passage of damaging fast-track legislation, to ensure that global trade agreements do not sweep away health and safety standards.

1998
- Public Citizen protests and helps force redesign of unethical AIDS research in Africa, which would have denied known effective treatment to HIV-positive pregnant women.
- Public Citizen again stops passage of undemocratic Fast Track trade legislation.
- Public Citizen played major role in stopping the Multilateral Agreement on Investment (MAI), a proposed treaty that would establish new rights for global investors.
- Campaign Finance Reform passes House with continued pressure from Public Citizen. Senate leaders kill it with a filibuster.
- Public Citizen played instru-mental role in enactment of a new law to require reengineered air bags to protect small adults and children.

1999
- Public Citizen publishes third edition of *Worst Pills, Best Pills*, a consumer's guide to avoiding drug-induced death or illness.
- Public Citizen wins release of historic grand jury records relating to the 1948 indictment of alleged Soviet agent Alger Hiss.

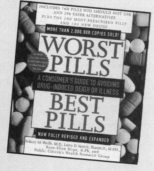

ORDER FORM

1600 20th Street, N.W. Washington, DC 20009-1001

Public Citizen Membership/Newsletter Subscription

QTY	ITEM DESCRIPTION	PRICE	SUBTOTAL
	Basic membership (includes PC News)	$20.00	
	Combination membership with Health Letter	$35.00	
	I want to help even more with an additional contribution of $_____	$_____	
	Membership/Subscription subtotal		

Publications from Public Citizen

QTY	ITEM DESCRIPTION	PRICE	SUBTOTAL
	MAI: The Multilateral Agreement of Investment and the Threat to American Freedom #E5558	$10.00	
	NAFTA at 5: School of Real-Life Results Report Card #E5562	$10.00	
	A Citizen's Guide to the World Trade Organization #E5563	$2.00	
	Worst Pills, Best Pills (3rd ed.) #F6672	$16.00	
	SUBTOTAL		
	SHIPPING/HANDLING CHARGES (see reverse)		
	TOTAL		

BWTOBK

CUT HERE

Name (please print)

_____

Mailing address

_____

City/State/Zip

_____

Phone number

Payment: All orders must be prepaid

Please make checks or money orders payable to Public Citizen

Charge to credit card: ☐ VISA ☐ MC ☐ AMEX ☐ DISC

_____

Credit Card Number

_____

Signature (as it appears on card)

Expiration Date: _____

Charge will appear on statement as Public Citizen

Publications Subtotal	*Shipping & Handling*		*Mail to:*	PUBLIC CITIZEN
$1.00—$5.99	add $1.00			1600 20th Street, N.W.
$6.00—$11.99	add $2.50			Washington, D.C. 20009
$12.00—$24.99	add $3.50			
$25.00—$99.99	add $5.00			
$100.00—$150.00	add $7.50			

Please allow 4-6 weeks for delivery of publications; 6-8 weeks for your first issue of subscriptions.

These titles represent only a portion of our current publications. For a complete brochure, to order publications by phone, get information on overnight delivery orders or orders outside the continental U.S., or for information on membership/subscriptions, call (800) 289-3787 or (202) 588-1000, M-F 9 a.m- 5 p.m. EST, or check our Web site at www.citizen.org.

Contributions to Public Citizen Foundation, which supports Public Citizen's education, litigation, research and public information activities, are tax-deductible in excess of your annual $20 membership dues. Contributions to Public Citizen, Inc., a nonprofit membership organization that lobbies for strong citizen and consumer protection laws, are not tax-deductible.

A copy of our latest financial statement may be obtained by sending a large, self-addressed, stamped envelope to Public Citizen, 1600 20th Street, N.W., Washington, D.C. 20009

Please remember that this is a library book,
and that it belongs only temporarily to each
person who uses it. Be considerate. Do
not write in this, or any, library book.